THE VIETNAM EXPERIENCE

A Concise Encyclopedia of American Literature, Songs, and Films

KEVIN HILLSTROM
and
LAURIE COLLIER HILLSTROM

Greenwood Press
Westport, Connecticut • London

Library of Congress Cataloging-in-Publication Data

Hillstrom, Kevin, 1963–
      The Vietnam experience : a concise encyclopedia of American
   literature, songs, and films / Kevin Hillstrom and Laurie Collier
   Hillstrom.
          p.   cm.
      Includes bibliographical references and index.
      ISBN 0–313–30183–2 (alk. paper)
      1. Vietnamese Conflict, 1961–1975—Motion pictures and the
   conflict—Encyclopedias.   2. Vietnamese Conflict, 1961–1975—
   Literature and the conflict—Encyclopedias.   3. Vietnamese
   Conflict, 1961–1975—Music and the conflict—Encyclopedias.   4. War
   films—United States—History and criticism—Encyclopedias.
   5. American literature—20th century—History and criticism—
   Encyclopedias.   6. Popular music—United States—1961–1970—History
   and criticism—Encyclopedias.   7. Popular music—United
   States—1971–1980—History and criticism—Encyclopedias.
   I. Hillstrom, Laurie Collier, 1965– .   II. Title.
   DS557.73.H55   1998
   959.704'3—dc21   97–21965

British Library Cataloguing in Publication Data is available.

Library of Congress Catalog Card Number: 97–21965
ISBN: 0–313–30183–2

First published in 1998

Greenwood Press, 88 Post Road West, Westport, CT 06881
An imprint of Greenwood Publishing Group, Inc.

Printed in the United States of America

The paper used in this book complies with the
Permanent Paper Standard issued by the National
Information Standards Organization (Z39.48–1984).

10 9 8 7 6 5 4 3 2 1

Contents

OTHER NOTABLE WORKS CONCERNING
THE VIETNAM WAR

Advisory Board

Michael Anderegg
Department of English
University of North Dakota
Grand Forks, North Dakota
Editor of *Inventing Vietnam: The War in Film and Television*

Pat Browne
Editor, *Journal of American Culture*
Bowling Green State University
Bowling Green, Ohio

Tobey Herzog
Department of English
Wabash College
Crawfordsville, Indiana
Author of *Vietnam War Stories: Innocence Lost* and *Tim O'Brien*

Philip K. Jason
Department of English
U.S. Naval Academy
Annapolis, Maryland
Author of *Fourteen Landing Zones: Approaches to Vietnam War Literature*

Preface

The Vietnam War remains one of the most traumatic and painful events in all of American history. Throughout much of its duration, the bitterly contested conflict, which would ultimately result in the loss of fifty-eight thousand American lives, provoked profound debate in the streets and households of America. Supporters of intervention in Indochina contended that U.S. involvement was both necessary and just, whereas critics insisted that the U.S. military effort there was ill-considered or immoral. Both sides brought healthy quantities of passion and invective to the debate, and the resulting split in American society shook the country to its core. This division never wholly healed. Long after the U.S. withdrawal from Vietnam in 1973—and South Vietnam's fall in 1975—Americans continue to grapple with the lingering impact of the conflict on its participants, both in Vietnam and at home, and with the repercussions of the war on notions of national identity and character.

Some of the most dramatic and compelling efforts to explore the Vietnam War's impact on its participants and on the collective American psyche have been made by American writers, filmmakers, and musicians. The themes of these works reflect no emerging national consensus; indeed, the best of the songs, novels, poems, plays, and films that rose to prominence during and after the war are notable not only for their power but for their diversity of opinion and ideological orientation. Yet all of these works' creators sought to convey some fundamental truth about the war as they saw it, and this passion is evident in works as diverse as Larry Heinemann's novel *Paco's Story*, Oliver Stone's film *Platoon*, and Bruce Springsteen's song "Born in the U.S.A."

The Vietnam Experience: A Concise Encyclopedia of American Literature, Songs, and Films is intended to provide readers with a comprehensive guide to the most notable of these American creative works (two works covered in this volume—Graham Greene's *The Quiet American* and The Animals' "We Gotta Get Out of This Place"—are not of American origin, but an examination of these vastly disparate works provides valuable insights into the American experience in Vietnam). *The Vietnam Experience* includes forty-four essays, each providing detailed information on a noteworthy film, song, or literary work. The information provided includes

- Insights into the Vietnam-era experiences and views of the work's primary creative force
- Discussion of the circumstances surrounding the creation of the work
- Plot summary (when appropriate)
- Critical reaction to the work
- Sources for further reading

In addition, each essay includes a historical background section that is intended to familiarize readers with actual events or themes underlying the creative work under discussion. The essay on Creedence Clearwater Revival's "Fortunate Son," for example, includes a section exploring the role that socioeconomic circumstances played in determining the composition of American combat troops in Vietnam; the essay on Bobbie Ann Mason's novel *In Country*, which includes a climactic scene at the Vietnam Veterans Memorial, details the controversy surrounding the creation of "the Wall."

This historical background component is designed to increase the reader's understanding of both the Vietnam War and the works it inspired. But the fact that a single historical event or aspect of the war is discussed in a certain essay should not be construed as an indication that the work in question is the only one that explores that event or subject. John Del Vecchio's *The 13th Valley*, for instance, is not the only work covered in *The Vietnam Experience* that details American soldiers' struggles to adapt to the inhospitable climate and terrain of Vietnam. Nor is Del Vecchio's book concerned with that subject to the exclusion of all else; the novel explores numerous other aspects of the American combat soldier's experiences in Vietnam. But by focusing on one or two historical aspects of the conflict in each essay, *The Vietnam Experience* provides its users with information on a wide range of Vietnam War issues and events, including

- The Battle of Khe Sanh and the Tet Offensive (in Michael Herr's *Dispatches*)
- Drug abuse within the U.S. Army during Vietnam (in Stephen Wright's *Meditations in Green*)
- The Kent State shootings (in Crosby, Stills, Nash, and Young's "Ohio")
- Atrocities in Vietnam (in Brian DePalma's *Casualties of War*)
- "Americanization" of the war (in Philip Caputo's *A Rumor of War*)

- Experiences of African Americans in Vietnam (in Wallace Terry's *Bloods*)
- The Vietnam War as surrealist event (in Francis Coppola's *Apocalypse Now*)

Finally, *The Vietnam Experience* includes an appendix listing more than 275 other films (both fictional and documentary), songs, and works of literature (including novels, memoirs, oral histories, plays, and poetry collections) that deal with the Vietnam War.

The inclusion list for *The Vietnam Experience* was determined in consultation with our distinguished advisory board. Their comments and suggestions were most valuable in settling upon a final list for essay treatment, and we offer our thanks for their time and consideration.

After Our War

Poetry Collection

Author: John Balaban

Facts of Publication: Pittsburgh: University of Pittsburgh Press, 1974

In 1967, at the height of American involvement in the Vietnam War, graduate student John Balaban gave up his student deferment in order to secure a deferment based on his moral opposition to the war. He successfully negotiated the hurdles associated with making such a change and subsequently spent two years in Vietnam as a civilian teacher and medical aid worker. His experiences during those long months, coupled with his unwavering philosophical opposition to the war, proved vital in shaping the works that would comprise *After Our War*, an award-winning book of poetry published in 1974.

HISTORICAL BACKGROUND

An estimated 170,000 Americans received "conscientious objector" (CO) deferments from the draft during the Vietnam War, but "as many as 300,000 other applicants were denied CO deferments," contended James W. Tollefson, a CO who authored *The Strength Not to Fight: An Oral History of Conscientious Objectors of the Vietnam War*. "Nearly 600,000 illegally evaded the draft; about 200,000 were formally accused of draft offenses. Many of these lawbreakers were men who had been denied CO deferments or who refused to cooperate with the draft on grounds of conscience." Tollefson noted that as a result, as many as fifty thousand draft-age Americans fled to Canada, and approximately twenty thousand others took up residence in other countries or assumed underground identities in America.

The number of conscientious objectors granted deferments expanded dramatically over the course of the war, more than tripling from 1964 to 1971. This increase was spurred by the growth of American military involvement in Vietnam. As American troop deployments grew—and media coverage of the conflict expanded—the domestic antiwar movement experienced a corresponding surge in energy and influence, and their message of draft resistance came to be regarded as an increasingly viable one. Pacifist groups such as the American Friends Service Committee (AFSC) subsequently established counseling centers in which volunteers discussed CO deferments and other options with draftees, and many university campuses became repositories of information and strategies on eluding the draft.

Another important factor in the growth of CO deferments was a change in the legal definition of conscientious objection. Prior to 1967, CO deferments were given only to young men who opposed all wars based upon their faith in a Supreme Being. As a result, "most successful CO applicants were from the traditional peace churches—Mennonite, Quaker, and Brethren," noted Tollefson. In 1967, however, the definition of conscientious objection was broadened to include objections based on "religious training and belief," rather than faith in a Supreme Being. Tollefson pointed out that other legal changes had an impact as well: "In the 1965 Seeger decision [*United States v. Seeger*], the [Supreme Court] expanded the definition of religious training and belief to include philosophical and moral beliefs that occupy a place in one's life 'parallel to that filled by orthodox belief in God.' In 1970, the Supreme Court ruled in *Welsh v. United States* that the central requirement for CO deferments was a deeply held conviction that participation in the military violated one's 'religious or moral' beliefs." Moral objections to the Vietnam War in particular—as opposed to war in general—were not entertained.

Some of the young men who applied for CO deferments requested to be excused from any military duty, though others stated their willingness to serve provided that they did so in a noncombatant capacity (the latter sometimes became combat medics in Vietnam). For those whose CO applications were rejected by their draft board, the pressure to submit to the draft was great. In many cases, these CO applicants had already experienced significant deterioration in their relationships with family, friends, or community as a result of their stance, and the rejection of their applications only added to their distress. But whereas some relented, others departed for the Canadian border or—after exhausting other legal avenues—submitted to prosecution for draft evasion. By the early 1970s, federal prosecutions of draft evaders had reached five thousand cases annually, and thousands of draft resisters were sentenced to prison terms for their violations of draft law. From 1965 to 1975, more than twenty-two thousand Americans were indicted for draft law violations; of these, approximately four thousand faced imprisonment.

BALABAN AND VIETNAM

"For all the confusion that engulfed me as soon as I arrived in Vietnam, I had come with clear conviction," wrote Balaban in his memoir *Remembering Heaven's Face*. "I was opposed to the taking of human life. I was opposed to all war and, in particular, opposed to this war. It seems odd to me now that I could have developed such notions in the late fifties and early sixties, especially growing up as I did in a rough housing project rife with violence." But a Quaker friend from high school and antiwar friends at Pennsylvania State University dramatically influenced his views and philosophy. After graduating from Penn State, Balaban secured a scholarship to attend graduate school at Harvard. He settled into a routine shortly after his arrival at the school. "I studied hard, happily immersed in Chaucer, Ovid, *Beowulf*, and the Scottish poets of the later Middle Ages," he recalled. "As the war droned on and Vietnam was filling up with American troops, I would have been content occupying myself with the literature of past centuries if it had not been for Robert Strange McNamara."

Balaban's decision to go to Vietnam was sparked when he witnessed a campus clash between antiwar activists and Secretary of Defense McNamara, whom Balaban characterized as a figure of crowd-baiting arrogance. "[McNamara's] public insolence [during the altercation] made me suddenly ashamed of my books, my university, and the safety of my student deferment," Balaban said in *Remembering Heaven's Face*. Convinced that the antiwar movement of that time was having no effect, "it occurred to me that the only place to learn anything, to *do* anything about Vietnam was in Vietnam." He subsequently traded in his student deferment for that of a conscientious objector. With that hurdle cleared, he joined International Voluntary Services (IVS), a private volunteer agency under contract to the U.S. Agency for International Development (USAID). Arriving in South Vietnam in the summer of 1967, Balaban served as an instructor at the University of Can Tho until the 1968 Tet Offensive, during which he was wounded by a cluster bomb. Musing on his wound, Balaban wrote that "the best guess, given its shape and the silence that attended its flight to me, was that a snippet from a cluster bomb that had been dropped on the outskirts of town, almost spent, had nevertheless strayed my way, as if to remind me of the pure cheekiness of standing close to so much pain and death and expecting I would come out whole."

In the aftermath of Tet—which had severely damaged the campus of the University of Can Tho—Balaban became a field representative for the Quaker and Mennonite Committee of Responsibility to Save War-Burned and War-Injured Children (COR), a group dedicated to providing medical care to wounded Vietnamese children. He completed his alternative service in 1969 and returned to the United States, but two years later he made the first of several return trips to Vietnam, doing research on Vietnamese folk poetry. These trips, wrote Ronald Baughman in *American Poets since World War II*, "yielded not only his award-winning translations of Vietnamese folk poetry but also a new perspective on the country and all those—Vietnamese and American—inextricably bound by a shared history. In the unified country of Vietnam, he found extensive healing of both landscape and people. Such healing he views as an affirmation of the Vietnamese resolve to move beyond tragedy and into the sanity of a hopeful future."

Still, Balaban acknowledged in *Remembering Heaven's Face* that he remains haunted by the war: "Often images from my COR days come floating up on mental backwaters: the napalmed mother and her lovely infant daughter with the blackened arm; the pajamaed girl throwing her thigh over her old father to keep him warm as he lay dying beneath her. . . . Now, twenty years after these events, I can't imagine how I could ever have thought I could look on that carnage of children and not be hurt forever by what I saw."

CREATION OF *AFTER OUR WAR*

Balaban composed poetry throughout his two years of volunteer service in South Vietnam, and upon returning home to the United States he quickly set about having his work published. His first collection, *Vietnam Poems*, appeared in 1970. Balaban's background in classical literature was apparent at this early juncture, and it became even more evident in 1974, when *After Our War* was published by the University of Pittsburgh Press. But a quick perusal of the poems contained in *After Our War* made it clear that the Vietnam War was the preeminent factor in shaping Balaban's poetic vision.

CRITICAL RECEPTION

After Our War won the Lamont Award from the Academy of American Poets in 1974, and years later, it continues to be recognized as one of the finest collections of American poetry to grow out of the Vietnam War, along with the works of such luminaries as Yusef Komunyakaa, W. D. Ehrhart, and Bruce Weigl. Commenting on *After Our War* and *Blue Mountain*, a 1982 collection by Balaban, Ehrhart observed in his essay "Soldier-Poets of the Vietnam War" that "Balaban is an anomaly: a soldier-poet who was not a soldier," but who was "as much a veteran of Vietnam as any soldier I have ever met." Moreover, contended Ehrhart, Balaban's volunteer work with IVS and COR gave him a unique, invaluable perspective on the war that is reflected in his poetry: "Balaban reveals the depth of his feeling for the Vietnamese—born of the years he spent interacting with them in ways no soldier-veteran ever could—his astounding eye for detail, his absorption of the daily rhythms of life in a rural, traditional world, and the terrible destruction of those rhythms and traditions." Indeed, many critics praised him for his emphasis on the war's impact on the Vietnamese people. Other reviewers hailed him for his skillful introduction of classical poetic traditions into modern verse and his postwar moral vision. As Ehrhart wrote, Balaban's poetry articulates a "remarkable promise of hope, a refusal to forget the past and 'go on.' . . . Balaban absorbs Vietnam and incorporates it into a powerful vision of what the world *ought* to be.''

Critic Philip Beidler speculated in *Re-Writing America* that the 1974 collection established the tone and direction of much of Balaban's post-Vietnam career. ''*After Our War*, both in the title itself and the long single poem from which it derives, defines from the outset the essential character of his career as post-Vietnam cultural mythmaker,'' wrote Beidler. ''His attempt . . . was to project memory into the grand contexts of imaginative and mythic comprehension that have traditionally marked the major poetic art of a given age. He has been, truly, the figure of the poet after our war.''

FURTHER READING

Balaban, John. *After Our War*. Pittsburgh: University of Pittsburgh Press, 1974.

————. *Remembering Heaven's Face: A Moral Witness in Vietnam*. New York: Poseidon Press, 1991.

Baskir, Lawrence, and William A. Strauss, *Chance and Circumstance: The Draft, the War, and the Vietnam Generation*. New York: Alfred A. Knopf, 1978.

Baughman, Ronald. ''John Balaban.'' In *American Poets since World War II, Third Series*, Vol. 120 of *Dictionary of Literary Biography*. Detroit: Gale Research, 1992.

Beidler, Philip D. *Re-Writing America: Vietnam Authors in Their Generation*. Athens: University of Georgia Press, 1991.

Ehrhart, W. D. ''Soldier-Poets of the Vietnam War.'' In *America Rediscovered: Critical Essays on Literature and Film of the Vietnam War*. Owen W. Gilman, Jr. and Lorrie Smith, eds. New York: Garland, 1990.

McReynolds, David. ''Pacifists and the Vietnam Antiwar Movement.'' In *Give Peace a Chance: Exploring the Vietnam Antiwar Movement*. Melvin Small and William D. Hoover, eds. Syracuse: Syracuse University Press, 1992.

Smith, Lorrie. ''Resistance and Revision by Vietnam War Veterans.'' In *Fourteen Landing Zones: Approaches to Vietnam War Literature*. Philip K. Jason, ed. Iowa City: University of Iowa Press, 1991.

Surrey, David S. *Choice of Conscience*. New York: Praeger, 1982.

Tollefson, James W. *The Strength Not to Fight: An Oral History of Conscientious Objectors of the Vietnam War*. Boston: Little, Brown and Company, 1993.

Apocalypse Now

Film

Director: Francis Ford Coppola

Screenplay: John Milius and Francis Ford Coppola, with narration by Michael Herr; suggested by the novella *Heart of Darkness* by Joseph Conrad

Principal Cast: Marlon Brando, Martin Sheen, Frederic Forrest, Albert Hall, Sam Bottoms, Laurence Fishburne, Dennis Hopper

Year of Release: 1979 (United Artists)

American cultural treatments of the Vietnam War have often given the conflict—and the experiences of those who fought in it—a uniquely hallucinatory or surrealistic quality. The best-known of these works is probably Francis Coppola's epic film *Apocalypse Now*. The controversial film, which follows the strange voyage of an American military assassin who has been ordered to kill a fellow soldier gone mad, continues to stand as one of the most influential depictions of Vietnam in American culture. Indeed, both supporters and detractors of Coppola's work acknowledge that the film contributed greatly to the belief, widely held across much of America, that service in Vietnam had uniquely bizarre and nihilistic qualities that had been absent in other wars.

HISTORICAL BACKGROUND

Writing in *The Perfect War: The War We Couldn't Lose and How We Did*, historian James William Gibson noted that "much war culture reflects upon the 'unreality' of Vietnam, the sense in which nothing seemed to meet preconceived concepts of rationality. Soldiers always spoke of what they were going to do when their one-year tours of duty were up and they returned to 'the world.' Vietnam by implication was 'unworld,' another place. Two common names for Vietnam were 'Brown Disneyland' and 'Six Flags Over Nothing'; the country was like a playground or amusement park where social rules had been suspended, but the fun was gone.''

Participants and observers alike attributed this disorientation to myriad factors. Some cited the unique nature of the Vietnam battlefield, in which the large-scale battles of previous wars were largely absent, replaced instead by a system of often brutal guerrilla warfare that blurred the lines between friend and foe. Other aspects of combat duty were cited as well, from the energy-leeching climate to the military's flawed system of troop replenishment, which many felt honed instincts for self-preservation while simultaneously undercutting allegiance to military units beyond one's own platoon or squad. Veterans and historians also cited the incorporation of various elements of American culture (such as rock music and drugs) into Vietnam as a factor in the ''surrealization'' of the war. Finally, the knowledge that large segments of the American public disapproved of the war—and that the home front at times seemed to be in danger of exploding over the conflict—lent the whole enterprise an exceedingly strange quality.

In the years following the American withdrawal from Vietnam, a number of creative works appeared that seemed to confirm this characterization of the war as one fundamentally different from its predecessors. Some of the most critically lauded of these works—Michael Herr's *Dispatches*, Tim O'Brien's *Going After Cacciato*, Larry Heinemann's *Paco's Story*—employed original narrative techniques and devices to tell their Vietnam stories, and critics began to ponder whether, as C. D. B. Bryan wrote in *Harper's*, conventional realism might be ''inadequate for conveying the moral and political ambiguities of the war in Vietnam.'' In the meantime, other, more traditional narratives of Vietnam were released to acclaim as well, but even many of these dwelled at length on the dark, hallucinatory quality of the Vietnam War. ''The voice of Vietnam literature,'' concluded Bryan, ''is that of a barely suppressed scream. There is an intensity to these books similar to that which pervades the literature of the Holocaust. One is always conscious of the authors' efforts to stay calm, to contain the shriek.''

But some observers (including Bryan) contended that statements about Vietnam's uniqueness when compared to other wars were overblown. They pointed out that the Civil War and World Wars I and II were replete with tragic and horrifying incidents, and that war literature from these earlier eras had provided many sadly enduring insights into the savagery of all wars, whatever their time and place. Others, meanwhile, speculated that characterizations of the war in Vietnam as singularly otherworldly or fantastical in nature made it easier for America to dismiss it as an aberration or a sort of bad dream. Vietnam veteran Tim O'Brien, author of several Vietnam books (including the aforementioned

Going After Cacciato), summarized the objections of this camp in an interview with Eric James Schroeder for *Modern Fiction Studies*: "For me Vietnam wasn't an unreal experience. It wasn't absurd. It was a cold-blooded, calculated war. Most of the movies about it have been done with this kind of black humorish, *Apocalypse Now* absurdity: the world's crazy; madman Martin Sheen is out to kill madman Marlon Brando; Robert Duvall is a surfing nut. There's that sense of 'well, we're all innocent by reason of insanity; the war was crazy, and therefore we're innocent.' That doesn't go down too well."

CREATION OF *APOCALYPSE NOW*

The first script for *Apocalypse Now* was written in the late 1960s by John Milius. The script was in effect an attempt to merge Joseph Conrad's novella *Heart of Darkness*, an allegorical exploration of man's darkest psychic places, with the war that was raging over in Southeast Asia. According to *Film Comment* contributor Brooks Riley, "Milius fashioned a script that structured itself in general terms after the Conrad work, but which incorporated many references to his own interests." Filmmaker Francis Ford Coppola was interested in the project even at this early juncture, but he later told *Rolling Stone* interviewer Greil Marcus that Milius's original script, though it included several scenes and characters that would appear in the final version of the film, ultimately depicted a "comic-strip Vietnam War."

Preoccupied with other projects and with his fledgling American Zoetrope film company, Coppola did not devote much attention to the script for several years. Indeed, Coppola did not begin work on the story in earnest until the mid-1970s (George Lucas was slated to direct the film for a time, but he drifted away from the project, devoting his energies instead to *Star Wars*). By 1975, however, Coppola was being hailed as a master filmmaker for his work on *The Godfather* (1972) and *The Godfather II* (1974). His subsequent announcement that he was ready to tackle Vietnam—a subject that had been avoided by Hollywood since 1968's *The Green Berets*—thus sparked a ripple of anticipation throughout the film world.

Despite the hefty budget attached to the film ($12 million), Coppola decided to finance it himself. "I had this idea that if I took this war film, and put some terrific stars together with me as a director, I could make a picture and own it, too," he told the *New York Times'* Tony Chiu. "I'd been around a long time, done a lot of good work, but I still had to go hat in hand to the movie companies. However, if this picture made a lot of money, I could use that money to build my own movie studio." He confessed to Chiu that he thought the scenario would be easy to carry out.

Coppola was able to secure advances from U.S. and foreign distributors to cover the film's budget, but other problems cropped up immediately. Horrified by the script, the U.S. Defense Department refused to cooperate with Coppola, and the director was forced to look elsewhere for the necessary military hardware and technical assistance he would need to make the film. He finally made arrangements with the government of President Ferdinand Marcos of the Philippines to use its American-made military aircraft and other equipment, but this would prove to be a fateful choice.

Coppola and his family arrived in the Philippines in early March 1976, and he quickly set about filming various battle scenes and special-effects sequences. But he was troubled by the heavily revised script, which he still regarded as unsatisfactory, and by his inability to secure the actors that he wanted for the film. He approached several marquee names to play the central roles of Kurtz and Willard, but all of them—Steve McQueen, Al Pacino, Jack Nicholson, James Caan, Robert Redford, and Gene Hackman—turned him down for one reason or another. By the end of March, however, he had finally settled on a cast that included Marlon Brando as Kurtz and Harvey Keitel as Willard.

Coppola, though, found himself besieged on many fronts. The region's energy-sapping climate and widespread poverty had a demoralizing effect on both cast and crew, and the director's arrangement with Marcos quickly proved problematic. "Marcos and his air force . . . were charging Coppola a fortune in helicopter rentals, but at the same time the generals seemed to regard the movie as a free pilot training program," wrote Michael Goodwin and Naomi Wise in *On the Edge: The Life and Times of Francis Coppola.* "They sent a different set of novice airmen every day, so the previous day's flying rehearsals were useless; thousands of dollars' worth of shots were ruined. To make matters worse, Philippine Air Force generals got into the habit of showing up amid a retinue of ladies in sundresses, to sit in directors' chairs, watch the show, and generally get in the way." Bribery of Philippine officials soon became standard operating procedure. Other aspects of the production were unsettling as well. Coppola quickly recognized that special-effects costs and miscellaneous expenses associated with the massive production might send the total price tag for the film far higher than had been anticipated. The director also was unhappy with Keitel's work, so he fired him and replaced him with Martin Sheen. Finally, Coppola remained dissatisfied with the script, and he spent many hours working feverishly to shape it more to his liking. One crew member later recalled in *On the Edge* that "it was hell for a while at the beginning of the movie. Artistically, Coppola didn't know what he was going for, and he was a pretty hard guy to be around. The crew didn't know he didn't know. But when you'd see him typing away in his houseboat in the mornings, you suspected as much. It created a sense of chaos."

That sense of chaos was heightened with the arrival of Hurricane Olga in late May 1976. The storm destroyed Coppola's two main sets, further adding to the movie's spiraling costs. In the aftermath of Olga, Coppola and his wife Eleanor checked into a Manila hospital, both of them suffering from malnutrition and dehydration. Upon his release, Coppola announced a six-week halt to the production, despite the fact that it was behind schedule and already far over budget. The cast and crew returned home, grateful for the reprieve. But all knew they would have to return eventually, and they awaited word of the resumption of the shoot with outlooks that ranged from apprehension to outright dread.

After making arrangements for the construction of a new set, Coppola departed for the United States as well. Back in America, he secured an agreement with United Artists in which they agreed to cover any cost overruns associated with the film, but the arrangement placed Coppola under greater financial risk, because he was personally responsible for repayment of the loan if the film did not cover costs after its release.

The resumption of filming did little to ease Coppola's growing panic over the uncertain direction and progress of the film. The script was in a constant state of flux (though Coppola was haltingly moving it ever closer both in tone and substance to Conrad's *Heart of Darkness*), and the original budget was a distant memory. Coppola's behavior became erratic as well, a development that was hardly helped by Brando's corpulent appearance when he arrived in the Philippines to do his scenes. Coppola was dismayed by the actor's excess weight as well as his lack of preparation for the role, but he quickly sat down with Brando to discuss the part. "Marlon's first idea—which almost made me vomit—was to play Kurtz as a Daniel Berrigan: in black pajamas, in VC clothes," Coppola told Marcus. "It would be all about the *guilt* [Kurtz] felt at what we'd done [in Vietnam]. I said, 'Hey, Marlon, I may not know everything about this movie—but one thing I know it's not about is *'our guilt'*!'" The production ground to a halt once again as Coppola engaged in long, exhausting sessions of improvisation and negotiation with the actor.

By the fall of 1976 the project's health was a topic of intense speculation and gossip back in the United States, both within and without the filmmaking community. Newspaper reports suggesting that the film was out of control popped up with increasing frequency, and Coppola himself admitted to several people that a part of him just wanted to walk away. "Inevitably, the film began to be compared to the endless war it meant to depict, and Coppola to the men who prosecuted that war—or to Kurtz himself," wrote Marcus. But Coppola slogged on, and by Christmas three-quarters of the shoot had been completed. After a month-long holiday break, Coppola returned to complete the shoot, only to have one final monstrous obstacle rise up in his path. Shortly after the production resumed, Martin Sheen suffered a major heart attack that nearly killed him (at one point a Philippine priest performed last rites over his body). Then, while recovering from the heart attack, the actor suffered a nervous breakdown. "I completely fell apart," Sheen told Jean Vallely in *Rolling Stone*. "My spirit was exposed, I cried and cried. I turned completely gray—my eyes, my beard—all gray. . . . [But] no one put a gun to my head and forced me to be there. I was there because I had a big ego and wanted to be in a Coppola film." Sheen's condition put the production in limbo once again, and the director was forced to wait anxiously for word of his star's progress. "Marty's heart attack . . . severely traumatized my nervous system," Coppola told Marcus. "If he'd gone to the U.S. for treatment, he might not have come back—his family might not have let him. I was scared shitless. The shooting was three-quarters done; it was all him, what was left.''

To Coppola's immense relief, Sheen returned to the production in April 1977, and the filming of *Apocalypse Now* was finally completed a month later. Coppola commented at the wrap party that he'd never seen so many people so happy to be unemployed. In June 1977 the *Apocalypse Now* crew finally left the Philippines, armed with 1.1 million feet of film—nearly eight times the norm—and countless harrowing stories about the nature of the shoot and the sometimes strange behavior of its director. As Goodwin and Wise noted, the departure from the Philippines did little to quell speculation about the film: ''Back in the United States, the newspaper exposés continued. Many people who cared for Coppola and his body of work wondered if the talented filmmaker had gone stark raving loony. Film critics speculated about his mental health and tried to diagnose his dilemma; reporters swarmed around his cast and crew, trying to get the dirt on the shoot and on Coppola's mental state. Nobody had the slightest idea whether the movie would be a masterpiece, a failure, or something in between.''

Coppola had finally concluded the scandalously expensive shooting of the film, but the task of converting the mountains of footage into a cohesive work was a daunting one. Intimidated by the sheer size of the task before him, Coppola seized on various excuses that kept him out of the editing room, and United Artists repeatedly was forced to push back the film's opening date. Growing marital difficulties between Coppola and his wife only added to the pressure and confusion at this time.

In 1979 Coppola permitted scattered screenings of the film; but even though he took pains to call the film a work in progress at these previews, his decision to trot out three different endings at the various screenings only added to the speculation surrounding the film. The controversy reached new heights when it was announced that Coppola was entering *Apocalypse Now* in the 1979 Cannes Film Festival. The unveiling of the film—still unfinished, and at an international competition, no less—caused a tremendous uproar, but Coppola, though still struggling to decide on the ending he wanted for the film, was determined to show it. Still, a Coppola press conference at the festival nearly overshadowed the screening of the much-anticipated film. During the course of the press conference, which was later reprinted in the October 1979 issue of *Millimeter*, the director castigated American journalism as ''the most decadent, totally lying kind of profession that I've ever come across'' and charged that ''there was never a truthful thing written about *Apocalypse Now* in four years.'' He also defended the film as ''the first $30 million surrealist movie'' ever made, while also alluding to the now-famous difficulties associated with the making of the film. ''My film is not a movie; it's not about Vietnam. It *is* Vietnam. It's what it was really like; it was crazy. . . . We were in the jungle, there were too many of us, we had access to too much money, too much equipment; and little by little, we went insane. I think you can see it in the film. . . . The film was making itself; the jungle was making the film.'' Coppola's film, though still unfinished, shared the festival's Golden Palm grand prize with *The Tin Drum*.

A few months later the final version of *Apocalypse Now* was at long last released to the public. But despite the controversy that had long swirled around the film—and an expensive marketing campaign on its behalf—public reaction was tepid. Critics reacted far more strongly: Some hailed it as a visionary evocation of man's darkest impulses and the madness of war; others assailed it as an ultimately empty monument to its maker's hubris.

THE PLOT OF *APOCALYPSE NOW*

The film opens with a disturbing portrait of Captain Willard (played by Martin Sheen). Alone in a Saigon hotel room, the drunken Willard is besieged with visions of the war that bring him to tears. It is then revealed that Willard is an assassin for the American military and that he has been assigned to travel upriver into Cambodia and eliminate Colonel Walter Kurtz (Marlon Brando), a once-valued Special Forces officer who has apparently gone insane.

Willard begins his journey on a patrol boat commanded by Chief (Albert Hall) and operated by a few young soldiers: Chef, a cook from Louisiana (Frederick Forrest); Lance, a surfer from California (Sam Bottoms); and Clean, an inner-city black youth (Laurence Fishburne). As the boat makes its way up the river, Willard muses on the nonsensical aspects of his mission: Kurtz is to be killed because he has allegedly gathered a band of marauding tribesmen about him, but "charging a man with murder in this place was like handing out speeding tickets at the Indy 500.''

As the patrol boat glides on, its inhabitants have a series of increasingly surrealistic encounters. First they witness the wholesale destruction of a Vietnamese village by a cavalry unit led by Lieutenant Colonel Kilgore (Robert Duvall), a larger-than-life figure who proclaims that he "loves the smell of napalm in the morning.'' Resuming their journey, they witness a bizarre USOish stage show that dissolves into chaos with the introduction of a trio of Playboy bunnies. Willard and the patrol boat crew press on until the crew decides to stop a lone sampan on the river. The crew suspects that the family might be smuggling supplies for the Communists, but their search of the vessel turns up nothing untoward. The encounter ends in tragedy, though, as the nervous Clean mows the sampan's passengers down after one of them makes a move toward one of the baskets on board (the basket contained a puppy). Chief wants to take the lone survivor to a medical post, but Willard insists on continuing the mission. The argument continues until Willard abruptly puts a bullet in the wounded woman's head.

The boat moves on and reaches the border of Cambodia, where yet another surrealistic scene awaits them: an apparently leaderless force of black GIs firing aimlessly into the night beneath the stark lights of a massive bridge. Willard disembarks in search of intelligence information, only to come upon a demoralized soldier who mutters that "this is the asshole of the world." Willard returns to the patrol boat and continues on. The crew becomes increasingly uneasy, especially after ominously silent tribesmen begin to appear along the river's shores. The natives eventually attack, slaying Clean and Chief, but Willard and the survivors continue on and finally reach Kurtz's jungle stronghold. Willard quickly realizes that Kurtz, who is attended by a vast tribe of strangely painted natives, has gone insane. The captain and the crew members also meet a free-lance photographer (Dennis Hopper) who incessantly blathers on about Kurtz's twisted genius.

Kurtz and Willard subsequently engage in a quiet battle of wills, exploring questions of morality and human nature in Kurtz's darkly lit chambers. Kurtz's decision to execute Chef only adds to the tension between the two men. Eventually, however, Willard carries out his mission, murdering the haunted Kurtz with a machete (this scene is intercut with footage of the natives' simultaneous slaughter of a water buffalo in a religious ritual). He then leaves the compound with Lance, whose mind has been destroyed by the ordeal, and disappears down the river. The film then returns to Kurtz, who in his last moments of life is staring off into space, whispering "the horror, the horror."

CRITICAL RECEPTION

Apocalypse Now remains one of the most controversial works ever to be made about Vietnam in any medium. Some members of the critical community praised it extravagantly when it was released, calling the film a masterwork and its creator a visionary. *Newsweek* critic Jack Kroll, who termed Coppola "a wonderfully gifted filmmaker," called *Apocalypse Now* "a stunning and unforgettable film. . . . *Apocalypse Now* is the ultimate war movie, a riveting adventure story, a searching and deeply committed probing of the moral problem of the Vietnam War—and something more than all of these, transcending categories and genres in a way that only true art, and specifically true movie art, does at its best. The film seethes with violence, horror, madness, irony, humor, sweetness, anger, despair and hope, but the seething is controlled by the hand of a master."

But many other critics, though impressed with certain aspects of the film— such as the cinematography, the performances, or Coppola's sheer ambition— offered more-qualified praise. *New York Times* reviewer Vincent Canby, for instance, wrote that "*Apocalypse Now* is a stunning work. It's as technically complex and masterful as any war film I can remember, including David Lean's *Bridge on the River Kwai*." But Canby contended that the film's later scenes, in which Willard meets with Kurtz, amounted to a "profoundly anticlimactic intellectual muddle." This complaint, which was echoed in the reviews of a great many other critics, ultimately emerged as a cornerstone of much of the negative reaction to the film. Indeed, a sizable percentage of the film community contended that Coppola's grandiose work was ultimately a failure, albeit a stunningly filmed one. "While much of the footage is breathtaking," wrote Frank Rich in *Time*, "*Apocalypse Now* is emotionally obtuse and intellectually empty. It is not so much an epic account of a grueling war as an incongruous, extravagant monument to artistic self-defeat." Other critics were not so absolute in their condemnation, but many of them contended that the film was a flawed one.

The central premise of the film—that Vietnam was a sort of surrealistic madhouse—was a subject of intense debate as well. Some critics (and veterans) argued that Coppola had done a superb job of conveying the moral ambiguities and hallucinatory qualities of the Vietnam War. Defenders of Coppola's vision claimed that even its most fantastic scenes (the Kilgore-led helicopter assault, the USO show, Kurtz's eerie stronghold) accurately symbolized certain larger truths about the intellectual and ethical dissolution of U.S. armed forces in Vietnam. Others, though, resented Coppola's representation of the war. Robert Hatch wrote in the *Nation* that "at the heart of *Apocalypse Now* [is] an assertion that the war was one bloody huge circus, with clowns, acrobats, fire-eaters and a big brass band." *Atlantic* reviewer Ward Just took Coppola to task as well. Though acknowledging that "a special kind of madness prevailed [in Vietnam], particularly toward the end," Just wrote that "in every important way the Vietnam War was like any other war. . . . Nothing in my reading or experience indicates that madness was peculiar to Vietnam. . . . *Apocalypse Now* is a cartoon, arguably the most wonderfully photographed cartoon in film history, but still a cartoon." The problem, Just insisted, was that "[the film] reduces the profound complexities of heart and mind to caricature, and in the end the audience can brush it all off with the explanation that it *couldn't* have been like that. And the audience is right, it couldn't and wasn't."

FURTHER READING

Bryan, C. D. B. "Barely Suppressed Screams: Getting a Bead on Vietnam War Literature." *Harper's* (June 1984).

Carby, Vincent. Review of *Apocalypse Now*. In *New York Times* (August 17, 1979).

Chiu, Tony. "Francis Coppola's Cinematic 'Apocalypse' Is Finally At Hand." *New York Times* (August 12, 1979).

Conrad, Joseph. *Heart of Darkness and the Secret Sharer*. New York: Knopf, 1993.

Coppola, Eleanor. *Notes: On* Apocalypse Now. New York, 1979.

Cowie, Peter. *Coppola: A Biography*. New York, 1994.

FitzGerald, Frances. "*Apocalypse Now*." In *Past Imperfect: History According to the Movies*, edited by Mark Carnes. New York, 1995.

Gibson, James William. *The Perfect War: The War We Couldn't Lose and How We Did*. New York: Atlantic Monthly Press, 1986.

Goodwin, Michael, and Naomi Wise. *On the Edge: The Life and Times of Francis Coppola*. New York: Morrow, 1989.

Grenier, Richard. "Coppola's Folly." *Commentary* (October 1979).

Hatch, Robert. Review of *Apocalypse Now*. In *Nation* (August 25, 1979).

Just, Ward. "Vietnam: The Camera Lies." *Atlantic* (December 1979).

Kroll, Jack. "Coppola's War Epic." *Newsweek* (August 20, 1979).

Levin, G. Roy. "Francis Ford Coppola Discusses *Apocalypse Now*." *Millimeter* (October 1979).

Lomperis, Timothy. *"Reading the Wind": The Literature of the Vietnam War*. Durham, N.C.: Duke University Press, 1987.

Marcus, Griel. "Journey up the River: An Interview with Francis Coppola." *Rolling Stone* (November 1, 1979).

Phillips, Gene. "Darkness at Noon: *Apocalypse Now*." In *Conrad and Cinema: The Art of Adaptation*. New York, 1995.

Pratt, John Clark. *Vietnam Voices: Perspectives on the War Years 1941–1982*. New York: Penguin, 1984.

Rich, Frank. "The Making of a Quagmire." *Time* (August 27, 1979).

Riley, Brooks. "Heart Transplant." *Film Comment* (September 1979).

Schroeder, Eric James. "Two Interviews: Talks with Tim O'Brien and Robert Stone." *Modern Fiction Studies* (Spring 1984).

Vallely, Jean. "Martin Sheen: Heart of Darkness, Heart of Gold." *Rolling Stone* (November 1, 1979).

The Armies of the Night

Nonfiction

Author: Norman Mailer

Facts of Publication: New York: New American Library, 1968

On the weekend of October 21, 1967, a huge antiwar demonstration was held in Washington, D.C. The protest culminated with a march across the Potomac River into Virginia and to the steps of the Pentagon, the country's military heart. Author Norman Mailer took part in the raucous, violent, confusing march on the Pentagon; his account of that turbulent weekend, called *The Armies of the Night*, continues to be hailed as one of the writer's best works.

HISTORICAL BACKGROUND

Growing Protests

After America's military involvement in Vietnam escalated in 1965, protests against U.S. policies registered a corresponding increase. By the fall of that year, antiwar demonstrations were held in dozens of U.S. cities, and "teach-ins" sprouted at American colleges and universities. Antiwar demonstrations continued to gain momentum in 1966 and 1967, galvanized by ever-growing public ambivalence with the war and increasing faith in the power of dissent. Charles DeBenedetti noted in *An American Ordeal*, though, that "between 1965 and 1967 protest remained largely respectful, its tactics designed to build an antiwar consensus. Facing hostile prowar majorities, most activists talked, taught, and marched without disruption." By 1967, however, the antiwar movement's disillusionment with the Johnson Administration, coupled with the growing influence of radical activists within the movement, sparked a pronounced shift to the left.

The best-known of the groups within the antiwar movement was Students for a Democratic Society (SDS), an organization that was born on the campus of the University of Michigan in 1960. In its early years, SDS's primary thrust had been in the realm of civil rights, but by the mid-1960s it had emerged as a major force in the antiwar movement, and some of its leaders (Tom Hayden, Todd Gitlin, Rennie Davis) were among the cause's most-visible figures. By 1967 some members of the organization had adopted increasingly revolutionary philosophies based on Marxism. (By the end of the decade the changing SDS leadership had dismissed participatory democracy in favor of a course of radical—and sometimes violent—revolution. The group folded soon after, crippled by internal disagreements.)

In mid-1967 the National Mobilization Committee to End the War in Vietnam (Mobe)—the latest incarnation of an umbrella organization that had been formed a few years before to engender cooperation among the myriad antiwar groups— announced plans to hold a massive protest in Washington, D.C., on October 21. Mobe, which had been beleaguered by clashes of philosophy and temperament between its many members since its inception, found that the planned protest was most unpopular with a number of its more moderate members, partly because of the committee's decision to appoint Jerry Rubin, widely viewed as an inflammatory figure of the counterculture, as its coordinator. But plans for the event proceeded, fanned by the frustrations of the previous few years.

The Pentagon, located across the Potomac River in Virginia, eventually emerged as the central target of the protest. The highlight of the weekend, which organizers hoped would draw up to a million people, was to be a march on the Pentagon itself. In the weeks leading up to the protest, statements by demonstration leaders made it clear that civil disobedience would be a strong component of the weekend and that the action would likely be far more confrontational than past protests. "There's nothing to explain about the war in Vietnam," said activist Abbie Hoffman. "Those days are over. The time has come for resistance." The U.S. government made its plans for defense of the Pentagon accordingly.

Debate over the wisdom of the upcoming protest—and its growing counterculture feel—intensified within the antiwar movement. DeBenedetti noted that while Mobe leaders negotiated with the government over details of the upcoming demonstration, "radical pacifists threatened that 'the peace movement has developed a strong backbone and means to fight,' and hippies dreamed about levitating the Pentagon and exorcising the demons in it or conducting 'looting' at nearby department stores. Worried by irresponsible rhetoric, SANE [National Committee for a Sane Nuclear Policy], SDS, and WILPF [Women's International League for Peace and Freedom] declared that they would neither endorse nor repudiate the October action, and antiwar military veterans and religious leaders hotly reminded leftist militants that the Mobilization was a coalition formed to help end the war in Vietnam, not to begin revolution in America.''

The weekend was kicked off with a fundraising event at Washington, D.C.'s Ambassador Theater on Friday evening, October 20. The program included an antagonistic, expletive-filled speech delivered by a visibly inebriated Norman Mailer. Later that evening, as the nation's capital went to sleep, its population swollen by thousands of demonstrators preparing for the next day, an atmosphere of tense expectation hovered over the city. Tom Wells, author of *The War Within*, noted that the tension was even felt in the White House: ''At dinner that evening, amidst the tinkle of fine china and the shuffling of servants' feet, there was 'much talk of tomorrow,' Lady Bird Johnson jotted in her diary. 'There is a ripple of grim excitement in the air, almost a feeling of being under siege.' ''

The March on the Pentagon

The following day began peacefully, with a huge crowd turning out for a day of music and speeches at the Lincoln Memorial. This rally had been insisted upon by moderate elements of the antiwar movement, because it allowed antiwar people who were uninterested in taking part in the upcoming Pentagon march to still register their opposition to American policies in Vietnam.

Later that afternoon the chaotic march on the Pentagon began. Between thirty-five thousand and fifty thousand demonstrators marched across the Arlington Memorial Bridge to the Pentagon, where they were met by a line of soldiers deployed to protect the building. The marchers were a remarkably diverse lot; they included religious leaders, celebrities (including Mailer), young professionals, and militant radicals, some of them brandishing flags of North Vietnam's National Liberation Front (NLF).

Mailer, who several months hence would go on to write the definitive account of the march on the Pentagon, was arrested fairly quickly, though some militants dismissed it as a ''celebrity arrest.'' As activist Dotson Rader told Mailer biographer Hilary Mills, ''It hurt Norman's reputation amongst the youngsters that he wasn't beaten up, that he was protected in a certain way because of his celebrity. It's no reflection on Norman's bravery, but it was seen by a lot of the kids as grandstanding.'' Mailer was released the following morning, as were most of those arrested.

As leaders of America's military looked on apprehensively from their office windows or the roof, militants made several dashes through the ring of security, and though most of these assaults were repulsed, a few protestors actually gained entrance into the Pentagon for a short time before being hauled off. ''It was terrifying,'' Defense Secretary Robert McNamara later told the *Washington Post*. ''Christ, yes, I was scared. You had to be scared. A mob is an uncontrollable force. It's terrifying. Once it becomes a mob, all the leaders are useless. It was a mess.''

The afternoon degenerated into confusion as thousands of protestors milled about the Pentagon mall area, taunting, cajoling, and conversing with the army troops standing before them. ''Without leadership or direction, most demonstrators became involved in sincere but aimless efforts,'' wrote DeBenedetti. ''Some tried to win the troops over with talk of 'flower power' and generational solidarity, or courted peaceable arrest. People sang, shrieked, or went limp in the arms of arresting federal marshals. A few cursed or flung missiles at the soldiers over the heads of front-line demonstrators. Troops responded in force, and protestors retreated, sometimes caught in clouds of tear gas, shaken by the very nakedness of the power they had provoked.''

As the day wore on, the size of the demonstration dwindled away. ''As darkness fell,'' wrote Wells, ''the force assailing the Pentagon shrank. Buses were leaving, stomachs were growling, it was getting cold. Soon there were only four hundred hardy souls left on the plaza and a few thousand on the stairs and mall. But the confrontation was far from over.'' The scene quieted somewhat as the remaining demonstrators settled in for the evening, but tensions between the troops and the protestors remained high; observers noted that a number of draft cards were burned, and some later said that female protestors made explicit offers of sex to soldiers if they would change sides.

Around midnight, the government forces moved to take back the area around the Pentagon. Moving in a V-shaped formation, they waded into the protestors to disperse them and make arrests. Some troops used excessive force to subdue demonstrators, and even some government officials later registered their dismay at the instances of brutality they witnessed. A number of accounts indicated that young women were singled out for particularly harsh treatment. A small number of militants, including Rubin, called for the demonstrators to fight back, but their appeals were ignored by the frightened demonstrators, who seemed to recognize that such steps might only worsen the situation.

The troop action effectively ended the siege of the Pentagon, though the repercussions of the demonstration would be felt for some time to come. More than 680 people were arrested during the clash (a few dozen were hospitalized, and many others suffered from minor injuries), and the march triggered a storm of criticism from media outlets. Whereas the actions of the troops received generally favorable reviews, the demonstrators were vilified on a number of counts (though some critics divided the protestors into two camps: ''good'' protestors and ''bad'' protestors). Some news organizations accused the demonstrators of harboring Communist sympathies, and others, such as the *New York Times*, speculated that the radicals had been spurred more by a thirst for media attention than genuine concern about the situation in Vietnam.

Post-march polls indicated that, as some antiwar leaders had feared, the march on the Pentagon had actually hurt the movement's position in the public eye. Indeed, that charge has been a hot topic of debate over the last few decades. Some participants and observers insist that the actions of the antiwar movement, though controversial, ultimately pushed the United States out of the war, if only to keep itself from bursting apart. Others, however, have contended that some of the protestors' actions actually hindered their efforts to stop the war. Adam Garfinkle, for instance, remarked in *Orbis* that "at the very time when the war's unpopularity was growing in the country at large, the image of irresponsibility and antipatriotism conveyed by the antiwar movement muted what might otherwise have been a louder expression of disaffection on the part of both elite and public opinion." Looking back on the antiwar movement as a whole, SDS leader Todd Gitlin concurred, though he maintained his belief in the legitimacy of the protestors' moral opposition to the war. "The movement sloppily squandered much of its moral authority," he said in *Mother Jones* in 1983. "Too much of the leadership, and some of the rank-and-file, slid into a romance with the other side. If napalm was evil, then the other side was endowed with nobility. If the American flag was dirty, the NLF flag was clean." As a result, he said, the radical fringe became "mirror images of the absolutist authority they detested."

Although the media's largely critical interpretation of the march helped the administration survive the Pentagon clash, the weekend's events nonetheless sent a shudder through the White House. The march on the Pentagon was the clearest indication yet that the United States was "coming apart" over the war. But as Mel Small noted in *Covering Dissent*, "The antiwar movement, never very cohesive, was coming apart as well. In the wake of the Pentagon action and especially the perceived brutality of the authorities, many doves threatened even greater militance in the future. Others, who were frightened by the government's response and the reaction of the public to media reports, vowed to continue the struggle using traditional means. . . . Both the administration and the antiwar movement were at a crossroads."

In the aftermath of the clash, analyses and summaries of that fateful October weekend proliferated, but none was able to fully articulate the many cultural and political aspects of the tumultuous Pentagon March. As Mailer himself would write in *The Armies of the Night* a few months later, "It may be obvious by now that a history of the March on the Pentagon which is not unfair will never be written, any more than a history which could prove dependable in details!"

MAILER AND VIETNAM

A writer renowned for bursts of both outspoken perceptiveness and unattractive belligerence, Mailer had been a remarkable literary voice in America ever since his epic World War II novel *The Naked and the Dead* was published in 1948 (he served as an infrantryman in the Phillippines from 1943 to 1945). Fueled by huge reservoirs of talent and ambition, he emerged during the 1950s and early 1960s as what Seymour Krim called "a kind of literary Frank Sinatra," a man sometimes known as much for his personal excesses as his talent.

As critic Anatole Broyard once remarked in the *New York Times*, "[Mailer's] career seems to be a brawl between his talent and his exhibitionism."

During the mid-1960s, Mailer, who had explored a variety of leftist political philosophies and shown a strong antiauthoritarian voice in much of his work, emerged as one of the literary arena's most passionate detractors of American policies in Vietnam. At one point Mailer and the *New York Herald Tribune* even discussed sending him over to file regular reports on the war, but the proposal eventually faded away, done in by concerns about the famous author's safety and the newspaper's financial woes.

In recognition of Mailer's position regarding the war, organizers of the Vietnam Day antiwar protest scheduled for Berkeley, California, on May 2, 1965, asked him to speak to the crowd. "The traditional left did not consider Norman to be a political person," organizer Jerry Rubin told Mills, "but I insisted on him because I thought he was a very important cultural statement of the reality of America at the time. Like a rock star, he interested a larger audience than the people who were just against the war."

Mailer's cutting remarks—heavily spiced with blunt put-downs of President Lyndon Johnson's new book, *My Hope for America*—proved tremendously popular with the thousands of protestors arrayed before him. His suggestion that opponents of the war turn portraits of the president upside down as a form of protest went over particularly well. "When Norman got up and gave his speech—an extraordinary speech—the crowd went crazy," Rubin told Mailer biographer Peter Manso. "It was the first time anybody had made fun of the President, and here he was telling the country to take LBJ's photo and turn it upside down." Activist Abbie Hoffman later remarked that Mailer's idea of turning the president's picture upside down "helped lead us into the guerrilla theater that the counterculture became noted for in the late sixties," according to Mills.

A few months later, Mailer penned a scathing article that appeared in the *Partisan Review* (and eventually his book *Christians and Cannibals*). A portion of his piece was devoted to ridiculing the magazine's editors, who had recently published an editorial objecting to American policies in Vietnam in what Mailer thought were exceedingly mild terms ("Three cheers lads. Your words read like they were written in milk and milk of magnesia," he wrote). Much of the rest of Mailer's words, however, concerned his fear that the war presented a tremendous risk to America's well-being: "If World War II was like *Catch-22*, this war will be like *Naked Lunch*. Lazy Dogs, and bombing raids from Guam. Marines with flame throwers. Jungle gotch in the gonorrhea and South Vietnamese girls doing the Frug . . . Unless Vietnam is the happening. Could that be? . . . Cause if it is, Warbucks, couldn't we have the happening just with the Marines and skip all that indiscriminate roast tit and naked lunch, all those bombed-out civilian ovaries . . . America will shoot all over the shithouse wall if this jazz goes on, Jim."

CREATION OF *ARMIES OF THE NIGHT*

Shortly after the October 1967 march on the Pentagon, Mailer's agent, Scott Meredith, met with representatives of *Harper's* magazine, who told the agent about their new emphasis on securing well-known literary contributors as part of an overall effort to burnish the magazine's image. Meredith told Hilary Mills, author of *Mailer: A Biography*, about the ensuing conversation: "Mailer had just come back from the Pentagon march in Washington and had told me all about it. I told them I thought it would make an absolutely marvelous article, but that we would never do it for a thousand dollars [the top fee for *Harper's* contributors at that time]. They asked me what I wanted, and I told them ten thousand dollars, which was much more than they had ever paid. They both got very gloomy and changed the subject, but apparently they went home and thought about it." A *Harper's* representative called the next day, agreeing to Meredith's financial terms; a deal was negotiated wherein Mailer would submit a twenty-thousand-word article in a month.

At the end of the month, however, Mailer had written ninety thousand words on the subject. The editors at *Harper's*, enthralled with the author's work, made the daring decision to run the whole thing in one issue. Mailer's article, "The Steps of the Pentagon," which appeared in the periodical's March 1968 issue, thus became the longest work ever to run in a magazine, said Mills. Shortly after completing the *Harper's* piece, Mailer began work on a twenty-five-thousand-word epilogue, "Battle of the Pentagon."

Harper's editor Willie Morris and the rest of the magazine's editorial staff knew that "The Steps of the Pentagon" would be a controversial piece, both for its provocative, opinionated nature and its New Journalism trappings (Mailer portrayed himself as the protagonist in the third person, among other things). "Oddly enough," Morris told Mills, "the cancellations we got were not over his stand on the Vietnam involvement but over the language. That piece broke new ground for American letters; it was a watershed issue because of the language. I knew when I read it that this was going to be a singular leap, but I also knew we'd have to go all the way and not compromise."

CRITICAL RECEPTION

In May 1968 New American Library published "The Steps of the Pentagon" and "Battle of the Pentagon" together as *The Armies of the Night: History as a Novel, The Novel as History*. *Armies of the Night* and its unconventional author received praise from many quarters when the book was published, although the work was not universally hailed; some critics found fault with the New Journalism quality of his prose, and some took issue with his interpretation of the events of that famous October weekend. *Dissent* founder Irving Howe, for instance, told Manso that he found *The Armies of the Night* to be an "irresponsible" book: "[Mailer] didn't take into account that those kids were brought down to a confrontation that they weren't prepared for, that the leaders were not just against the war—which I was too, of course—but in many cases actively supported the Vietcong." But most reviewers found it to be a powerful document that provided keen insights into a chaotic time. *New Republic* critic Richard Gilman wrote that "all the rough force of [Mailer's] imagination, his brilliant gifts of observation, his ravishing if often calculating honesty, his daring and his *chutzpah* are able to flourish on the steady ground of a newly coherent subject." *Saturday Review* writer H. S. Resnik commented that the book "is probably the truest picture we have of what has been happening to America. . . . [It features] the objectivity of journalism and the intimacy of a memoir. . . . Some people will never be able to overcome their repugnance for Mailer's public role, a combination of Tamburlaine, Faust, and Cassius Clay, but for those who can, the rewards are rich."

Influential critic Alfred Kazin was particularly impressed. Writing in the *New York Times Book Review*, he said that "only a born novelist could have written a piece of history so intelligent, mischievous, penetrating, and alive, so vivid with crowds, the great stage of American democracy." He called *The Armies of the Night* "a work of personal and political reportage that brings to the inner and developing crisis of the United States at this moment admirable sensibilities, candid intelligence, the most moving concern for America itself. Mailer's intuition in this book is that the times demand a new form. He has found it."

Years later, *The Armies of the Night*, which won the Pulitzer Prize for nonfiction and the National Book Award in arts and letters, continues to be one of Mailer's most highly regarded and influential books. Critic and writer Diana Trilling, for instance, told Manso that "[Mailer] was in the very midst of what I call the revolutionary Establishment, and yet in *The Armies of the Night* he was able to get above it and look at it." Citing the author's ability to see both the frail reality and the potent symbolism of both the soldiers and protestors who clashed outside the Pentagon, Trilling concluded that "*The Armies of the Night* was his greatest book without any question."

FURTHER READING

DeBenedetti, Charles, with Charles Chatfield. *An American Ordeal: The Antiwar Movement of the Vietnam Era*. Syracuse: Syracuse University Press, 1990.

Garfinkle, Adam. "Aftermyths of the Antiwar Movement." *Orbis* (Fall 1995).

Gilman, Richard. Review of *The Armies of the Night*. In *New Republic* (June 8, 1968).

Gitlin, Todd. *Mother Jones* (November 1983).

Kazin, Alfred. Review of *The Armies of the Night*. In *New York Times Book Review* (May 5, 1968).

Lennon, J. Michael, ed. *Conversations with Norman Mailer*. Jackson: University Press of Mississippi, 1988.

Mailer, Norman. *The Armies of the Night*. New York: New American Library, 1968.

———. *Cannibals and Christians*. New York: Dial, 1966.

Manso, Peter. *Mailer: His Life and Times*. New York: Simon and Schuster, 1985.

Mills, Hilary. *Mailer: A Biography*. New York: Empire Books, 1982.

Resnik, H. S. Review of *The Armies of the Night*. In *Saturday Review* (May 4, 1968).
Sale, Kirkpatrick. *SDS*. New York: Random House, 1973.
Small, Melvin. *Covering Dissent: The Media and the Anti–Vietnam War Movement*. New Brunswick, N.J.: Rutgers University Press, 1994.
Wells, Tom. *The War Within: America's Battle over Vietnam*. Berkeley: University of California Press, 1994.

"The Ballad of the Green Berets"

Song

Artist: Barry Sadler

Written by: Barry Sadler

Original Release: January 12, 1966 (as single)

Album Release: January 19, 1966 (On *The Ballad of the Green Berets*, RCA Victor)

One of the most famous of the Vietnam-era songs to hit the American charts was "The Ballad of the Green Berets," Barry Sadler's ode to his fellow Special Forces soldiers. A decidedly patriotic song, "Ballad" proved immensely popular upon its release. Sadler himself, though, developed a profound ambivalence toward his creation. Relegated to public relations appearances by his superiors, he became disenchanted and left the military.

HISTORICAL BACKGROUND

The U.S. Army's Special Forces units were elite troops trained in various counterinsurgency and unconventional warfare tactics. The soldiers in these units, nicknamed "Green Berets" in recognition of their distinctive headgear, proved adept at executing many of their unconventional assignments during the course of the war. Operating primarily in small teams along the borders of Laos and Cambodia, the Green Berets embarked on many intelligence-gathering missions into those countries. Their responsibilities also included training various South Vietnamese peoples in counterinsurgency tactics behind enemy lines.

U.S. Army Special Forces involvement in Vietnam began in 1957 with the arrival of the 1st Special Forces Group (Airborne) in Nha Trang. For the next four years, the Green Berets' primary responsibility was to train regular members of the Army of the Republic of Vietnam (ARVN) in guerrilla warfare and counterinsurgency tactics; these early trainees eventually became the nucleus of the ARVN's own Special Forces units. The Green Berets were bolstered during this time by President John Kennedy, who was an enthusiastic supporter of the military's counterinsurgency programs.

In 1962 the Green Berets' responsibilities were expanded to include training of other Vietnamese peoples, most notably Montagnard tribesmen. "The Special Forces found the Montagnard aborigines incredibly simplistic and superstitious," wrote Shelby Stanton in *Green Berets at War*. "To gain their allegiance, the Special Forces soldiers carefully learned tribal customs and studied the local dialects, ate the tribal food, endured the cold, mixed indigenous garb with their uniforms, and participated in the rituals and ceremonies. Many senior MACV [Military Assistance Command Vietnam] officers viewed this latest rugged and independent Special Forces effort with extreme displeasure, but the CIA [Central Intelligence Agency] heartily approved." The Civilian Irregular Defense Group (CIDG), which became an important element in defending South Vietnam from NVA infiltration, originated out of these efforts.

By late 1965, Special Forces camps dotted western South Vietnam, many of them in enemy dominated regions. Despite their vulnerability, the Special Forces units stationed in these areas continued to provide key intelligence information to MACV, and by the summer of 1966 MACV estimated that Green Beret–led units accounted for about half of its ground intelligence reports. Indeed, throughout the war American Special Forces units had an impact that was disproportionate to their small numbers. In 1968, however, the CIDG program ended, in part because South Vietnam's government felt that it was promoting separatism among the Montagnards.

SADLER AND VIETNAM

Sadler dropped out of high school and joined the Air Force in the late 1950s at the age of seventeen. He left the service after four years, but an unrewarding six-month stint picking fruit spurred him to return to military service. This time he enrolled with the Army, eventually making his way into the Green Berets, the Special Forces branch of the Army. He subsequently transferred to Vietnam, where he was wounded. It was during his convalescence that he penned and recorded "The Ballad of the Green Berets," an unabashedly patriotic song that rocketed to the top of the charts upon its release in January 1966. Any subsequent inclination he might have had to return to active duty in Vietnam was squelched by superior officers who recognized his public relations value (and the corresponding blow that the service would suffer if Sadler were killed in Vietnam). But even though Sadler soon emerged as the war's best-known soldier on the strength of the single and his various public relations appearances, "he anguished over the role he'd acquired,'' according to *GQ* contributor John Ed Bradley. ''At appearances, he often was introduced as the most decorated soldier yet produced by the Vietnam War, which was a flat-out lie. Some members of the Special Forces complained that he was exploiting them, making bags of money singing his overly sentimental dirge while every day in the field they put their asses on the line. . . . At times, racked with guilt, he expressed a searing hatred of the ballad [and] said he wished he'd never written it.'' In 1967, after a year of public relations–oriented assignments, Sadler left the service with an honorable discharge.

In 1978 Sadler, who was married, was convicted of voluntary manslaughter in the shooting of the ex-boyfriend of a girlfriend (Sadler claimed that he mistook the man's car keys for a handgun). Originally sentenced to a four- to five-year prison term, he served only twenty-one days due to the intervention of a sympathetic appeals judge. Sadler eventually established himself as a writer of military adventures. He was named a contributing editor to *Soldier of Fortune* magazine, and he penned two dozen military-flavored pulp novels during the 1970s and 1980s. In September 1988, however, while living in Guatemala, Sadler was shot in the head under mysterious circumstances. Some accounts blame the shooting on an unhappy business partner, whereas others attribute it to a poorly executed suicide attempt. In any event, the wound partially paralyzed him and left him incoherent at times. He died of an apparent cardiac arrhythmia in November 1989, fourteen months after the shooting.

CREATION OF "THE BALLAD OF THE GREEN BERETS"

Sadler was a noted barracks performer among his friends, though he had no formal musical background. Word of his patriotic, pro-military music eventually reached Army officials, who subsequently encouraged him to record some of his compositions. Armed with a bundle of songs, including the ''Green Berets'' song, Sadler traveled to the New York City recording studios of RCA Victor. There he recorded ''Green Berets'' with a minimum of musical accompaniment.

''The Ballad of the Green Berets'' was released into a fertile environment. Robin Moore's *Green Berets* novel—which featured a photograph of Sadler on its cover—had already sold more than a million copies by January 12, 1966, when Sadler's record was released, and those who favored American involvement in Vietnam were increasingly troubled by rising antiwar rhetoric. The single was an immediate sensation, selling two million copies in its first five weeks of sale (it eventually sold about eight million copies). It quickly became the top-selling single in the nation, regardless of musical genre, its popularity aided tremendously by Sadler's successful appearance on the ''Ed Sullivan Show'' and a joint marketing arrangement with the publisher of Moore's novel. The song pulled its biggest fans from that segment of the American population that concurred with the song's salute-to-the-brave-American-soldier sentiments, but its popularity extended beyond this base of support. ''Performed to a simple guitar and martial drum accompaniment by an actual member of the U.S. Army Special Forces, it had a ring of authenticity that made it popular among people who were not even passionately devoted to the successful conclusion of the conflict,'' contended Jens Lund in "Country Music Goes to War: Songs for the Red-Blooded American.''

CRITICAL RECEPTION

As was the case with antiwar songs of the same period, reaction to the song from American music-buyers was predicated in large measure on their own views of the war. Dismissed by critics of the war as laughably simplistic, "The Ballad of the Green Berets" was embraced as a patriotic and stirring anthem by America's "silent majority." Indeed, observers of the single's phenomenal popularity characterized the song as an undeniably potent articulation of traditional American military themes. The song, wrote Lund, was "a skillful sentimentalization of the American soldier's task, full of effective cliches of *machismo*.''

FURTHER READING

Bradley, John Ed. "Barry Sadler, with a Bullet." *GQ-Gentleman's Quarterly* (April 1990).

Dimaggio, Paul, Richard A. Peterson, and Jack Esco, Jr. "Country Music: Ballad of the Silent Majority." In *The Sounds of Social Change: Studies in Popular Culture*. Serge Denisoff and Richard A. Peterson, eds. Chicago: Rand McNally, 1972.

Donahue, Deirdre. "The Balladeer of the Green Berets, Sgt. Barry Sadler, Now Pens Pulp Novels." *People Weekly* (July 7, 1986).

James, David. "The Vietnam War and American Music." In *The Vietnam War and American Culture*. John Carlos Rowe and Rick Berg, eds. New York: Columbia University Press, 1991.

Lund, Jens. "Country Music Goes to War: Songs for the Red-Blooded American." *Popular Music and Society* (Summer 1972).

Santoli, Al. *To Bear Any Burden*. New York: Dutton, 1985.

Stanton, Shelby L. *Green Berets at War*. Novato, Calif.: Presidio Press, 1985.

The Best and the Brightest

Nonfiction

Author: David Halberstam

Facts of Publication: New York: Random House, 1972

In September 1962 *New York Times* reporter David Halberstam arrived in South Vietnam; by the time he left the country about fifteen months later, he had emerged as an extremely controversial figure both in South Vietnam and back in the United States. Dismayed at the disparity between official accounts of the war's progress and their impressions of the true nature of events in Vietnam, Halberstam and several other correspondents—notably Homer Bigart, Neil Sheehan, Charles Mohr, and Malcolme Browne—filed increasingly pessimistic accounts of both the war and the regime of Ngo Dinh Diem. These accounts differed dramatically from the optimistic statements of government officials in both America and South Vietnam. As the star reporter of America's flagship newspaper, Halberstam became the lightning rod for much of the criticism that subsequently rolled in from the U.S. military and the Kennedy Administration.

After returning to the United States at the end of 1963, Halberstam received the Pulitzer Prize for his Vietnam reporting. He remained with the *New York Times* for another three and one-half years before moving on to *Harper's*. During this time, he also launched a very successful book writing career. In early 1969, intrigued by the personalities that had led America into the Vietnam fray, Halberstam began work on the book that would be known as *The Best and the Brightest*. The finished product was a searing examination of key figures in the Kennedy and Johnson Administrations.

HISTORICAL BACKGROUND

When John F. Kennedy assumed the presidency of the United States in 1961, he observed that his election marked a generational change in the leadership of the nation: "The torch has been passed to a new generation of Americans— born in this century, tempered by war, disciplined by a cold and bitter peace, proud of our ancient heritage—and unwilling to witness or permit the slow undoing of those human rights to which this nation has always been committed, and to which we are committed today at home and around the world." Indeed, the Kennedy Administration's top appointees—many of whom were pulled from prestigious universities and think tanks—were on average nearly twenty years younger than those who had served in the Eisenhower White House. Administration supporters characterized these men as the bright and self-confident cream of a new generation of leaders, proud Americans who had already proved their mettle in World War II and the subsequent Cold War years.

"It was a glittering time," wrote Halberstam in *The Best and the Brightest*. "They literally swept into office, ready, moving, generating their style, their confidence—they were going to get America moving again. There was a sense that these were brilliant men, men of force, not cruel, not harsh, but men who acted rather than waited. There was no time to wait, history did not permit that luxury; if we waited it would all be past us. Everyone was going to Washington, and the word went out quickly around the Eastern seacoast, at the universities and in the political clubs, that the best men were going to Washington. Things were going to be done and it was going to be great fun; the challenge awaited and these men did not doubt their capacity to answer that challenge."

The talents of the men Kennedy gathered around him were unquestioned; men such as Robert S. McNamara (the Ford executive turned secretary of defense), McGeorge Bundy (the dean of Harvard turned special assistant for military affairs), and many others (Walt Rostow, Maxwell Taylor, John McNaughton, Dean Rusk, etc.) were lauded for their vigor and intelligence. Indeed, wrote Halberstam, "their image was of virility; they played squash and handball to stay in shape, wrote books and won prizes (even the President had won a Pulitzer Prize), climbed mountains to clear their minds. Many of them read poetry and some were said to be able to quote it. Day after day we read about them, each new man more brilliant than the last." Still, as always, there were doubters. House Speaker Sam Rayburn, for instance, commented to Vice President Lyndon B. Johnson that "they may be every bit as intelligent as you say, but I'd feel a whole lot better about them if just one of them had run for sheriff once."

The new Administration settled in, armed with an ambitious agenda that symbolized the can-do atmosphere that permeated the capital. Kennedy's domestic program called for civil rights expansion, increased education spending, tax reform, and medical care for the elderly. Key aspects of the program, however, were slowed by Congress and a series of international crises of a distinctly Cold

War flavor, in Cuba and Berlin. But even though the Bay of Pigs, the Cuban Missile Crisis, and the Berlin Wall grabbed the headlines in the early 1960s, Southeast Asia concerned the Administration as well.

American foreign policy in Southeast Asia was predicated on the "domino theory," which held that if one nation fell to Communism, others would follow, like a string of dominoes. Determined to show America's resolve to hold the line on Communism—and mindful of the need for a foreign policy success—the Kennedy Administration chose Vietnam as the place to make its stand in the region. During Kennedy's first months in office, he approved increased U.S. financial and military aid for the South Vietnamese government, which was struggling with Communist insurgents from North Vietnam (and in its own land). In November 1961 General Maxwell Taylor and foreign policy advisor Walter Rostow were sent to South Vietnam on a fact-finding mission. When they returned, they assured the president that the Communist insurgents could be defeated with an increase in U.S. military and economic assistance.

Project Beef-Up was subsequently launched. Shrouded in secrecy, the initiative dramatically increased U.S. involvement in South Vietnam. By the fall of 1962, the American military commitment in South Vietnam had risen to about ten thousand men, and as William Prochnau noted in *Once Upon a Distant War*, "the civilian contingent had also grown substantially, with American bureaucrats advising on everything from rice production to land reform." Secretary of Defense Robert McNamara supervised the gradual escalation of American military involvement in the country.

McNamara was "perhaps the brightest star in Kennedy's constellation of advisers," wrote William J. Rust in *Kennedy in Vietnam*. "A brilliant administrator and statistician, he dazzled other officials with his energy, intensity, and, above all, quantifiable facts." McNamara had taken the Pentagon by storm when he had arrived in Washington. Dismissive of the military, he had surrounded himself with analysts plucked from civilian life and established a philosophy of measuring the war's progress in which quantitative data held sway.

Stanley Karnow noted in *Vietnam: A History* that when McNamara made "the first of his many trips to Vietnam in May 1962, he looked at the figures and concluded optimistically after only forty-eight hours in the country that 'every quantitative measurement . . . shows that we are winning the war.' " Increased American aid, it was felt, would surely ensure victory. But the war dragged on nonetheless. In late 1963 Diem and Kennedy were assassinated within weeks of one another. In 1965 America's role in Vietnam underwent a dramatic shift as President Lyndon B. Johnson approved the deployment of American ground troops in the country. And still the escalation continued, propelled by the continued assurances of U.S. officials that victory was right around the corner. Instead, the war claimed rising numbers of American and Vietnamese casualties, and it ultimately claimed the presidency of Johnson as well.

For much of this time, McNamara and his prowar allies continued to cite their data analyses as proof that the war was being won. But as Karnow remarked, "the missing element in the 'quantitative measurement' that guided McNamara and other U.S. policy makers was the qualitative dimension that could not easily be recorded. There was no way to calibrate the motivation of Vietcong guerrillas. Nor could computers be programmed to describe the hopes and fears of Vietnamese peasants." Finally, the numbers themselves were often inaccurate, falsified to appease public opinion, bolster officers' careers, or blunt growing doubts about the war's progress. "Two and two always make four," admitted one CIA analyst to Prochnau. "But first someone has to decide that two actually is two."

HALBERSTAM AND VIETNAM

The Press in Vietnam before Diem's Fall

In the early 1960s a relatively small number of print correspondents had a major impact on the tone of U.S. press coverage of the Vietnam War. "Television news was still in the process of inventing itself," remarked Prochnau. "Television remained an *enfant trouvé*, a journalistic foundling that still yielded status, wisdom, and influence to the written press." The commitment of American ground troops remained far in the future as well, so Vietnam remained beneath the radar of American citizens preoccupied with events in Cuba and other international hot spots. The U.S. news community subsequently devoted relatively few resources to Vietnam. In early 1962, then, the American press contingent in the country consisted of little more than a few wire service stringers, the *New York Times'* Homer Bigart, and a smattering of traveling correspondents who rarely troubled to fully acquaint themselves with the dynamics of the unfolding situation.

The war in Vietnam, commented Prochnau, was unlike any other war that the American press had covered. "Neither officialdom nor media had worked out rules for untidy covert conflicts that were not so covert. The mutual confidentiality [seen in earlier wars] disappeared in the government's paranoia over its own actions. In Saigon, American officials refused to confirm, on or off the record, the most obvious facts. The reporters, quite naturally, scrambled for secondary and sometimes less-reliable sources (although, as time wore on, the information from those sources often proved to be more accurate than the highly politicized official reports going to Washington). It was an extraordinarily self-destructive policy, one that began with lies to the public and press and soon led to the government lying to itself."

Indeed, relations between U.S. diplomatic and military officials and the correspondents soured with remarkable speed. The Saigon press corps felt that official accounts of individual clashes with the Vietcong and updates of big-picture progress too often showed an appalling disregard for the facts, and they chafed under information restrictions imposed by U.S. officials and the South Vietnamese government. U.S. officials, meanwhile, were preoccupied with the possible impact of the press on military security and public opinion. As William Hammond noted in *The Military and the Media, 1962–1968*, "If enthusiasm for the conflict in South Vietnam began to fade because of negative reporting in the press, the American effort to defeat Communist aggression in Southeast Asia would also begin to slip and might even fail for lack of support. A low profile, achieved through restraints on the press at the scene of conflict and designed to sustain the American public's support for the war, seemed a safer course."

By the time Halberstam replaced Homer Bigart for the *New York Times* in the fall of 1962, however, correspondents such as UPI's Neil Sheehan, AP's Malcolme Browne, and *Time*'s Charlie Mohr had learned to find the story themselves. Their reports reflected growing concern about the weakness of the shaky Diem regime, the ineptitude and passivity of its armed forces, and the reservoir of support for the Communists present in some areas of the South Vietnamese countryside. For their part, angry U.S. officials charged that the correspondents were inexperienced and misinformed malcontents who insisted on putting the worst possible light on everything they reported.

Criticism of Halberstam, Other Correspondents

Much of the criticism was targeted at Halberstam, who had emerged as a vocal—and highly visible—dissenter from administration gospel concerning the war effort and the Diem regime within months of his arrival. As the primary voice from Vietnam for the *New York Times*, America's most influential newspaper, Halberstam's damning reports had a tremendous impact back in Washington, D.C. At one point President Kennedy—who once complained that Halberstam's *New York Times* reports provided more complete and timely coverage of events than did his own intelligence reports—even asked Arthur Sulzberger, the paper's publisher, to reassign the young reporter. Sulzberger, however, declined to follow through on the suggestion, and Halberstam continued to roam across Vietnam until his regularly scheduled departure time of December 1963.

Halberstam remained the biggest target among the correspondents during his tenure, but Browne, Sheehan, and others in the press corps felt the heat as well. "What began as sniping turned into an orchestrated attack," Halberstam told Prochnau. "It became a full-fledged war with more fronts than Vietnam. We were getting cannon fire from a different direction every day: the Pentagon regiment, the White House regiment, the embassy regiment, the press regiment, the right-wing regiment—and all of it feeding the regiments from our own offices."

Through it all, the correspondents continued to put together a far more accurate portrait of the situation in Vietnam than did most official sources. This was due in part to the unique "hail-a-cab" nature of the war; one could drive mere miles out of Saigon and be confronted with grim evidence of the war. Indeed, the Diem government's hold on the entire Mekong Delta area was a tenuous one even at this early stage of the war: "What the government controlled nominally by day, including the highway, slipped easily back to the rebels at night," wrote Prochnau. "After dark, people disappeared at roadblocks, snipers operated more boldly, crudely efficient land mines blew up reckless intruders."

The best of the correspondents stationed in Saigon were energetic and brave (often to the point of recklessness) reporters who refused to be intimidated by pressure from U.S. officials, the Diem government, or their own sometimes-nervous news organizations. Determined to solicit the opinions of frontline military personnel and other less savory but nonetheless knowledgeable sources, the reporters were rewarded with information that continually reinforced their impressions that the effort against the Vietcong was not going nearly as well as officials seemed to believe. As Halberstam once remarked for the *New York Times*, "It should be reported that there is considerably less optimism out in the field than in Washington or in Saigon and that the closer one gets to the actual contact level of this war, the farther one gets from official optimism." Ironically, despite ample evidence of their dangerous backcountry forays, some critics of the press contingent insisted that the correspondents were hiding in Saigon and thus misinterpreting the information they heard. "The idea that the correspondents sat around Saigon bars cooking up stories to aggravate the government became a Washington fixation" said Prochnau. "The problem was quite the opposite. The government couldn't keep the correspondents *in* Saigon because they didn't believe anything they heard there." But instead of looking into the warning flares launched by the reporters, members of the Kennedy Administration concentrated on discrediting the correspondents.

As Halberstam, Sheehan, and the others continued to dig, grumblings about their competence gave way to complaints about their patriotism. This charge would dog the American press corps throughout the rest of the conflict. As Clarence R. Wyatt noted in *Paper Soldiers*, the American press in Vietnam has over the years past been cast as a "villain, one inspired by political and ideological biases to misrepresent the nature and the progress of the war, thus leading the American people to turn their backs on a 'noble cause.'" Such charges were leveled from all quarters, from Administration officials to military leaders to other journalists who supported the war.

Defenders of the American correspondents, though, dismiss such charges. "The idea that this early group carried with them an antimilitary bent, polluting a generation of reporters, is one of the enduring myths of the war," said Prochnau. "In the great dispute between the government and the press that built to an explosion in 1963, then festered throughout the war and long afterward, none of the young resident correspondents challenged U.S. involvement in Vietnam or the war itself." Sheehan later commented on those who questioned Halberstam's patriotism. "David was a *very* intense guy and *very* patriotic," he told Prochnau. "That was what produced all that anger. You've got to understand, we thought these people were *losing* the war!" Mohr, Halberstam, and others later echoed these sentiments: They weren't angry about the war; they were angry because they felt that decisions based on ignorance and self-deception were jeopardizing American chances to win the war.

By 1963 relations between the leading members of the Saigon press corps and U.S. officials and the Diem government were abysmal. The correspondents were contemptuous of General Paul Harkins and Ambassador Frederick Nolting, the leading American officials in Vietnam, and the feeling was mutual. As Prochnau observed, relations disintegrated into a "mutual standoff of cold fury and hot shouts—Liar! Traitor! Scoundrel! Fool!—with an American foreign policy teetering precariously in the void between." The animosity between the two sides congealed into a bitter wall of anger that remained in place until 1964, when relations between the two camps began to improve somewhat.

Press relations with the Diem regime were even worse. In 1961 and 1962 the Saigon press corps wrote numerous articles that embarrassed or angered Diem, his brother Ngo Dinh Nhu, and his brother's wife, Madame Ngo Dinh Nhu (Diem's brother and sister-in-law wielded significant power in the South Vietnamese government). The reports, said Wyatt, contended that Diem's government "had 'so far failed to win the active support of South Vietnam's population,' that he was personally isolated from his people, that his methods mirrored those of the communists in their authoritarianism, their constant suspicion and surveillance, and their implied threats, and that his administration was riddled with gross inefficiency, nepotism, and corruption. But he was also, it was written, the only real alternative to the Vietcong." The unfavorable coverage infuriated Diem and his family, who took to dismissing the press as agents of Communism. They also refused to believe U.S. officials, who insisted that they did not have the power to silence their country's press representatives. Unable or unwilling to differentiate between the American press and the American government, Diem sometimes equated press criticism with U.S. government maneuverings to undermine his rule.

By the summer of 1963, when a string of ritual Buddhist suicides by self-immolation rocked Saigon, correspondents were painting a picture of a country in dire straits. Even stateside editorials lambasted the Diem government in the wake of the Buddhist crisis (the *Washington Post*, for instance, called Diem's policies "morally repugnant and politically suicidal"). As tensions mounted around the capital, key correspondents were placed under government surveillance and subjected to intimidation and physical violence. Disquieting rumors of government assassination lists circulated; it was said that the lists included the names of Sheehan, Halberstam, U.S. embassy press liaison John Mecklin, and others (including Ambassador Henry Cabot Lodge, who had succeeded Nolting earlier in the year).

On November 1, 1963, the South Vietnamese military overthrew Diem and his family. A day later Diem and his brother were assassinated, opening the door for a succession of civilian and military governments. Both the U.S. government, which had begun distancing itself from Diem in the preceding months, and the press seemed to recognize that Diem's death signaled the end of a chapter in Vietnam. A rapprochement of sorts was reached between the two antagonists. As Halberstam recalled in his book *The Making of a Quagmire*, "Those first few weeks after the coup were a time of great frankness and soul-searching, of mutual trust in many areas." U.S. officials subsequently took a different tack in handling the press. "They saw that their obstructionism had cost them a significant degree of influence and control over what the reporters eventually wrote," said Wyatt. "By figuratively taking the reporters into the house, they could defuse much of the ill will and antagonism that had plagued both parties."

As a result, the working relationship between the Vietnam press and the U.S. government thawed somewhat during the next few years. Still, the fundamentally different mandates of the two entities—and the emergence of television news coverage of the war—ensured that clashes would erupt down the road.

CREATION OF *THE BEST AND THE BRIGHTEST*

The Best and the Brightest actually grew out of a Halberstam article on McGeorge Bundy written for *Harper's* magazine in January 1969. Halberstam felt that an examination of Bundy, whom he called "the most glistening of the Kennedy-Johnson intellectuals," would provide readers with a potentially fascinating glimpse into the Kennedy Administration. "I thought it was a good idea," Halberstam remarked in *The Best and the Brightest*, "since the Kennedy intellectuals had been praised as the best and the brightest men of a generation and yet they were the architects of a war which I and many others thought the worst tragedy to befall this country since the Civil War."

As Halberstam launched the piece on Bundy, however, he realized that the article had "turned out to be much broader than a profile of a man, in effect [it was] the embryonic profile of an era. . . . When the article was finished I had the feeling of having just started." Halberstam subsequently decided to write an entire book on the leaders of the Kennedy and Johnson Administrations. "The men intrigued me because they were fascinating," wrote Halberstam. "They had been heralded as the ablest men to serve this country in this century—certainly their biographies seemed to confirm that judgment—and yet very little had been written about them. . . . I felt that if I could learn something about them, I would learn something about the country, the era and about power in America."

For the next two and one-half years, Halberstam worked on the book, determined to find out "why it had all happened." As the months passed, though, the author found that the work was "not a book about Vietnam, but a book about America, and in particular about power and success in America, what the country was, who the leadership was, how they got ahead, what their perceptions were about themselves, about the country, and about the mission."

CRITICAL RECEPTION

Halberstam's book received largely favorable reviews, although there were some notable exceptions. Critics praising the book included W. W. MacDonald of *Library Journal*, who called *The Best and the Brightest* a "brilliant, imaginatively conceived, lucidly organized, and gracefully written work," and *Newsweek*'s P. S. Prescott, who wrote that the volume was "a staggeringly ambitious undertaking that is fully matched by Halberstam's performance; it is also a staggeringly long book which, thanks to Halberstam's technical virtuosity and narrative skill, is seductively readable." *Life, Business Week*, the *New York Times*, and the *Washington Post* weighed in with complimentary reviews as well.

Even though a number of Halberstam's critics granted that the book made for often fascinating reading, they contended that in the final analysis the book was flawed. Several prominent periodicals—including the *Wall Street Journal*, the *New York Review of Books*, and *Newsday*—took Halberstam to task for alleged transgressions ranging from a subjective, bombastic tone to overreliance on personal interviews at the expense of other documentation.

FURTHER READING

Halberstam, David. *The Best and the Brightest*. New York: Random House, 1972.
———. "Getting the Story in Vietnam." *Commentary* (January 1968).
———. *The Making of a Quagmire*. New York: Random House, 1965.
Hallin, Daniel C. *The "Uncensored War": The Media and Vietnam*. New York: Oxford University Press, 1986.
Hammond, William M. *The Military and the Media, 1962–1968*. Washington, D.C.: Center of Military History, 1988.
Karnow, Stanley. *Vietnam: A History*. New York: Viking Press, 1983.
MacDonald, W. W. Review of *The Best and the Brightest*. In *Library Journal* (November 1, 1972), 85.
Mecklin, John. *Mission in Torment: An Intimate Account of the U.S. Role in Vietnam*. Garden City, N.Y.: Doubleday, 1965.
Prescott, P. S. Review of *The Best and the Brightest*. In *Newsweek* (November 20, 1972), 125.
Prochnau, William. *Once Upon a Distant War*. New York: Random House, 1995.
Rust, William J. *Kennedy in Vietnam: American Vietnam Policy, 1960–1963*. New York: Charles Scribner's Sons, 1985.
Schandler, Herbert Y. *Lyndon Johnson and Vietnam: The Unmaking of a President*. Princeton, N.J.: Princeton University Press, 1977.
Wyatt, Clarence R. *Paper Soldiers: The American Press and the Vietnam War*. New York: W. W. Norton, 1993.

Bloods: An Oral History of the Vietnam War by Black Veterans

Nonfiction

Author: Wallace Terry (editor)

Facts of Publication: New York: Ballantine, 1984

African-American soldiers who served in Vietnam struggled with many of the same issues of life and death that confronted their white, Hispanic, and Native American counterparts, but they also grappled with matters unique to the black experience, for the treatment of black soldiers in that conflict became a source of considerable controversy both during and after the war. Determined to explore all aspects of the black vet experience, Wallace Terry spent several years interviewing African Americans who had seen combat in Vietnam. The final result was *Bloods: An Oral History of the Vietnam War by Black Veterans*.

HISTORICAL BACKGROUND

In the late 1960s relations between black and white U.S. soldiers in all branches of the military deteriorated alarmingly in some regions of Vietnam. Only a few years earlier, the U.S. military had seen race relations within its ranks as a point of pride; indeed, many black men felt that the Army or Navy provided greater opportunities to use one's talents—and be compensated accordingly—than did civilian society. As Clark C. Smith remarked in *Brothers: Black Soldiers in the Nam*, "Military service was for blacks a vehicle for social equality in which rank replaced race as a measure of respect and accomplishment." But Wallace Terry noted in *Bloods* that by 1969, "a new black soldier had appeared." Having exhausted its supply of professional blacks who had entered into military service for career reasons, the United States was forced to take "black draftees, many just steps removed from marching in the Civil Rights Movement or rioting in the rebellions that swept the urban ghettos from Harlem to Watts."

This influx of new soldiers, coupled with growing disillusionment about the war, dramatically changed the tone of black-white race relations in Vietnam. Angered by events back in America (urban riots, the assassination of Martin Luther King, Jr.), perceived discrimination in military assignments and promotions, instances of outright racism, and the widespread feeling that the war had degenerated into a wasteful stalemate, growing numbers of black GIs adopted an increasingly militant stance. Particularly galling to black soldiers was evidence that they accounted for a disproportionate percentage of Vietnam casualties, especially in the conflict's early years. (By 1967, blacks—who accounted for about 11 percent of the U.S. military's enlisted strength in Vietnam—accounted for more than 20 percent of its casualties; by 1970, however, military efforts to correct this inequity had cut the percentage of black casualties in half.) Some white soldiers dismissed these concerns, their perspective influenced by racist feelings, genuine doubts about the legitimacy of the complaints, or the conviction that the military had overcompensated for the earlier inequities.

Black soldiers were also keenly aware of the war's unpopularity with black leaders back in America. King emerged as a vocal and eloquent opponent of the war prior to his murder in April 1968, and advocates of "black power" such as Stokely Carmichael bitterly denounced the conflict as nothing more than "white people sending black people to make war on yellow people in order to defend the land they stole from red people," as he told the *National Guardian* in 1967. The decline in race relations was particularly noticeable in support/rear-echelon base camps, where the threat of injury or death from VC or North Vietnamese Army troops was not so great. After visiting the huge Camp Tien Sha base facility in Danang, *New Republic* reporter Zalin B. Grant reported that "the camp's biggest threat is race riots, not Vietcong. . . . Past favorable publicity about integration of U.S. troops has shimmered and disappeared like paddy water under a tropic sun." He went on to describe several examples of racial animus, ranging from an incident wherein a Confederate flag was hoisted above Navy headquarters on a day of national mourning for the assassinated King to a full-scale race riot that erupted at the Long Binh Detention Center between white and black inmates. Grant's conclusions about the dismal state of relations between blacks and whites in rear areas were echoed by countless other reporters and soldiers. By 1970 significant numbers of black soldiers were practicing a self-imposed brand of segregation, and the chasm in social interaction subsequently widened.

Out in the bush, however, the situation was much better. "In a combat situation the goal of survival transcends and overshadows all other problems," noted Byron Fiman, Jonathan Borus, and Duncan Stanton in the *Journal of Social Issues*. "Everyone was constantly confronted by the potentially overwhelming threat of death; they needed each other for survival. . . . Interpersonal contact between races became quite intimate as a result of the pressures of the combat environment. Consequently, it is not surprising that those soldiers in combat units experienced a more positive racial milieu." Both black and white soldiers confirmed that the harrowing environment out in the field provided fertile ground for nourishing respect and friendship between the races. In an interview with Wallace Terry for *Bloods*, black Vietnam veteran Harold Bryant recalled one instance in which a self-proclaimed Ku Klux Klan member joined his field unit. "That pissed a lot of us off," he said, " 'cause we had gotten real tight. We didn't have racial incidents like what was happening in the rear area, 'cause we had to depend on each other. . . . Well, we got out into a fire fight, and Mr. Ku Klux Klan got his little ass trapped. . . . So we laid down a base of fire to cover him. But he was just immobile. He froze. And a brother went out there and got him and dragged him back. Later on, he said that action had changed his perception of what black people were about."

TERRY AND VIETNAM

Journalist Wallace Terry provided reports from Vietnam for *Time* magazine for two years, from late 1967 to mid-1969. He was one of the few black correspondents to submit stories from Vietnam (the *New Republic* noted that in 1969 he was the only black among the two hundred accredited journalists in the country). During his time in Vietnam, Terry witnessed a profound deterioration in the relationship between America's white and black soldiers. In 1967 the relationship had been one of "foxhole brotherhood," but by 1969 the two races were frequently wary adversaries, especially in rear-echelon areas. But whereas the U.S. military's fractious race relations became a subject of considerable discussion back home, Terry felt that other aspects of the black soldier's Vietnam experience were not being adequately aired. He subsequently went out in the field to interview hundreds of black and white soldiers, canvassing them about their thoughts on a variety of social and political issues.

CREATION OF *BLOODS*

Wallace Terry admitted to Eric James Schroeder in *Vietnam, We've All Been There* that at one point he convinced himself that his grim assessments of black-white relations in the U.S. military might have a major impact on America's perspective on the war. Upon returning to America, however, Terry was unable to secure a book contract. He attributed this failure to publishers' perceptions that black Americans "don't buy books."

Eventually, though—after reorganizing the book as a sort of oral history—Terry secured a contract. He subsequently interviewed black men who had served in Vietnam in all sorts of combat capacities. Some of the men were veterans whom he had met during Vietnam, and others were men whom he contacted back in America. He would later note in the introduction to his book that the only requirement was that they had "won a badge of courage in combat, whether on a patrol boat or in a POW camp, on a night ambush or in the skies above North Vietnam." He also sought out soldiers from all branches of the service, and of all ranks and backgrounds. The final result was a collection of twenty stories called *Bloods: An Oral History of the Vietnam War by Black Veterans*.

Many of the issues discussed in *Bloods* transcended race. Vietnam was a war of horrific violence and destruction, and all U.S. soldiers stationed in the field— whether African American, white, Hispanic, Native American, or some other ethnicity—faced moments of immense physical and emotional stress. In his interview with Schroeder, Terry remarked that this reality was a large component of the book. "I've had people tell me that I was an advocate journalist. So what? So I'm reporting things in a way, or selecting material to use to try to convince you of something. What I'm trying to do in this book is convince you of the sacrifice of the men who went to Vietnam—whatever their color—and of the respect they deserve for that sacrifice."

Nonetheless, Terry contended that the black American combat soldier faced additional pressures and moral ambiguities that made the circumstances of his service that much more complex. "[The black Vietnam veteran] fought at a time when his sisters and brothers were fighting and dying at home for equal rights and greater opportunities," Terry wrote in his introduction, "for a color-blind nation promised to him in the Constitution he swore to defend. He fought at a time when some of his leaders chastised him for waging war against a people of color, and when his Communist foe appealed to him to take up arms instead against the forces of racism in America. The loyalty of the black Vietnam War veteran stood a greater test on the battleground than did the loyalty of any other American soldier in Vietnam; his patriotism begs a special salute at home."

CRITICAL REACTION

Most reviewers—and more significantly, many black Americans—saw *Bloods* as a long-overdue document of the black soldier's experiences in Vietnam and back home. Critics found Terry's book to be a powerful, if often disquieting, collection. The *Atlanta Journal & Constitution* called the work "a major contribution to the literature of [Vietnam]. For the first time a book has detailed the inequities blacks faced at home and on the battlefield. Their war stories involve not only Vietnam, but Harlem, Watts, Washington, D.C., and small-town America." Sam Cornish remarked in the *Christian Science Monitor* that "Terry shows skill and sensitivity in giving us a platoon of men who shared a common experience and help illuminate an era. Like good fiction, *Bloods* presents these men and their histories in a firm but objective tone, without apology."

Other critics commented that the book, though valuable for its insights into the thoughts and feelings of black soldiers, provided valuable insights into the pressures faced by all American combat personnel in Vietnam. Stanley Karnow remarked in the *New York Times Book Review* that even though the book cast a much-needed spotlight on the black soldier and his contributions to the war effort, its "broader value . . . is that it demonstrates that blacks and whites in Vietnam, whatever their differences, went through essentially the same ordeal." Reviewer Paul Gray, writing in *Time*, concluded that "the composite that [emerges in the book] is a portrait not just of warfare and warriors but of beleaguered patriotism and pride. . . . Their experience finally transcends race; their dramatic monologues bear witness to humanity."

FURTHER READING

Boyle, Richard. *The Flower of the Dragon: The Breakdown of the U.S. Army in Vietnam.* San Francisco: Ramparts Press, 1972.

Cornish, Sam. Review of *Bloods*. In the *Christian Science Monitor* (October 26, 1984).

Ebert, James R. *A Life in a Year: The American Infantryman in Vietnam, 1965–1972.* Novato, Calif.: Presidio, 1993.

Fiman, Byron G., Jonathan F. Borus, and M. Duncan Stanton. "Black-White and American-Vietnamese Relations among Soldiers in Vietnam." *Journal of Social Issues* 31, no. 4 (1975).

Goff, Stanley, and Robert Sanders, with Clark C. Smith. *Brothers: Black Soldiers in the Nam.* Novato, Calif.: Presidio, 1982.

Grant, Zalin B. "Whites against Blacks in Vietnam." *New Republic* (January 18, 1969).

Gray, Paul. Review of *Bloods*. In *Time* (August 20, 1984).

Johnson, Thomas A. "Negroes in 'The Nam.' " *Ebony* (August 1968).

Karnow, Stanley. Review of *Bloods*. In the *New York Times Book Review* (October 14, 1984).

Mullen, Robert W. *Blacks and Vietnam.* Washington, D.C.: University Press of America, 1981.

Schroeder, Eric James. *Vietnam, We've All Been There: Interviews with American Writers.* Westport, Conn.: Praeger, 1992.

Taylor, Clyde, ed. *Vietnam and Black America: An Anthology of Protest and Resistance.* Garden City, N.Y.: Anchor Press, 1973.

Terry, Wallace, ed. *Bloods: An Oral History of the Vietnam War by Black Veterans.* New York: Ballantine, 1984.

"Born in the U.S.A."

Song

Artist: Bruce Springsteen

Written by: Bruce Springsteen

Recorded: 1984

Album Release: June 4, 1984 (on *Born in the U.S.A.*, Columbia)

Many Vietnam veterans found it difficult to find their place in postwar America. Saddled with their own memories of a grim war and their status as a symbol of one of the nation's most tumultuous periods, veterans struggled against an undertow of social isolation and economic hardship. Thousands and thousands of veterans triumphed upon returning home; they built meaningful lives for themselves and their families. Some, though, were not so fortunate. These latter figures were the subject of Bruce Springsteen's "Born in the U.S.A.," which became a widely discussed (and widely misunderstood) song within weeks of its release.

HISTORICAL BACKGROUND

After completing their tours in Vietnam, many American soldiers returned home to receptions that bore little resemblance to the dreams they no doubt harbored while overseas. Instead of welcoming parades, returning veterans were greeted with indifference, uneasiness, or outright hostility. Indeed, in the years during and immediately following the war, the Vietnam veteran seemed to personify the conflict in a way that made him or her a target for all sectors of the political spectrum. "Vietnam veterans have carried the heaviest sense of responsibility for the conduct and outcome of the war," remarked Christian Appy, author of *Working-Class War*. "They have felt blamed on all sides—by conservatives for losing the war and by liberals for having participated in its immorality." Supporters of the war were perhaps more welcoming than America's antiwar factions, but even there, veterans found their support eroded by widely circulated tales of breakdowns in military discipline in Vietnam (in the form of drug abuse, "fraggings" [the murder of officers at the hands of their own soldiers], atrocities, disrespect for the uniform, etc.) and the visibility of those vets who renounced the war after returning home.

Vietnam had wracked the nation's internal workings and rattled its confidence, and many Americans saw those who had fought in the conflict as unpleasant reminders of a sad chapter in the nation's history. "Ignoring the Vietnam vet was just one part of the more general phenomenon of ignoring the nation's entire, shattering, unhappy Vietnam experience in all of its aspects—a phenomenon that hits at a need to suppress, a deep wish to forget," wrote David Levy, author of *The Debate over Vietnam*. Even veterans organizations such as the VFW and the American Legion were cool toward the returning veterans, who were too often branded as losers by a culture unfamiliar with military defeat. Author Tim O'Brien would later recall that the very words "American Legion" made many Vietnam veterans "shudder."

Some veterans reciprocated by adopting a cynical view of the country and nurturing a deep anger toward those who had protested against the deadly war from the safety of America's shores. Even those who came to agree that the war was an ill-conceived one bridled at the antiwar movement's characterizations of American soldiers as ignorant pawns with a taste for mayhem. Appy commented that "for veterans torn by confusion about the war they had fought, and struggling to feel some pride in what they had done, the protesters' passion, self-assurance, and sense of purpose could generate a nagging—if unspoken— envy. Faced with people so sure the war was wrong, vets were convinced their own morality was under siege."

In addition to grappling with their abandonment by large segments of American society, veterans also were confronted with proliferating portrayals of Vietnam veterans as demented, disturbed figures in mainstream culture, and, even more importantly, with often-bleak economic circumstances that made it difficult for some to regain their footing back home. "Drugs were frequently mentioned as a reason for the high unemployment among the veterans of Vietnam," said Richard Severo and Lewis Milford in *The Wages of War*. "But the truth was that jobs were hard to get even for veterans who had no drug problem, veterans unwelcomed by a people who did not want to be reminded of the war. Perhaps 250,000 Vietnam veterans between the ages of twenty and twenty-nine were unable to find work." They also pointed out that the Vietnam generation of soldiers—the vast majority of whom did not have a college degree when they departed for Southeast Asia—received less help from the government when they returned than had previous generations of soldiers. "More stringent fiscal management was ordered for the soldiers who had survived the free-spending combat that took place during the Johnson and Nixon administrations. When the fathers and uncles of Vietnam veterans came home from World War II, the G.I. Bill had paid all tuition and given veterans $75 a month, in a time when $75 a month could pay the rent and then some. Now, in a period of considerable inflation, the veterans were to get $200, which was to pay for higher tuition *and* the cost of staying alive. Some of the veterans thought that was not a very fair arrangement. The Defense Department's red carpet had been rolled up and stored away." The government's reluctance to pursue health issues affecting Vietnam veterans (post-traumatic stress disorder, exposure to Agent Orange) added to their bitterness and sense of abandonment.

In the late 1970s and early 1980s, however, the reputation of the Vietnam veteran began to change. Vietnam veterans groups played a large role in this transformation. They noted that veterans comprised a vital, contributing sector of American society, and their tireless efforts on behalf of those who had been victimized by Agent Orange and other poisonous chemicals during their tours garnered national attention. In addition, works of literature, films, and other media of popular culture increasingly presented sympathetic portraits of vets (and harrowing descriptions of the pressures they endured). By 1985, the nation's attitude towards those who fought in Vietnam had changed so dramatically that *Newsweek* was moved to remark that "America's Vietnam veterans, once viewed with a mixture of indifference and outright hostility by their countrymen, are now widely regarded as national heroes." Levy noted that both supporters and opponents of the war effort have subsequently adjusted their stances. Opponents of the war, "while holding to the view that the war was immoral and unnecessary . . . began to see the eighteen year olds who fought there less as perpetrators of evil and more as victims of a callous and misguided policy. In short, the animosity that was once, in part, directed against common soldiers has gradually become focused against politicians, technical planners, and the Pentagon." Some supporters of the war effort, meanwhile, abandoned efforts to justify the war. "The anger they felt against all who opposed the war now tends to be concentrated on those who abused and vilified the fighting men," Levy stated.

SPRINGSTEEN AND VIETNAM

Bruce Springsteen grew up in Freehold, New Jersey, a working-class town located about fifteen miles inland from the Atlantic coast. Recalling his teenage years to biographer Dave Marsh, author of *Glory Days*, Springsteen characterized Freehold as "no different than probably any other provincial town. It was just the kind of area where it was real conservative." The musician remembered his hometown as a stagnant place dominated by "some factories and some farms

and stuff that, if you didn't go to college, you ended up in. There really wasn't
that much.''

Springsteen later recalled in an interview with Kurt Loder for *Rolling Stone*
that the Vietnam War seemed a very distant phenomenon during his high school
years. ''I was aware of it through some friends that went. The drummer in my
first band was killed in Vietnam . . . Bart Hanes was his name. He was one of
those guys that was jokin' all the time, always playin' the clown. He came over
one day and said, 'Well, I enlisted. I'm goin' to Vietnam.' I remember he said
he didn't know where it *was*. And that was it. He left and he didn't come back.
And the guys that did come back were not the same.''

Springsteen ultimately received a medical deferment from the draft as a result
of a concussion he had suffered in a motorcycle accident. But he acknowledged
to Loder that until he got his 4-F, the specter of the war was a constant companion. A brief stint at a community college had not worked out—Marsh noted
that Springsteen's classmates ''petitioned for his dismissal on grounds of un-
acceptable weirdness''—and his departure from higher education's protective
walls left him vulnerable to the draft. He subsequently found himself on a bus
with a few dozen other young men on their way to take a physical. As he sat,
watching the scenery roll by, the young man brooded over the machinations of
the draft, which he felt suggested that a college boy's life was more valuable
than his own. ''And it was funny,'' he told Loder, ''because my father, he was
in World War II, and he was the type that was always sayin', 'Wait till the
army gets you. Man, they're gonna get that hair off of you. I can't wait. They
gonna make a *man* outta you.' We were really goin' at each other in those days.
And I remember I was gone for three days, and when I came back, I went in
the kitchen, and my folks were there, and they said, 'Where you been?' And I
said, 'Well, I had to go take my physical.' And they said, 'What happened?'
And I said, 'Well, they didn't take me.' And my father sat there, and he didn't
look at me, he just looked straight ahead. And he said, 'That's good.' It was,
uh . . . I'll never forget that. I'll *never* forget that.''

CREATION OF "BORN IN THE U.S.A."

The album that preceded Springsteen's *Born in the U.S.A.* was *Nebraska*, a
collection of bleak, evocative meditations on wrecked dreams and frail hopes in
the American heartland. ''*Nebraska* . . . was a record about the basic things that
keep people functioning in society, in a community, or in their families or in
their jobs,'' Springsteen told Marsh. ''The idea is that they all break down. They
fail. The record was a spiritual crisis—families fail, your job fails, and then
you're gone, you're lost, you don't have any connection to anything. Everything
just goes out the window. I was interested in finding out what happens then—
what do my characters do, what do I do?''

''Born in the U.S.A.'' was actually first recorded during the studio sessions
for *Nebraska*, but the lyrics were initially backed by spare acoustic accompa-

niment (as were all the songs on *Nebraska*). No one—including Springsteen—was satisfied with the song in its first incarnation. "To me, it was a dead song," manager/producer Jon Landau told Marsh. "Clearly the words and the music didn't go together." But as the months passed, and Springsteen began work on a new album, the songwriter continued to ponder the song's possibilities. Returning to the studio, Springsteen decided to give the song another try, but with a different melody and a pounding wave of musical accompaniment. "An acoustic guitar wasn't gonna get you there on this song. He needed a band that could feel the way this song was supposed to feel," said Landau. "To me it was one of the most ultimate things of Bruce's gift, the way he had not let go of this song—he had so fully seen its potential and he had just somewhere on his own, instinctively, found his way to the solution. Because it was the same words, the music was different."

The result was a powerful, bittersweet anthem about the grim lives that some Vietnam veterans faced after returning home to America. Wielding plain-spoken lyrics that echoed his own blue-collar upbringing, Springsteen touched on several aspects of the postwar plight of veterans, from unemployment ("Come back home to the refinery / Hiring man said 'Son if it was up to me' ") to the sense that all of that war's heartaches had been for naught ("I had a brother at Khe Sanh / Fightin' off the Viet Cong / They're still there, he's all gone . . . ''). Loder called the track "one of those rare records: a rousing rock and roll song that also gives voice to the pain of forgotten people." Robert Hilburn, author of *Springsteen*, called it "one of the most strident pieces of social commentary ever to become a Top 10 single in America."

For his part, Springsteen told Marsh that "I knew that that particular song was just a song that comes along once in a while, even if you write good songs. It had some power to it that seemed to speak to something that was so essential, similar to the way that 'Born to Run' [his biggest hit to that point] did. It's not that you have better songs or worse songs, but that's a particular type of song."

POPULAR RECEPTION

The *Born in the U.S.A.* album—which featured Springsteen's jeans-clad backside and an American flag on the cover—was phenomenally successful, with both the record-buying public and music critics. The title track was one of the album's most popular cuts, but ironically, much of its popularity was due to the fact that its sentiments were so fundamentally misunderstood or ignored. In the mid-1980s, noted Loder, "there was a new patriotism upon us, a great flexing of the national pecs." This changing self-image was fueled by several factors, including the Reagan Administration's interpretation of the nation's standing, concerns about the possible economic threat that Japan posed, and a sense that America had grown weary of carrying the twin millstones of Vietnam and Watergate. Supporters of this shift in attitude hailed it as a burst of self-recognition that the United States was still the world's greatest nation; critics of the new national mood dismissed much of it as jingoism masquerading as patriotism. Marsh, for instance, charged that ''any popular song that honored the American Vietnam veteran in the age of Reagan and *Rambo* was going to be misconstrued as celebrating the war. Issued in the teeth of a presidental election being sold as a plebiscite on national virtue, such a song could expect to be misappropriated.''

Released into this environment, the message of ''Born in the U.S.A.'' was warped with stunning speed. Seizing on the song's refrain (''Born in the U.S.A. / I was born in the U.S.A.''), the public embraced it as an anthem of the nation's renewed pride. The rest of the song's somber lyrics received far less attention, to the dismay of those who understood Springsteen's central point—that America's Vietnam veterans had been badly served by their country. ''Perhaps because of the emotional primacy of his writing—and the irresistible exhilaration of his music—it is easy to overlook Springsteen's intentions,'' wrote Loder. ''Easy, for example, to forget the bitter irony of a title like 'Born in the U.S.A.' . . . and to perceive it in the beer-pumped heat of Springsteen's live show as a simple, house-rocking salute to the big country whose name it so ambivalently invokes.''

In September 1984 conservative syndicated columnist George Will wrote an article in which he praised Springsteen as a purveyor of hard-working patriotism. A week later, at a campaign stop in New Jersey, Ronald Reagan remarked that ''America's future rests in a thousand dreams inside your hearts. It rests in the message of hope in songs of a man so many young Americans admire: New Jersey's own Bruce Springsteen.'' The songwriter's initial reaction to Reagan's remarks was little more than a shrug of bemusement, but as the days passed, the controversy over the conservative politician's implicit linkage of Springsteen's work with his own campaign lingered.

Springsteen finally responded a few days later during a concert performance. ''The president was mentioning my name the other day,'' he told his audience, ''and I kinda got to wondering what his favorite album musta been. I don't think it was the *Nebraska* album. I don't think he's been listening to this one.'' He then launched into one of that album's many dark songs of survival in America's have-not neighborhoods. Gleeful about Springsteen's remarks, Democrats suggested that his words amounted to an endorsement of Walter Mondale, who was challenging Reagan for the presidency. But the Springsteen camp quickly moved to squelch those claims as well.

FURTHER READING

Appy, Christian G. *Working-Class War: American Combat Soldiers and Vietnam.* Chapel Hill: University of North Carolina Press, 1993.

Figley, Charles R., and Seymour Leventman, eds. *Strangers at Home: Vietnam Veterans since the War.* New York: Praeger, 1980.

Flippo, Chet. ''Bruce Springsteen, A Rock 'n' Roll Evangelist for Our Times Crusades for Patriotism and Puritanism of a Different Stripe.'' *Musician* (November 1984).

Hilburn, Robert. *Springsteen*. New York: C. Scribner's Sons, 1985.

Levy, David W. *The Debate over Vietnam*. Baltimore: Johns Hopkins University Press, 1995.

Loder, Kurt. "Jingo Bells." *Rolling Stone* (December 19, 1985).

———. "The Rolling Stone Interview." *Rolling Stone* (December 6, 1984).

Marsh, Dave. *Glory Days: Bruce Springsteen in the 1980s*. New York: Pantheon, 1987.

Pareles, Jon. "Bruce Springsteen's Mass Appeal." *New York Times* (August 18, 1985).

Severo, Richard, and Lewis Milford. *The Wages of War: When America's Soldiers Came Home—From Valley Forge to Vietnam*. New York: Simon and Schuster, 1989.

Will, George. "A Yankee-Doodle Springsteen." *New York Daily News* (September 13, 1984).

Born on the Fourth of July

Film

Director: Oliver Stone

Screenplay: Oliver Stone and Ron Kovic; based on the book by Kovic

Principal Cast: Tom Cruise, Willem Dafoe, Raymond J. Berry, Caroline Kava, Kyra Sedgwick

Year of Release: 1989 (Universal)

One of the best-known memoirs of the Vietnam experience was written by Ron Kovic, a Marine lieutenant who was crippled in action. His book, *Born on the Fourth of July*, provided an illuminating look into the consciousness of a young man who was transformed from an enthusiastic supporter of the war into one of its most visible critics over the course of a decade. Director Oliver Stone, himself a Vietnam veteran, released a film version of Kovic's book in 1989, more than a dozen years after it had first been published. It won generally positive reviews and a large audience, although Stone's decision to alter some facts aroused controversy. Even though certain aspects of the film became subjects of hot debate, most who saw the film concurred that it provided powerful depictions of some of the hurdles that awaited veterans—and especially those with debilitating injuries—upon their return to the United States.

HISTORICAL BACKGROUND

John Hellman wrote in *American Myth and the Legacy of Vietnam* that "Vietnam is an experience that has severely called into question American myth. Americans entered Vietnam with certain expectations that a story, a distinctly

American story, would unfold. When the story of America in Vietnam turned into something unexpected, the true nature of the larger story of America itself became the subject of intense cultural dispute. On the deepest level, the legacy of Vietnam is the disruption of our story, of our explanation of the past and our vision of the future." The Americans who suffered most from this unseen deviation were undoubtedly Vietnam veterans, young men who grew up in a culture that emphasized patriotism and American hegemony. As Ralph Nader noted in his introduction to Paul Starr's *The Discarded Army*, disillusioned veterans returned home to an America that too often viewed them as unpleasant reminders of an embarrassing national failure: "They were not seen as the returning heroes of the 'Johnny Comes Marching Home' cadence; if they were seen in imagery at all, it was as broken drug addicts or demoralized unemployed."

America's wary, ambivalent reaction to returning veterans only exacerbated the soldiers' suspicions that their sacrifices in Vietnam had been meaningless. "Men are willing to bear great discomfort and pain, even death, if they believe their actions have legitimate and important purpose . . . and that their own sacrifices will be respected, or at least remembered," wrote Starr. "To most men these rewards are much more important than any material compensation." Bobby Muller, a paraplegic veteran who founded Vietnam Veterans of America (VVA), remarked in Karen Willenson's *The Bad War: An Oral History of the Vietnam War* that for those veterans who returned home with permanent injuries, the sense that their sacrifices had been for naught made acceptance of their new physical status particularly difficult. "[Crippled veterans such as quadriplegics] were married, some of them. They had kids, some of them. They got nowhere to go and nothing coming down the road except more staring at the ceiling. And what do they do? They console themselves by the thought that goddamnit, it's a bitch but that's what you got to do to fight for freedom, for democracy. . . . And when you go to that guy and say, 'Hey, pal, guess what? You lost what you lost for nothing. There was no purpose, no reason, and what happened to you is a total, fucking waste,' well, that's a bitter pill to swallow."

Other veterans, and particularly volunteers such as Kovic, struggled with their conviction that America's government and culture had sold them a false bill of goods. "I realized in Vietnam that the real experience of war was nothing like the comic books or movies I had watched as a kid," Kovic said in an interview with Robert Seidenberg for *American Film*. "I realized when the war was over and I had come home in a wheelchair that these movies had romanticized war, made war seem like a glorious and heroic thing. . . . The whole goddamn thing was a sham. My best intentions, my innocence, my youth, my beautiful young spirit had been desecrated by men who never went where I went, men who would never have to go through what I was about to endure."

Veterans Administration Hospitals

As members primarily of America's poor and working-class communities, disabled Vietnam veterans did not have the financial strength to secure good medical care on their own. Instead, they were forced to rely on the generosity of the country they served. Unfortunately, most observers agree that the U.S. government performed inadequately in this area. Indeed, in the years since the end of the Vietnam War, the poor medical care that many veterans received has emerged as a source of considerable national embarrassment. Ron Kovic's memoir *Born on the Fourth of July* included a graphic account of the deplorable conditions at the Bronx VA (Veterans Administration) hospital in which he convalesced; unfortunately, his experiences were all too typical. Many VA hospitals were understaffed, underfunded, and inattentive to their patients, sometimes scandalously so. Even before the influx of Vietnam veterans under its roofs, the VA hospital system struggled to meet its patients' needs. The introduction of the Vietnam contingent only worsened the situation.

The unique medical needs of the Vietnam veteran further strained the resources of VA hospitals, many of which had become oriented toward caring for chronically ill and elderly veterans of earlier wars. Starr noted that this orientation did not always make them ideal institutions for treating young veterans still in the process of coming to terms with crippling injuries. "There is no question that we need facilities for chronic disease," he said, "but one may doubt whether we need to treat young veterans in them and whether such institutions afford an optimal climate for their therapy and rehabilitation."

Starr and others have also noted that the circumstances of Vietnam casualties differed somewhat from those of previous wars in which America had been engaged. "Rapid helicopter evacuation and sophisticated medical science . . . combined to save thousands of soldiers in Vietnam who would have died in previous wars," reported Starr, who noted that whereas the ratio of American wounded to killed in World War II had been 3.1 to 1, the ratio in Vietnam had been 5.6 to 1. "But progress in reducing deaths has not been matched by progress in restoring health. More men come home, but more come home with severe and permanent injuries. Among wounded Army men discharged for disability, the proportion of amputees has risen from 18 percent in World War II to 28.3 percent in Vietnam."

The VA also proved ill-equipped to respond to the psychological toll that the war (and their country's tepid reaction to their return) took on Vietnam veterans. "Until 1979," wrote historian Christian Appy in *Commonweal*, "the VA did not even acknowledge the *existence* of post-traumatic stress syndrome, a condition (the VA later conceded) that has afflicted some five hundred thousand veterans. The long list of symptoms—chronic depression, rage, guilt, self-doubt, sleeplessness, nightmares, social detachment—were typically treated with drugs alone. Psychiatric help has improved somewhat, but the best programs still have long waiting lists. No one knows precisely how many Vietnam veterans have committed suicide, but some experts believe the number is at least as great as the sixty thousand who died in the war."

CREATION OF *BORN ON THE FOURTH OF JULY*

Ron Kovic's memoir *Born on the Fourth of July* was regarded as one of the finest accounts yet written about the experiences of Vietnam veterans when it was published in 1976. His story, in which he moves from enthusiastic enlistee to crippled, haunted veteran to dedicated antiwar activist, was hailed by many critics for its honesty and candidness. C. D. B. Bryan commented in the *New York Times Book Review* that ''[Kovic is] a mature, perceptive, contemplative man who has written the most personal and honest testament published thus far by any young man who fought in the Vietnam War. . . . What is so remarkable about Kovic's writing is that whereas one is perfectly prepared to forgive him occasional lapses into bitterness, self-pity, or excesses of rage, he retains the most extraordinary self-control throughout.''

In 1978 a film version of Kovic's memoir was discussed, and Oliver Stone was secured to write the screenplay. But the project, which had Al Pacino slated for the lead role, collapsed only days before shooting was to commence because of concerns about its financial viability. Over the course of the next several years, however, Stone established himself as a director, and in the late 1980s he resurrected the project, to Kovic's delight. ''Ron's story is a coherent vision of the whole Vietnam experience, before, during, and after the war,'' Stone told Alan Mirabella in the *New York Daily News*. ''The concept being, there was a second war when we came back. It was a real booby trap, we came back and got slammed in the back of the neck. We were out of step. People didn't care about Vietnam.''

The film opens with several scenes that show the ''All-American'' small-town atmosphere in which young Kovic (played by Tom Cruise) grew up. He plays ''army'' with his friends, swoons under the heady atmosphere of 1950s-era Fourth of July parades, agonizes over his infatuation with a classmate named Donna (Kyra Sedgwick), and incorporates the patriotic, winning-is-everything mind-set espoused by those he admires (his parents, his wrestling coach, a square-jawed Marine recruiter) into his own world view. Determined to prove his manhood and defend his country from the Communist threat in Vietnam, Kovic joins the Marines.

The film then picks up the story in Vietnam. Kovic, now a Marine sergeant, is part of a military unit advancing on a Vietnamese village that is thought to be a haven for VC troops. A number of innocent villagers are slain in a sudden eruption of gunfire from the unit. Angered and saddened by the unnecessary violence, Kovic advances into the village with the others. In the village, though, the soldiers are suddenly raked by enemy fire. In the ensuing firefight, Kovic accidentally shoots and kills one of his own men. He subsequently tries to report his action to his superior, only to have the officer angrily cut him off. Kovic is ordered to return to his unit. Several months later he is shot in the spine during another battle.

Paralyzed from the mid-chest down by his wound, Kovic is shipped home to the United States. He spends the next several months at the Bronx Veterans Hospital. This harrowing segment of the film would later be singled out by many film critics and veterans as one of its most powerful—and sadly accurate—sections. As John Simon remarked in the *National Review*, ''for intimate horror nothing can surpass the scenes in the [hospital]: understaffed and rat-infested, the mostly black personnel shooting up behind not even locked doors, the antiquated equipment failing and nearly costing Ron one of his nonfunctional but still precious legs.''

Kovic eventually returns home in a wheelchair, where he and his parents struggle to come to terms with his injury. His sense of loss is further deepened by his awareness that many of his countrymen now view him with either indifference or outright hostility. A series of encounters with old acquaintances (including Donna, who is now an antiwar activist), and strangers unmoved by the sacrifices that he and others made in Vietnam, push him into a spiral of destructive behavior that culminates with a stint in Mexico, where he joins a group of similarly crippled Vietnam veterans. Upon returning to the United States, Kovic visits the family of the soldier he accidentally killed and confesses.

Kovic eventually joins the antiwar movement and quickly emerges as a spokesmen for other antiwar veterans. During a protest rally held outside the Republican National Convention in Miami in 1972, he bitterly criticizes America's treatment of its Vietnam veterans before a group of television reporters. The rally dissolves into a confusing clash between protestors and police, but despite being knocked out of his wheelchair, Kovic rallies the activists to storm the convention hall. The film then shifts to the 1976 Democratic National Convention, and it is clear that his status has changed dramatically in the period between the two events. He is a scheduled speaker at the convention, and the film ends as he wheels himself up to the speaker's platform, bathed in bright light and a thunderous ovation.

CRITICAL REACTION

The film version of *Born on the Fourth of July* received accolades from many reviewers, and it proved popular with the movie-going public. Bolstered by Cruise's marquee value—and largely admiring reviews of his performance—the film played to large audiences; and like *Platoon*, it garnered eight Academy Award nominations, winning four (the Directors Guild of America also named Stone Director of the Year for his work on the film).

Many of those critics who liked *Fourth of July* emphasized the film's visceral power in their reviews. ''I have been anything but a fan of this director,'' admitted John Simon in the *National Review*, ''but the new film . . . is a gripping, unrelenting but extremely powerful work, whose shortcomings evaporate from the memory, but whose strengths are indelible.'' *Cineaste*'s Christopher Sharrett said that the film ''may be the most incisive indictment to date of the American adventure in Vietnam'' because of its focus on ''the ideological character underlying not just American policy in Vietnam but American society overall, particularly in the decade or so before the war." And *Village Voice* reviewer J. Hoberman, though troubled by perceived excesses in the film, nonetheless called it "powerful and unflinching, crude but compelling."

Some reviewers, however, registered far harsher assessments. Robert Stone wrote in the *New York Review of Books* that "the movie is all glib explanation: the paradoxes of populist democracy, the corruptions attendant on patriotism and world power, and the spiritual limitations of the American working class are reduced to stereotypes and subjected to a Hollywood treatment, banal in its obviousness and crass in its moralizing." *New Yorker* critic Pauline Kael also offered a scathing critique. She castigated Stone as a merchant of melodrama and questioned the film's (and the autobiography's) account of Kovic's prewar views. "It's inconceivable that Ron Kovic was as innocent as the movie and the 1976 autobiography on which it's based make him out to be. Was this kid kept in a bubble? At some level, everybody knows about the ugliness of war," she wrote. "We come out [of the film] knowing nothing about [Kovic] except that his self-righteousness—his will to complain and make a ruckus—is rather glorious. I don't think I've ever seen another epic about a bad loser." Oliver Stone reacted to Kael's comments with a mixture of anger and incredulity. "You think your country needs you and you do it," he told Stone biographer James Riordan. "There are still people who play football and break their limbs because they think it's a noble thing to do. I guess that's hard for some people to understand. They didn't grow up in that world so they don't relate, especially to a kid from a working-class family."

The film's adherence to the facts also became a subject of some controversy in the months following its release. Critics of Stone's film noted that his characterization of the village scene was markedly different from the incident as described in Kovic's memoir, and they observed that if Kovic ever made a confession to the parents of the GI he accidentally killed, he made no mention of it in his book. Stone claimed that much of the controversy surrounding the film could be traced to Kovic's unsuccessful bid to secure the U.S. House seat then held by California Republican Robert Dornan. "That politicized everything," he said in Riordan's *Stone*. "It became instant news. Dornan was terrified of Ron, he hated him. He immediately attacked the movie everywhere he could, on public radio, in the newspaper. Then all the conservatives attacked it. George Will wrote about it, Patrick Buchanan, William Buckley went after it, and that hurt the movie a lot."

FURTHER READING

Appy, Christian. "Vietnam according to Oliver Stone." *Commonweal* (March 23, 1990).

Bryan, C. D. B. Review of Kovic's *Born on the Fourth of July*. In the *New York Times Book Review* (August 15, 1976).

Hellman, John. *American Myth and the Legacy of Vietnam*. New York: Columbia University Press, 1986.

Hoberman, J. "The Worst Years of Our Lives." *Village Voice* (December 9, 1989).

Kael, Pauline. "Potency." *New Yorker* (January 22, 1990).

Kovic, Ron. *Born on the Fourth of July.* New York: McGraw-Hill, 1976.

MacPherson, Myra. *Long Time Passing: Vietnam and the Haunted Generation.* Garden
City, N.Y.: Doubleday, 1984.

Mirabella, Alan. "The War Within." *New York Daily News* (January 20, 1990).

Riordan, James. *Stone: The Controversies, Excesses, and Exploits of a Radical Filmmaker.* New York: Hyperion, 1995.

Seidenberg, Robert. "To Hell and Back." *American Film* (January 1990).

Sharret, Christopher. Review of Stone's *Born on the Fourth of July.* In *Cineaste,* no. 4
(1990).

Simon, John. Review of Stone's *Born on the Fourth of July.* In the *National Review*
(February 5, 1990).

Starr, Paul. *The Discarded Army: Veterans after Vietnam; The Nader Report on Vietnam
Veterans and the Veterans Administration.* New York: Charterhouse, 1974.

Stone, Robert. "Oliver Stone's USA." *New York Review of Books* (February 17, 1994).

Willenson, Kim. *The Bad War: An Oral History of the Vietnam War.* New York: New
American Library, 1987.

A Bright Shining Lie: John Paul Vann and America in Vietnam

Nonfiction

Author: Neil Sheehan

Facts of Publication: New York: Random House, 1988

Both John Paul Vann and Neil Sheehan went to Vietnam in the early 1960s, Vann as a military advisor, Sheehan as a reporter for United Press International (UPI). As the months passed, Vann's disillusionment with the war's progress eventually led him to share his frustrations with Sheehan and other reporters, and the advisor became one of the correspondents' most valuable sources of information on the true dynamics of the situation out in the countryside. In the mid-1960s Sheehan left Vietnam for assignments in the United States, but Vann remained and, after assuming a civilian position, rose to become one of the most powerful Americans in the country. In 1972, a short time after Vann's death in a helicopter crash, Sheehan began work on a biography of the soldier. Sixteen long years later, the book was finally published to a chorus of critical praise.

HISTORICAL BACKGROUND

John Paul Vann's First Vietnam Tour

John Paul Vann went to Vietnam in March 1962 at age thirty-seven. A lieutenant colonel in the U.S. Army, he served as senior advisor to the South Vietnamese Army's 7th Infantry Division, which was headquartered at My Tho in the Mekong Delta south of Saigon. An intelligent, fearless man possessed of terrific stamina and a deeply held belief in the legitimacy of U.S. involvement in Vietnam, Vann was an ideal advisor in many respects. Sheehan wrote in *A Bright Shining Lie* that the military man's character and education had "combined to produce a mind that could be totally possessed by the immediate task and at the same time sufficiently detached to discern the root elements of the problem. He manifested the faith and the optimism of post–World War II America that any challenge could be overcome by will and by the disciplined application of intellect, technology, money, and, when necessary, armed force."

But as the months passed and the Army of the Republic of Vietnam (ARVN) troops that he was advising continued to flounder, Vann's frustration grew. South Vietnamese commanders proved reluctant to commit troops to confrontations because of political concerns back in Saigon and their own instinct for self-preservation, and the rosy forecasts of American policymakers troubled him as well. Moreover, Vann felt that both the South Vietnamese government and U.S. officials did not appreciate the significance of the social problems plaguing the country, and he argued that U.S. bombing policies and the Strategic Hamlets program (in which peasants were forcibly removed from their homes and placed in group encampments) were eroding already tenuous support for the Diem regime out in the countryside. By the end of his first year in Vietnam, wrote Sheehan, "Vann saw that the war was being lost. The ambassador and the commanding general in South Vietnam were telling the Kennedy administration that everything was going well and that the war was being won. Vann believed then and never ceased to believe that the war could be won if it was fought with sound tactics and strategy."

When Vann's superiors disregarded his warnings, he turned to the Saigon press corps to get his message out. The American's candor and knowledge attracted correspondents like moths to a flame. As Clarence Wyatt noted in *Paper Soldiers*, Vann and the reporters shared "mutually reinforcing self-interests. Vann's impatience with [South Vietnamese General Huynh Van] Cao and an unresponsive American military command grew, and he carefully used the press to air his concerns publicly. The equally frustrated reporters came to respect and protect jealously an invaluable source. Soon the frustrations of Vann and the reporters exploded."

Ap Bac

On January 2, 1963, the ARVN 7th Infantry Division, which was under the command of General Huynh Van Cao, carried out orders to destroy a Vietcong radio transmitter located in the hamlet of Tan Thoi in the Mekong Delta. Acting on intelligence that indicated that the transmitter was protected by a force of about one hundred Vietcong in nearby Ap Bac, Vann and his staff settled on a plan of attack that featured his usual precise calculations. "Vann saw an opportunity to use the ARVN's advantages in mobility, firepower, and armor to destroy a Viet Cong unit," noted Harry G. Summers, Jr. in the *Historical Atlas of the Vietnam War*. But instead of wreaking havoc on the guerrillas (whose hit-and-run tactics had frustrated the American advisors over the preceding months), the operation proved disastrous for Cao's troops.

Larger-than-expected Vietcong forces at Ap Bac and Tan Thoi were ready for the attack, having intercepted radio messages concerning the upcoming operation. When the raid's first helicopters arrived, they were met with withering ground fire, and three of the H-21 helicopters and one Huey (UH-1) gunship were promptly downed. The first few minutes of the battle set the pattern for the rest of the clash. As the hours dragged by, ARVN forces committed a series of strategic blunders—some over the objections of Vann and his staff—that served to further deteriorate their position. Finally, Vann felt that Cao's forces showed little appetite for battle, a factor that further contributed to the debacle. By the next morning the Vietcong guerrillas had slipped away, leaving behind eighty ARVN dead and another one hundred wounded. Significantly, three Americans had been killed as well. Later in the morning, Cao ordered a fraudulent air strike on the area, nearly killing Sheehan and two other Americans who were surveying the long-abandoned battlefield.

In the battle's aftermath, U.S. and South Vietnamese officials tried to call the clash at Ap Bac a victory, but Vann and his staff quickly disabused the press corps of any such notions. Enraged by the whole operation, Vann called the ARVN effort "a miserable damn performance," and even though correspondents who used the quote did not reveal his identity, U.S. officials familiar with Vann knew whose voice it was.

"As a battle it did not amount to much, but Ap Bac would have profound consequences for the later prosecution of the war," wrote Summers. "Prior to Ap Bac," Sheehan pointed out, "the Kennedy administration had succeeded in preventing the American public from being more than vaguely conscious that the country was involved in a war in a place called Vietnam. . . . Ap Bac was putting Vietnam on the front pages and on the television evening news shows with a drama that no other event had yet achieved."

Vann retired from the army several months later. When those who knew him learned of his departure, many assumed that he had selflessly sacrificed his military career so that he could comment on the war with greater freedom, and his reputation was further enhanced. His admirers were unaware that Vann's myriad sexual indiscretions (including a valid statutory rape charge that he ultimately beat) had permanently scarred his record, effectively limiting his advancement anyway.

Vann Returns to Vietnam as a Civilian

In 1965 Vann returned to Vietnam as a civilian, serving as a provincial pacification representative for AID (the Agency for International Development). As American involvement in the war expanded, Vann's authority increased, even though he continued to be an outspoken critic of some aspects of the war's prosecution. "His leadership qualities and his dedication to the war had assisted his promotion, as had a realization by those in power in Saigon and Washington that his dissent over tactics or strategy was always meant to further the war effort, not hinder it,'' wrote Sheehan. In May 1971 Vann was promoted to an advisory position that gave him authority over all U.S. military forces in Vietnam's Central Highlands and adjacent provinces along the central coastline. The unprecedented arrangement gave Vann more power than he could have ever wielded had he stayed in the army.

By this point, some people who knew Vann felt that the years of involvement in the war had changed the man, and not for the better. They noted that Vann had adopted a much more lenient philosophy about appropriate methodologies for winning the bitter war. Those who recalled his harsh criticisms of bombing strategies earlier in the conflict for the toll that they exacted on civilians found that he had become an enthusiastic proponent of intensive bombing campaigns. Sheehan wrote about an exchange between Vann and *Washington Post* reporter Larry Stern that dramatically reflected Vann's change of heart: ''Anytime the wind is blowing from the north where the B-52 strikes are turning the terrain into a moonscape, you can tell from the battlefield stench that the strikes are effective,'' Vann reportedly told Stern.

In March 1972, North Vietnamese forces launched the three-pronged Easter Offensive, a bold effort to overwhelm South Vietnam by attacks on three strategic regions. All three thrusts were ultimately turned back, however, as the NVA (North Vietnamese Army) was handed a major setback. Vann was widely credited with being a key figure in the defense of An Loc, a site seventy-five miles north of Saigon that had been one of the NVA's primary targets in the offensive. In June of that year, however, Vann was killed in an air crash when his helicopter, flying low over an otherwise treeless valley at night, hit a small group of trees standing over a primitive Montagnard cemetery (Montagnards are aboriginal tribespeople who make their homes in some of Vietnam's more mountainous areas).

SHEEHAN AND VIETNAM

Years after his reporting stints in Vietnam, Sheehan was asked by *Publishers Weekly* interviewer Walter Gelles to comment on the reasons for America's unsuccessful efforts in Vietnam. ''In World War II, our leadership was attuned to reality, but in the postwar period we became so rich and powerful that our leadership lost its ability to think creatively—and arrogance replaced reality,'' he replied. ''In Vietnam, our political and military leaders simply could not conceive the possibility that we could lose. Successive administrations deluded themselves into the fantasy that we could somehow perpetuate an American presence in the country. The American soldier became a victim of his own leadership, which is a bitter lesson to face.'' The former UPI and *New York Times* reporter had not always viewed U.S. policymakers so harshly.

Sheehan first arrived in Vietnam in April 1962 as Saigon bureau chief for

UPI. Sheehan and the other members of the Saigon press corps bucked attempts by U.S. and Vietnamese officials to spoon-feed the media information on the war's progress, and relations between the camps quickly deteriorated. Within a matter of months, however, the adventurous UPI reporter had developed an effective network of independent sources and established a productive partnership with David Halberstam of the *New York Times*.

One of the correspondents' best sources in the U.S. military was John Paul Vann. "Vann played it smart," wrote William Prochnau, author of *Once Upon a Distant War*. "He actually *admitted* screw-ups, *conceded* losses, because they were part of the game, part of any game. The admissions, of course, made him more believable. [American General Paul] Harkins was disbelieved on *everything* because he would never admit that *anything* went wrong." Writing in *A Bright Shining Lie*, Sheehan described the relationship between Vann and the reporters in similar terms: "Vann taught us the most, and one can truly say that without him our reporting would not have been the same. . . . He gave us an expertise we lacked, a certitude that brought a qualitative change in what we wrote. He enabled us to attack the official optimism with gradual but steadily increasing detail and thoroughness."

Sheehan noted that he and most of the other correspondents initially supported America's presence in Vietnam. "We believed in what our government said it was trying to accomplish in Vietnam, and we wanted our country to win this war just as passionately as Vann and his captains did," Sheehan said. But the reports of Vann and other sources, coupled with their own firsthand observations out in the field, convinced the press corps that the U.S. prosecution of the war was fundamentally flawed.

As the months passed, and disastrous events such as the Ap Bac debacle and the Buddhist uprising erupted, Sheehan emerged as one of the war's finest—and most controversial—correspondents. He did so despite struggling with an almost paralyzing certainty that death would claim him when he went out into the field. When he first arrived in Vietnam, Sheehan had been exhilarated by violent, dangerous excursions out in the countryside, but the events at Ap Bac changed his attitude in dramatic fashion. While surveying the scene of the battle, Sheehan and two others (reporter Nick Turner and Brigadier General Robert York) had nearly been blown apart by General Cao's fraudulent attack against the abandoned Vietcong positions in the area. As the friendly fire rained down around them, Sheehan's attitude toward the war was transformed. "His belief in the American goal held fast," wrote Prochnau. "But not in the heroics. 'I never saw glory in war again,' [Sheehan] said later, 'and I never again went into battle unafraid.'"

In the fall of 1963, Sheehan was forced by his UPI superiors to take a week-long vacation in Tokyo after he submitted a report suggesting (accurately) that the United States was giving the green light to conspirators plotting a coup against the South Vietnamese government. Sheehan resisted, because he and the other reporters sensed that Ngo Dinh Diem's regime was tottering. In the end, however, he was forced to go; as he dreaded, the coup took place during his absence. (During the next two years, a series of coups brought South Vietnam seven different governments and new heights of political instability.)

In June 1964 Sheehan left UPI for the *New York Times*. A year later he returned to Saigon, where he stayed until 1966, when he was transferred to Washington, D.C. That same year he wrote an article, "Not a Dove, but No Longer a Hawk," that reflected his growing disillusionment with America's involvement in Vietnam. In the late 1960s he served as the newspaper's Pentagon and White House correspondent. By 1971 Sheehan had come full circle; he emerged as a critic of the war. "Even at that late date the passion of his conversion shook *The Times* and all its establishment," remarked Prochnau.

The Pentagon Papers

Sheehan thus attracted the attention of Daniel Ellsberg, a McNamara "whiz kid" in the Pentagon whose view of the war had undergone a transformation that bore some similarity to the one experienced by Sheehan. Formerly an ardent supporter of the war, Ellsberg had decided that American involvement in Vietnam was a tragic mistake. In 1971 Ellsberg's disenchantment with U.S. policies led him to give Sheehan a massive collection of confidential government memorandums and reports on the war that came to be known as the Pentagon Papers. To opponents of the war, the records in this archive—commissioned by Defense Secretary McNamara back in 1967, they included reports dating back to the 1940s—provided stark evidence that U.S. involvement in Southeast Asia had too often been characterized by deceit, misjudgments, and bureaucratic arrogance.

On June 13, 1971, after weeks of analysis of the documents, the *New York Times* published the first in a series of installments on the Pentagon Papers. Embarrassed and angry at the publication of the papers, "the government responded with a vengeance," said Prochnau. "Sheehan's honesty and patriotism were questioned. The government accused him of theft. A federal grand jury, looking for violations of the Espionage Act, targeted him. Federal officials subpoenaed his bank records and hounded his friends and neighbors. He faced, then avoided, jail." Sheehan's work on the Pentagon Papers further enhanced his already high reputation in journalistic circles (the *New York Times* received a Pulitzer Prize in the public service category in 1972 for its publication of the documents), but the whole controversy seemed to deepen his growing preoccupation with Vietnam.

CREATION OF *A BRIGHT SHINING LIE*

While attending the funeral for John Paul Vann in 1972, Sheehan was struck by the stature of those in attendance (from General William Westmoreland, who served as a pallbearer, to Ellsberg, who had been one of Vann's closest friends). Upon returning home, Sheehan secured a two-year leave of absence from the *New York Times*, along with a contract from a publisher, and began work on a biography of Vann. The writer felt that by studying Vann's life, he would also be able to examine America's role in Vietnam. As he wrote in *A Bright Shining Lie*, "The intensity and distinctiveness of his character and the courage and drama of his life had seemed to sum up so many of the qualities Americans admired in themselves as a people. By an obsession, by an unyielding dedication to the war, he had come to personify the American endeavor in Vietnam. He had exemplified it in his illusions, in his good intentions gone awry, in his pride, in his will to win."

Sheehan began research on the book immediately. He made a visit to Vietnam, where he was chilled by the nihilism that seemed to permeate the land. Soon after his return to the United States, obstacles cropped up. In 1974 he was sued for libel by a man who had been the subject of an earlier Sheehan book (the suit was eventually dismissed, but not before Sheehan wasted several months defending his research work). Later that year, a youth driving on the wrong side of the road smashed into Sheehan's vehicle in a head-on collision. The writer suffered eleven fractures, including two broken arms, and spent a good portion of the following year in recovery.

As the 1970s blurred into the early 1980s, Sheehan's obsession with Vann's story grew. Month after month passed by as the writer tried to reconcile Vann's dark secrets (a troubled childhood, a sexual appetite that doomed his army career) with the honorable soldier he had known in the Mekong Delta. And over it all lay the shadow of the war itself, the contradictions of which Sheehan continued to see encapsulated in Vann. Sheehan fell into a reclusive routine in which his waking hours were dominated by the book. Wracked by anxiety attacks, insomnia, and the knowledge that his obsession was taking a toll on his family and friends, Sheehan slogged on. "It went on year after year. The only way to control it is to get up and YOU MARCH," he told Prochnau. "It may be raining, it may be snowing, the sun may be shining, but you get up and YOU MARCH. The army taught me some of that. Get up! The ten-minute break is over! Get up! March! And so I slapped myself in the face, threw water over my face, and went on." Prochnau later commented that "the ordeal of [writing *A Bright Shining Lie*] became a legend that surpassed the legend of John Paul Vann. . . . He found a man who personified the national trip into moral quicksand and, in the writing, Sheehan became the personification of the inability to get out."

In August 1986 Sheehan finally completed the manuscript for *A Bright Shining Lie*. Over the course of the next year, the author pared the book down to 360,000 words, still a massive work. In 1988—sixteen years after Sheehan began work on the Vann biography—*A Bright Shining Lie* was finally published.

CRITICAL RECEPTION

Sheehan's massive tome garnered many awards (Pulitzer Prize, National Book Award for nonfiction, Columbia Journalism Award, Robert F. Kennedy Book Award, and others) and laudatory reviews in the months following its publication. Boosted by the recognition, the book became a best-seller.

Reviewers were almost unanimous in their praise for Sheehan's work (the harshest dissent with the critical consensus appeared in the *National Review). New York Times Book Review* critic Ronald Steel commented that "if there is one book that captures the Vietnam War in the sheer Homeric scale of its passion and folly, this book is it." *New Republic* contributor Richard Holbrooke added that "Sheehan has produced a book of vast ambition and scope that tells the entire story of the American tragedy in Vietnam through Vann's life and death."

Indeed, reviewers recognized that the book worked in large measure because of its choice of subject matter. Critics felt that, in John Paul Vann, Sheehan had found a larger-than-life figure whose experiences in Vietnam offered valuable insights into the character and nature of American involvement in the conflict. Steel commented that "Sheehan has created in John Paul Vann a man as complex and ambiguous as the war itself, a brave man of decent instincts in the grip of a compulsion that defied, and ultimately overwhelmed, reason." *Washington Monthly* reviewer Taylor Branch concurred: "By capturing within the life of one small obsessive daredevil the essence of something so vast and benumbing as Vietnam, Sheehan has written by far the best single account of the war."

FURTHER READING

Branch, Taylor. Review of *A Bright Shining Lie*. In *Washington Monthly* (October 1988).

Brimelow, Peter. "Out of Control." *National Review* (March 10, 1989).

Gelles, Walter. "Publishers Weekly Interview." *Publishers Weekly* (September 2, 1988).

Halberstam, David. *The Making of a Quagmire*. New York: Random House, 1965.

Holbrooke, Richard. "Front Man." *New Republic* (October 24, 1988).

Prochnau, William. *Once Upon a Distant War*. New York: Times Books, 1995.

Sanoff, Alvin P. "Vietnam, and the Battle for Reality" (interview with Sheehan). *U.S. News & World Report* (October 24, 1988).

Sheehan, Neil. *A Bright Shining Lie: John Paul Vann and American in Vietnam*. New York: Random House, 1988.

Steel, Ronald. Review of *A Bright Shining Lie*. In the *New York Times Book Review* (September 25, 1988).

Summers, Harry G., Jr. *Historical Atlas of the Vietnam War*. New York: Houghton Mifflin, 1995.

———. "Troubled Apostle of Victory" (interview with Sheehan). *Vietnam* (Spring 1989).

Wyatt, Clarence R. *Paper Soldiers: The American Press and the Vietnam War*. New York: W. W. Norton, 1993.

Casualties of War

Film

Director: Brian DePalma

Screenplay: David Rabe; based on the book by Daniel Lang

Principal Cast: Michael J. Fox, Sean Penn, Don Harvey, John C. Reilly, John Leguizamo, Thuy Thu Le

Year of Release: 1989 (Columbia)

Late in 1969, American learned of a horrible massacre that had taken place in Vietnam some eighteen months earlier: American troops had descended on the village of Son My, located in Quang Ngai Province, and wiped out hundreds of unarmed Vietnamese civilians, mostly women and children. Most of the violence was visited upon a hamlet of Son My known as My Lai. The incident touched off a storm of controversy back in the United States, as both hawks (supporters of the war) and doves (critics) grappled with its implications. In the wake of My Lai, reporters and soldiers who earlier had been reluctant to speak volunteered stories of other atrocities that they had witnessed, heard of, or been involved in.

One such incident—in which a squad of American soldiers kidnapped, raped, and murdered a young Vietnamese woman—was detailed by reporter Daniel Lang for the *New Yorker*. The author later wrote a book, *Casualties of War*, about the incident. Filmmaker Brian DePalma expressed interest in adapting the book for the screen, and in 1989 the film *Casualties of War* was released. By this time, other Vietnam films had included scenes of atrocities, but none had made a war crime the centerpiece of the story being told. Predictably, *Casualties of War* provoked great debate upon its release.

HISTORICAL BACKGROUND

Atrocities in Vietnam

By the early 1970s, Americans had gained a certain mind-numbing familiarity with tales of atrocities committed by U.S. soldiers in Vietnam. Proliferating media reports of misconduct, coupled with events such as the 1971 "Winter Soldier" Investigation—wherein dozens of veterans testified about incidents of rape, torture, and murder of innocent civilians—rocked the nation as its citizenry grappled with questions about the frequency of and reasons for such awful episodes.

"During the summers of 1965 and 1968, I took part—as a press correspondent—in numerous military operations and patrols in Vietnam," recalled Charles C. Moskos, Jr. in *War Crimes and the American Conscience*. "Cruel acts occurred on both sides with nauseating frequency. As a day-to-day participant in the combat situation, I was repeatedly struck by the brutal reactions of soldiers to their participation in the war. To understand the way in which combat soldiers' attitudes and behavior are shaped, however, one must try to comprehend the conditions under which they must manage. The misery of these conditions is so extreme that conventional moral standards are eclipsed in a way difficult for the noncombatant to appreciate. . . . The ultimate standard rests on keeping alive—a harsh standard which can sanction atrocities." Vietnam veteran Philip Caputo concurred with this evaluation in his memoir, *A Rumor of War*: "Whether committed in the name of principles or out of vengeance, atrocities were as common to the Vietnamese battlefields as shell craters and barbed wire."

Other observers pointed to the military's emphasis on "body counts" to gauge progress or to the uncertainty that soldiers felt about the sympathies of the Vietnamese they encountered. This latter factor gave rise to a particularly virulent brand of racism embodied in a grim joke that was popular among U.S. Marines: The "loyal" Vietnamese should be put out to sea in a raft. Everyone left in the country should then be killed and the nation paved over with concrete. The raft should then be sunk. "[American soldiers] were repeatedly told they could trust no one—not the bar girl, nor the sidewalk peddler, nor the farmer. They must be on guard against six-year-old children, for some of that age had been known to be armed and ready to kill," said Cecil B. Curry (writing as Cincinnatus) in *Self-Destruction: The Disintegration and Decay of the United States Army during the Vietnam Era*. "When GIs couldn't tell friend from foe, they came to hate and despise them all. All slopes are dirt. Viewing all Vietnamese as less than human released American boys from their own humanity." William Calley, who would emerge as the most visible figure associated with the My Lai massacre, voiced similar sentiments in his memoir *Body Count*: "We weren't in My Lai to kill human beings, really. We were there to kill an ideology that is carried by—I don't know. Pawns. Blobs. Pieces of flesh. . . . I was there to destroy an intangible idea. To destroy communism. . . . I looked at communism as a southerner looks at a Negro, supposedly. It's evil. It's bad.''

Many veterans and other defenders of U.S. military conduct, though, while acknowledging that atrocities did occur, resented the insinuation that all American soldiers were guilty of such activities. Many American soldiers conducted themselves honorably throughout their tours of duty, and they were terribly angered by insinuations that lumped all U.S. personnel into the same ''war criminal'' bag. Other analysts discounted many of the atrocity stories as exaggerations of events or outright fabrications. Finally, some observers made a distinction between atrocities committed by American troops and those committed by their adversaries. ''It is important to note that for American forces such actions were aberrations in direct violation of U.S. military law and specific MACV directives,'' wrote Col. Harry G. Summers, Jr. in *Vietnam War Almanac*. ''For the Viet Cong and the North Vietnamese Army, however, atrocities were a deliberate, sanctioned tactic.''

The My Lai Massacre and Its Aftermath

The most infamous of the Vietnam atrocity incidents was the one that took place on March 16, 1968, in the hamlet of My Lai. On that morning, a platoon of soldiers from Charlie Company, First Battalion, 20th Infantry, commanded by Lieutenant William Calley, Jr. massacred between three hundred and four hundred innocent Vietnamese men, women, and children.

Even before entering My Lai, some members of Charlie Company had become dangerously violent in their encounters with villagers. In his book *My Lai 4*, Seymour Hersh, the reporter who eventually broke the story of the My Lai massacre, included a letter from one soldier in the company to his father that read in part: ''On [the platoon's] way back to [Landing Zone Dotti] they saw a woman working in the fields. They shot and wounded her. Then they kicked her to death and emptied their magazines in her head. They slugged every little kid they came across. Why in God's name does this have to happen? These are all seemingly normal guys; some were friends of mine. . . . This isn't the first time, Dad. I've seen it many times before . . . My faith in my fellow men is shot all to hell. I just want the time to pass and I just want to come home.'' Another soldier told Hersh that My Lai was the culmination of a spiraling circle of violence that had been growing for months. ''It was like going from one step to another, worse one. First, you'd stop the people, question them, and let them go. Second, you'd stop the people, beat up an old man, and let them go. Third, you'd stop the people, beat up an old man, and then shoot him. Fourth, you go in and wipe out a village.''

When Charlie Company, spearheaded by a platoon under the command of Calley, swept into My Lai on the morning of March 16, many of the soldiers were braced for a fight. The company had suffered several recent casualties from mines and booby traps, and intelligence reports indicated that the village of Son My was a possible base for a dangerous Vietcong battalion. Upon arriving in the hamlet, however, Calley and his men encountered no resistance. But even though the villagers—largely women and children—made no hostile moves, Calley and his men launched a vicious attack on the hamlet's unarmed inhabitants. Huts were destroyed, women and children were raped and sodomized, and villagers were shot or bayonetted by the score. The slaughter went on for hours, and when the orgy of violence had finally concluded, hundreds of villagers had been slain.

Warrant Officer Hugh C. Thompson, who was piloting a reconnaissance helicopter during the operation, stumbled upon the nightmarish scene when it was still in progress. He and his door gunner, Lawrence Colburn, quickly descended into the hamlet and landed. Thompson subsequently loaded a group of terrified villagers into the helicopter, directing Colburn to shoot Calley or any of his men if they interfered. Sickened by what he had witnessed, Thompson filed a report on the slaughter. It was ignored, however, and Charlie Company's Commander, Ernest L. Medina, made no mention of civilian casualties in his report on the operation. My Lai would remain a secret for the next several months.

In the spring of 1969, however, rumors about the massacre reached the ears of ex-GI Ronald Ridenhour. Appalled by the accounts that he heard, Ridenhour wrote letters to the White House, the Pentagon, and a number of congressmen about the incident. The letters triggered an investigation, and a formal board of inquiry headed by Lieutenant General William R. Peers was eventually established.

The investigation remained out of the public's eye until November 13, when newspapers across the nation ran a story by Hersh on the massacre. But even though news of the massacre sparked a shudder of disgust and shame across much of the country, many Americans flatly refused to believe that the incident had occurred (a statewide poll conducted by the *Minneapolis Tribune* in late December 1969 found that 49 percent felt that the My Lai story was false). Others, meanwhile, defended Calley, Medina, and the other soldiers who were being investigated, contending that they were mere pawns in the larger struggle taking place in the United States over the war. Ironically, this view of Calley-as-scapegoat transcended ideological lines. Supporters of the war argued that Calley and his men were being unfairly persecuted by the antiwar movement, and members of the antiwar faction contended that Calley should not be unfairly singled out for actions that some felt were commonplace in Vietnam. The true criminals, said some left-wing voices, were the generals and politicians who gave the orders.

Over the next few months, a groundswell of support for Calley—who had come to personify the men under investigation—could be seen in many areas of America. Scattered American Legion groups made public declarations of support for the lieutenant, and public opinion polls indicated that a majority of Americans believed that incidents such as My Lai were inevitable in war. A pro-Calley song called "The Battle Hymn of Lt. Calley" sold two hundred thousand copies in three days, and Saigon's armed forces radio network played it regularly until they were ordered to desist. "Free Calley" bumper stickers materialized on American cars, and resolutions urging the president to offer clemency to the soldier were introduced in several state legislatures. Writing in their book *Four Hours in My Lai*, Michael Bilton and Kevin Sim remarked that the title of one chapter in a book that touched on My Lai—"It Never Happened—Besides, They Deserved It"—"seemed perfectly to capture the attitude of many Americans who believed Calley was truly innocent." In February former Alabama Governor George Wallace made a public statement of support for Calley, and some pro-war congressmen bitterly criticized his treatment (Democratic Senator Allen Ellender remarked that the My Lai villagers "got just what they deserved," and Senate colleague Ernest Hollings "publicly wondered if all soldiers who made 'a mistake in judgment' were going to be tried 'as common criminals, as murderers,' " Hersh reported in *My Lai 4*).

Calley and twelve other officers and enlisted men were eventually charged by the U.S. Army with war crimes, and another dozen soldiers were charged with covering up the atrocity, but Calley was the only man who was found guilty. Convicted of murdering 22 unarmed civilians, he was sentenced to life in prison. Heeding the political winds, President Richard Nixon arranged for Calley to be released from the stockade pending his appeal. His sentence was upheld, but on April 15, the Secretary of the Army reduced his sentence to ten years. Seven months later, Nixon set Calley free on parole. Calley subsequently returned to his hometown of Columbus, Georgia, where he continues to live quietly.

CREATION OF *CASUALTIES OF WAR*

Daniel Lang's nonfiction article for the *New Yorker* on the court-martial of a group of American soldiers who had raped and murdered a young Vietnamese woman was a chilling report of military misconduct. A few screenplays based on the story were subsequently written, but the idea for a film treatment of the incident languished until 1979, when playwright David Rabe, a Vietnam veteran who had written a number of Vietnam-related plays, volunteered to write a new screenplay for filmmaker Brian DePalma. DePalma had made several controversial films prior to *Casualties of War*, and some critics contended that his work was marked by elements of misogyny and an excessive taste for violence. The seeds of controversy were thus planted very early in the production process. Unfazed, DePalma set out for Thailand, where *Casualties of War* was filmed.

DePalma had actively worked to avoid being drafted for Vietnam. Prior to his visit to the draft board, he worked hard to ensure that his asthma would appear debilitating. "I did have asthma, actually. But I really had a case when I went to the draft board. I could hardly breathe. I had taken everything in the world to make me . . . asthmatic," he admitted to *New York Times Magazine* writer Bruce Weber. But though he had not served in Vietnam, its lingering shadow over the United States attracted him to the subject. "To me, the Vietnam experience is the sore that will never heal," he told Weber. "I think I was lucky I didn't go to Vietnam. Maybe it would have given me an understanding of some things I only understand secondhand. But I think you'd be so horribly scarred by it. . . . How close do you want to get to the fire in order to be able to write about it?"

The story that unfolds in *Casualties of War* is triggered when a Vietnam veteran named Eriksson (played by Michael J. Fox) sees a young Asian woman on the San Francisco subway who reminds him of his experiences in the war. The viewer is thus transported back to Vietnam, where the action opens with a firefight between American soldiers and Vietcong gurrillas. Private Eriksson, an inexperienced soldier newly arrived in Vietnam, is saved from death by his squad leader, Sergeant Meserve (Sean Penn). A short time later, however, another man in the squad is felled by a sniper's bullet. The loss deeply angers Meserve, who is dedicated to the welfare of the men under his command.

Meserve's five-man squad is subsequently given a long-range reconnaissance mission. Warned away from a brothel with alleged VC connections, the squad descends on a nearby village and kidnaps a young woman named Oahn (Thuy Thu Le) to serve as "portable R and R (rest and recreation)." The woman is subsequently gang-raped over the objections of a horrified Eriksson. Helpless to prevent the rape, he provides what little comfort he can to Oahn. The squad then encounters the enemy, and the woman—now regarded as no more than a piece of unnecessary equipment—is quickly murdered.

Upon returning to base camp, an anguished Eriksson reports the incident to his superiors. He initially meets with resistance from his commanding officers and death threats from his fellow soldiers, but he is ultimately successful in seeing that Meserve and the other squad members are punished for their actions.

CRITICAL REACTION

The merits of *Casualties of War* were furiously debated among critics and veterans (several veterans organizations registered formal objections to the film). Reviewer Peter Travers commented in *Rolling Stone* that the "flawed but overwhelming" film paints a "portrait of hell so harrowing it's impossible to shake." Weber, meanwhile, remarked that *Casualties of War* "is gravely and potently distinct from all [DePalma's] earlier work. . . . [It] is, in fact, different from the other celebrated movies about Vietnam. . . . It is not a 'journey' film, or an allegory of good and evil, that uses the war to track its characters' descent into inhumanity. Nor is it a surrealist portrait of the horrors of combat. Rather, almost from the start, it asks the viewer simply to accept the fundamental amorality that our soldiers embraced in order to survive."

Others, though, weighed in with far more critical evaluations. Vietnam reporter Frances FitzGerald dismissed the film as a cliché-ridden mess with overtones of sadism and pornography. *Time*'s Richard Schickel commented that the film's "distant and curiously monotonous tone . . . numbs the conscience instead of awakening it." Many reviewers of the film were particularly critical of Rabe's dialogue, which they characterized as riddled with platitudes and obvious sermonizing. Rabe, meanwhile, was apparently unhappy with some aspects of the film as well, because he made an effort to disassociate himself from the final version prior to its release.

FURTHER READING

Bilton, Michael, and Kevin Sim. *Four Hours in My Lai*. New York: Viking, 1992.

Hammer, Richard. *One Morning in the War: The Tragedy at Pinkville*. London: Hart-Davis, 1970.

Hersh, Seymour M. *My Lai 4: A Report on the Massacre and Its Aftermath*. New York: Random House, 1970.

Knoll, Erwin, and Judith Nies McFadden. *War Crimes and the American Conscience*. New York: Holt, Rinehart and Winston, 1970.

Lewy, Guenter. *America in Vietnam*. New York: Oxford University Press, 1978.

Sack, John. *Body Count: Lt. Calley's Story as Told to John Sack*. London: Hutchinson, 1971.

Schickel, Richard. Review of *Casualties of War*. In *Time* (August 21, 1989).

Simon, John. Review of *Casualties of War*. In *National Review* (September 29, 1989).

Smith, Gavin. "Body Count: Rabe and De Palma's Wargasm." *Film Comment* (July-August 1989).

Travers, Peter. "The Wounds of War." *Rolling Stone* (September 7, 1989).

Weber, Bruce. "Cool Heads, Hot Images." *New York Times Magazine* (May 21, 1989).

Coming Home

Film

Director: Hal Ashby

Screenplay: Waldo Salt and Robert C. Jones; based on a story by Nancy Dowd

Principal Cast: Jane Fonda, Jon Voight, Bruce Dern, Penelope Milford, Robert Carradine

Year of Release: 1978 (United Artists)

American veterans of the Vietnam War adopted dramatically different interpretations of the war and their roles in it upon returning to the towns and cities that they had left a few years before. Some affirmed that the cause was a noble one, a worthy effort hamstrung by bureaucratic dissembling and tentativeness, treacherous media, and ignorant—and often cowardly—radicals. Others raged that American policies in Vietnam had been fatally flawed from the outset; they contended that the war had amounted to nothing more than a tragic waste of life of breathtaking scale. The sentiments of many vets, though, fell somewhere in between, as they tried to attach meaning to their wartime experiences. One of the first cinematic examinations of this struggle is found in *Coming Home*, a 1978 film that featured Jane Fonda—a very unpopular figure with veterans' groups—and Jon Voight, as a wheelchair-bound veteran who emerges over the course of the film as a passionate antiwar activist.

HISTORICAL BACKGROUND

After interviewing more than two hundred Vietnam veterans in the late 1960s, author Murray Polner remarked in *No Victory Parades* that "not one of them—

hawk, dove, or haunted—was entirely free of doubt about the nature of the war and the American role in it. . . . Never before have so many questioned as much, as these veterans have, the essential rightness of what they were forced to do.'' Many veterans continued to support the war effort after returning to the United States, but for others, nagging doubts blossomed into active opposition to the war in Vietnam. The voices of these men added a dose of authority to the stances taken by antiwar demonstrators. As Christian Appy observed in *Working-Class War*, however, many antiwar veterans continued to harbor some skepticism about their place within the civilian antiwar movement, convinced that any evaporation in their ''ideological purity'' would render them immediate outcasts.

Many antiwar Vietnam veterans combined their voices under the banner of Vietnam Veterans Against the War (VVAW). Founded in June 1967 by veteran Jan Barry, the group, which eventually grew to include several thousand members, came to wield considerable clout both within and without the antiwar movement. The members' tours gave them a greater measure of credibility than their civilian allies enjoyed, and recollections of their own wartime experiences and homecomings gave them insights into counterproductive attitudes within the antiwar community. ''They . . . convinced other protesters to reach out to soldiers rather than berate them,'' wrote Tom Wells in *The War Within*, ''thereby advancing antiwar sentiment inside the U.S. military.'' As Barry told Wells, ''When we would meet other people in the peace movement we constantly said to them, 'Stop screaming at the GIs! Talk to them. Listen to them. They might really agree with you.' That's exactly what started to happen.''

Antiwar Vietnam vets inevitably drew fire from conservatives who questioned their patriotism or grit—especially after some of the vets adopted the clothing styles and rhetoric of the larger antiwar community—but members of the VVAW and other activist veterans dismissed charges that they were being disloyal to their country or their fellow soldiers. Instead, they contended that they were simply trying to put an end to a doomed and misguided war. As VVAW member Jack Smith explained in an interview with Myra MacPherson, author of *Long Time Passing*, he saw his antiwar activities with the organization as ''*continuing* my responsibility as a marine. If we were there to 'win hearts and minds' and I saw that mission distorted, I had an *obligation* to come back and tell the people it was being thwarted.''

Though the VVAW gained strength throughout the latter part of the 1960s, it was in the early 1970s, when many other antiwar groups were struggling with infighting and dwindling constituencies, that the group had its greatest impact. In 1970 the VVAW angrily protested against horrid conditions in VA hospitals; Barry recalled to Wills that when he would pay visits to such institutions, ''I didn't know what to say. You walk into a ward full of guys in wheelchairs who have got no arms and legs—mad as hell! And you don't know if they're mad at you. But, oh no, they're mad at the government.''

In February 1971 the group held its widely publicized ''Winter Soldier'' hearings in Detroit, Michigan, in the wake of assertions that the notorious My

Lai Massacre had been an aberration. During the hearings, which lasted three days, veterans provided grim testimony about atrocities that they had witnessed or participated in during their tours. Two months later, the VVAW launched Operation Dewey Canyon III, a week-long series of demonstrations in Washington, D.C., in which women who had lost sons in Vietnam joined with disabled veterans for a series of rallies and other actions. The protest culminated on April 23, when about one thousand veterans marched to the Capitol and flung their Vietnam war medals over a hastily erected barricade onto the building's steps. Wells noted that it was a difficult day for the protestors: "Many of the veterans made emotional statements about the war or dead comrades before tossing their medals over the fence. Afterward, the emotions of some burst. 'It was like two hours before I could stop crying,' one recalled. 'It was very, very, very heavy.'"

In the aftermath of Dewey Canyon III, government operatives tried to discredit the VVAW, and a smear campaign against VVAW leader John Kerry (who would go on to serve Massachusetts in the U.S. Senate) was launched. The organization persevered, but internal disputes over governing philosophies and efforts to broaden VVAW's membership soon wracked the group, and by the mid-1970s its influence had diminished considerably.

FONDA AND VIETNAM

Jane Fonda, daughter of Hollywood icon Henry Fonda and sister of Peter Fonda of *Easy Rider* fame, was easily the most visible and controversial of the celebrities in the antiwar movement in the early 1970s. A frequent speaker at antiwar rallies around the country, she became romantically involved with (and eventually married and divorced) Tom Hayden, founder of Students for a Democratic Society (SDS). In 1971 she kicked off a tour of skits, songs, and other entertainment under the banner of FTA (Fuck the Army). The tour, dubbed "political vaudeville," targeted coffeehouses located near military bases boasting large numbers of GI customers. The FTA cast played to large and enthusiastic crowds at many of these venues. Fonda also helped sponsor the VVAW's Winter Soldier Investigation into alleged military atrocities in Vietnam early in 1971.

But all of Fonda's other antiwar activities paled next to her decision to visit North Vietnam in July 1972. During her two-week stay there, her North Vietnamese hosts showed her how American bombing campaigns had devastated hospitals, schools, and villages across the country. This tour shook her deeply. A carefully scripted meeting was also arranged in which Fonda spoke with several American prisoners of war (who later charged that their appearance and statements at the meeting had been forcibly extracted by the threat of torture), and she subsequently pronounced that American POWs were being treated well.

Other elements of her trip provoked considerably stronger criticism. Years after her return to the United States, she would continue to be haunted by widely broadcast film footage that showed a smiling Fonda posing aboard a North Vietnamese antiaircraft gun, surrounded by applauding NVA soldiers. Finally, she willingly made a broadcast over Radio Hanoi in which she castigated American soldiers as pawns and war criminals. Radio Hanoi aired various portions of her statements from July 14 to July 22, reaching American (and South Vietnamese) soldiers, pilots, and POWs alike. "It's difficult to put into words how terrible it is to hear that siren song that is so absolutely rotten and wrong," said Colonel George Day, ranking officer at the notorious Hanoi Hilton POW camp, in an interview with Christopher Anderson, author of *Citizen Jane*. "It was worse than being manipulated and used. She got into it with all her heart. . . . She caused the deaths of unknown numbers of Americans by buoying up the enemy's spirits and keeping them in the fight. That's not what you'd expect from Henry Fonda's daughter."

Fonda returned home to a firestorm of criticism and a new nickname: Hanoi Jane. Supporters of American involvement in Vietnam viewed her actions as treasonous, and even some people who strongly opposed the war viewed her visit as ill-considered. Veterans' organizations and conservative politicians called for a boycott of her films, and some critics urged stronger punishment. "Incensed by Jane's actions, congressmen . . . urged that she be indicted," wrote Anderson. "Meanwhile, resolutions censuring Jane were promptly introduced in the Colorado and Maryland legislatures. An editorial in the right-wing Manchester (New Hampshire) *Union Leader* called for her to be tried for sedition and, if convicted, shot." Unfazed by the criticism, Fonda joined Hayden in forming the Indochina Peace Campaign (IPC), a speaking tour that touched down in nearly one hundred cities over an eight-week period in the fall.

In the spring of 1973, following a January cease-fire agreement, American prisoners of war returned to the United States to a rousing welcome. Upon their return, they provided harrowing accounts of the torture they endured at the hands of their North Vietnamese captors, but Fonda was unconvinced. She told the Associated Press that "I think that one of the only ways that we are going to redeem ourselves as a country for what we have done [in North Vietnam] is not to hail the POWs as heroes, because they are hypocrites and liars. History will judge them severely." Over the ensuing weeks, she repeatedly defended the Hanoi government, dismissing the POWs as liars and professional killers. Fonda, though, found that she had staked out a lonely position regarding the character of the POWs, some of whom had been held for the better part of a decade. She was widely rebuked in the press (and by voices from across the political spectrum) for her statements, and hatred for her reached new levels among veterans and other sectors of American society.

In 1975 North Vietnam invaded the South and, following the fall of Saigon, established their rule in brutal fashion, executing thousands of South Vietnamese and consigning millions more to labor camps or panicked flight. Stunned by this turn of events, singer Joan Baez and other antiwar activists launched an "Appeal to the Conscience of Vietnam," but Fonda declined to join them; instead she criticized the activists for the move, suggesting that they were being manipulated by the U.S. government.

Years later, Fonda acknowledged in an interview with Barbara Walters for ABC that she remained a controversial figure as a result of her Vietnam-era activities. ''The war was a very divisive and very confusing tragedy for all of us, but because I don't think we've ever resolved what the war meant, there are still festering wounds and a lot of pain, and for some I've become a lightning rod. . . . I am proud of most of what I did and I am very sorry for some of what I did.'' Before the interview concluded, she offered an apology to ''men who were in Vietnam who I hurt or whose pain I caused to deepen because of things that I said or did. . . . My intentions were never to hurt them or make their situation worse. It was the contrary. I was trying to help end the killing, end the war, but there were times when I was thoughtless and careless about it, and I'm very sorry that I hurt them.''

CREATION OF *COMING HOME*

In 1972 Fonda, who had been wanting to do a film on Vietnam, hired Nancy Dowd to write a script about the war as seen from the perspective of a veteran's wife. After the script was reworked by Robert C. Jones and Waldo Salt to add a greater love story element, it was accepted by IPC (Indochina Peace Campaign) Films, the production company that had been formed by Fonda and Bruce Gilbert, one of her activist friends, several months previously. Fonda and Gilbert then secured the highly-regarded Hal Ashby to direct, and lined up Bruce Dern and Jon Voight to play the two male leads, Fonda's Marine husband and a crippled Vietnam vet, respectively (Voight was originally slated to play Fonda's husband, but he grabbed the role of the paraplegic veteran when a number of other actors passed).

Fonda recognized that *Coming Home* was a gamble. The filming was done at a time when memories of ''Hanoi Jane'' were still fresh in many people's minds, a reality that was brought home to the production crew when all requests to film scenes at VA hospitals and military bases were denied. Still, Fonda was determined to make the movie.

The film opens with a scene in which a group of young disabled veterans argue passionately about the merits of America's involvement in Vietnam. It then introduces the viewer to Bob Hyde (played by Dern), a Marine captain who is decidedly gung-ho about his impending Vietnam tour. After his departure, his wife, Sally Hyde (played by Fonda), volunteers at the base hospital. While there, she becomes acquainted with Luke Martin (played by Voight), a bitter Vietnam veteran consigned to a wheelchair by injuries suffered in the war.

Over the ensuing weeks, a relationship between Sally and Luke develops, and the veteran's rage fades. At the same time, Sally undergoes a transformation of her own in her husband's absence, changing from a docile housewife into a newly independent person with a dawning recognition of the toll that the war is taking. A brief visit with her husband in Hong Kong further shakes her, because Bob's experiences in Vietnam have left him dazed and uncomprehending.

Meanwhile, the suicide of a fellow vet transforms Luke into an antiwar activist. Sally bails him out after he is arrested for chaining himself to the gate of a Marine recruiting station. They subsequently have sex for the first time, and Sally finds the experience much more pleasurable than she ever did with Bob. By the time Bob returns home as the result of an accident in which he shot himself in the leg, Sally and Luke have fallen in love. Informed of their relationship by FBI agents who have kept the wheelchair-bound veteran under surveillance since his arrest, an enraged Bob loads his combat rifle and confronts his wife. Luke arrives, though, and disarms the distraught man with calming words. The film climaxes with two intercutting scenes: in one, Luke tells a group of high school boys about his traumatic experiences in Vietnam; in the other, a haunted Bob wades into the ocean and drowns himself.

CRITICAL RECEPTION

Coming Home garnered largely positive reviews, though several aspects of the film (an obtrusive soundtrack, an unsatisfying conclusion, and the one-dimensional quality of Dern's character) were faulted by a number of critics. The film was nominated for several Academy Awards; it received three, for best actress (Fonda), best actor (Voight), and best screenplay.

As one might expect, impressions of the film were colored somewhat by the reviewers' politics—and, by extension, their feelings toward Fonda. Arthur Schlesinger, Jr., for example, commented in *Saturday Review* that "*Coming Home* seems to me a valiant though stammering attempt to speak to profound national perplexity and guilt. . . . More than any other fiction film, it recalls, however imperfectly, the horrid waste and destructiveness of the most shameful war in American history, the worst years of our lives. I salute Jane Fonda for insisting that it be made." Others, though, felt that the film offered only a simplistic examination of Vietnam issues. *America* reviewer Richard Blake remarked that "[the world in *Coming Home*] is a world drained of ambiguity and complexity, where you can always tell people of conscience by their blue chambray shirts, and lackeys of repressive capitalism because the tops of their ears show." Appy commented in *Working-Class War* that "despite some fine moments, the film finally reduced the complexity of veterans' experiences to a sanctimonious political parable," a sentiment echoed by others (especially those embittered by the activities and statements of Fonda and other opponents of the war).

But even though critics granted that the film was flawed, most felt that it nonetheless made an honorable attempt to examine the effects of war on veterans and their families. *Time* reviewer Frank Rich contended that in its best moments, *Coming Home* "reminds us of the choices everybody made during those harrowing war years—and of the price the nation paid thereafter." Blake, though offering only lukewarm comments on the execution of the film, allowed that "*Coming Home* deserves all the applause it has been receiving for daring to touch those wounds that still ache."

FURTHER READING

Anderson, Christopher. *Citizen Jane: The Turbulent Life of Jane Fonda*. New York: Henry Holt, 1990.

Appy, Christian G. *Working-Class War: American Combat Soldiers and Vietnam*. Chapel Hill, N.C.: University of North Carolina Press, 1993.

Blake, Richard A. "The Revolution Is Forever." *America* (March 18, 1978).

Crandell, William F. "They Moved the Town." In *Give Peace a Chance: Exploring the Vietnam Antiwar Movement*, Melvin Small and William D. Hoover, eds. Syracuse, N.Y.: Syracuse University Press, 1992.

Emerson, Gloria. *Winners and Losers*. New York: Random House, 1976.

Kerry, John, and Vietnam Veterans Against the War. *The New Soldier*. New York: Macmillan, 1971.

MacPherson, Myra. *Long Time Passing: Vietnam and the Haunted Generation*. Garden City, N.Y.: Doubleday, 1984.

Polner, Murray. *No Victory Parades: The Return of the Vietnam Veteran*. New York: Holt, Rinehart and Winston, 1971.

Rich, Frank. "The Dark at the End of the Tunnel." *Time* (February 20, 1978).

Rosenblum, Ron. "Dangerous Jane." *Vanity Fair* (November 1988).

Schlesinger, Arthur, Jr. "The Worst Years of Our Lives." *Saturday Review* (April 29, 1978).

Wells, Tom. *The War Within: America's Battle over Vietnam*. Berkeley: University of California Press, 1994.

The Deer Hunter

Film

Director: Michael Cimino

Screenplay: Deric Washburn; based on a story by Michael Cimino, Deric Washburn, Louis Garfinkle, Quinn Redeker

Principal Cast: Robert De Niro, Christopher Walken, Meryl Streep, John Savage, John Cazale, Chuck Aspegren

Year of Release: 1978 (Universal)

Director Michael Cimino had only one feature film to his credit (the 1974 Clint Eastwood film *Thunderbolt and Lightfoot*) when he unveiled *The Deer Hunter* in December 1978. The film follows a small group of working-class friends from the wedding of one of their own to the harrowing terrain of Vietnam, culminating with a nightmarish vision of the fall of Saigon. *The Deer Hunter* garnered extravagant praise from large segments of the critical community, many of whom cited it as the best of the several Vietnam films that appeared in the late 1970s, and it went on to win a number of prestigious awards, such as the New York Film Critics' Circle Award for best English-language film and five Academy Awards, including Best Picture and Best Director. But the work also elicited severely negative reactions, and within weeks of its release a significant body of critics—including a number of prominent Vietnam correspondents—had denounced the film as racist, jingoist, and manipulative. Nearly two decades after its release, the debate over the film's merits and faults has not subsided.

HISTORICAL BACKGROUND

The Last Days of South Vietnam

In March 1975, the North Vietnamese decided to test the United States' 1973 pledge to react "with full force" if North Vietnam violated the terms of the Paris peace accords. The United States had made the pledge in order to get a reluctant South Vietnam to agree to the accords, but subsequent events had called that resolve into question. Later in 1973 the U.S. Congress passed both the Case-Church Amendment, which explicitly forbade funding of direct or indirect combat activities by U.S. forces in Southeast Asia, and the War Powers Act, which limited the president's authority to commit troops outside U.S. borders without congressional approval. President Nixon was unhappy with both pieces of legislation; the latter bill, in fact, required Congress to override his veto in order to pass it into law. U.S. military aid to South Vietnam dropped dramatically between 1973 and 1975 as well, plummeting from $1.6 billion in fiscal year 1973 to $700 million for fiscal year 1975. Some observers bitterly criticized this drop in support. Defense Secretary James Schlesinger, for instance, argued that "it would be a serious error on the part of the United States, and I believe, a serious moral lapse for us to contemplate the semi-abandonment of an ally by failure to provide them with the appropriate financial resources." Others, however, argued that the United States had already invested far too much in South Vietnam, and that it was time for the government of President Nguyen Van Thieu to stand on its own. North Vietnam observed all these developments with growing confidence, and its military leaders revised their strategy accordingly. Buoyed by the power of the Ho Chi Minh Trail, the departure of the Americans, and the advantageous terms of the Paris accords, the NVA presence in South Vietnam increased dramatically in 1974. The massive incursion, however, went largely undetected by Saigon.

Encouraged by America's tepid response to their late December 1974 assault on and capture of Phuoc Long Province, located midway down South Vietnam's border with Cambodia, the North Vietnamese made another offensive thrust on March 10, 1975. This assault, on Ban Me Thuot, a provincial capital in the central highlands, proved to be a profoundly important battle. The Communists' confidence soared when they saw that this second cease-fire violation would not bring America's dreaded B-52s back to the skies of Vietnam. Conversely, the U.S. decision to stay on the sidelines was a severe blow to South Vietnam.

An ARVN counterattack against the now NVA-controlled Ban Me Thuot failed, and on March 15 Thieu ordered his troops to abandon the central highlands and consolidate their defenses further south. He thus ceded the northern half of the country to the North Vietnamese in a single day, and set in motion a chaotic withdrawal that decimated the South Vietnamese military and triggered a torrent of refugees. Hundreds of thousands of civilians and soldiers—many of the latter burdened with family members who had been permitted to live near where they were stationed—merged together in a vast southward-winding torrent that came to be known as the "Convoy of Tears." The retreat down Highway 7, a rough, narrow road, became even more miserable when "the North Vietnamese shelled the congested drawn-out convoy—and half a million people began pushing and fighting for the vanguard," wrote Michael Maclear in *The Ten Thousand Day War*. "Survivors told of old people and babies crushed and left to die as military vehicles bulldozed through the slowly trudging civilians, who still clutched at cartloads of lifetime possessions. In the stampede countless lost children died from the shells and from hunger. Only one in four of the vast human convoy reached the coast, with most of the civilians having fallen behind to await capture."

By the end of March, the northern coastal cities of Quang Tri, Hue, and Da Nang were firmly in the possession of NVA forces, and other South Vietnamese coastal holdings (Qui Nhon, Nha Trang, Cam Ranh Bay) fell in short order. The North Vietnamese thus marched steadily southward, gulping up huge swaths of territory. Valiant attempts to halt the advance, such as the ARVN stand at Xuan Loc, only slowed the Communists, and by April 22, when Xuan Loc finally fell to the North Vietnamese, it was clear that South Vietnam's days were numbered.

The Fall of Saigon

On April 21—four days after the U.S. Senate Armed Services Committee declined a request by President Gerald Ford for $722 million in emergency aid to the South Vietnam government—Thieu gave a bitter resignation speech in which he excoriated America for abandoning his regime. His elderly vice president, Tran Van Huong, took his place for a few days, but he was in turn replaced by General Duong Van Minh. Both Minh and the Ford administration held out hope that Thieu's departure and the general's ascension might convince Hanoi to accept a negotiated settlement to the violence, but that last tattered hope soon fell away before the advancing NVA forces. By April 27 Saigon was completely surrounded, and the evacuation of American civilian personnel and selected South Vietnamese civilians—which had started weeks before—intensified. (An estimated 120,000 Vietnamese and 20,000 Americans were evacuated during Saigon's final month of existence.) On April 28 Communist pilots manning captured American warplanes bombed Saigon's Tan Son Nhut Airport, and in the early morning hours of April 29, an additional barrage of NVA rockets slammed into the air base, rendering it inoperable for the fixed-wing aircraft that had been the primary mode of transportation for the evacuation.

U.S. Ambassador Graham Martin continued to resist calls for a final helicopter evacuation of American and Vietnamese personnel. Later on the morning of the 29th, however, Armed Forces Radio played Bing Crosby's "White Christmas." This was the signal to execute "Operation Frequent Wind"—the Pentagon's call for the final evacuation of American personnel from Saigon.

The next twenty-four hours were tremendously chaotic, as thousands of South

Vietnamese soldiers and civilians commandeered ARVN aircraft and barges and boats in an effort to reach the U.S. fleet waiting off the coast. Back in Saigon, meanwhile, confusion reigned. Attempts to execute helicopter pickups of Americans and selected South Vietnamese civilians and their families at designated spots around the city were complicated by the deteriorating situation, as desperate Vietnamese cast about for some avenue of escape. "I saw on the streets— you wouldn't believe it," recalled one Vietnamese reporter in *Time*. "You can hear the bombs, the guns. Everyone running out in the street, shouted, cried. They run, run, run, look for a boat, someplace to move. I saw—right now I remember—their eyes open, suffering."

The scene was particularly bad around the U.S. embassy, where thousands of Vietnamese milled around its gates in hopes of gaining deliverance. One Marine sergeant recalled in *Newsweek* that there were "thousands of people screaming, begging, throwing money at us. . . . They were throwing babies over the walls. But hell, those walls were eight to ten feet tall with double strands of concertina wire. Some of them couldn't get the kids over. They just hung up on the wire. Babies, screaming."

The frantic helicopter lift continued throughout April 29 and into the early hours of April 30 as NVA forces prowled along the city's outskirts. Martin and others were determined to evacuate as many Vietnamese people as possible, but Ford finally ordered an end to the evacuation on the morning of the 30th. The timing of the order left an estimated 420 Vietnamese in the compound, waiting for helicopters that never arrived. About one hour after the departure of the last American helicopter, NVA General Tran Van Tra ordered his troops to move into the helpless city. By noon the North Vietnamese had seized the airwaves. As their tanks rolled through Saigon's streets, the NVA announced that the city, which it renamed Ho Chi Minh City, had been captured. The war was over.

CIMINO AND VIETNAM

Around the time of *The Deer Hunter*'s release, director Michael Cimino indicated in interviews that he had voluntarily joined the U.S. Army in early 1968, dropping out of Yale shortly before completing work on a doctoral degree. "I was a medic with a Green Beret unit that trained in Texas and I was called up to go to Vietnam, but, for a number of reasons, wound up not going," Cimino wrote in *American Cinematographer*. "However, it was largely my experience with the Special Forces troops while I was taking this training that influenced the spirit of *The Deer Hunter* and my feeling toward the men portrayed in it. Vietnam was, after all, the war of my generation, and so I feel extremely privileged to have had a chance to make a major film about something so important."

According to Pentagon records, however, Cimino enlisted in the U.S. Army Reserve in 1962—not 1968—while taking classes at Yale University. Defense Department records indicate that he spent six months on active duty, with the bulk of it at Fort Dix in New Jersey (he did take a month of medical training at Fort Sam Houston in Texas). In 1963 he graduated from Yale with an M.F.A. degree; the university has no records that indicate that Cimino did any doctoral work at the school. Cimino's apparent misrepresentation of his service record was seized upon by critics of *The Deer Hunter* in the months following its release.

CREATION OF *THE DEER HUNTER*

After his 1963 graduation from Yale, Cimino spent the remainder of the 1960s immersing himself in the production of commercials and industrial and documentary films on the East Coast. In 1971 Cimino moved to California in an attempt to break into the motion picture business. After collaborating on the scripts for *Silent Running* (1971) and *Magnum Force* (1973), Cimino served as the scriptwriter and director for *Thunderbolt and Lightfoot* (1974).

In November 1976 Cimino struck a deal with EMI Film Distributors, Ltd., an English company interested in expanding their involvement in American films, for the film that would become *The Deer Hunter*. Armed with only an outline of the story that he wanted to tell, Cimino scrambled to secure locations in order to meet EMI's ambitious production schedule. He subsequently wrote large sections of the script during these frantic scouting excursions (Deric Washburn wrote the final version of the screenplay). "*The Deer Hunter* was an enormously difficult picture to make for all of the obvious reasons, but mainly because I had decided early on to work only in real locations and to go to places where film crews had not shot before," Cimino recalled in *American Cinematographer*. The script for the film, which eventually featured scenes shot in such diverse locales as the Ohio River Valley, Washington state's Cascade Mountains, and Thailand, changed as he discovered new locations. "As we came across various places in the process of surveying locations, the script began to change," Cimino wrote. "We were actually laying out the physical production and writing the script simultaneously. As a result, the script, instead of describing locations that had been conjured up, described real places."

The actual filming of *The Deer Hunter* took place under often arduous circumstances. Winter scenes filmed in the Pittsburgh area actually had to be made in the heat of summer because of production delays, and several of the war scenes filmed in Thailand proved very dangerous for the film's actors. "We were risking our lives," actor Robert De Niro told *Esquire*'s Jean Vallely. "You want it to look authentic but it is a movie. You don't want to be a jerk about it. It just got all confusing."

The film came in over budget as well, but by mid-1978—after months of exhausting editing sessions and intense negotiations with EMI and Universal Pictures, the film's distributor, over the movie's three-hour length—*The Deer Hunter* was completed. "My film has nothing to do with whether the war should or should not have been," Cimino told the *New York Times'* Leticia Kent in

December 1978, only days before its release. "This film addresses itself to the question of the ordinary people of this country who journeyed from their homes to the heart of darkness and back. How do they survive that? If they're lucky enough to survive, how do they return home? And after they return home, how do they go on without committing suicide, having seen and been through what they've seen and been through? And how do they go on with some sense of hope, with their spirits intact? And still believe in something?"

The Plot of *The Deer Hunter*

The film opens with a glimpse of the insides of a fiery Pennsylvania steel mill, where three Ukrainian-American steelworkers—Michael (played by Robert De Niro), Steven (John Savage), and Nick (Christopher Walken)—are completing their last day of work before entering the Army and, it is strongly suggested, going on to Vietnam. After knocking off work, Michael, Steven, and Nick join several other friends at a local tavern. They then prepare for the wedding of Steven, who is being married that night. As Michael and Nick dress, they make plans to embark on one last deer hunt before reporting for duty. Michael, in particular, discusses the subject with great feeling, and it becomes clear that he adheres to a rigid ethical code when he hunts. The deer must be slain "with one shot," he states flatly.

The film then moves on to the wedding and the raucous reception that follows. During this long sequence, it becomes clear that Michael has strong feelings for Nick's girlfriend, Linda (Meryl Streep), but he remains silent on the subject. The revelry continues well into the night, dampened only by Steven's ambivalence about his new status and the brief appearance of a bitter Vietnam veteran who turns aside all questions about his tour. At the end of the evening, Nick secures a promise from Michael: If "something happens" to Nick in Vietnam, his friend will stand by him, no matter the cost. The next morning Michael leads a ragtag hunting party into the mountains, where, in accordance with his code, he bags his quarry with a single shot.

The Deer Hunter then moves to Vietnam, where Michael, Nick, and Steven are captured by the enemy. Housed in wretched conditions, the three men watch in horror as their Vietcong captors force other prisoners to play Russian roulette against one another. The VC wager on each contest, and those who refuse to take part are thrown into a rat-infested cage in the river, where death will simply come more slowly. Eventually, Michael and Nick are pitted against one another, but Michael tricks the VC into loading the gun with three bullets. He subsequently shoots all three of the guards, and Michael, Nick, and Steven all escape (although Steven is crippled during the flight). The three men then part ways. Steven and Michael return to Pennsylvania, where each grapples with their Vietnam experiences. Nick, meanwhile, remains in Vietnam. Emotionally scarred by the trauma of his captivity, his psyche receives yet another blow when he discovers that a civilian version of the deadly Russian roulette game is popular in Saigon's gambling community. Shattered by the discovery, Nick subsequently disappears into the city's shadows.

Michael's relationship with his hometown community, meanwhile, has changed in fundamental ways. He finds it difficult to interact with his old friends, and while he and Linda become lovers, the ghost of Nick hangs over their relationship. Michael also finds that he can no longer hunt. Presented with an opportunity to kill a trophy buck, he allows the animal to live.

Michael subsequently decides to return to Vietnam in hopes of finding Nick. He arrives in Saigon in mid-1975, during the last desperate hours before the arrival of the North Vietnamese Army. Michael roams the streets, heedless of the chaos and carnage around him, and finally finds his old friend at a gambling den. The blank-eyed Nick has become a professional Russian roulette player, and Michael's feverish attempts to talk with him are drowned out by the voices of the excited gamblers and Nick's blasted mental state. Michael subsequently buys his way into the game against Nick, risking his own life in an effort to save his friend. Both men survive the first round. Frantic, Michael pursues and discards several different avenues of conversation as he tries to reach Nick. He finally asks Nick if he remembers the afternoons they spent deer hunting together. Nick smiles crookedly in recognition and brings the gun to his head. "One shot," he says, and pulls the trigger, killing himself.

The film's climactic scene takes place at a local tavern back in Pennsylvania, where mourners from Nick's funeral have gathered. The atmosphere in the bar is sad and restless, but after a time one of the people gathered there begins to render a tentative version of "God Bless America." The rest of the mourners, including Michael, Linda, and Steven, join in, and the film comes to a close.

CRITICAL RECEPTION

The Deer Hunter sparked a tremendous amount of controversy upon its release. Many reviewers praised it as a powerful, skillfully executed treatment of the war and its impact on a small American community, and it won several major awards, including Best Picture and Best Director Academy Awards. But other reviewers—including several commentators closely associated with Vietnam—castigated it as a warped, misleading representation of the war. International reaction to the film was often critical, too; several foreign delegations withdrew from the Berlin Film Festival when *The Deer Hunter* was named the official American entry in the event. The remarks of Vietnam War reporter Gloria Emerson encapsulated the two dramatically different responses to the film. Writing in the *National Catholic Reporter*, she noted that "many Vietnam veterans I know and respect were deeply moved and saddened by scenes in *The Deer Hunter*," but she herself felt that the film was "an appalling sham."

Most people who were unhappy with the picture centered their complaints on three aspects of the film: the factual accuracy of the Russian roulette sequences and other scenes; the movie's overall depiction of the Vietnamese people; and the film's use of "God Bless America," seen in some quarters as an approving benediction on American intervention in Indochina. John Pilger commented in the *New Statesman & Society* that Cimino presents "a suffering, courageous people as sub-human Oriental brutes and dolts. . . . The orgiastic Russian roulette scenes that recur throughout the film . . . leave an audience with the impression that the Vietnamese gamble on human life as casually as the British gamble on the pools. How odd: in Vietnam, I never heard about this game. I have asked other correspondents and they have never heard about this game. And interviews with POWs never mentioned this game; but much of Cimino's picture is given over to this 'meaningful horror,' which he insists happened and which is meant to be somehow redemptive." Vietnam reporter Tom Buckley offered a harsh assessment as well, charging in *Harper's* that "[Cimino's] characters, their milieu, his version of the Vietnam war, all suffer from the same defect. They are neither real nor surreal—merely pretentious and false. . . . *The Deer Hunter* does not examine cruelty, it exploits it," continued Buckley. "To invent forms of cruelty—the Russian roulette game—where so much suffering actually occurred seems doubly perverse." Such prominent journalists as Peter Arnett and Studs Turkel also registered their unhappiness with the film. "Absent are the disillusion at home, the bitterness of those who served, the destruction of a country, and any other factors that might lessen the epic theme," argued Arnett in the *Times-Picyune*.

"Vietnam is a hell on earth, but was not made so—the film seems to suggest—by the American presence," concluded Gilbert Adair in his *Vietnam on Film*. "If American involvement was wrong-headed and even criminal, it was only because it exposed 'our boys' to contamination by a continent so irredeemably mired in moral corruption and the debilitating lethe induced by opium that it hardly deserved to be saved. The unspoken question hanging over the movie would seem to be less 'Why are we in Vietnam?' than 'How can the President allow our soldiers to be contaminated by gooks?' "

Cimino, though, also had a substantial number of admirers. *New York Times* critic Vincent Canby echoed the thoughts of many when he wrote that with *The Deer Hunter*, Cimino had emerged as a major new filmmaker. Numerous reviewers pointed to specific sections of the film as evidence that a significant new cinematic voice had arrived: "Throughout the film, Cimino draws visual parallels between the grimy blue-collar town of Clairton and the mess America created in Asia, until finally America and Vietnam seem to share a single bastard culture," wrote Frank Rich in *Time*. "This surreal device reaches brilliant fruition when the film re-creates the fall of Saigon: in the holocaust the city starts to resemble a Western ghost town."

Other defenders of the film suggested that much of the critical reaction stemmed from Cimino's refusal to meekly adhere to expected Vietnam themes. When *The Deer Hunter* was released, wrote Robert E. Bourdette, Jr. in *America Rediscovered*, "there were rigid expectations about what such a film that involved that conflict should convey. These demands, often contradictory, were reflected in the early criticism: such a film was expected to be single-minded in opposing our involvement in Vietnam; it was expected to portray a literal, even documentary-like, record of events; it should demonstrate overtly and with no ambiguity our moral failure as a nation." Bourdette went on to charge that what many critics demanded was a reproduction of their version of history rather than an illumination of the meaning of that history. Critic Frank Burke agreed. Writing in *Literature/Film Quarterly*, Burke contended that the film was "a supremely moral act of imagination . . . depicted with empathy and integrity."

For his part, Cimino insisted that he never meant to create a film governed by actual events. "The film is not realistic," he told Leticia Kent. "It's surrealistic. Even the landscape is surreal. . . . In trying to compress the experience of the war into a film, even as long as this one, I had to deal with it in a nonliteral way. You're right. I used events from '68 and '75 as reference points rather than as fact. But if you attack the film on its facts, then you're fighting a phantom, because literal accuracy was never intended." The director also took exception to criticisms that *The Deer Hunter* espoused a right-wing interpretation of the war. The film's characters, he told *Time*'s Lance Morrow, "are not endorsing anything except their common humanity—their common frailty, their need for each other."

FURTHER READING

Adair, Gilbert. *Vietnam on Film: From* The Green Berets *to* Apocalypse Now. New York: Proteus, 1981.

Anderegg, Michael, ed. *Inventing Vietnam: The War in Film and Television*. Philadelphia: Temple University Press, 1991.

Arnett, Peter. "War Reporter Compares Deer Hunter to Reality." *Times-Picyune* (New Orleans, Louisiana) (April 13, 1979).

Auster, Albert, and Leonard Quart. *How the War Was Remembered: Hollywood and Vietnam*. New York: Praeger, 1988.

Bourdette, Robert E., Jr. "Reading *The Deer Hunter*: Michael Cimino's Deliberate American Epic." In *America Rediscovered: Critical Essays on Literature and Film of the Vietnam War*, Owen W. Gilman, Jr. and Lorrie Smith, eds. New York: Garland Publishing, 1990.

Buckley, Tom. "Hollywood's War." *Harper's* (April 1979).

Burke, Frank. "In Defense of *The Deer Hunter* OR: The Knee Jerk Is Quicker than the Eye." *Literature/Film Quarterly* (January 1983).

Butler, David. *The Fall of Saigon*. New York: Simon and Schuster, 1985.

Church, George A. "A Lost War." *Time* (April 24, 1995).

Cimino, Michael. "Ordeal by Fire and Ice." *American Cinematographer* (October 1978).

Dittmar, Linda, and Gene Michaud, eds. *From Hanoi to Hollywood: The Vietnam War in American Film*. New Brunswick, N.J.: Rutgers University Press, 1990.

Emerson, Gloria. "How Films Lie about Vietnam." *National Catholic Reporter* (November 14, 1980).

Kent, Leticia. "Ready for Vietnam? A Talk with Michael Cimino." *New York Times* (December 10, 1978).

Maclear, Michael. *The Ten Thousand Day War: Vietnam, 1945–1975*. New York: St. Martin's Press, 1981.

Morrow, Lance. "Viet Nam Comes Home: Two Winning Films Signal the Struggle to Learn from a Lost War." *Time* (April 27, 1979).

Pilger, John. "Why *The Deer Hunter* Is a Lie." *New Statesman & Society* (March 16, 1979).

Rich, Frank. "In Hell without a Map." *Time* (December 18, 1978).

Snepp, Frank. *Decent Interval*. New York: Random House, 1977.

Strasser, Steven, et al. "55 Days of Shame." *Newsweek* (April 15, 1985).

Summers, Harry G., Jr. "Final Days of South Vietnam." *American History* (April 1995).

Vallely, Jean. "Michael Cimino's Battle to Make a Great Movie." *Esquire* (January 2, 1979).

Dispatches

Nonfiction

Author: Michael Herr

Facts of Publication: New York: Alfred A. Knopf, 1977

During the first months of 1968, events in Vietnam dramatically altered the military and political landscape, both in that country and in the United States. North Vietnam's Tet Offensive was launched on January 30–31, violating a Tet (lunar new year) cease-fire that had been agreed to by both sides. This massive NVA campaign, which had been undertaken in hopes of sparking a popular uprising among the peasantry of the South against the Saigon government, consisted of simultaneous assaults on more than 150 cities, hamlets, and military installations in South Vietnam, including such major urban centers as Saigon and Hue. For more than a month, fierce battles were waged up and down the length of Vietnam as U.S. and ARVN (Army of the Republic of Vietnam) forces responded to the offensive. Tet ultimately proved to be a decisive military victory for the United States and its South Vietnamese allies, but it wreaked heavy damage on America's domestic front, where it was widely regarded as a rebuke of official assurances of impending victory.

Writer Michael Herr witnessed the impact of Tet on the country firsthand, accompanying American troops through the decimated, sniper-riddled streets of Hue. His wide-ranging journeys in the country also took him to Khe Sanh, a U.S. Marine base that endured a brutal and highly publicized seventy-seven-day siege in the early months of 1968. Years after his return to the United States, he completed *Dispatches*, a harrowing memoir about his experiences in Hue, Khe Sanh, and other areas of Vietnam. The book shunned standard reporting

conventions in favor of impressionistic war stories and frank, often grim, musings on life and death. "Conventional journalism could no more reveal this war
than conventional firepower could win it," wrote Herr.

HISTORICAL BACKGROUND

Khe Sanh

The Khe Sanh combat base was located in the northwestern corner of the
mountainous Quang Tri Province, which was in the northernmost section of
South Vietnam. By 1967 Khe Sanh, which overlooked a major highway and
possible NVA infiltration route, had begun to loom as a potentially vital interest
for both sides. During April and May of 1967, Marine air and ground forces,
ably assisted by Army artillery and Air Force B-52 strikes, consolidated their
control of Khe Sanh by taking several strategic hills in the area.

In late 1967, however, U.S. intelligence indicated that NVA troops—an estimated forty thousand—were converging on the region. By this time, U.S. commanders had begun to refer to Khe Sanh as the anchor for much of its defensive
strategy against NVA incursions from the jungles of adjacent Laos. The stakes
at Khe Sanh were thus very high, and by the end of 1967 the atmosphere at the
base was a tense one, because the Marines stationed there were entirely surrounded and outnumbered by an estimated eight-to-one margin.

The defense of Khe Sanh was predicated on air support. As Herr wrote in
Dispatches, "air support was everything, the cornerstone of all our hopes at
Khe Sanh, and we knew that once the monsoons lifted, it would be nothing to
drop tens of thousands of tons of high explosives and napalm all around the
base, to supply it without strain, to cover and reinforce the Marines."

On January 21, 1968—ten days before Tet—the NVA began the siege of Khe
Sanh. Rockets, mortars, artillery, and sniper fire pummeled the base on a daily
basis as NVA troops constructed a maze of slowly advancing trenches. President
Johnson reacted to news of the assault angrily, telling General Earle G. Wheeler,
the chairman of the Joint Chiefs of Staff (JCS), that he did not want "any damn
Dien Bien Phu" to unfold at Khe Sanh. (The siege of Dien Bien Phu had been
decisive in pushing France out of Indochina fourteen years before; Harry G.
Summers, Jr., writing in the *Historical Atlas of the Vietnam War*, called it "the
denouement of the eight-year First Indochina War and . . . the *coup de grâce* to
faltering French public support for hostilities.") Johnson subsequently insisted
upon and received a guarantee from the JCS that Khe Sanh would not fall.

The Marines and South Vietnamese Rangers stationed at Khe Sanh held fast,
but they absorbed a good deal of punishment. Then, on February 7, word
reached the base that Communist forces supported by tanks had decimated a
well-fortified Special Forces camp at Lang Vei, only five kilometers away. News
of the attack chilled the defenders of Khe Sanh. As Ronald Spector remarked

in *After Tet*, "the swift fall of Lang Vei sent psychological shock waves through many Americans already apprehensive about the safety of Khe Sanh."

But the American response to the siege was a decisive one. In the weeks preceding the siege, Westmoreland and his staff had settled upon a plan for massive aerial bombardment of NVA positions surrounding Khe Sanh. This campaign, known as Operation Niagara, was unveiled immediately after the siege began. Over the next several weeks, noted Summers, the campaign sent an estimated 24,000 Air Force and Marine bombing sorties over regions surrounding Khe Sanh. Operation Niagara also included 2,700 B-52 bomber sorties over enemy positions, dropping an estimated 110,000 tons of bombs in the process (some of these bombs were dropped within one-sixth of a mile of the base perimeter in an effort to knock out enemy bunkers).

The siege—and the Operation Niagara response—became one of the most heavily covered events of the Vietnam War. Television and print correspondents flocked to the base to post stories, and major American media outlets devoted a great deal of time and energy to Khe Sanh and possible Dien Bien Phu correlations. "Khe Sanh said 'siege,' it said 'encircled Marines' and 'heroic defenders,' " wrote Herr. "It could be understood by newspaper readers quickly, it breathed Glory and War and Honored Dead. It seemed to make sense. It was good stuff."

But the anticipated "big battle" never came. Instead, NVA forces began to withdraw from the area in mid-March (though they continued to bedevil the base with rocket attacks from afar), and by April 8 the base was declared secure. "Journalists and some military men speculated that the enemy's sudden withdrawal indicated that the attack on Khe Sanh had been a feint to draw U.S. attention and troops away from the areas of the impending Tet attacks," wrote Spector. "Westmoreland and his commanders contended that the heavy losses the enemy had suffered were what compelled him to break off the siege. Twenty years later the argument over the Communists' real intentions and their degree of success at Khe Sanh still rages."

The Tet Offensive

The Tet Offensive was a dual NVA-Vietcong campaign of immense proportions that was designed to trigger a countrywide popular uprising against their "oppressors" in Saigon. According to the Tet plan, Vietcong guerrillas already in the South would be joined by thousands of NVA troops who would swing into South Vietnam from various points on the Ho Chi Minh Trail, the famous Communist supply line that ran through Laos and Cambodia along South Vietnam's border. As the NVA and VC forces attacked in concert, the citizenry would rise up in support, and the South Vietnamese government in Saigon would be toppled.

But the Communists never received the popular support they had been expecting. The attackers wreaked heavy damage on dozens and dozens of cities, towns, and villages all across South Vietnam, but after the first few days most of these offenses had been beaten back. Even in Saigon, where Communist troops had breached the walls of the American embassy to the horror of American television audiences, the city was never in danger of falling (thanks in part to the foresight and tactical decisions of Lt. General Fred C. Weyand, the commander in charge of defending the capital). The North Vietnamese forces proved unable to hold any of the cities they had gained, and Tet is now widely regarded as a decisive defeat for the NVA forces (some officials and historians estimate that they may have lost fifty-thousand of their eighty-thousand-man force). Some observers even interpreted the results of Tet as a repudiation of much of the rhetoric that the Communists had been espousing over the previous years. As reporter Don Oberdorfer noted in his *Tet!*, "the Viet Cong lost the best of a generation of resistance fighters, and after Tet increasing numbers of North Vietnamese had to be sent south to fill the ranks. . . . Because the people of the cities did not rise up against the foreigners and puppets at Tet—indeed they gave little support to the attack force—the Communist claim to moral and political authority in South Vietnam suffered a serious blow."

Despite the heavy losses sustained in the campaign, however, Tet still proved beneficial for the Hanoi government. "In all honesty, we didn't achieve our main objective, which was to spur uprisings throughout the south," explained NVA General Tran Do in Stanley Karnow's *Vietnam: A History*. "Still, we inflicted heavy casualties on the Americans and their puppets, and that was a big gain for us. As for making an impact in the United States, it had not been our intention—but it turned out to be a fortunate result."

Stunned by the scale of the offensive—and the disconcerting war footage that was soon flickering across U.S. television sets—American audiences who had repeatedly been assured that victory was near began to look to the execution of the war with a newly skeptical eye. Some observers contend that the often critical tone of much of America's press coverage of Tet hastened this shift in public opinion (the performance of the news media during and after Tet continues to be a subject of great debate). News that General William Westmoreland was requesting additional troops further exacerbated public discomfort with the war, and American public sentiment toward the war increasingly moved toward a "Win it or get out" stance. Dogged by plummeting popularity, President Lyndon B. Johnson abruptly announced that he did not intend to run for a second term later that year.

The Battle for Hue

Some of the most brutal fighting during the Tet Offensive took place in Hue, the old imperial capital located in central Vietnam. Upon taking the city, the Communist forces had rounded up a wide range of Vietnamese military officers and government officials, clergymen, intellectuals and merchants. Thousands of those arrested were executed in sometimes brutal fashion—the graves of about three thousand victims were eventually found, but another three thousand were never accounted for. ARVN, Marine, and U.S. Cavalry forces quickly counter-attacked, but the Communist invaders dug in. U.S. Marine Myron Harrington later recalled to Karnow that "we were new to this type of situation. We were accustomed to jungles and open rice fields, and now we would be fighting in a city, like it was Europe during World War II." The scene that confronted the allied forces was a grim one. "My first impression [of the city] was of desolation, utter devastation," said Harrington. "There were burnt-out tanks and trucks, and upturned automobiles still smoldering. Bodies lay everywhere, most of them civilian. The smoke and stench blended, like in some kind of horror movie. . . . You felt that something could happen at any minute, that they would jump out and start shooting from every side."

For the next three weeks the city was reduced to rubble as allied troops took the city back street by street under withering sniper fire. "For days now, [the Marines] have been fighting their way, bloody inch by inch, down Le Loi Street," reported one CBS news correspondent, as recounted in Peter Braestrup's *Big Story*. "Much is left in shambles as the Marines advance building after building, the North Vietnamese retreat building after building, giving up nothing without a fight." As the grim march forward continued, the Marines absorbed one casualty for every yard gained. "On the worst days," wrote Herr in *Dispatches*, "no one expected to get through it alive. A despair set in among members of the battalion that the older ones, the veterans of two other wars, had never seen before."

Finally, though, the American and ARVN troops retook the ruined, smoking city. By early March the battle for Hue was officially over. An estimated 5,000 Communist troops were killed in the struggle, while South Vietnamese forces lost 384 (with another 1,830 wounded). American casualties included 142 Marines killed (857 wounded) and 74 U.S. Army killed (507 wounded).

HERR AND VIETNAM

Herr arrived in Vietnam in 1967 with the purpose of providing regular columns on the war for *Esquire* magazine, but he and his editor soon agreed to suspend the monthly column idea, and Herr was given the freedom to explore the war in whatever way he desired. For the next eleven months, Herr traveled around the country by helicopter, immersing himself in the war around him. Much of his time was spent in the company of soldiers out in the field, and as Herr freely admitted later, the dark, frightening nature of their daily existence fundamentally altered his perspective. "After a year I felt so plugged in to all the stories and the images and the fear that even the dead started telling me stories," he recalled in *Dispatches*. "However many times it happened, whether I'd known them or not, no matter what I'd felt about them or the way they'd died, their story was always there and it was always the same: it went, 'Put yourself in my place.' "

As the months passed, and the carnage of Khe Sanh, the Tet Offensive, and countless unnamed firefights washed over the country, Herr's desire to write about the war became inextricably intertwined with a sense of obligation to the American soldiers he met. "And always," he wrote, "they would ask you with an emotion whose intensity would shock you to please tell it, because they really did have the feeling that it wasn't being told for them, that they were going through all of this and that somehow no one back in the World knew about it." Years after his stint in Vietnam, Herr told *Vietnam, We've All Been There* author Eric James Schroeder that the voices of the soldiers he had met served as the inspiration for the writing of *Dispatches*. "Most of the soldiers . . . were very open. They always found the subject. I didn't pose the subjects of our conversations. They would tell you. They would tell you *very* eloquently and *very* beautifully." Journalistic detachment, he noted, was an early casualty. "In the situation, in the moment, not politically, not geopolitically, not ideologically, but humanly I was on their side because they were in a real shitstorm and you'd have to be some kind of monster not to be on their side."

CREATION OF *DISPATCHES*

Herr left the escalating bloodshed in Vietnam for the sanctuary of the United States in 1968. He published a few magazine articles soon after his return (in *Esquire, Rolling Stone*, and *New American Review*), but he found it more difficult to complete the book that he had been hoping to write about Vietnam. After writing about two-thirds of the book over an eighteen-month period, Herr underwent what he himself called in his conversation with Schroeder "a massive collapse, a profound paralysis that I can't *directly* attribute to Vietnam, although Vietnam was certainly the catalyst." A period of psychiatric therapy followed, and Herr was eventually able to resume his work on the book.

The final result, published in 1977, was a marked departure from the conventions of standard journalism. Forsaking discussions of ideology and strategy, Herr instead offered up a stunning blend of nightmarish vignettes and introspective musings about the war and its corrosive effect on the humanity of its participants. *Dispatches* concentrated on "the characters and images of Vietnam residing in [the author's] retrospective consciousness," wrote John Hellmann in *American Myth and the Legacy of Vietnam*. The book's chaotic narrative form, Hellmann suggested, "actually represents a 'howling' mental wilderness through which a heroic narrator journeys toward the grail of self-knowledge."

CRITICAL RECEPTION

Dispatches is widely regarded as one of the essential works of literature about the Vietnam War. The book, which wedded novelistic elements to journalism to create a wholly original narrative, was a best-seller, and it was eventually nominated for the 1978 National Book Award in nonfiction. Most critics hailed the book and its author, citing everything from his examination of the dark allure of war to his skillful renderings of the tumult of Khe Sanh and the deadly streets of Hue.

Author C. D. B. Bryan remarked in the *New York Times Book Review* that "Vietnam required not only new techniques of warfare, but new techniques in writing as well. Newscameramen and photographers could show us sometimes what the war looked like, but an entirely new language, imagery and style were needed so that we could understand and feel. . . . *Dispatches* is the best book to have been written about the Vietnam War." *Newsweek* reviewer Raymond Sokolov called it "an oddly delicate book preoccupied, beautifully, with death and pain and violence." The *New York Times'* John Leonard wrote that "*Dispatches* is beyond politics, beyond rhetoric. . . . It is as if Dante had gone to hell with a cassette recording of Jimi Hendrix and a pocketful of pills: our first rock-and-roll war. Stunning." Perhaps most tellingly, many other writers who have tackled the Vietnam War as a subject called Herr's book a masterpiece. Robert Stone wrote in the *Chicago Tribune* that "I was overwhelmed [by the book]. What a passionate, compassionate, brilliant book this is. With uncanny precision it summons up the very essence of that war—its space diction, its surreal psychology, its bitter humor—the dope, the dexedrine, the body bags, the rot, all of it."

FURTHER READING

Beidler, Philip. *American Literature and the Experience of Vietnam*. Athens: University of Georgia, 1982.

Braestrup, Peter. *Big Story: How the American Press and Television Reported and Interpreted the Crisis of Tet 1968 in Vietnam and Washington*. Boulder, Colo.: Westview Press, 1977.

Bryan, C. D. B. Review of *Dispatches*. In the *New York Times Book Review* (November 20, 1977).

Hellmann, John. *American Myth and the Legacy of Vietnam*. New York: Columbia University Press, 1986.

Herr, Michael. *Dispatches*. New York: Knopf, 1977.

Karnow, Stanley. *Vietnam: A History*. New York: Viking, 1983.

Leonard, John. Review of *Dispatches*. In *New York Times* (October 28, 1977).

Oberdorfer, Don. *Tet!*. New York: Doubleday, 1971.

Prados, John, and Ray W. Stubbe. *Valley of Decision: The Siege of Khe Sanh*. New York: Houghton Mifflin, 1991.

Schroeder, Eric James. *Vietnam, We've All Been There: Interviews with American Writers*. Westport, Conn.: Praeger, 1992.

Sokolov, Raymond. Review of *Dispatches*. In *Newsweek* (November 14, 1977).

Spector, Ronald H. *After Tet: The Bloodiest Year in Vietnam*. New York: Free Press, 1993.

Summers, Harry G., Jr. *Historical Atlas of the Vietnam War*. New York: Houghton Mifflin, 1995.

Fields of Fire

Novel

Author. James Webb

Facts of Publication: New York: Prentice-Hall, 1978

Vietnam veteran James Webb once remarked that "in my mind, I am a writer. In my heart I am a soldier, and always will be." This soldier's perspective has been evident throughout his life, both in his work as a government official and in the pages of the novels he has written. The first and best-known of these novels was *Fields of Fire*, a work grounded in Webb's experiences as a combat Marine in Vietnam. Lauded for its battlefield realism and sympathetic characterizations of the U.S. soldiers who served in Asia during that conflict, the novel was also notable for its unflattering depiction of the American antiwar movement. Webb's portrayal of the protestors reflected a viewpoint held by many military personnel who served in Vietnam.

HISTORICAL BACKGROUND

American soldiers who saw combat in Vietnam reacted to the protests and proclamations of the antiwar movement back home in a variety of ways. A number of soldiers chose to block out the growing turmoil in the United States over the war, noting wryly that they had more immediate concerns. Others found the protestors' questions about the morality and prosecution of the war more difficult to ignore, because the statements that filtered out of the antiwar movement's camp to Vietnam echoed their own doubts about the violent, chaotic world in which they found themselves. Finally, some soldiers were outraged by the actions and statements of America's antiwar movement. This latter group tended to view the protestors as either uninformed, unappreciative, or degenerate (or some combination of all three). For example, in *Dear America: Letters Home from Vietnam*, Bernard Edelman included a 1970 letter published in the *Greenfield* (Mass.) *Recorder* from twenty servicemen that castigates the American public for their callous attitude toward the soldiers serving in Vietnam. "Why don't your hearts cry out and shed a tear for the 40-plus thousand red-blooded Americans and brave, fearless, loyal men who have given their lives so a bunch of bloody bastard radicals can protest, dissent and generally bitch about our private and personal war in Vietnam and now Cambodia? . . . How in the hell do you think that we in Vietnam feel when we read of the dissension and unrest in our country caused by young, worthless radicals and the foremost runner of them all: the vile and disease ridden SDS?" Other soldiers angered by the antiwar movement offered less-emotional criticism, but they shared the letter-writers' conviction that their service was being unjustly stained. This anger was slow to dissipate, even years after the war's end.

Some of this resentment stemmed from the socioeconomic composition of both the soldiers and the protestors. As Philip Caputo remarked in a 1996 post-script to his classic memoir *A Rumor of War*, "the establishment that got us involved in Vietnam did not send its sons and daughters there; in fact, its sons and daughters were in the forefront of the antiwar movement." Stung by the rhetoric of antiwar activists, and a profound awareness of their own often-miserable circumstances, many soldiers needed little prodding to conjure up a vision of the antiwar protestor as a spoiled figure of debauchery from the right side of the tracks.

But what angered soldiers most was the conviction that those who had not served in Vietnam had no right to cast aspersions on the performances of those who did. As Paul Starr noted in *The Discarded Army*, "[Veterans] feel over-whelmingly that people who were not in Vietnam have no right to judge them, that such judgments are a luxury of those who stayed at home and had nothing to do with the situation they confronted." This resentment could be found even within the sizable ranks of soldiers who had themselves concluded that the war was a mistake of epic proportions, in part because they often felt that antiwar rhetoric was aimed at soldiers rather than the architects of the war, America's policymakers.

Other observers contended, however, that the antiwar movement—though characterized by excesses at times—had staked out a legitimate moral position, and that its memberships' geographic location or military pedigree was imma-terial. "The mingling in the Vietnam War of the debating and the fighting sowed bitterness in the field and at home," concluded Jonathan Schell in *The Real War*. "The soldiers were carrying out their professional obligation to fight a war into which they had been sent by their democratically elected commander-in-chief. The citizens who opposed the war were faithfully carrying out their no less solemn obligation to decide whether it was in the nation's best interest to be in the war. The tragedy was that the two things were going on at the same time.''

WEBB AND VIETNAM

Webb arrived in Vietnam in March 1969 as a second lieutenant with the Marines. As a platoon commander in the Fifth Marines' First Battalion, Delta Company (and later, as leader of the entire company), the young officer quickly impressed both his superiors and the troops under his charge with his coolness and dedication. He spent the next year leading his troops through the VC-infested terrain of Vietnam's An Hoa Basin, a region known to the Americans as the Arizona Valley. The valley was, even by Vietnam standards, a deadly region to patrol, because land mines, booby traps, and ambushes were commonplace. Webb, though, proved to be an excellent soldier and officer. ''Webb's medals attest to his bravery and composure in combat,'' wrote Robert Timberg in *The Nightingale's Song*. ''He is cited time and again for rallying his men under fire, capturing VC single-handedly, and pulling wounded troops to safety. 'I never did so much award writing as I did for Jim Webb on that tour,' said company commander Mike Wyly.''

Webb left Vietnam in March 1970. The wounds that he had accumulated during his tour forced him to accept a medical discharge from the Marines in 1972. He subsequently enrolled at Georgetown Law School, where he found himself interacting on a daily basis with students and professors who opposed the war. Webb, who continued to support the war, clashed with the campus's antiwar contingent on a number of occasions. Timberg later remarked that though the former Marine ''viewed opposition to the war as a legitimate philosophical position,'' he was appalled by classmates who actively promoted the cause of the Vietcong and the North Vietnamese at a time when ''the VC and NVA were killing and maiming other young Americans.'' Most perplexing to Webb, said Timberg, was his sense ''that his antiwar classmates not only opposed the war but reviled, truly reviled, the men who fought it.'' Webb would eventually conclude that the antiwar movement was primarily characterized by ignorance, cowardice, and a brand of self-righteousness that stemmed from guilt about their own fears. ''I think [the antiwar movement] *extended* [the war],'' he told Myra MacPherson, author of *Long Time Passing: Vietnam and the Haunted Generation*. ''They were irresponsible in the way they conducted dissent. There is a principled place for dissent—it should be done in a context that *embraces* our value system.'' He went on to speculate that those Americans who avoided service by going to Canada or claiming phantom ailments were largely responsible for the emergence of veterans who expressed anger, doubt, or shame about their Vietnam tours during and after the war. ''The major unspoken problem in our generation is that too many of these people who didn't go have transferred their guilt on the people who did!''

After graduating from Georgetown, Webb emerged as one of the nation's most prominent spokesmen for Vietnam veterans, though some who disagreed with his conservative, anticommunist rhetoric took exception to this characterization. In the 1970s and 1980s, he worked in several different capacities while simultaneously launching a productive career as a novelist. He served as a professor of literature at the U.S. Naval Academy in 1979, and served in several defense-related government positions as well, culminating with a stint as Secretary of the Navy in 1987–88. He remained outspoken about issues concerning the war and the military throughout this period and became known as a spokesman for veterans who contended that American intervention in Vietnam *was* warranted and that the war could have been won had domestic will been more resolute. His critical remarks about such subjects as Maya Lin's Vietnam Veterans Memorial design and women in the military—and his contention that PTSD (Post Traumatic Stress Disorder) was less prevalent than some studies indicated—also aroused considerable controversy. Throughout it all, Webb remained unwavering in expressing pride in his service in Vietnam, although he has decried certain aspects of American military operations there, such as the socioeconomic makeup of the troops. "I honestly believe the ultimate responsibility for Calley [Lieutenant William Calley, who led the infamous massacre of Vietnamese civilians at My Lai] is Lyndon Johnson," he told MacPherson. "Not because he conducted an immoral war, but because he conducted it on the cheap and did not *require* the better, talented people to go in the military. Why did a guy like Calley, who had flunked out of college, almost all F's after one semester, become an officer in the military? Because the other people *weren't there*."

CREATION OF *FIELDS OF FIRE*

"I wrote *Fields of Fire* with a desire to convey certain truths about human nature that become illuminated in a combat environment," Webb told *Contemporary Authors*. "Combat to me represents not the discovery of courage, but the limitations of heroism. Most people have the capacity for bravery. But in a war of attrition such as Vietnam, the greatest acts of courage often yielded nothing more than a corpse-strewn ridgeline that would be abandoned immediately after being attained. Courage in this environment . . . became a waste [and] heroic acts became limited to the preservation of the unit and the man's friends."

Webb began work on the novel that would become *Fields of Fire* in the early 1970s. Spurred by the antiwar rhetoric of that time, which he saw as self-serving and uninformed, "[Webb] aspired to depict the war as he knew it," wrote Timberg, "a conflict in which young men, some just months removed from the high school gridiron, the local bowling alley, or the steamy back seat of the family car, faced ethical dilemmas, made moral judgments, at times horrible ones, and struggled to survive into adulthood. . . . He also wanted to impart dignity to the rifleman's service without enmeshing him in the tangled politics of the war.''

The final result, published in 1978, was an episodic work that sought to convey the moral ambiguities and dark disillusionments that dogged American soldiers in Vietnam. The novel details the experiences of one squad of soldiers stationed in the An Hoa Basin. The group is led by Lietenant Robert E. Lee Hodges, Jr., a skilled officer who—like Webb—hails from a long line of military men. Other significant characters include Snake, a hardened young man whose difficult prewar life in the streets of America ironically makes him a valued member of the platoon out in the bush, and Goodrich, a sensitive Harvard drop-out who joined the Marines in the mistaken belief that he would be able to sail through the war in the service's band. As the novel's action unfolds, the size of Hodges's squad is eroded by a succession of violent events. Goodrich—a shaky soldier with antiwar leanings—becomes increasingly alienated from the rest of the squad. After witnessing an event in which Snake and a few other Marines shoot a Vietnamese couple that are suspected of being VC, Goodrich reports the incident and an investigation is launched. In the meantime, the squad clashes with the enemy in a fierce firefight. Goodrich's poor performance during the battle leaves him injured and helpless and results in the death of another Marine, but Snake sacrifices his own life to save him. A troubled Goodrich subsequently returns to America, where he angrily castigates a group of antiwar protestors who are dismissive of the sacrifices being made by their countrymen in the war.

CRITICAL REACTION

Webb's autobiographical novel was hailed by reviewers as a riveting, convincing portrait of the infantry soldier's experiences of Vietnam upon its publication, and it continues to be regarded as one of the finest of literary works about the war (it was nominated for a Pulitzer). *New Republic* critic Raphael Sagalyn wrote that ''Webb has fashioned a searing vision of [this] tragic and futile war. Like all good war novels, *Fields of Fire* pulsates with the horror, comraderie, and yes, the joy of men at war. . . . *Fields of Fire* deserves to be read . . . as a vivid reminder of what it was like to live through the war most everyone would now like to forget.'' Gene Venable, writing in *West Coast Review of Books*, remarked that ''Webb tells horrifying tales, which seem closely modeled on actual experiences, to give readers a picture of the war which will haunt them for a long time.'' Still others, such as *Newsweek*'s Richard Boeth, praised the author's characterizations: ''In swift, flexible prose that does everything he asks of it—including a whiff of hilarious farce, just to show he can—Webb gives us an extraordinary range of acutely observed people, not one a stereotype, and as many different ways of looking at that miserable war.'' The book's realistic grit and sympathetic tone made it immensely popular with veterans as well.

Some critics did pan certain aspects of the book, however. Foremost among these was the novel's climatic scene, in which Goodrich angrily berates the student protestors. Some reviewers, such as Sagalyn, felt that even though Webb certainly conveys his "contempt" for the protestors, "Goodrich is too stylized and the climactic scene too contrived to be totally convincing." Others objected to the message itself. Venable contended that "the end of the novel is uncalled for. . . . Webb trys to give his novel a moral. The moral is that antiwar protestors had no right to put down a war they didn't understand. . . . Webb should have stuck with the war, which he knew and understood." Not surprisingly, however, those who supported Webb's contentions about the character of the antiwar movement looked on the scene more favorably.

FURTHER READING

Boeth, Richard. Review of *Fields of Fire*. In *Newsweek* (October 9, 1978).

Edelman, Bernard, ed. *Dear America: Letters Home From Vietnam*. New York: Norton, 1985.

Lemley, Brad. "Never Give an Inch: James Webb's Struggles with Pen and Sword." *Washington Post Magazine* (December 8, 1985).

Locher, Frances Carol, ed. *Contemporary Authors, Volumes 81–84*, Detroit: Gale Research, 1979.

MacPherson, Myra. *Long Time Passing: Vietnam and the Haunted Generation*. New York: Doubleday, 1984.

Puhr, Kathleen M. "Four Fictional Faces of the Vietnam War." *Modern Fiction Studies* (Spring 1984).

Sagalyn, Raphael. Review of *Fields of Fire*. In *New Republic* (October 21, 1978).

Schell, Jonathan. *The Real War: The Classic Reporting of the Vietnam War*. New York: Pantheon, 1987.

Starr, Paul. *The Discarded Army*. New York: Charterhouse, 1974.

Timberg, Robert. *The Nightingale's Song*. New York: Simon and Schuster, 1995.

Venable, Gene. "Fiction: *Fields of Fire*." *West Coast Review of Books* (November 1978).

Webb, James. *Fields of Fire*. New York: Prentice-Hall, 1978.

———. "The Invisible Vietnam Veteran."*Washington Post* (August 4, 1976).

———. "Viet Vets Didn't Kill Babies and They Aren't Suicidal." *Washington Post* (April 6, 1986).

Fire in the Lake

Nonfiction

Author: Frances FitzGerald

Facts of Publication: Boston: Atlantic-Little, Brown, 1972

Many Americans, especially government officials and those who served in Vietnam, realized that there were vast differences between American and Vietnamese cultures, traditions, and values. But because few Americans had the time or opportunity to immerse themselves in a study of the Vietnamese people and way of life—and, in fact, most military personnel were strictly segregated from the local population—it was not generally known to what extent these cultural differences complicated or impeded the war effort. "Brief tours of duty, ignorance of the language, and lack of meaningful interaction [did not] enable most Americans who served in Vietnam to gain more than a superficial understanding of this ancient people," Edward Doyle and Stephen Weiss wrote in their book *Collision of Cultures: The Americans in Vietnam, 1954–1973.* "The very real differences between them led to a gulf of misunderstanding that was never satisfactorily overcome." The pernicious effects of this clash of cultures were perhaps most apparent in Vietnam's cities—particularly Saigon, which was utterly transformed by a rapid influx of American personnel and dollars in the mid-1960s. "Saigon became a symbol of how the United States ruined a nation that it meant to save," Glen Gendzel commented in the *Encyclopedia of the Vietnam War.*

In her critically acclaimed study *Fire in the Lake: The Vietnamese and the Americans in Vietnam,* American journalist Frances FitzGerald examines the tragic results of this basic misunderstanding. Based upon academic research as well as her own observations during several visits to Vietnam, FitzGerald's book traces the development of Vietnamese culture, discusses the people's struggle to solve their own problems following the overthrow of French colonialism, and shows how Americans—given their different cultural background—misinterpreted the Vietnamese revolution and thus applied policies to the situation that were doomed to fail. FitzGerald also chronicles the changes that took place in Vietnamese society during the war, in both rural and urban settings. *Fire in the Lake*, which won several prestigious awards and became a best-seller upon its publication in 1972, added fuel to the fires of protest against the Vietnam War.

HISTORICAL BACKGROUND

Besides the obvious differences in size, wealth, power, and technological development, the United States and Vietnam differed dramatically in terms of culture and ideology by the mid-twentieth century. These latter differences—though often difficult to perceive and understand in superficial dealings between members of the two populations—significantly affected the relationship between the two countries during the Vietnam War. At the most basic level, a gulf emerged in the way that Americans and Vietnamese viewed the struggle that was taking place. The Vietnamese tended to see their society as organic in form, ever growing and occasionally shedding its skin, and so were less alarmed than the Americans by the revolutionary changes that were underway. "Revolution for Westerners is an abrupt reversal in the order of society, a violent break in history. But the Vietnamese traditionally did not see it that way at all. For them revolution was a natural and necessary event within the historical cycle; the problem of revolution was merely one of timing and appropriateness," Fitz-Gerald explained in *Fire in the Lake*. "The French and the Americans tried to stop the revolution, and in doing so they created an interregnum of violence unparalleled in Vietnamese history."

Because American policies toward Vietnam were based upon the Americans' fundamentally different view of the revolution, they sometimes seemed illogical, contradictory, or futile to the military personnel who were charged with implementing them. "By intervening in the Vietnamese struggle the United States was attempting to fit its global strategies into a world of hillocks and hamlets, to reduce its majestic concerns for the containment of Communism and the security of the Free World to a dimension where governments rose and fell as a result of arguments between two colonels' wives," FitzGerald wrote in *Fire in the Lake*. "For the Americans in Vietnam it would be difficult to make this leap of perspective, difficult to understand that while they saw themselves as building world order, many Vietnamese saw them merely as the producers of garbage from which they could build houses."

Complicating the already considerable distance between the Americans and the Vietnamese was the fact that they largely remained separate. For the first several years of American involvement—prior to the large-scale infusions of troops in the mid-1960s—very few Americans lived or worked outside of Saigon. There they tended to cluster in American enclaves, known as "Yankee Ghettos," where they enjoyed a high style of living that contrasted with that of the locals. After the war escalated and American soldiers began to arrive in Vietnam in large numbers, this sort of segregation was built into military policy. American military bases were routinely located away from Vietnamese cities and towns in order to reduce conflicts with the locals, and troops were restricted to base whenever possible. This enforced distance from the Vietnamese people contributed to the feelings of detachment and unreality that affected many American soldiers who served in Vietnam.

Cultural differences often complicated even the most innocuous interactions between individual Americans and Vietnamese. Many Vietnamese were insulted that the Americans appeared to reject their traditional way of life (by refusing to eat dog meat, for example), and many Americans felt that the Vietnamese were ungrateful. In fact, both of these generalized feelings could be attributed to cultural misunderstanding. In the Vietnamese culture, accepting charity was considered undignified, so the simple act of an American soldier giving a Vietnamese child a toy could be misinterpreted. Ignorant of such nuances in Vietnamese culture, American soldiers often reacted with anger and puzzlement when their generous gestures were rebuffed.

The Transformation of Saigon

Nowhere were the differences between the American and Vietnamese cultures and life-styles—and the negative impact of one upon the other—more apparent than in the nation's cities, particularly Saigon. By 1965, according to Doyle and Weiss, there were sixty thousand American military personnel living in the city, as well as thousands of civilian aid workers, missionaries, and journalists. The city also saw an influx of five thousand businessmen and construction workers, most of whom came in pursuit of the $300 million in contracts that the U.S. Defense Department awarded that year. The Americans in Saigon created a huge demand for Western goods and transformed the elegant Asian capital into a "carnival of Western decadence," according to Gendzel. "The mood was infectious and it was hard to remember that the country was at war," American nurse Marva Hasselbad recalled in Doyle and Weiss's book. "Beautiful Vietnamese girls in lovely and often expensive aodais walked along the streets . . . looking into shop windows full of all kinds of merchandise—stereo sets and radios, and cosmetics and clothes mostly imported from Europe and the United States." Saigon's streets were crowded with new cars, taxis, motorbikes, and bicycles, and lined with fine restaurants, banks, and theaters featuring American movies.

The flow of American dollars into Saigon's economy created tens of thousands of jobs for the Vietnamese, most in service-oriented positions catering to the needs of the Americans. Some Vietnamese, notably landlords and business owners, were able to attain unprecedented standards of living in the transformed city. A privileged urban class previously unseen in Vietnamese society thus formed. Jobs created by the American presence in Saigon raised the incomes of some middle- and working-class residents as well, so that ordinary Vietnamese households suddenly began to include such modern conveniences as electric rice cookers, radios, and even televisions.

But most aspects of Saigon's transformation were not so positive. Many Vietnamese blamed the Americans for the materialism that overcame the city's residents, leading to rampant corruption and declining morality. They also resented the changes that sudden wealth created in the traditional Vietnamese social structure. In the transformed city of 1965, a policeman's income of $25 per month paled in comparison with that of a construction worker employed by an American firm, who might earn $300 per month; some prostitutes took in over $800 per month. Commenting on this state of affairs in 1967, Senator J. William Fulbright charged that ''Saigon has become an American brothel.''

Whether seeking to achieve a luxurious life-style or to escape the destruction in the countryside, hundreds of thousands of rural Vietnamese were drawn to Saigon each year. The city's population more than tripled from eight hundred thousand in 1957 to three million in 1970, and by 1972 its population density of seventy thousand per square mile surpassed that of Hong Kong, Tokyo, and New York, noted Doyle and Weiss. ''The dark side of this rapid urbanization was starkly dramatic,'' they added. ''There were insufficient housing, sanitation, transportation, social services, and jobs to accommodate the tens of thousands of newcomers who settled in each month. In Saigon this provoked a state of emergency. Huge shantytowns encircled the city's prosperous center.''

With a lack of adequate housing and triple-digit inflation making it impossible for many Vietnamese to obtain the necessities of life, huge throngs of people were forced to beg or scavenge on the streets of Saigon in order to survive. Doyle and Weiss estimated that 300,000 Vietnamese women resorted to prostitution, and 150,000 children—unable to attend school due to a lack of facilities—had to fend for themselves as beggars, pickpockets, or members of youth gangs. The number of desperate people in Saigon contributed to the development of an enormous black market for stolen goods, many of them from American military stocks, as well as a billion-dollar drug industry. ''Saigon was an addicted city, and we were the drug: the corruption of children, the mutilation of young men, the prostitution of women, the humiliation of the old, the division of the family, the division of the country—it had all been done in our name,'' James Fenton wrote in *Granta*. ''The French city . . . had represented the opium stage of the addiction. With the Americans had begun the heroin phase.''

Despite the more pernicious effects of the American influence on Saigon, many Vietnamese felt ambivalent about returning to the old ways. In fact, large numbers of rural Vietnamese were reluctant to leave the city after the war ended, either because their land had been destroyed or because they had grown accustomed to the conveniences of urban life. This attitude was indicative of the far-reaching changes that took place in Vietnamese society as a result of the war. "The rapid process of modernization and the impact of the American presence had unsettled traditional Vietnamese social relationships and standards of behavior," Doyle and Weiss explained. "In a society of familial responsibility and strong parental authority there now existed a profusion of urban youth gangs, boys and girls neither disciplined by nor dependent upon their parents. In a society of puritan social mores there was now an entire class of prostitutes and bar girls, pimps and drug pushers whose very presence called into question the vitality of traditional social norms. In a society of limited resources and communal arrangements, a new materialism had emerged, an unfettered pursuit of wealth and luxury that strained families, fostered crime, and . . . accentuated the contrast between the cities and the rural areas."

FITZGERALD AND VIETNAM

Frances FitzGerald was born into a prominent East Coast family in 1940. Her father, Desmond FitzGerald, was a Wall Street attorney and a deputy director of the CIA; her mother, Marietta Tree, was an urban planner and a delegate to the United Nations. "Both believed strongly in the importance of public service; and both were very much engaged with the big issues. So what else could I do?" FitzGerald told Jean W. Ross in an interview for *Contemporary Authors*. She was exposed to political ideas from an early age, and she met many important figures in world affairs during her childhood, including Winston Churchill, Adlai Stevenson, and Albert Schweitzer. FitzGerald excelled in her studies, graduating magna cum laude from Radcliffe in 1962 with a major in Middle Eastern history. She considered various careers but eventually decided to become a writer. By 1964 she was publishing articles regularly in the *New York Herald Tribune, Vogue*, and *Village Voice*.

FitzGerald first traveled to Vietnam in February 1966, when American involvement in the war, as well as the number of American reporters covering it, was escalating rapidly. She claimed that she was prepared to view the conflict objectively at the time of her first visit. "I hadn't any fixed opinions," she told Ross. "The war was just building up, and whatever I came up with really came from my experience there." Rather than following the other American reporters and listening to the official government reports, FitzGerald used her fluency in French to interview numerous Vietnamese, from villagers to bureaucrats, in order to gain a different perspective on the conflict. "My attempt was . . . to try and understand the politics of Vietnam and the effect of the American presence and the war on Vietnamese society. At the time there was little American scholarship on Vietnam and few Americans were engaged in a serious effort to understand the political, economic, and social issues at stake for the Vietnamese," she noted in *Fire in the Lake*. "I thought to myself, Here's this American war being fought in a place that no one understands at all," she stated in the interview with Ross. "It looks like there are two entirely separate enterprises going on here, the Vietnamese one and the American."

Though FitzGerald originally planned to stay in Vietnam for only a month or two, long enough to write a few articles to help pay for her trip, her search for answers ended up taking most of a year. During this time, she produced a number of articles exposing "the incongruity of what Americans were saying with what actually existed out there," as she explained to *Esquire*'s Robert Friedman.

"From the beginning FitzGerald's articles from South Vietnam stressed the negative aspects of American involvement in the war," Virginia Elwood-Akers wrote in her book *Women Correspondents in the Vietnam War*. "She was not interested in battlefield action, but in the effect of the war upon the Vietnamese people." Many observers felt that FitzGerald's ability to see the war from the Vietnamese perspective gave her unique insight into the perils of American involvement. One fellow correspondent noted in *Esquire* that she "was able to understand better than any of us why the American government was doomed to fail."

Upon returning to the United States, FitzGerald continued her study of Vietnamese history and culture under the French anthropologist Paul Mus. She also began compiling her observations into a book. In 1971, FitzGerald returned to Vietnam and visited many of the sites she had seen during her first trip nearly five years earlier. She noted that this experience left her feeling overwhelmed by the futility of war. "America had damaged Vietnam very badly when I was first there," she stated in *Newsweek*. "But it's astonishing how much more suffering has been caused since then." FitzGerald traveled to Vietnam yet again in February 1973, during a time when the Saigon government and the Vietcong (by this time known as the Provisional Revolutionary Government, or PRG) had declared a cease-fire. She was invited to tour PRG zones of control along with other journalists, and she found that many people in the Vietnamese countryside still favored the Vietcong. "After thirty years of war," she wrote in the *Atlantic*, "the people in those areas that first supported the revolution continue to do so today." FitzGerald made a final trip to Vietnam in 1974, when she went to Hanoi and met with Communist officials who informed her that the reunification of Vietnam was inevitable.

CREATION OF *FIRE IN THE LAKE*

Many of FitzGerald's writings on Vietnam first appeared as a series of articles in *New Yorker*. "The articles she wrote concentrated on the war's devastating effect on the structure of Vietnamese society. She wrote of the refugees who had swelled the population of Saigon, of people clinging to habits of their no longer existent society," Elwood-Akers related. "FitzGerald sounded the warning that the American failure to understand the Confucian-based politics and psychology of the Vietnamese would prove disastrous." FitzGerald compiled these writings, along with other observations and the results of her research, into a book over the course of five years. The result was *Fire in the Lake*, FitzGerald's first full-length work, published in 1972. "I wanted it to be scholarly and I wanted it to be popular, but I didn't want to go too far toward either of those poles," she told Jane Howard of *Life*. "I had no idea it would take so long. It's much more of a history than I meant it to be, but who could have guessed the war would last so long?"

FitzGerald took the title of *Fire in the Lake* from the image of revolution in the *I Ching*, the ancient Chinese Book of Changes. The book begins with an in-depth analysis of the development of Vietnamese culture, then goes on to show how Vietnamese traditions and ideas inevitably clashed with American notions of progress and urbanization, with tragic results. Elwood-Akers stated that FitzGerald's book concludes that "fundamental differences between Eastern and Western culture and thought had doomed the American–South Vietnamese alliance from the start. The war was futile from the beginning, she wrote, and therefore, as thousands died and no end was accomplished, the war was immoral."

Though the war brought horrendous physical destruction upon the Vietnamese land and people, FitzGerald argues that the destruction of Vietnamese society was equally tragic. "The physical suffering of South Vietnam is difficult to comprehend, even in statistics. The official numbers—650,000 'enemy' dead, over 110,000 ARVN soldiers and 350,000 civilians killed—only begin to tell the toll of death this war has taken. Proportionately, it is as though twenty million Americans died in the war instead of the 45,000 to date," she wrote in *Fire in the Lake*. "Still, the physical destruction is not, perhaps, the worst of it. . . . Physical death is everywhere, but it is the social death caused by destruction of the family that is of overriding importance." She describes many of the negative changes that took place within Vietnamese society as a result of the war. "Out of a population of seventeen million there are now five million refugees. Perhaps 40 or 50 percent of the population, as opposed to the 15 percent before the war, live in and around the cities and towns. The distribution is that of a highly industrialized country, but there is almost no industry in South Vietnam," she commented in *Fire in the Lake*. "South Vietnam is a country shattered so that no two pieces fit together."

CRITICAL RECEPTION

Fire in the Lake became an immediate hit with critics and the reading public alike. It was a best-seller, going into a second printing within days of its release, and also won many prestigious literary awards, including the Pulitzer Prize and the National Book Award. Michael Mok of *Publishers Weekly* attributed the book's popularity to FitzGerald's ability "to get under the skin of this ugly war which has left so many Americans feeling bewildered and morally bankrupt."

Many reviewers praised FitzGerald's research, her straightforward writing style, and her insight into the differences between Vietnamese and American culture. Stanley Hoffmann, writing in the *New York Times Book Review*, called *Fire in the Lake* "a compassionate and penetrating account of the collision of two societies that remain untranslatable to one another, an analysis of all those features of South Vietnamese culture that doomed the American effort from the start, and an incisive explanation of the reasons why that effort could only disrupt and break down South Vietnam's society—and pave the way for the revolution that the author sees as the only salvation." Christopher Lehmann-Haupt of the *New York Times* found FitzGerald's work "lucid, exhaustive, dramatic, penetrating, and even witty (in a bitterly ironic sort of way)." Jane Howard quoted historian Arthur Schlesinger, Jr. as saying, "If Americans read only one book to understand what we have done to the Vietnamese and to ourselves, let it be this one."

Thanks to the attention her book received, FitzGerald became "one of the most outspoken and well-known critics of American policy in the Vietnam War," according to Elwood-Akers. *Fire in the Lake*, in addition to FitzGerald's many later articles and speeches, helped turn American public opinion against the war. The book became "gospel for the antiwar movement," as David Brudnoy observed in the *National Review*. "The sheer weight of Miss FitzGerald's documentation and the undeniable effectiveness of her remarkably persuasive style cannot but commend her book to those who've told us all along that our cause in Vietnam was and is hopeless."

FURTHER READING

Brudnoy, David. Review of *Fire in the Lake*. In *National Review* (September 29, 1972).

Buck, D. D. Review of *Fire in the Lake*. In *Library Journal* (June 15, 1972).

Butler, David. *The Fall of Saigon*. New York: Simon and Schuster, 1985.

Doyle, Edward, and Stephen Weiss. *A Collision of Cultures: The Americans in Vietnam, 1954–1973*. Boston: Boston Publishing Company, 1984.

Elwood-Akers, Virginia. *Women Correspondents in the Vietnam War, 1961–1975*. Metuchen, N.J.: Scarecrow Press, 1988.

Fenton, James. "The Fall of Saigon." *Granta*, no. 15 (1985).

FitzGerald, Frances. "The End Is the Beginning." *New Republic* (May 3, 1975).

———. *Fire in the Lake: The Vietnamese and the Americans in Vietnam*. Boston: Little, Brown, 1972.

———. "Lessons from a War." *Intervention* (Spring 1984).

———. "The Tragedy of Saigon." *Atlantic Monthly* (December 1966).

———. "Vietnam: Behind the Lines of the 'Cease-Fire' War." *Atlantic* (April 1974).

———. "Vietnam: Reconciliation." *Atlantic* (June 1974).

Friedman, Robert. "Frances FitzGerald Is Fascinated with Failure." *Esquire* (July 1980).

Gendzel, Glen. "Saigon." In *Encyclopedia of the Vietnam War*, Stanley I. Kutler, ed. New York: Charles Scribner's Sons, 1996.

Hassler, Alfred. *Saigon, U.S.A.* New York: R. W. Baron, 1970.

Hoffmann, Stanley. Review of *Fire in the Lake*. In the *New York Times Book Review* (August 27, 1972).

Howard, Jane. "Frankie's 'Fire.' " *Life* (October 27, 1972).

Lehmann-Haupt, Christopher. "Awakening to the Nightmare." *New York Times* (August
     17, 1972).
Mok, Michael. "Frances FitzGerald." *Publishers Weekly* (October 16, 1972).
"Reporter at a Fire." *Newsweek* (August 7, 1972).
Ross, Jean W. Interview with Frances FitzGerald. In *Contemporary Authors, New Re-
     vision Series*, Volume 32. James G. Lesniak, ed. Detroit: Gale Research, 1991.
White, Peter T. "Saigon: Fourteen Years After." *National Geographic* (November 1989).

"Fortunate Son"

Song

Artist: Creedence Clearwater Revival

Written by: John Fogerty

Recorded: 1969

Original Release: October 1969 (as single)

Album Release: December 1969 (on *Willy and the Poor Boy's Fantasy*)

As the Vietnam War escalated during the 1960s, members of the antiwar movement and administration critics increasingly charged that poor and working-class Americans (and especially minorities) accounted for a disproportionate percentage of the U.S. soldiers serving in Vietnam. They complained that inequities in socioeconomic circumstances ultimately spared the vast majority of wealthier and better-educated young men in America at the expense of their less fortunate contemporaries in the inner-city and in rural areas. Late in 1969, as the controversy over the legitimacy of these charges continued to boil, critics of the war were presented with a new anthem that commented on the alleged "working-class war" in the harshest of terms: "Fortunate Son," by John Fogerty and Creedence Clearwater Revival.

HISTORICAL BACKGROUND

Approximately 58,000 Americans died in Vietnam during the war; another 270,000 were wounded. Most studies indicate that a disproportionate share of these deaths and injuries were borne by members of the United States' poor and working-class economic sectors. As James Fallows (who evaded the draft himself) noted in the *Atlantic Monthly*, Vietnam reporter David Halberstam once remarked that "All you had to do was *see* [the American soldiers] to know that this was America's lower-middle class. Vietnam was a place where the elite went as reporters, not as soldiers. Almost as many people from Harvard won Pulitzer Prizes in Vietnam as died there." This state of affairs was not lost on the American soldier out in the field. As Vietnam veteran Steve Harper told Murray Polner, author of *No Victory Parades*, "The critics are picking on us, just 'cause we had to fight this war. Where were their sons? In fancy colleges? Where were the sons of all the big shots who supported the war? Not in my platoon. Our guys' people were workers and things like that. . . . If the war was so important, why didn't our leaders put everyone's son in there, why only us?" The activities of antiwar demonstrators—most of whom came from middle- and upper-class families—only exacerbated the resentments of the American soldier in Vietnam.

Christian G. Appy, author of *Working-Class War: American Combat Soldiers and Vietnam*, remarked that American troops were primarily pulled from poor or working-class settings because the institutions that were responsible for channeling young men into the military erected a two-tiered system. Appy charged that whereas the government (through the draft), the nation's universities, and the job market took steps to protect middle-class youth and their wealthier peers, they offered no such shelter to the children of working-class families. This arrangement ultimately produced an army composed overwhelmingly of young men from modest or impoverished socioeconomic circumstances.

Citing government data, Appy noted that 80 percent of the American men who went to Vietnam had a high school education or less at a time when opportunities for higher education were hitting new heights across the country (45 percent of all Americans between the ages of eighteen and twenty-one had some college education in 1965; by 1970 the figure had risen to 50 percent). Appy observed that even in the late 1960s, when draft calls increased and many graduate school deferments ended, the percentage of American forces in Vietnam with some college education still fell well below the 50 percent figure for the age group as a whole.

The Draft

The United States Selective Service System draft directly inducted more than two million men into the military. In addition, the long shadow of the draft convinced thousands of others unshielded by exemptions or deferments to enlist before receiving their induction notices in hopes of securing more desirable terms of service (in 1968 a U.S. House Committee on Armed Services study indicated that 54 percent of that year's enlistees were motivated to enlist by the looming pressure of the draft).

Nearly 16 million men—about 60 percent of the 26.8 million draftable men who came of age during the war—avoided service by legal means. Members of the middle and the upper classes proved particularly adept at securing exemptions. The student deferment was, of course, a very popular option. It had its limitations—students with poor grades could lose their deferments, for instance—but successful students found it to be a haven, and they recognized that graduate school could further extend their immunity from the draft. In addition, students entering fields of engineering, science, and education could then acquire occupational deferments. But whereas full-time students who maintained good grades enjoyed draft immunity, part-time students who had to work their way through school had no such protection. These part-time students overwhelmingly came from working-class backgrounds.

Another 3.5 million American men were exempted from military service because of medical conditions. Most of these exemptions were secured by young men from the middle and upper classes, even though their working-class peers often did not enjoy the same advantages in health care, nutrition, and physical environment. But whereas men from poor or working-class backgrounds most often went to military induction centers, where exemptions were given only grudgingly, men from America's middle and upper classes could often turn to family physicians and friends with medical credentials to secure medical exemption claims.

In addition, college campuses and other centers of white, middle-class social activity often provided young men seeking to evade the draft with valuable information. In working-class neighborhoods, however, Appy noted that such methods were both less well-known and far more controversial: "Avoiding the draft was more likely to be viewed as an act of cowardice than as a principled unwillingness to participate in an immoral war" in working-class homes. Years later, former Secretary of Defense Donald Rumsfeld told James M. Fallows that "it was very clear what had happened with the draft. There was an accommodation between the government and the academic community. Students, teachers, and people who figured out how to work the system were exempted. It is inconceivable that a system designed and operating the way the draft did could have produced a true cross-section of America in the military."

Still another way of avoiding Vietnam was to secure a place in the National Guard or the Reserves (although this option did not guarantee deliverance; about fifteen thousand men from these outfits were sent to Vietnam over the course of the war). Nonetheless, Lawrence Baskir and William Strauss, authors of *Chance and Circumstance*, noted that these remained highly popular destinations for college graduates who had exhausted their student deferments. By 1968 the National Guard had a waiting list of one hundred thousand, while in the army reserves, the percentage of college graduates among enlisted men was three times higher than in the regular army. Finally, young men often started families to secure deferments.

Young men blessed with good academic or financial backgrounds, then, were far less likely to find themselves in the war. Nonetheless, some pockets of

Vietnam battered even upper-class American families. "Service-academy graduates came from relatively privileged backgrounds and suffered heavy casualties
in Vietnam," acknowledged Fallows. "Two of the most dangerous specialties
in Vietnam were those of pilots (especially helicopter) and infantry lieutenants.
Because of the educational requirements for those jobs and the role of ROTC
in providing lieutenants, they drew many men from affluent backgrounds, many
of whom died."

Those Who Served

On the whole, however, young men from poor and working-class families
were far more likely than their peers from wealthier families to see action in
Vietnam. The sanctuary of college remained out of the reach of many of these
young men, in part because the overall economic boom of the 1960s generally
failed to reach America's working class. Economic circumstances precluded
many families from sending their sons on to college, and the job market made
it difficult for young men to save for tuition themselves. For some young men
of draft age, it was hard to secure any kind of job at all. As Appy and others
noted, employers in construction and other blue-collar industries were sometimes
reluctant to hire draft-age men—in part because they did not want to take the
time and effort to train them, only to see them shipped off to Vietnam. Government programs such as the controversial Project 100,000 drive—in which
minimum intelligence and physical fitness requirements were lowered to help
meet military quotas—also ensured that the disadvantaged would bear the brunt
of the war's impact.

American troops in Vietnam included a disproportionate number of representatives from two regions of America that do not typically boast large upper-
class populations: rural towns and the inner city. Rural areas were particularly
hard-hit; the National Opinion Research Center (NORC) noted that whereas
about 5 percent of the American labor force was engaged in farming in the
1960s, about 12 percent of America's enlisted men came from agricultural backgrounds (in the army that figure reached almost 15 percent in the 1960s). Con-
sidering such skewed representation, then, it is no surprise that whereas 2 percent
of Americans lived in towns with fewer than one thousand people in the 1960s,
8 percent of American deaths in Vietnam came from towns of that size.

Modest economic and educational circumstances also led many minorities—
and especially blacks—from urban centers to serve in Vietnam. Blacks initially
accounted for a disproportionate percentage of Vietnam casualties (in the war's
early years blacks—who accounted for about 11 percent of the U.S. population—accounted for 20 percent of American casualties), but by the end of the
war black casualty rates had dropped to a figure that was only slightly higher
than their percentage of America's civilian population. Defenders of U.S. policies toward black soldiers contended that the end-of-the-war figures showed that
they were not victims of institutional racism. But civil rights leaders (Martin

Luther King, Jr., Malcolm X, Julian Bond, and others) and other critics pointed out that blacks overwhelmingly served in Vietnam as enlisted combat soldiers (only 2 percent of Vietnam officers were black), and argued that if it were not for their highly public criticisms of government policies in the mid-1960s, blacks would have continued to account for a disproportionate percentage of total American casualties throughout the war.

All these factors combined to ensure that most American soldiers in Vietnam "came from the ragged fringes of the Great American Dream, from city slums and dirt farms and Appalachian mining towns," wrote ex-Marine Philip Caputo in his Vietnam memoir *A Rumor of War*. But Caputo also noted that despite the various circumstances that worked to propel them to Vietnam, military service did have an alluring quality for many poor and working-class youth: "The Marines provided them with a guaranteed annual income, free medical care, free clothing, and something else, less tangible but just as valuable—self-respect. A man who wore that uniform was somebody. He had passed a test few others could. He was not some down-on-his-luck loser pumping gas or washing cars for a dollar-fifty an hour, but somebody, a Marine."

CREATION OF "FORTUNATE SON"

The members of Creedence Clearwater Revival—John Fogerty, Tom Fogerty, Stu Cook, and Doug Clifford—toiled in musical obscurity for much of the 1960s, playing in small bars and other venues under a variety of names. In June 1968, however, the band released an eponymous LP that reached gold record status on the strength of CCR's first single, "Suzy Q (Parts I and II)." In 1969 Creedence released three more successful albums and a number of hit singles, including the fabulously popular "Proud Mary." Much of the band's music, an inspired hybrid of rock and country blues that came to be known as "Swamp Rock," was regarded as terrifically tuneful material. Critics also complimented lyricist John Fogerty for the evocative quality of his songs, but Creedence's first three albums were not notable for their trenchant social commentary. Indeed, when some listeners tried to put a political spin on the CCR song "Bad Moon Rising," Fogerty quickly moved to dispel any such notions: "It's not political," he told *Melody Maker* magazine. "It's just meant to be a statement on the good and bad sides of life. It's not a protest song, like the sort of protest songs we've had over the last few years."

The band's fourth LP, *Willy and the Poor Boys*, thus marked a new direction for the band. The group's rollicking Delta blues–flavored music remained as strong as ever, but listeners found that Fogerty's lyrics had expanded to include observations about various aspects of contemporary American culture. Reviewers pointed to songs such as "Fortunate Son," "Effigy," and "It Came Out of the Sky" as evidence that the band was striking out in new thematic directions. Of these, "Fortunate Son" easily garnered the most attention.

CRITICAL RECEPTION

"Fortunate Son" reflected the widespread belief that America's poor and working-class segments were bearing a disproportionate share of the burden for the fight in Vietnam. Antiwar voices charged that the sons of the rich and privileged were able to parlay their connections into educational deferments or health-related disqualifications, but families with limited socioeconomic options were far less able to protect their sons from the war. This viewpoint was evident in Fogerty's lyrics, which lamented that the sons of millionaires remained safe while others were pushed into the war. Moreover, the song made it clear that Fogerty was unswayed by the efforts of some Americans to equate patriotism with support for the war. Finally, "Fortunate Son" set such accusations to a driving, percussion-heavy beat that seemed wholly in keeping with its angry sentiments.

In the months following the release of the popular "Fortunate Son," Fogerty—who was in the Reserves—insisted that he was no more "political" than he had ever been. "They put too much weight on political references in songs," he told *Rolling Stone* interviewer Ralph J. Gleason in 1970. "They think a song will save the world. That's absurd." Despite such sentiments, however, Fogerty acknowledged a certain hope that his lyrics might strike a chord with some of his listeners. "Some of the . . . things I write, I'm sure people don't agree with," he told Gleason. "But I manage sometimes to be, purposely, like in the middle. Not because I'm coppin' out, but because there's things on both sides that're wrong. . . . I'm not trying to polarize hippies against their parents, or youth against their parents . . . because I think music, my concept of what music is supposed to be, shouldn't do that. It should unite, as corny as that is."

FURTHER READING

Appy, Christian G. *Working-Class War: American Combat Soldiers and Vietnam*. Chapel Hill: University of North Carolina Press, 1993.

Barnett, Arnold, Timothy Stanley, and Michael Shore. "America's Vietnam Casualties: Victims of a Class War?" *Operations Research* (September/October 1992).

Baskir, Lawrence M., and William A. Strauss. *Chance and Circumstance: The Draft, the War, and the Vietnam Generation*. New York: Knopf, 1978.

Fallows, James M. "Low-Class Conclusions." *Atlantic Monthly* (April 1993).

———. "What Did You Do in the Class War, Daddy?" *Washington Monthly* (October 1975).

Gleason, Ralph J. "The Rolling Stone Interview." *Rolling Stone* (February 21, 1970).

Gottlieb, Sherry Gershon. *Hell No, We Won't Go: Resisting the Draft during the Vietnam War*. New York: Viking, 1991.

Interview with John Fogerty. *Los Angeles Times* (April 8, 1973).

MacPherson, Myra. "McNamara's 'Other' Crimes." *Washington Monthly* (June 1995).

Polner, Murray. *No Victory Parades*. New York: Harcourt, Brace and World, 1971.

"Vietnam: Who Served and Who Did Not." *Wilson Quarterly* (Summer 1993).

Friendly Fire

Nonfiction

Author: C. D. B. Bryan

Facts of Publication: New York: Putnam, 1976

The Vietnam War took a devastating toll not only on its participants but also upon their loved ones back home. Among the most tragic victims of the war were those whose lives were shattered by "friendly fire," the sadly ironic name applied to casualties caused by American or South Vietnamese weapons. C. D. B. Bryan's 1976 book *Friendly Fire* explores the circumstances surrounding the death of one American soldier, Sergeant Michael Mullen, due to friendly fire, as well as its effect on his Iowa farm family. Grief and rage over their son's senseless death transformed Michael's parents, Peg and Gene Mullen, from prototypical patriotic Americans into prominent antiwar activists. In fact, within a year of Michael Mullen's death, his formerly unobtrusive parents appeared on the FBI's list of people to watch. Bryan's book chronicling this tragic family saga was well-received by critics and became an award-winning television movie, though the Mullens disavowed the conclusions the author reached about the cause of their son's death.

HISTORICAL BACKGROUND

Of the approximately 58,000 American lives lost during the Vietnam War, about 10,000 were classified as "nonhostile casualties," meaning that the deaths had not been caused by the enemy. This classification included such causes of death as vehicle accidents, suicide, homicide, and drug abuse, as well as "friendly fire." In Vietnam, this term—which Albert E. Stone called one of the "more egregious euphemisms of modern warfare" in his foreword to Peg Mullen's memoir *Unfriendly Fire*—referred to accidental death due to American or South Vietnamese weapons. "The soldier's vulnerability is never more dramatically apparent than when artillery, bombs, or napalm intended to support troops in a fight with the enemy kill the very men they are meant to protect," Jonathan Shay noted in *Achilles in Vietnam*. Though official sources have estimated the number of lives lost to friendly fire during the Vietnam War at about 3,700, Colonel David H. Hackworth claimed in *About Face* that friendly fire accounted for 15 to 20 percent of overall American deaths in the conflict.

Military experts tend to view friendly fire casualties as inevitable, though unfortunate, consequences of warfare. But for soldiers and their families back home, deaths by friendly fire seem like an inexcusable and negligent waste of human lives. Thanks to Bryan's book, the tragic case of Michael Eugene Mullen became one of the most widely publicized incidences of death as a result of friendly fire in the Vietnam years. Mullen was drafted into the army in September 1968, shortly before he was to have begun graduate studies in agricultural biochemistry. After basic training in Fort Polk, Louisiana, he remained in the United States to attend Noncommissioned Officers School and complete advanced infantry training. In September 1969, Mullen was sent to Vietnam, where he was stationed near Chu Lai as a sergeant in the 198th Infantry, Americal Division. He was killed in the early morning hours of February 18, 1970, when an artillery shell ostensibly fired in support of his unit landed short of its target and exploded near the foxhole where he was sleeping. A tiny piece of shrapnel from the shell pierced his back and severed a vital artery near his heart. Afterward, there was considerable confusion about who had ordered the artillery fire, what had caused the shell to miss its target, and why the sleeping soldiers along the defensive perimeter had not been warned in advance.

Back home in Iowa, Sergeant Mullen's parents, Peg and Gene Mullen, found the circumstances surrounding his death impossible to accept. "Our son's life had been taken for no reason in a war without definition," Peg Mullen wrote in *Unfriendly Fire*, adding that the army "didn't even allow him the decency of dying at the hands of the enemy." Compounding their grief was frustration at their inability to obtain a complete and consistent account of his death from the army or the U.S. government. The Mullens' problems began when the notice informing them of their son's death misspelled his last name. When Michael's body arrived in Iowa, they were dismayed at the apparently minor nature of his wound, which seemed inconsistent with an artillery blast. They soon learned that Michael's name did not appear on the official casualty lists for the time period when he was killed—because, as a matter of policy, the government did not include nonhostile casualties among its official totals. The Mullens' frustration eventually turned to suspicion, as the conflicting reports they received from the vast military bureaucracy convinced them that they were the victims of a conspiracy to cover up what had really happened to their son.

The Mullens' anger grew even more bitter after several incidents made it appear that the government had little sympathy for their loss or appreciation for the sacrifice their son had made. For example, the army deducted nine days' wages from Mullen's final paycheck because he had not lived long enough to make up the advance leave he had taken. Later, an official condolence note the family received from President Richard Nixon's office was attached to copies of his recent speeches on "Vietnamization." And apparently the Mullens' persistent inquiries irritated Iowa Senator Jack Miller, whose response Bryan quoted in *Friendly Fire*: "It has been my observation that, with few exceptions, the persons bearing the real burden of this war—the men who have been doing the fighting, the wounded, their wives and parents—have been the least complaining of anyone over this tragic war. I regret that you are one of the exceptions." In time, the Mullens' anger and suspicion toward the government following their son's death transformed them from a patriotic farm family into dedicated antiwar activists. "Peg and Gene Mullen were casualties of the Vietnam War as surely as their son was," Amanda Heller noted in *Atlantic Monthly*.

BRYAN AND VIETNAM

Though Courtlandt Dixon Barnes Bryan did not serve in Vietnam, his experiences as a nuclear targeting officer in Korea helped shape his views of the conflict. Bryan joined the army shortly after earning his bachelor's degree from Yale University in 1958. During his two years in Korea, the corrupt government of President Syngman Rhee was overthrown and the ruler was expelled from the country. Shaken by mounting American losses, Bryan came to feel a sense of disillusionment about his country's involvement in Korea. Bryan was recalled for another year of active duty in 1961, during the Berlin crisis. He wrote short stories in his spare time at Fort Lewis, Washington; several of these were published in national magazines.

In 1965 Bryan won the Harper Prize for his first novel, *P. S. Wilkinson*, and in 1967 he began a two-year teaching term at the University of Iowa Writers Workshop. After moving to Connecticut, and seeing his second novel disappear shortly after publication in 1970, he decided to try his hand at nonfiction. He was particularly interested in exploring various aspects of the ongoing American involvement in Vietnam. "The Vietnam War had been on my mind, as it had been on everybody's, and I wasn't sure how to handle it—to sign more petitions, to make more protest marches, to write more letters just seemed inconsequential. Nothing had any effect," Bryan stated in an interview with Jean W. Ross for *Contemporary Authors*. "It had been month after month of watching Cronkite on the news with the casualty reports and realizing that I didn't quite care as much anymore as I should have. I knew the only way to make those casualty reports meaningful was to pick out one and write about the impact that it had on his family."

CREATION OF *FRIENDLY FIRE*

Bryan learned about the Mullen family's tragedy while visiting friends in Iowa in November 1970. In April of that year, Peg and Gene Mullen had used some of the money the government had provided them for their son's burial to place a half-page advertisement in the *Des Moines Register* admonishing Iowa families to speak out against the Vietnam War. The ad consisted of 714 crosses, each one representing an Iowan who had died in Vietnam, along with the message, "Fathers and mothers of Iowa. . . . How many more lives do you wish to sacrifice because of your SILENCE?" In the ensuing months, Peg Mullen had become a prominent figure in protests against the war, and several periodicals had run stories about her quest to uncover the truth about what had really happened to Michael.

When Bryan first met the Mullens in April 1971, he was amazed at the toll their son's death had taken on them and at the depth of their anger. "My own feeling was that if the government had lost the loyalty of a family like the Mullens, who had had five generations on the land, then the government was in serious trouble," he told Ross. Bryan arranged to tell the Mullens' story in a six-thousand-word article for *New Yorker*. As he explored the circumstances surrounding Michael's death, however, the story kept expanding. Finally, after five years of work that included several fresh starts, Bryan published *Friendly Fire* in 1976. (A shorter, more straightforward telling of the story had run as a three-part series in *New Yorker* earlier that year.)

The book begins with Bryan recounting the Mullen family's long history on their Iowa farm. He then describes the last few days Michael spent at home before departing for Vietnam. After a tense and traumatic scene in which Peg and Gene learn of their son's death, Bryan details the innumerable problems they encountered in dealing with the military bureaucracy and charts the course of their growing resentment toward the government. Bryan himself becomes a character in the drama about two-thirds of the way through the book, when he arrives at the Mullens' farm for the first time. The story then shifts to the author's attempts to uncover, on the family's behalf, the complete story behind Michael's death. After conducting extensive research and numerous interviews, Bryan becomes satisfied with the army's official explanation of events: The soldiers who had fired the artillery had failed to take the height of a nearby group of trees into account; the shell that killed Sergeant Mullen had deflected off one of the trees, causing it to fall near his position. The final chapter of the book consists of Bryan's reconstruction of what took place the night Michael Mullen died.

Bryan explained the purpose behind the book's structure to Ross: "*Friendly Fire* was not about Michael Mullen's death and it wasn't about what happened to Michael. It was about what happened to Peg and Gene Mullen and the impact of the Vietnam War on America. But nobody would want to read that book, so the way to handle it was to create the sense that it was a mystery. How did

Michael die? And it isn't until you're about two-thirds of the way through *Friendly Fire* that you realize this isn't what the book's about at all. But by that time you're hooked.'' Three years after its publication, *Friendly Fire* was adapted as an ABC-TV ''movie of the week,'' starring Carol Burnett as Peg Mullen, Ned Beatty as Gene Mullen, and Sam Waterston as C. D. B. Bryan. The film, which generally follows the *New Yorker* version of the story, attracted 64 million viewers and garnered six Emmy Awards.

CRITICAL RECEPTION

For the most part, the book *Friendly Fire* was well-received by critics. Many praised the way that Bryan used the story of one soldier's death to illuminate how the Vietnam War—perhaps uniquely among conflicts involving the United States—challenged and often changed the beliefs of American citizens. ''The great war stories do not deal solely with the death of soldiers but with the death of idealism, and Bryan's handling of that theme is certainly the finest that has come out of the Vietnam War,'' Robert Sherrill wrote in the *New York Times Book Review*. In the *Washington Post Book World*, Jane Howard noted that Bryan's book reflected ''the tarnishing . . . of a whole nation's comfortable self-image.''

Reviewers who disliked the book tended to focus on the last section, when Bryan reveals the results of his investigation to the Mullens. Some critics commented that Bryan seemed to run out of patience with the grieving parents when they refused to believe his explanation of their son's death. ''It was as if the Sinister Force had come and finished Bryan's book for him in the night,'' Diane Johnson claimed in the *New York Review of Books*. ''Nothing in our experience of reality or of this book prepares us for, or can reconcile us to, the conclusion of the author that the officers [in charge of the artillery unit that killed Michael Mullen] were 'fine men' and that Peg and Gene were, finally, tired fanatics whose obsession with their son's death was only their personal tragedy.''

Joining the dissenting voices about the merits of *Friendly Fire* were the Mullens themselves. ''During the five years that [Bryan] worked on our story, it simply became his story, and we definitely did not like his version,'' Peg Mullen wrote in *Unfriendly Fire*. ''There's no question that, after Michael's tragic death, I became so preoccupied with the Vietnam War and the peace movement that those things seemed to dominate my life. No one realized it more than I,'' she admitted. ''But it was that very preoccupation and sense of purpose that allowed me to carry on in spite of the pain.''

FURTHER READING

Bryan, C. D. B. *Friendly Fire*. New York: Putnam, 1976.
Hackworth, David H. *About Face*. New York: Simon and Schuster, 1989.
Heller, Amanda. Review of *Friendly Fire*. In *Atlantic Monthly* (July 1976).
Howard, Jane. ''An American Tragedy.'' *Washington Post Book World* (May 2, 1976).

Johnson, Diane. "True Patriots." *New York Review of Books* (August 5, 1976).

Mullen, Peg. *Unfriendly Fire: A Mother's Memoir*. Iowa City: University of Iowa Press, 1995.

Regan, Geoffrey. *Blue on Blue: A History of Friendly Fire*. New York: Avon Books, 1995.

Ross, Jean W. Interview with C. D. B. Bryan. In *Contemporary Authors, New Revision Series*, Vol. 13. Detroit: Gale Research, 1984.

Schroeder, Eric James. *Vietnam, We've All Been There: Interviews with American Writers*. Westport, Conn.: Praeger, 1992.

Shay, Jonathan. *Achilles in Vietnam: Combat Trauma and the Undoing of Character*. New York: Simon and Schuster, 1994.

Sherrill, Robert. Review of *Friendly Fire*. In the *New York Times Book Review* (May 9, 1976).

Full Metal Jacket

Film

Director: Stanley Kubrick

Screenplay: Stanley Kubrick, Michael Herr, and Gustav Hasford; based on Hasford's novel *The Short-Timers* (New York: Harper & Row, 1979)

Principal Cast: Matthew Modine, Lee Ermey, Vincent D'Onofrio, Adam Baldwin, Dorian Harewood, Arliss Howard

Year of Release: 1987 (Warner Brothers)

Immediately after the release of the film *Full Metal Jacket* in mid-1987, its merits became a subject of much debate. Some viewers regarded it as a powerful examination of war and the darker human impulses, but others saw the film as nihilistic and emotionally distant. Based on *The Short-Timers*, a grim, harrowing novel by Vietnam veteran Gustav Hasford, *Full Metal Jacket* examines two dramatically different, yet undeniably linked, phases in a Vietnam infantry soldier's life: basic training and combat. The basic training segment of the film takes place at the Marine training facility at Parris Island, North Carolina; the Vietnam action is centered on the city of Hue, site of some of the Tet Offensive's bloodiest fighting.

HISTORICAL BACKGROUND

Military service for the recruits who enlisted or were drafted into the United States military began with a roughly eight-week course of training and instruction. All activities during this period are undertaken with the ultimate goal of transforming civilians into soldiers. "It is a process that is not without accompanying pain," James Ebert dryly noted in his *A Life in a Year*. Indeed, the early stages of basic training were designed to strip away learned behavior governing even the most elementary of every-day practices (eating, speaking, attending to personal hygiene) so that the recruits could be reshaped in accordance with the military's desires.

Instruction in all matters was meted out by instructors who—especially in the Marine Corps—were renowned for their harsh treatment of recruits. Upon arrival at their assigned training facility, Marine trainees found themselves on the receiving end of a demoralizing torrent of verbal abuse that was matched only by the exhausting physical demands that were placed upon them. Gwynne Dyer wrote in *War* that "basic training is not really about teaching people skills; it's about changing them, so that they can do things they wouldn't have dreamt of otherwise. It works by applying enormous physical and mental pressure to men who have been isolated from their normal civilian environment and placed in one where the only right way to think and behave is the way the Marine Corps wants them to."

Individuality was an early casualty of such a training regimen. Recruits were forbidden from referring to themselves in the first person, and any sense of privacy was quickly obliterated by the communal environment in which they ate, slept, and trained. One army Vietnam veteran later recalled in an interview with Appy that the recruit "is ingrained with the spirit of the corps, but his own personal self is sacrificed. His personal identity is put on ice."

Basic training called for that sense of individual identity to wither under the hot glare of newly created feelings of loyalty to a larger community—the platoon, the Corps, the United States, etc. "The removal of one's identity was not a surgical process," wrote Ebert. "It was more a steady application of pressure, like squeezing the contents out of a sausage casing and then restuffing it with the substance of the training. Civilian identities, along with civilian clothing, were folded and stored away or shipped home for use in an inforeseeable future when, it was hoped, both might still be found to fit."

Trainee platoons, welded together by their shared experiences and the manipulations of their instructors, soon emerged as self-policing units that operated with the best interests of their community in mind. Individual recruits who performed poorly often brought punishment down on the larger platoon. In such instances, noted Ebert, these underachievers were mercilessly ostracized or bullied by their contemporaries into improving their conduct. "Much more rarely," he wrote, "group frustrations toward a recalcitrant 'screw-up' resulted in acts of violence, such as 'blanket parties' in which the target of the group's wrath was beaten. It is difficult to appreciate the destruction of self-esteem and the feeling of being utterly forsaken that failure in training could engender."

Although the methodologies employed in basic training were harsh, they were undertaken with the understanding that they were necessary to give trainees the greatest chance of survival in Vietnam. The military contended that those recruits who were not hardened, both mentally and physically, would not be adequately equipped for war. Only by providing these recruits with a "full metal jacket"—a reference to a special hard shell casing used to cover the soft lead interior of a bullet—would they be able to withstand the maelstrom of Vietnam.

CREATION OF *FULL METAL JACKET*

The Short-Timers, the book that would serve as the basis for *Full Metal Jacket*, was published in 1979. Written by Marine combat correspondent Gustav Hasford, the novel—which took its name from the term that soldiers used to refer to men nearing the conclusion of their one-year tour of duty in Vietnam—was a short, intense work that garnered a mixed critical reception. Some critics saw the book as an unremarkable addition to the Vietnam literary canon, charging that Hasford's characters were weakly drawn and that his brutally violent narrative was ultimately uncompelling. Others, such as *Newsweek*'s Walter Clemons, were more impressed. Wrote Clemons: "This brief, extremely ugly first novel is the best work of fiction about the Vietnam war I've read."

Hasford's book spurred Kubrick to make his first cinematic attempt at the subject of Vietnam. "[*The Short-Timers*] is a very short, very beautifully and economically written book," said the director in a *Rolling Stone* interview with Tim Cahill. "What I like about not writing original material—which I'm not even certain I could do—is that you have this tremendous advantage of reading something for the first time. You never have this experience again with the story. You have a reaction to it: it's a kind of falling-in-love reaction."

News that Kubrick was working on a Vietnam movie stirred a ripple of anticipation in the film world. A number of Kubrick's previous works (*2001: A Space Odyssey, Dr. Strangelove, A Clockwork Orange*) had explored the darker corners of human experience; his adaptation of Hasford's book, mused some critics, would provide him with material with which he would be immediately comfortable. "War offers Kubrick the spectacle of the lowest instinct deployed at the highest level of technical skill, the state in which the human yearning for extinction is pursued at the fullest throttle," wrote Richard Lacayo in *Film Comment.*

The film opens with a forty-five-minute segment devoted to the basic training experiences of a platoon of Marine recruits. Kubrick centers on two trainees, both of whom have been given nicknames by Sergeant Hartman, their profane, ferocious drill instructor. Joker (played by Matthew Modine) is a sharp, cynical recruit who soon emerges as the platoon leader; Pyle (Vincent D'Onofrio) is a dull-witted, overweight trainee who becomes the primary target of Hartman's abuse. Pyle's struggles to survive basic training reach a turning point when he is savagely beaten in a "blanket party" by the other members of the platoon. The attack unhinges Pyle, who kills Hartman and himself in a chilling nighttime encounter in the barracks latrine.

Full Metal Jacket then moves to Vietnam, where it follows Joker, now a *Stars and Stripes* correspondent, as he is sent to cover the battle for Hue during the Tet Offensive. Joker accompanies one besieged unit as it methodically sweeps through a section of the ruined city. (At one point a documentary crew that is accompanying the soldiers interviews Joker, who offers a twisted explanation for his presence in Vietnam: "I wanted to meet interesting, stimulating people from an ancient land . . . and kill them.") Shortly thereafter, an unseen sniper cripples a member of the unit, who sags to the ground. Subsequent attempts to rescue him only add to the body count, as the sniper uses the wounded men to lure would-be rescuers out in the open. The soldiers finally infiltrate the hiding place of the sniper, who turns out to be a young Vietcong girl. Terribly wounded by the gunfire of the Marines, she begs Joker to kill her. After hesitating, he does so, either out of a desire for retribution or a sense of compassion (talking with *American Film*'s Penelope Gilliatt, Kubrick referred to the scene as "humanity rearing its ugly head"). The film then ends with the Marines singing the theme to the *Mickey Mouse Club* as they wander through Hue's fire-lit streets. (*The Short-Timers* concludes in dramatically different fashion: Desperate to abort a suicidal plan to rescue four Marines who have been wounded by sniper fire, Joker finishes the men off himself.)

Perhaps the most interesting aspect of the creation of *Full Metal Jacket* was Kubrick's decision to cast Lee Ermey—a former Parris Island Marine drill instructor who had originally signed on to the production as a technical advisor—to play the crucial role of Gunnery Sergeant Hartman, the man charged with transforming the movie's recruits into soldiers. "I'd say fifty percent of Lee's dialogue, specifically the insult stuff, came from Lee," Kubrick told Cahill. "Lee came up with, I don't know, 150 pages of insults. Off the wall stuff: 'I don't like the name Lawrence. Lawrence is for faggots and sailors.' Aside from the insults, though, virtually every serious thing he says is basically true. When he says, 'A rifle is only a tool, it's a hard heart that kills,' you know it's true. Unless you're living in a world that doesn't need fighting men, you can't fault him."

CRITICAL REACTION

Reaction to *Full Metal Jacket* was mixed, to say the least. Many negative reviews contended that the film's bipartite structure did not work, and that the movie's core was essentially a cold and empty one, bereft of any worthwhile message. *The Nation*'s Terrence Rafferty wrote that "the characters remain dehumanized, the audience remains desensitized, and Vietnam has never seemed farther away." Pauline Kael's review in *New Yorker* was similarly scathing: "Here's a director who has been insulated from American life for more than two decades, and he proceeds to define the American crisis of the century. . . . This may be his worst movie. He probably believes he's numbing us by the power of his vision, but he's actually numbing us by its emptiness."

But other critics found the film—and particularly its gripping boot-camp scenes—to be a trenchant, white-knuckle exploration of the war's impact on its American participants. "The long boot-camp sequence is, in many ways, the most forceful work [Kubrick has] done in years—he's frighteningly into it," wrote Rafferty. Critic Penelope Gilliatt was similarly impressed. "[*Full Metal Jacket*] is a shapely and thoughtful achievement about the most disfigured and foolish notion of manliness that our gun-happy species has yet drummed up," she wrote in *American Film*. "*Full Metal Jacket* is about nothing less than the intellect, passions, and instincts of humanity." At the end of the year, Kubrick received Best Director recognition from the London Film Critics Circle for his direction of the film.

FURTHER READING

Appy, Christian G. *Working-Class War: American Combat Soldiers and Vietnam*. Chapel Hill, N.C.: University of North Carolina Press, 1993.

Cahill, Tim. "Stanley Kubrick: The Rolling Stone Interview." *Rolling Stone* (August 27, 1987).

Clemons, Walter. Review of *The Short-Timers*. In *Newsweek* (January 1, 1979).

Dyer, Gwynne. *War*. New York: Crown, 1985.

Ebert, James R. *A Life in a Year: The American Infantryman in Vietnam, 1965–1972*. Novato, Calif.: Presidio Press, 1993.

"*Full Metal Jacket* Section." *Literature/Film Quarterly* 16, no. 4 (1988).

Gilliatt, Penelope. "Heavy Metal: *Full Metal Jacket*—Or How Stanley Kubrick's Marines Learn to Stop Worrying and Love Vietnam." *American Film* (September 1987).

Gilman, Owen W., Jr. "Vietnam and John Winthrop's Vision of Community." In *Fourteen Landing Zones: Approaches to Vietnam War Literature*, Philip K. Jason, ed. Iowa City: University of Iowa Press, 1991.

Hammel, Eric. *Fire in the Streets: The Battle for Hue, Tet 1968*. Chicago: Contemporary Books, 1991.

Hasford, Gustav. *The Short-Timers*. New York: Harper & Row, 1979.

Kael, Pauline. Review of *Full Metal Jacket*. In *New Yorker* (July 13, 1987).

Lacayo, Richard. "Semper Fi." *Film Comment* (September-October 1987).

Rafferty, Terrence. Review of *Full Metal Jacket*. In *Nation* (August 1, 1987).

Reaves, Gerri. "From Hasford's *The Short-Timers* to Kubrick's *Full Metal Jacket*." *Literature/Film Quarterly* 16 (1988).

Go Tell the Spartans

Film

Director: Ted Post

Screenplay: Wendell Mayes; based on the novel *Incident at Muc Wa* by Daniel Ford

Principal Cast: Burt Lancaster, Craig Wasson, Jonathan Goldsmith, Marc Singer, Joe Unger, Evan Kim

Year of Release: 1978 (Avco Embassy)

The late 1970s brought a flurry of Vietnam films to American movie screens. But while *The Deer Hunter, Apocalypse Now*, and *Coming Home* received the bulk of the attention from American critics and moviegoers, a comparatively understated examination of the war, called *Go Tell the Spartans*, went largely unnoticed. Yet a number of reviewers felt that the film—which tells the story of an American advisory unit in Vietnam in 1964—was a work of some consequence in its own right, and some contended that it was superior to its better-known contemporaries in several significant respects.

HISTORICAL BACKGROUND

The American advisory presence in Vietnam began in 1950, when President Harry S. Truman directed the U.S. military to provide assistance to "the forces of France and the Associated States in Indochina" (Laos, Cambodia, and Vietnam) as part of a strategy to ward off Communism in that area of the world. The Military Assistance Advisory Group Indochina (MAAG-Indochina) was thus formed. This entity lasted until the mid-1950s, when Vietnam was partitioned along the seventeenth parallel into northern and southern entities. This "temporary" arrangement, agreed to as part of the 1954 Geneva Agreements, quickly hardened as American opposition to Ho Chi Minh's Communist government in North Vietnam became more evident. Determined to halt Communist expansion in the region, the United States threw its support behind the creation of a permanent, anticommunist government south of the seventeenth parallel. On October 26, 1955, South Vietnam became the independent Republic of Vietnam; within a week of that date, the United States had formed a military organization—termed the U.S. Military Assistance Advisory Group Vietnam (MAAG-Vietnam)—to provide assistance to the new nation. This organization, which replaced MAAG-Indochina, was responsible for providing strategic advice to all branches of South Vietnam's military, and it emerged as an important counselor to the Saigon government as well.

As MAAG expanded its efforts to train ARVN (Army of the Republic of Vietnam) troops and officers, the size of the organization itself swelled. The attendant growth in bureaucracy only complicated the jobs of frustrated field advisors, who encountered a range of obstacles in their efforts to nourish a self-sufficient South Vietnamese military. Advisors found it difficult to enlist the support of the rural population in defense initiatives, and corruption within the ARVN officer corps and the Saigon government created a discouraging environment for those within the ARVN who were dedicated to their duty and country.

In May 1964, MAAG was disbanded, its responsibilities folded into the U.S. Military Assistance Command Vietnam (MACV). Established in February 1962, the MACV had been formed to address the growing logistical issues associated with the American buildup in South Vietnam. In 1962 and 1963, MACV allowed MAAG to supervise the U.S. advisory effort in the country, devoting its energies to interactions with Saigon and oversight of the U.S. buildup. By 1964, however, it was felt that America's advisory efforts should be unified with its other Vietnam endeavors, and MAAG was eliminated.

The absorption of MAAG into MACV in 1964 had little practical effect on the day-to-day interactions between the American advisors and the Vietnamese armed forces. U.S. field advisors continued to counsel and negotiate with their South Vietnamese counterparts on military matters (mindful that American officers had no direct authority over South Vietnamese troops), and by 1968 nearly 9,500 U.S. Army personnel were engaged as field advisors in Vietnam. "With U.S. advisors assigned down to battalion level within SVNAF (South Vietnamese Armed Forces), U.S. assistance in the form of advice, coordination of artillery and air firepower as well as moral support was invaluable," wrote Harry G. Summers, Jr. in *Vietnam War Almanac*. Summers went on to note that most American advisors performed admirably despite the perilous circumstances of their assignments. "Five MACV advisors won the Medal of Honor for conspicuous battlefield bravery. From the U.S. Army element alone, 378 advisors were killed in action, and 1,393 were wounded in action. If there is a criticism of this field advisory effort, it is that U.S. advisors were too good, for they inadvertently helped to create a dependency that was to prove fatal once U.S. support was withdrawn in March 1973, after the Paris Accords were signed.''

CREATION OF *GO TELL THE SPARTANS*

Wendell Mayes wrote the screenplay for *Go Tell the Spartans*, which was based on Daniel Ford's book *Incident at Muc Wa*, in the early 1970s. But it languished for several years until Ted Post, best known for his direction of such action films as *Beneath the Planet of the Apes, Hang 'Em High*, and *Magnum Force*, was secured as director.

The film is set in Vietnam in the summer of 1964, less than a year before the arrival of the first American combat troops in the country. It opens by providing a portrait of Major Asa Barker (played by Burt Lancaster), commander of a U.S. military advisory team stationed in Penang. It quickly becomes clear that the gruff Barker, a veteran of World War II and the Korean War, is somewhat cynical about his present assignment and leery about the environment into which America is sinking. This viewpoint can also be detected in the words and manner of his ambitious aide, Captain Olivetti (Marc Singer).

After restraining Cowboy (Evan Kim), his outfit's Vietnamese interpreter, from torturing a Vietcong prisoner, Barker welcomes a group of new soldiers into his outfit. These soldiers range from the patriotic Lieutenant Hamilton (Joe Unger) to the haunted Sergeant Oleonowski (Jonathan Goldsmith) to Corporal Courcey (Craig Wasson), a college graduate who volunteered for Vietnam for reasons he seems unable or unwilling to articulate.

Barker initially assigns the new men to ridiculous make-work details such as ''mosquito patrol,'' wherein the soldiers roll up their sleeves and count the number of mosquito bites they receive. But circumstances soon change dramatically. Barker's superior, General Harnitz (Dolph Sweet), arrives, angry about Barker's submission of a false ''position paper'' on a nearby village called Muc Wa (disdainful of the position paper request, the major told Olivetti to file a report indicating that it was a busy little hamlet of no strategic importance). Harnitz orders Barker to establish a garrison at the village, which in fact is abandoned.

Barker subsequently assigns several of his men to serve as the advisory team for the mission, and the ragtag group, composed of an odd assortment of South Vietnamese soldiers, mercenaries, and farmers, sets off. Hamilton is given command of the team, but dysentery and inexperience take their toll, and Oleonowski soon emerges as the unit's de facto leader. The expedition soon reaches Muc Wa, which turns out to be an abandoned French outpost. The soldiers discover a French military cemetery on its outskirts; on its gate is a quote from Simonides that refers to Leonidas and his Spartan comrades, who fell at the battle of Thermopylae in 480 B.C. The college-educated Courcey recognizes the quote and translates it for his fellow soldiers: ''Stranger, when you find us lying here, go tell the Spartans we obeyed their orders.'' The sense of foreboding engendered by this inscription is heightened when Courcey, taking a walk through the cemetery, spots a withered, one-eyed Vietnamese man watching him.

The joint American-Vietnamese force subsequently erects a well-fortified garrison at Muc Wa, only to have Courcey bring a group of Vietnamese villagers inside its fortifications. Several members of the garrison insist that the motley crew of children, young women, and elderly people are Vietcong. The party is allowed to stay, but their visit proves a short one. Cowboy kills the group one night. Turning the bodies over, the Americans note that many of them were apparently smuggling weapons out of the camp, but an undercurrent of uncertainty about Cowboy's actions remains.

The death count grows a short time later, when VC attack a patrol led by Oleonowski. The patrol retreats to the garrison, leaving behind a wounded Vietnamese soldier. Hamilton rushes out to rescue him, only to be slain himself. This turn of events takes a heavy toll on the despondent Oleonowski, who subsequently commits suicide.

Concerned about the deteriorating situation at Muc Wa, Barker campaigns for additional support for the garrison. He makes a deal with a corrupt South Vietnamese colonel, but before he is able to bring these new resources to bear, he learns that the VC have launched a full-scale assault on Muc Wa. Barker's demands for air support are initially rebuffed, because the South Vietnamese military wants to hold its forces in reserve against a possible coup. He subsequently turns to Harnitz, who gives approval to the air support after receiving a strongly worded telegram from Barker.

The garrison successfully defends Muc Wa, but after the battle is over, Barker receives orders to withdraw his men from the outpost. Barker arranges for an evacuation of the Americans stationed there, but when it becomes clear that the Vietnamese will be left to fend for themselves, Courcey refuses to board the helicopter. Barker decides to stay as well, and the two of them organize the Vietnamese troops for the long walk ahead. Another VC ambush decimates the group, though, and Courcey awakens to find that he is the only survivor of the assault. The film concludes with Courcey's return to the cemetery at Muc Wa. There he encounters the silent, one-eyed Vietnamese man once again. "I'm going home, Charlie,'' Courcey says.

CRITICAL RECEPTION

Go Tell the Spartans was released shortly after *Coming Home*, and two other high-profile Vietnam films—*The Deer Hunter* and *Apocalypse Now*—appeared shortly afterward. Although those three films garnered far more critical and public attention, *Go Tell the Spartans* was welcomed by a number of reviewers who felt that the film, in its own modest way, addressed some important issues in an effective manner. "*Spartans* is no earth-shaking masterpiece,'' wrote *New*

Republic reviewer Stanley Kauffmann, "but in its small-scale way it's strong, hard, forthright—very much more incisive about its subject than the star-laden, flabby *Coming Home*. The final effect of *Spartans* is as if a war *movie* had actually gone to war." *Time* reviewer Richard Schickel suggested that the film's shortcomings actually served to bolster its effectiveness. "It is understated, lacking in powerful dramatic incident and high human emotion, and rather flatly written and directed," he wrote. "As a result, it has about it a realistically antiheroic air that is rare enough in any movie about any war, and a grubby brutality that matches memories of the news film that came out of Southeast Asia in the '60s. . . . *Go Tell the Spartans* is, within its limits, an earnest and honest little picture."

Arthur Schlesinger, Jr. agreed with Schickel's characterization of the film's mood but felt that *Go Tell the Spartans* packed a deceptively powerful punch. "The film is continually intelligent and interesting," he wrote in *Saturday Review*. "Its very understatement makes *Go Tell the Spartans* a more powerful anti-war film than *Coming Home*. It has no overt message. It recognizes the complexities of motive and discipline that made Americans fight in Vietnam. By concentrating with great intensity on a single, obscure incident, it illuminates a vast landscape. In sure, swift strokes, it shows the irrelevance of the American presence in Vietnam, the corruptions wrought by that irrelevance, and the fortuity, cruelty, and waste of an irrelevant war."

FURTHER READING

Ford, Daniel. *Incident at Muc Wa*. Garden City, N.Y.: Doubleday, 1967.
Halberstam, David. *One Very Hot Day*. New York: Houghton, 1968.
Kauffmann, Stanley. "Searching and Destroying." *New Republic* (June 24, 1978).
Kroll, Jack. "The Dirty Little War." *Newsweek* (October 2, 1978).
Palmer, Bruce, Jr. *The 25-Year War: America's Military Role in Vietnam*. Louisville: University of Kentucky Press, 1984.
Schickel, Richard. "Good Conduct." *Time* (September 25, 1978).
Schlesinger, Arthur, Jr. "An Incident of War." *Saturday Review* (June 22, 1978).
Summers, Harry G., Jr. *Vietnam War Almanac*. New York: Facts on File, 1985.

Going After Cacciato

Novel

Author: Tim O'Brien

Facts of publication: New York: Delacorte, 1978

Debate about the legitimacy of the Vietnam War triggered an unprecedented rebellion against the war within America's borders. At the forefront of the debate were the thousands of young draftees who refused to serve in Vietnam, choosing instead to flee to Canada, register as conscientious objectors (COs), or go to prison. Some opponents of the war claimed that a similar rebellion was taking place within America's military ranks, and antiwar activists offered up anecdotal evidence from military bases both in the United States and abroad to support their contention. As the war dragged on, and evidence of morale problems within the U.S. military increased, the issue of military absenteeism received additional attention.

"In the lexicon of military crimes, few are more serious than desertion in combat," wrote Lawrence Baskir and William Strauss, authors of *Chance and Circumstance: The Draft, the War, and the Vietnam Generation*. "[But] the unpopularity of the [Vietnam] war gave desertion an added dimension. By the late 1960s, the offense began to have political overtones, and desertion came to be seen as the military counterpart of draft resistance. . . . [Both the pro- and antiwar camps] used the image of battlefield desertion to make political and moral arguments that advanced their own points of view. This led to an 'either-or' stereotype of deserters, with the public assuming that most deserters left because they refused to participate in combat. The only thing in doubt was the rightness or wrongness of what they did." In 1978, Vietnam veteran Tim

O'Brien published *Going After Cacciato*, a novel that hinges on one soldier's decision to leave the battlefield.

HISTORICAL BACKGROUND

Approximately 100,000 U.S. soldiers were discharged for "absence offenses" during the Vietnam era (more than 450,000 others received less-than-honorable discharges for other reasons, ranging from drug abuse to disciplinary problems). But though critics of the war have cited the rate of desertion and incidents of AWOL (absent without leave) offenses during Vietnam as evidence of "grunt"-level opposition to the war, in reality, most of these cases involved desertion from posts where combat was not imminent. Indeed, the majority of soldiers convicted of desertion charges during the war were actually stationed in the United States, and researchers have contended that desertion and AWOL rates in the Marines actually crested *after* the United States completed its withdrawal from Vietnam in 1975, as troops struggled to assimilate back into American society.

Those soldiers based in the United States who went AWOL or deserted committed these infractions for any number of reasons. Family problems, romantic quandaries, financial difficulties, and inability to cope with the military life-style all took a toll. Some soldiers—an estimated seven thousand total—also went "over the hill" and fled to Canada after receiving orders to report to Vietnam. "Since these men did not seem to be opposed to the war in Vietnam until they had to go there, it is safe to assume that they were motivated by fear for their own survival rather than opposition to the war," wrote Baskir and Strauss. "It was a question of survival; they might get killed there."

Over in Vietnam, approximately five thousand U.S. soldiers were convicted of AWOL or desertion offenses during the war (Baskir and Strauss pointed out that in World War II about twenty thousand U.S. troops were convicted for desertion in combat). The comparatively low Vietnam figure was attributed in large part to the dearth of options available to American field troops—Baskir and Strauss quoted one soldier who sardonically asked, "What are you going to do? Walk through Cambodia?" Mid-tour rest-and-recreation leaves provided one of the few opportunities for combat troops to desert, and about half of the five thousand soldiers who were penalized for desertion offenses during the war are believed to have taken this route.

Some of the frontline soldiers who deserted from Vietnam left for reasons similar to those cited by deserters over in America—disintegrating romantic relationships, family finances, etc. Others, though, departed as a direct result of their combat experiences. Antiwar critics subsequently contended that these desertions were acts of conscience triggered by prolonged exposure to a defoliated wasteland and an amoral war. Hawks, meanwhile, argued that the deserters were simply cowards whose instincts for self-preservation proved stronger than their sense of duty.

In the years following the American withdrawal from Vietnam, defenders of U.S. military performance have pointed with satisfaction to the relatively low number of courts-martial for desertion offenses, as well as the number of short-term AWOL incidents (which was comparable to rates in previous wars). Other statistics painted a more sobering picture, however. Analysts noted that even though Vietnam-era courts-martial for desertion offenses were not excessive when compared with earlier wars, the military was forced to deal with an alarming number of AWOL and desertion incidents that did not reach the court-martial stage for one reason or another. Baskir and Strauss reported that incidents in the Army and Marines in which soldiers were AWOL for more than thirty days rose from about fifteen per thousand troops in 1966 to approximately seventy per thousand by 1972, and that during the Vietnam War the U.S. military experienced approximately 1.5 million AWOL incidents. At the peak of the war, an American soldier was going AWOL every two minutes, and deserting every six minutes. They went on to note that AWOL and desertion offenses accounted for a total loss of roughly one million man-years of military service, and that the Senate Armed Services Committee estimated that in 1968 alone, absenteeism was costing the military the equivalent of ten combat divisions of fifteen thousand men each.

CREATION OF *GOING AFTER CACCIATO*

Long after receiving his honorable discharge from the U.S. Army in March 1970, author Tim O'Brien grappled with his feelings about the Vietnam War and the events that he witnessed and participated in there. This struggle to come to terms with the moral and philosophical implications of service in a war that he came to hate became a central theme in much of his subsequent literary work, from his first book, the autiobiographical *If I Die in a Combat Zone*, to 1990's *The Things They Carried*.

In the years following his tour, O'Brien gave considerable thought to the forces that "seemed, almost physically, to push me into the war," as he told Larry McCaffery for the *Chicago Review*. These emotional pressures included the expectations of his family and community, and the implicit understanding that flight from the draft meant exile from the people he loved. Nonetheless, O'Brien researched the logistics of desertion prior to his tour in Vietnam—and mused at length upon the dark allure of deserting once he had arrived there. "In *Cacciato* the premise I started with was, what if I *had* deserted. Would I have been happy living in exile? Would I be happy running? What would I experience? Would I be able to live with myself? Was it *right* to run?"

The narrative structure of *Going After Cacciato* is a complex one. The principal character in the novel is Paul Berlin, an American soldier assigned to night watch at an observation post deep in Quang Nai Province. The solitary Berlin muses at length upon his doubts about the legitimacy of the war and the nature of duty and morality, but he also spends much of the night recalling the chaotic, violent events of the past few months and fantasizing about pursuing Cacciato, a private who has gone AWOL, all the way to Paris. As the novel progresses, it becomes clear that the latter fantasy—although profoundly influenced by the war (it includes an encounter in the bowels of a North Vietnamese tunnel and a heated debate on the merits of desertion at the Paris peace negotiation table)— serves as an escape from the traumatic events that have scarred Berlin over the preceding months. "We live in our heads a lot, but especially during situations of stress and great peril," O'Brien said in an interview with Eric James Schroeder for *Modern Fiction Studies*. "It's a means of escape in part, but it's also a means of dealing with the real world—not just escaping it, but dealing with it. . . . The central theme of the novel has to do with how we use our imaginations to deal with situations around us, not just to cope with them psychologically but, more importantly, to deal with them philosophically and morally." (For further information on O'Brien's wartime experiences, see the essay on his short story collection *The Things They Carried*.)

CRITICAL RECEPTION

"*Going After Cacciato* is, without reservation, one of the most challenging and powerful novels to find its way into print in some time," wrote Doris Grumbach in *The Chronicle Review*. "[The book] is about the power of the mind, about daydreaming in the presence of war in the pursuit of peace, and about the possibilities of escape through 'flights of imagination,' a phrase O'Brien uses again and again. . . . *Cacciato* contains the kind of truth that separates the shallow from fully realized and original fiction." Many other reviewers were equally appreciative, and the book eventually won the National Book Award for fiction. *Commentary* critic Pearl K. Bell called the novel a "remarkable piece of work, even though the alternating faces of its story—the one a cinematic daydream, the other a waking nightmare—do not fuse in a dramatically realized whole. In the end this matters a good deal less than O'Brien's profound understanding of the moral innocence that bewildered, then corrupted, and finally destroyed so many of the American soldiers in Vietnam."

Though Bell, John Updike, and a few other reviewers registered minor complaints, it was generally agreed that O'Brien's efforts to merge Vietnam's grim reality with Paul Berlin's imaginary journey were masterfully executed, and that Berlin's imagined pursuit of the deserter Cacciato lent the novel an urgency and poignancy absent from other war literature. Grumbach remarked that with *Going After Cacciato*, O'Brien "accomplished something of a miracle. By using all the authentic and bloody detail that he knows so well from the war he survived, he has created a narrative that borders on myth and theology, psychology and epic, a picaresque parable of the imagination." And Thomas R. Edwards, writing in the *New York Review of Books*, said that "it is a book about the imagination itself, one which both questions and celebrates that faculty's way of resisting the destructive powers of immediate experience. . . . At one point [in the novel] a medic feeds M&Ms to a dying soldier while telling him that they're medicine. The incident crystallizes many of the novel's attitudes—the dreadful absurdity of war in itself, the helplessness of technology to serve human ends, the persistence of compassion when rational purpose fails, the power of imagination (within limits) to serve living needs."

FURTHER READING

Baskir, Lawrence M., and William A. Strauss. *Chance and Circumstance: The Draft, the War, and the Vietnam Generation*. New York: Alfred A. Knopf, 1978.

Bell, D. Bruce, and Thomas J. Houston. *The Vietnam Era Deserter*. U.S. Army Research Institute for the Behavioral and Social Sciences, July 1976.

Bell, Pearl K. "Writing about Vietnam." *Commentary* (October 1978).

Edwards, Thomas R. "Feeding on Fantasy." *New York Review of Books* (July 19, 1979).

Grumbach, Doris. "Walking Away from the Horror." *The Chronicle Review* (February 13, 1978).

Kaplan, Steven. *Understanding Tim O'Brien*. Columbia, S.C.: University of South Carolina Press, 1994.

McCaffery, Larry. "Interview with Tim O'Brien." *Chicago Review* 33, no. 2 (1982).

Musil, Robert K. "The Truth about Deserters." *Nation* (April 16, 1973).

O'Brien, Tim. *Going After Cacciato*. New York: Delacorte, 1978.

———. *If I Die in a Combat Zone, Box Me Up and Ship Me Home*. New York: Delacorte, 1973.

———. "The Vietnam in Me." *New York Times Magazine* (October 2, 1994).

Schroeder, Eric James. "Two Interviews: Talks with Tim O'Brien and Robert Stone." *Modern Fiction Studies* (Spring 1984).

Updike, John. "Layers of Ambiguity." *New Yorker* (March 27, 1978).

The Green Berets

Film

Director: John Wayne

Screenplay: James Lee Barrett; based on novel by Robin Moore

Principal Cast: John Wayne, David Janssen, Jim Hutton, Aldo Ray

Year of Release: 1968 (Warner Brothers)

The American media's coverage of the Vietnam War was a subject of significant debate, both during the war and in the years following U.S. withdrawal. Observers both within and without the journalistic community who regarded the press's performance in generally favorable terms contended that anger toward media coverage was largely the product of a "kill the messenger" mentality: "Dispatches from the war zone reflected mostly what the reporters themselves saw, or heard from soldiers and officials," wrote Kim Willenson in *The Bad War*. "They may have emphasized what was going wrong, but it was an emphasis supplied by their sources. The press did not manufacture events, and its details came from the participants—often key figures who believed U.S. policy was in error, and who pushed their views by making public bad news the policymakers refused to heed in private."

Critics, however, argued that the press provided the American people with fundamentally flawed reports that contributed mightily to the country's polarization over Vietnam and its ultimate failure to win the war. These critics claimed that the media's thirst for high drama and controversy, its sometimes antagonistic relationship with military and administration leaders, its tendency to rush to judgment, and its liberal biases all resulted in slanted reporting that gave

Americans a warped perspective on the war. Such views even led some critics to question the patriotism of correspondents who filed stories that did not correlate with official versions of events.

One of the first depictions of the American newsman in Vietnam as an untrustworthy producer of misinformation could be found in John Wayne's *The Green Berets*. An unwavering supporter of American involvement in Vietnam, Wayne was, "depending on one's point of view, either a noble superpatriot or a neolithic ultraconservative," Michael Anderegg observed in *Inventing Vietnam*. Determined to make a picture that would rally Americans around their country's actions in Vietnam, Wayne created a film that followed the transformation of a journalist from ignorant skeptic to dedicated believer in the need for U.S. action in Vietnam. Widely decried as a trite and breathtakingly misleading portrait of the realities in Vietnam, the movie nonetheless was a popular success. Years later, historian Philip Taylor called *The Green Berets* "the most blatantly propagandist contemporaneous American feature film made about the Vietnam war."

HISTORICAL BACKGROUND

The American press's coverage of events in Vietnam was controversial from the very beginning. During the early 1960s, attempts by U.S. government and military officials to shape the tone and content of press coverage backfired, as reporters abandoned worthless official sources for more reliable (and often less optimistic) sources out in the field. The resulting stories—whether on the struggle against the Vietcong or the stability of the Diem government—often did not correspond with the rosy assurances of U.S. officials.

The introduction of U.S. troops into South Vietnam and the commencement of bombing of North Vietnam following 1964's Tonkin Gulf controversy significantly upped the stakes in Vietnam, and this, perhaps inevitably, further heightened tensions between the press and the Johnson Administration and the U.S. military. The rise of television journalism during this time was an additional factor. As Daniel C. Hallin wrote in *The "Uncensored War": The Media and Vietnam*, both supporters and detractors of the American media noted that "because it is a visual medium, television shows the raw horror of war in a way print cannot." Footage of vicious firefights, wounded children, bone-weary soldiers, and flaming villages were all broadcast into American living rooms, and nearly everyone agreed that these pictures packed a more visceral punch than did newspaper reports or radio broadcasts. Richard Nixon later commented in *RN: The Memoirs of Richard Nixon* that "In each night's TV news and each morning's paper the war was reported battle by battle, but little or no sense of the underlying purpose of the fighting was conveyed. Eventually this contributed to the impression that we were fighting in military and moral quicksand, rather than toward an important and worthwhile objective. More than ever before, television showed the terrible human suffering and sacrifice of war."

U.S. press coverage also had a cumulative effect, thanks to the ever-lengthening period of American involvement. With each passing month, officials offered new assurances that the tide was turning and that America's superior military and technological might was relentlessly closing in on victory. The media passed this version of events on to the American public, but as reporter Don Oberdorfer later observed in Kim Willenson's *The Bad War*, the war eventually spawned many competing versions of events: "For the American press, Vietnam was a learning experience—much as it was for the rest of the country and the government. We knew very little at the beginning, but as the war progressed people in the press, along with people in the government who were our sources after all, began to get this very hazy, fuzzy situation into focus. And this picture was not the same picture that was being portrayed in the official reports. We know now . . . that the picture portrayed in the official reports was not the one that was believed by many of the policymakers." Former U.S. press liaison Barry Zorthian concurred that it became increasingly difficult for the Johnson Administration to reconcile their predictions of imminent victory with the continued carnage that the news media saw. In an interview for *The Bad War*, he admitted that credibility became a problem: "There was a feeling 'Hell, we've been getting all this good news and, Christ, none of it's accurate.' And then came the realization, as the level of deaths went up, that this was not going to be a Sunday picnic. So things started to go sour and the military situation didn't move and skepticism about the war grew. But still, as far as public impact, the great devastation didn't come until Tet. That was the ultimate collapse."

Tet and the Press

The American press's performance during and after the Tet Offensive of 1968 has been the subject of a great deal of dissection and debate. Critics charge that even though the offensive was in reality a decisive military defeat for North Vietnam, the American press's emphasis on isolated components of that offensive (the attack on the American embassy in Saigon, the protracted battle for Hue, initial surprise about the strength of the assault) demoralized the American public and thus actually gave North Vietnam a significant political victory. Journalist Peter Braestrup, author of the highly critical *Big Story: How the American Press and Television Reported and Interpreted the Crisis of Tet 1968 in Vietnam and Washington*, wrote that "rarely has contemporary crisis-journalism turned out, in retrospect, to have veered so widely from reality. Essentially, the dominant themes of the words and film from Vietnam (rebroadcast in commentary, editorials, and much political rhetoric at home) added up to a portrait of defeat for the allies. Historians, on the contrary, have concluded that the Tet offensive resulted in a severe military-political setback for Hanoi in the South. To have portrayed such a setback for one side as a defeat for the other—in a major crisis aboard—cannot be counted as a triumph for American journalism."

Journalist Charles Mohr, however, echoed the thoughts of other defenders of the press when he wrote in the *Columbia Journalism Review* that "the revisionists ascribe the erosion [in public support for the war in the wake of Tet] to hysterical reporting from Vietnam; my own belief is that it was the result of strong public shock following the highly optimistic public claims of progress by American officials in the fall of 1967." Reporter Jonathan Schell offered a similar analysis in his *The Real War*: "The fact that [North Vietnam] lost the battle was nothing new—it had lost all the battles of the war since the Americans had arrived with their tremendous firepower; but the fact that, after three years of exposure to that firepower, it could still launch an offensive on the scale of Tet *was* new. It shed a light backward on American policy so far. . . . The precise target that was destroyed by the foe at Tet was not any military installation but a certain picture of the war that had been planted in the minds of the American people by their government."

Certainly, Tet triggered a reevaluation of the war in living rooms all across America. It sparked reassessments among the media as well, including a highly public one that is sometimes cited as a crucial turning point in American acceptance of the war. On February 27, 1968, Walter Cronkite, America's best-known and most-trusted press figure and a self-described "impartial" observer of the war prior to Tet, grimly reported from Vietnam that "to say that we are closer to victory today is to believe, in the face of the evidence, the optimists who have been wrong in the past. To suggest we are on the edge of defeat is to yield to unreasonable pessimism. To say that we are mired in stalemate seems the only realistic, yet unsatisfactory, conclusion." Upon hearing of Cronkite's remarks, President Lyndon B. Johnson reportedly lamented that if he had lost Cronkite, he had lost Middle America. Still, Johnson White House official and diplomat Richard Holbrooke contended in *The Bad War* that "the press didn't lose the war for us. Congress didn't lose the war for us. The war was lost because the strategy was wrong. The military lost the war; the political leadership of this country lost the war; Lyndon Johnson . . . and Richard Nixon and Henry Kissinger are the men who cost us this thing. Not the Case-Church Amendment, not David Halberstam and Walter Cronkite, and not the anti-war demonstrators. . . . The war was not lost, as Nixon always likes to write, in the halls of Congress and on the pages of *The New York Times*; it was lost in the rice paddies of Indochina."

"Journalism is an imperfect instrument," wrote Mohr. "Before and after Tet, the story did often tend to overwhelm the essentially conventional journalistic methods we employed." Mohr granted that the American press's coverage of the Vietnam War was flawed, but he contended that "the coverage seems sound in retrospect. Not only ultimately, but also at each major milestone of the war, the weight of serious reporting corresponds quite closely to the historical record. Revisionists seem to fault correspondents for distrusting the version of events propounded by the most optimistic senior officials in Vietnam. But what if the correspondents had believed that version and had been guided by it in carrying out their assignment? In that case, the reporters' reputations, which are not unblemished, would be irredeemably tarnished.''

WAYNE AND VIETNAM

John Wayne was a Hollywood icon known for his leading roles in a wide range of Westerns and World War II films. Indeed, his stature as a symbol of American patriotism and can-do spirit made his name a sort of shorthand for such sentiments in the Vietnam era, as countless participants attested. Journalist David Halberstam noted in *The Best and the Brightest* that the John Wayne persona ''influenced the officers and the men, everyone. The Wayne image of the guy cleaning up the town, the good guy standing alone was there . . . the swagger, the tough guy walk . . . there were a lot of guys out there playing John Wayne.''

Wayne, a political conservative, watched the growth of the American antiwar movement during the mid-1960s with a mixture of anger and incredulity: ''I think they oughta shoot [antiwar protestors] if they're carrying the Viet Cong flag,'' he told Joan Barthel for the *New York Times*. ''A lot of our boys are getting shot lookin' at that flag. As far as I'm concerned, it wouldn't bother me a bit to pull the trigger on one of 'em.'' Wayne felt that much of the domestic opposition to the war was based on ignorance of the true stakes. ''Duke's views on Vietnam were carved in stone and remained so throughout the 1960s and 1970s,'' wrote Randy Roberts and John S. Olson in *John Wayne, American*. ''The war was in the best interests of the United States and the free world. . . . To those who argued that Vietnam was really an internal civil war, or that nationalism, not communism, was the force driving the Viet Cong and North Vietnamese, Duke had one word: 'Horseshit!'''

Olson and Roberts noted that Wayne took the antiwar protests sprouting across America ''very personally. It went against the grain of every role he every played, as well as the man he tried to be. He determined to rally Americans to the cause of anticommunism and to the support of the boys going over to Vietnam to fight and die, in the best way he knew how—to make a pro-American, pro-soldier, guts-and-glory film, just as he had done so many times in the past.''

CREATION OF *THE GREEN BERETS*

In December 1965 Wayne sent a personal letter to President Lyndon B. Johnson, in which he laid out his proposal for a film ''that will inspire a patriotic attitude on the part of fellow Americans'' about U.S. military involvement in Vietnam. Johnson—who had increased American troop levels to nearly two hundred thousand men by this time—was understandably interested. Subsequent correspondence between the White House and Wayne resulted in an agreement in which the Defense Department would provide assistance in making the movie in return for approval of the script.

In 1966 Wayne acquired the film rights to Robin Moore's best-selling novel *The Green Berets*, a work that had reportedly aroused the ire of the Pentagon because of its factual accuracy. The Green Berets were undeniably a potent group for cinematic treatment. An elite counterinsurgency unit from army Special Forces that had been rejuvenated by President John Kennedy, the Green Berets enjoyed a certain mystique that made them immediately attractive to Wayne.

In June 1966 Wayne traveled to South Vietnam as part of a USO tour. One reporter who covered Wayne's visit recalled in an interview with Maurice Zolotow that the actor spent much of his time greeting American soldiers. The soldiers, said the reporter, would feel "this giant hand on their shoulder and a voice saying: 'Hello, soldier. I'm John Wayne and I just want you to know a hell of a lot of folks back home appreciate what you're doing.' These kids would turn around and break into tears. For fourteen days from six o'clock in the morning to ten at night, Wayne would walk around and introduce himself to GIs." Wayne returned to the United States more convinced than ever of the need for the American presence in Indochina. That conviction was evident from first frame to last of *The Green Berets*.

The film's action centers around two largely unrelated stories. The film's first section takes place in a Green Beret base camp, where the U.S. soldiers are teaching South Vietnamese people how to defend themselves; this section of the film ends with an assault on the camp by marauding Vietcong troops who murder all the Vietnamese civilians before finally being routed. The film then follows a group of Green Berets as they parachute into an area of Vietcong control to capture a Communist general. But the overarching plotline of *The Green Berets* concerns the enlightenment of a liberal journalist who, prior to his firsthand exposure to Vietcong atrocities, had been openly skeptical of the legitimacy of U.S. involvement in the country. Roberts and Olson called the awakening of the journalist George Beckwith (played by David Janssen) "the unifying focus of the movie." Jarred from his smug preconceptions about the war by Colonel Kirby (Wayne) and the depravities of the Vietcong, Beckwith dons military fatigues and joins the fight. He later tells Kirby that it will be difficult to publish a true account of what he has seen, implying that such a story would clash with the American media's agenda: "If I say what I feel, I may be out of a job."

POPULAR AND CRITICAL REACTION

The Green Berets was, as Wayne anticipated, pummeled by reviewers and America's antiwar contingent (which he generally placed in the same camp). *New York Times* reviewer Renata Adler called the film "vile and insane." Michael Korda, writing in *Glamour*, called it "immoral, in the deepest sense. It is a simple-minded tract in praise of killing, brutality, and American superiority over Asians. . . . [It] is racist in the hallowed tradition of Rudyard Kipling. . . . [It] is an insult to every man in uniform on *both* sides of the war.'' Many others contributed similar remarks. But whereas some critics were genuinely appalled by the film's political tone, others spent more time marveling at its ''cowboys and indians'' veneer and its heavy-handed execution. *Life* critic Richard Schickel commented that ''the war being fought here bears no resemblance whatever to the reality of Vietnam as we have all, hawks and doves alike, perceived it to be through the good offices of the mass media. That's why I can't really get very angry at Big John. He has wasted my time, but he is incapable of poisoning my mind, or anyone else's.'' *Cinema Magazine*'s Frank Martarella, meanwhile, remarked that ''*The Green Berets* is so wretched and so childishly sleazy that it is embarrassing to criticize its pretentiousness and banality.''

Perhaps the most stinging rebuke of the film, however, was delivered a few years later by Vietnam veteran Gustav Hasford in his novel *The Short-Timers* (upon which the film *Full Metal Jacket* was based). Hasford harshly ridicules the film in one scene, writing that ''this is the funniest movie we have seen in a long time. . . . At the end of the movie, John Wayne walks off into the sunset with a spunky little [South Vietnamese] orphan. The grunts laugh and whistle and threaten to pee all over themselves. The sun is setting in the South China Sea—in the East—which makes the end of the movie as accurate as the rest of it.''

Journalists and correspondents who had covered the war, meanwhile, were contemptuous of the film's insinuation that the American press was more interested in advancing their own liberal agendas than in accurately reporting the situation in Vietnam.

Wayne shrugged off the harsh reviews, dismissing them as the predictable hectoring of an ignorant ''liberal'' media. Instead he basked in the glow of *The Green Berets*'s undeniable popularity with the movie-going public. Though some movie houses showing the film were picketed by antiwar protestors, it was more common to see throngs of customers filling the seats to see the show. Wayne described himself as ''personally gratified by the box-office results,'' telling the *New York Times* that he was not ''surprised a bit by the reviews of that group who see Vietnam in their own, peculiar way. . . . *The Green Berets* simply says that a lot of our brave guys are fighting and dying for us out there. The ridiculously one-sided criticism of the picture only made people more conscious of it and they are proving that the reviews were not very effective.'' Certainly, the film's core audience was America's so-called ''silent majority,'' those who supported the U.S. military commitment in Vietnam and interpreted the antiwar movement as an unpatriotic one. ''The film's popularity was deeply rooted in both John Wayne's persona and in the pain his traditional audiences felt in 1968,'' wrote Roberts and Olson. Wayne was most popular in America's working-class communities, which were bearing the brunt of the war's pain and suffering. Working-class families were thus left with what Roberts and Olson called ''painfully ambivalent feelings. They loved their country, hated the war, loved their boys, and despised the antiwar movement.'' *The Green Berets* served as a salve to these communities, reassuring them that the cause of America— and their sons—in Vietnam was right and just.

The Green Berets was a financial success, but Hollywood would not return to Vietnam as a subject again until well after the war was over. As Philip Taylor remarked in *History Today*, ''the fusion of denunciation and mockery surrounding *The Green Berets* probably contributed to Hollywood's subsequent reluctance to tackle the Vietnam war again until after it was all over. A suitable period of mourning was prompted by America's 'first military defeat,' when the impact not just on the veterans and their families but also on U.S. public confidence generally prompted a reappraisal of the war, its causes and course.''

FURTHER READING

Barthel, Joan. ''John Wayne, Superhawk.'' *New York Times* (December 24, 1967).

Braestrup, Peter. *Big Story: How the American Press and Television Reported and Interpreted the Crisis of Tet 1968 in Vietnam and Washington*. Boulder, Colo.: Westview Press, 1977.

Hallin, Daniel C. *The ''Uncensored War'': The Media and Vietnam*. New York: Oxford University Press, 1986.

Korda, Michael. Review of *The Green Berets*. In *Glamour* (October 1968).

Levy, Emanuel. *John Wayne: Prophet of the American Way of Life*. Metuchen, N.J.: Scarecrow, 1988.

Mandelbaum, Michael. ''Vietnam: The Television War.'' *Daedalus* (Fall 1982).

Mohr, Charles. ''Once Again—Did the Press Lose Vietnam? A Veteran Correspondent Takes on the New Revisionists.'' *Columbia Journalism Review* (November/December 1983).

Nixon, Richard. *RN: The Memoirs of Richard Nixon*. New York: Grosset & Dunlap, 1978.

Roberts, Randy, and James S. Olson. *John Wayne, American*. New York: Free Press, 1995.

Schickel, Richard. ''Duke Talks through His Green Beret.'' *Life* (July 19, 1968).

Taylor, Philip. ''*The Green Berets*.'' *History Today* (March 1995).

Weiler, A. H. ''*Green Berets* Triumphant at Box Office.'' *New York Times* (January 3, 1969).

Willenson, Kim. *The Bad War: An Oral History of the Vietnam War*. New York: New American Library, 1987.

Wills, Garry. *John Wayne's America: The Politics of Celebrity*. New York: Simon and Schuster, 1997.

Zolotow, Maurice. *Shooting Star: A Biography of John Wayne*. New York: Simon and Schuster, 1974.

The Hanoi Hilton

Film

Director: Lionel Chetwynd

Screenplay: Lionel Chetwynd

Principal Cast: Michael Moriarty, Jeffrey Jones, Paul Le Mat, Stephen Davies, David Soul

Year of Release: 1987 (Cannon)

Some of the most horrifying stories that came out of Vietnam were told by American aviators who had been taken prisoner by the North Vietnamese. Some of these POWs spent years of their lives in miserable living conditions, buffeted by isolation, torture, and the gnawing fear that they would die inside the prison in which they were held. The most famous of the North Vietnamese prisons was Hoa Lo Prison, commonly referred to as the Hanoi Hilton. Lionel Chetwynd's 1987 film *The Hanoi Hilton* was an attempt to convey the grim realities of imprisonment in that facility. The merits of the work, which painted decidedly unflattering portraits of the American press and antiwar movement, became a subject of hot debate in the months following its release.

HISTORICAL BACKGROUND

Because the Vietnam War was fought on South Vietnamese soil, the numbers of American soldiers who were captured and imprisoned by North Vietnam were relatively few. Of the hundreds of American servicemen who became prisoners of war, then, the vast majority were downed airmen, pilots who had been shot out of the skies of North Vietnam during bombing runs. Beginning with Navy pilot Everett Alvarez, Jr., who was captured in August 1964, the numbers of captured airmen steadily rose, and by 1968 more than three hundred Americans were in North Vietnamese prison camps.

The Communists maintained several camps, many of them in or around Hanoi. These included Cu Loc Prison (dubbed "the Zoo" by the POWs), Xam Ap Lo (the "Briarpatch," where prisoners were tortured to the point of near-insanity), Alcatraz, Plantation Gardens, and the Rockpile. Perhaps the most notorious of the camps, though, was downtown Hanoi's Hoa Lo Prison, which came to be known as the "Hanoi Hilton." Hao Lo Prison, which had been a French penitentiary back in the nineteenth century, was the cornerstone of North Vietnam's POW prison system.

In the years following their return home, American POWs who were imprisoned in the Hilton and elsewhere told harrowing tales of systematic and brutal mistreatment that endured for year after year. (For much of the war, the Communists insisted that their captives were being treated well; at other times they contended that although they believed in the tenets of the Geneva Convention of 1949—which held that prisoners of war should receive "decent and humane" treatment—the Americans who bombed North Vietnam were committing crimes against humanity and were thus not protected by the Geneva guidelines.) The North Vietnamese were unrelenting in their efforts to force prisoners to sign confessions of criminal wrongdoing or broadcast statements that cast their captors in a favorable light.

Treatment of American prisoners varied. Some reported that they were treated humanely, but many reported enduring extensive sessions of torture at the hands of their captors (this latter group often bore physical ailments and scars that supported their contentions). John G. Hubbell's book *P.O.W.: A Definitive History of the American Prisoner-of-War Experience in Vietnam, 1964–1973*, provided many accounts of such incidents, including the following all-too-representative episode, in which Air Force pilot Lawrence Guarino endured savage treatment for day after day: "He was denied sleep, once for a solid week. He was rope-tortured. He was repeatedly flogged with rubber whips. Guards were set upon him to administer long, terrible beatings with their fists. Bamboo clubs were used to smash the cartilage in his shins. He was denied water until he was nearly dehydrated. He was kept in leg irons and on his knees until they were swollen to basketball size, with holes gouged out to the bones. . . . When he confessed to all the things his captors demanded he confess to, he was accused of lying, and the torture went on."

Creeping awareness of the growing domestic tumult over the war rocked the POWs as well. The antiwar movement in America left the prisoners feeling "bewildered, depressed, betrayed," wrote Hubbell. "Many POWs could not fathom the basis for the dissent. They could not understand what was 'treasonous,' 'blasphemous,' or even questionable about helping a small, weak ally resist a forcible Communist takeover." Indeed, most of the prisoners maintained a fierce belief in the legitimacy of the U.S. mission in Vietnam throughout their captivity.

Many American POWs remained defiant even during periods of blackest despair. Sometimes this defiance took dramatic form—as when Navy pilot Jeremiah Denton blinked the word "torture" in Morse Code with his eyelids during a televised interview that was shown in the United States—but on other occasions it manifested itself in a simple determination to maintain dignity and unity no matter how appalling the circumstances. Using the quadratic alphabet, American prisoners adopted inventive codes to communicate with one another from cell to cell through tapping or coughing and other throat-clearing variations. Such communication was a lifeline for many prisoners. "Among the American prisoners in North Vietnam, the appetite for knowledge was insatiable, not merely as a diversion but as an intellectual stimulant, a device to keep their minds from going to seed," wrote Robert Timberg in *The Nightingale's Song*, a book that provided a detailed account of the experiences of POW (and eventual U.S. Senator) John McCain. "The POWs had one mental exercise in common. They committed to memory the name of every prisoner they knew of, which eventually included almost all of the nearly six hundred aviators in captivity. The mind game was serious business. Suspicious of Vietnamese claims that they had made public an accurate prisoner list, the Americans wanted to be ready for any opportunity to smuggle out a complete roster. Instead of counting sheep, John McCain dozed off reciting names to himself."

In late 1969, treatment of American prisoners suddenly improved at some of the camps. Many theories about the impetus for this change have been offered. The 1969 death of Ho Chi Minh, which shocked the people of North Vietnam, is often cited as a factor. Others, meanwhile, feel that Hanoi came to a belated recognition that their stance on the POW issue was hurting the larger war effort. As Hubbell remarked in *P.O.W.*, "Ho seems badly to have misjudged the feeling of the American people for their captured military men. Thus, bitterly divided though America was about the war, he provided the one rallying point around which the most ardent protagonists on both sides of the war issue could unite, the well-being of the POWs. Indeed, it is difficult to imagine how Hanoi, whose purpose with its American prisoners was to exploit them for maximum political gain, could have managed the situation worse than it did."

The Christmas Bombing of Hanoi

In April 1972, in the wake of the North Vietnamese Easter Offensive, American forces resumed their bombing of North Vietnam. American prisoners viewed the new bombing campaign, code-named Operation Linebacker, as a decidedly positive event, because they interpreted it as a signal that the long stalemate that had kept them imprisoned for so long might finally end. "We knew at the time that unless something very forceful was done that we were never going to get out of there," McCain told Timberg. "We were fully aware that the only way we were ever going to get out was for our government to turn the screws on Vietnam. So we were very happy. We were cheering and hollering.'' The sound of the B-52s flying over Hanoi lifted their spirits immeasurably, even though they knew that the bombs might end their lives in an instant. ''Some [prisoners] were so excited that they simply could not bring themselves to lie down, and went several days without any sleep,'' wrote Hubbell. ''Others slept all day, through the tactical aircraft assaults, so as to be able to stay awake all night and watch the big B-52 show.'' By the time the operation was terminated, Air Force, Navy, and Marine air assaults had dropped more than 125,000 tons of bombs.

In the fall of 1972, speculation grew that a significant breakthrough was imminent in discussions between American representative Henry Kissinger and Le Duc Tho, North Vietnam's chief negotiator, at the Paris Peace Talks. And indeed, by October of that year, a basic agreement had been made in which, among other things, American POWs would be freed. South Vietnam's President Nguyen Van Thieu objected to the terms of the proposed agreement, though, and the accord fell apart. Determined to secure a negotiated settlement, President Richard Nixon directed that a new bombing campaign be instituted against Hanoi. This controversial action, code-named Linebacker II and commonly known as the Christmas Bombing, began on December 18 and lasted for eleven days (excluding Christmas day). By the time the last sortie had been flown on December 30, B-52s and other American aircraft had dropped forty thousand tons of bombs.

Kissinger and Le Duc Tho resumed negotiations in early January 1973 and quickly reached agreement on a treaty. Wary that Thieu might object to the terms once again, Nixon sent him a strongly worded warning: ''You must decide now whether you desire to continue our alliance or whether you want me to seek a settlement with the enemy which serves U.S. interests alone.'' Thieu reluctantly fell in line, and the peace agreement was formally signed on January 27, 1973. The accord opened the door for the American POWs, some of whom had been imprisoned for eight or nine years, to finally return home, where they were hailed as heroes. In accordance with the U.S. Military Code of Conduct, which stipulated that prisoners who had been held captive the longest should leave first, the first group of POWs to be flown out of Hanoi included Alvarez.

Controversy over the imprisonment of American soldiers in Indochina has never wholly subsided, however. A significant percentage of the American public came to believe that some U.S. soldiers listed as ''missing in action'' (MIA) continued to be held by their Communist captors after 1973. The U.S. and Vietnamese governments, as well as many other observers, insisted that all POWs had been released, but groups like the National League of Families of American Prisoners and Missing in Southeast Asia formed to push for further investigation. By the mid-1980s the United States government was prodding Vietnam to provide the ''fullest possible accounting'' for American POW/MIAs from the war. Some observers attributed this shift to political opportunism, but others applauded it as an overdue response to the MIA issue. The government of Vietnam, eager to normalize economic and political relations with the United States, subsequently launched a new investigation into their archives for additional information on American MIAs. In 1993 Vietnam released a detailed report on U.S. pilots and soldiers who died in captivity or combat, but these new efforts did little to ease the suspicions of those Americans who believe that U.S. POWs remain in Southeast Asia.

CREATION OF *THE HANOI HILTON*

The Hanoi Hilton is often cited as one of the American films that typified the 1980s-era popular reevaluation of the Vietnam War and the forces that caused U.S. defeat there. Buoyed by a general shift to the right in American politics, as exemplified by Ronald Reagan's two terms as president, conservative interpretations of the war gained new currency. This newly ascendant version of Vietnam held that the war was a just cause carried out by patriotic Americans, but that the cowardice and duplicity of the country's left wing dragged them down to defeat. The *Rambo* trilogy, *Hamburger Hill*, and *The Hanoi Hilton* are among the best known of these works.

Chetwynd's *The Hanoi Hilton* follows the brutal day-to-day existence of a small group of downed American pilots who have been consigned to Hanoi's notorious "Hanoi Hilton." The pilots endure torture, long stretches of solitary confinement, horrible food, and generally wretched conditions at the hands of their cruel captors, but for the most part the POWs refuse to crack. Relying on each other for spiritual strength, the prisoners battle to survive as wave after wave of atrocity and indignity is visited upon them. The awful nature of their plight is intensified by the arrival at the prison of an American antiwar activist and members of the American media. Both the activist (a Jane Fonda-like figure) and the press are characterized as near-treasonous dupes of the North Vietnamese government, pawns in the Communist plan to undermine domestic support for the war in the United States. (At one point in the film, a prison commander proclaims that "This war will not be won in the Delta. We will win it in Berkeley, California, on the Washington Mall. . . . Your journalists will win the war for us.")

CRITICAL REACTION

The Hanoi Hilton endured a poor critical reception from many quarters, as reviewers posted objections both to the film's political leanings and to Chetwynd's execution of the story. Lawrence O'Toole remarked in *Maclean's* that "however well-meaning, Chetwynd's work is crude and pummelling, devoid of subtlety." Other critics were considerably more vituperative. "Anyone can make a boring movie, but it takes real talent—a special aptitude for instilling stupefaction—to make a boring POW movie," wrote *New York* critic David

Denby. "The picture is a dogged celebration of the intrepid American fliers held by the North Vietnamese—a mix of noble suffering, anti-liberal finger-pointing, and sheer exploitation. . . . *The Hanoi Hilton* has the grinding vindictiveness of an old Patrick Buchanan column."

Perhaps the most scathing review of the film was submitted by *New Republic* reviewer Stanley Kauffmann (who alludes that he was a participant in the antiwar movement that the film portrays so negatively). "*The Hanoi Hilton* is filth," he charged. "It exploits the sufferings—and deaths—of American POWs in North Vietnam in order to promote a distortion of history: that the peace movement in the United States and elsewhere prolonged the imprisonment of those men by impeding American victory. . . . For the sufferings of these men, there cannot possibly be anything but compassion, together with respect for their courage. . . . But the point of *The Hanoi Hilton* is elsewhere."

The film did have its defenders. Those who supported the film's central contentions about the character of the antiwar movement and American press coverage of the conflict saw *The Hanoi Hilton* as a welcome antidote to other, more "liberal" accounts of the war, and they noted that the film's viewpoint reflected the attitudes of many American POWs. Other reviewers, meanwhile, contended that the film was a more effective and less reactionary film than its detractors would admit. *Time* critic Richard Schickel wrote that "it is as an earnest attempt to redress a festering grievance, not as film art, that *The Hanoi Hilton* deserves attention," and *Playboy*'s Bruce Williamson called the film a "dynamic drama" that is "inarguably an important picture," whatever one's political orientation.

FURTHER READING

Denby, David. "Flea-Bagged." *New York* (April 13, 1987).

Denton, Jeremiah A. *When Hell Was in Session*. New York: Reader's Digest Press, 1976.

Hubbell, John, with Andrew Jones and Kenneth Y. Tomlinson. *P.O.W.: A Definitive History of the American Prisoner-of-War Experience in Vietnam, 1964–1973*. New York: Reader's Digest Press, 1976.

Kauffmann, Stanley. "Hanoi and Elsewhere." *New Republic* (April 27, 1987).

O'Toole, Lawrence. "Cellmates in Hell." *Maclean's* (May 11, 1987).

Schickel, Richard. Review of *The Hanoi Hilton*. In *Time* (April 13, 1987).

Timberg, Robert. *The Nightingale's Song*. New York: Simon & Schuster, 1995.

Williams, Tony. "Narrative Patterns and Mythic Trajectories in Mid-1980s Vietnam Movies." In *Inventing Vietnam: The War in Film and Television*, Michael Anderegg, ed. Philadelphia: Temple University Press, 1991.

Williamson, Bruce. Review of *Hanoi Hilton*. In *Playboy* (June 1987).

Hearts and Minds

Documentary
Director: Peter Davis
Year of Release: 1974 (Warner Bros.)

Following the withdrawal of American troops from Vietnam in early 1973, the U.S. government quickly turned its attention to other foreign policy issues and the emerging Watergate scandal. Many members of the American media—and even of the antiwar movement—soon followed suit, and the Vietnam War began to fade from the public consciousness. It was into this atmosphere that director Peter Davis released his documentary film *Hearts and Minds*, which he hoped would break through American apathy about the ongoing conflict in Indochina. The film, which "contains probably the most horrendous compilation of war footage ever assembled," according to Peter Biskind in *Cineaste*, powerfully juxtaposes the suffering of the Vietnamese with the actions of U.S. soldiers and policymakers. *Hearts and Minds*, which received an Academy Award for best documentary, was surrounded by controversy both before and after its release.

HISTORICAL BACKGROUND

On March 29, 1973, the U.S. government completed the repatriation of 653 American POWs and the withdrawal of the last twenty-four thousand American troops from Vietnam, thus ending direct U.S. military intervention in Indochina. The conclusion of this chapter in the nation's history was largely attributed to the diplomacy of Secretary of State Henry Kissinger, who had made the withdrawal of troops conditional upon the release of prisoners in the Paris peace agreements.

Immediately after the troop withdrawal was completed, the U.S. government began focusing its attention elsewhere, although it continued to provide significant financial assistance to the Saigon government. Noting in a speech before Congress that "Vietnam no longer distracts our attention from the fundamental issues of global diplomacy," President Richard Nixon proclaimed 1973 to be the "Year of Europe." Meanwhile, Kissinger began making frequent trips to the Middle East in an attempt to negotiate peace between the Arabs and Israelis. "The strategy of the president and his advisers was clear: to reunite America after the divisiveness and debate of Vietnam in order to pursue other foreign policy goals," Samuel Lipsman and Stephen Weiss noted in *The False Peace*. "The method was to encourage the nation in forgetting events in the country the U.S. had spent more than a decade trying to save."

The sudden lack of government interest in Vietnam soon spread to the American media. "The major news media played their role in the new silence about Vietnam," according to Lipsman and Weiss. "With American troops no longer engaged in combat, the Saigon bureaus of countless smaller newspapers closed. Only the country's major periodicals maintained full-time, although reduced, staffs in Saigon." Coverage in weekly news magazines, which for years had devoted special sections to Vietnam, declined to occasional, brief mentions. In fact, Lipsman and Weiss noted that the total amount of media coverage given to Vietnam between June 1973 and December 1974 was less than what normally would have appeared in a single issue of a news weekly during the height of American involvement. "It was difficult for the American people to become concerned about events in Indochina when they were told so little about what was transpiring there," they concluded.

Some observers claimed that many Americans—who had long felt frustrated and embarrassed by the war—were eager to put Vietnam out of their minds. A March 1973 Gallup poll revealed that only 7 percent of American adults placed Vietnam among the country's most important problems, compared to 35 percent who had called it the single most important problem just a few months earlier. Instead, more than half the people surveyed cited the cost of living as the most pressing issue facing the nation. In her book *Winners and Losers*, Gloria Emerson recalled encountering similar attitudes among the average Americans she interviewed about the war: "Some people said that because of Vietnam nothing would ever be the same, but others said this was not true. The war is boring, they said, it is much like having rheumatism, which will not kill you or quite go away. You learn to live with it."

As the war slipped from the American public consciousness—and was replaced by concern about the Watergate scandal—the antiwar movement seemed to lose momentum. "The country became more quiet," Edward Shils remarked in *The Vietnam Legacy*. "Large-scale demonstrations against the war decreased in size and frequency. Riots in the black quarters of the large cities diminished in size and practically halted.... The uproar in the universities also calmed down.'' As Peter Osnos noted in the same volume, ''By the spring of 1973, the Vietnam War had already been largely forgotten by many people.''

CREATION OF *HEARTS AND MINDS*

Producer Bert Schneider originally envisioned the documentary that became *Hearts and Minds* as an examination of the U.S. government's attempts to suppress the Pentagon Papers. He selected Peter Davis—a professor of film at Yale University and director of the hard-hitting 1972 CBS documentary ''The Selling of the Pentagon''—to direct the project. By this time, Nixon had responded to public pressure and withdrawn most American forces from Vietnam. But Schneider and Davis, who remained adamantly against the war even after the ''Vietnamization'' process was complete, were dismayed to note that the American public quickly seemed to lose interest in the conflict after the troops came home—despite the fact that the war continued, with the U.S. government providing support to the South Vietnamese army. ''By the early seventies, we were destroying Indochina as a reflex action; most people didn't even want the war anymore but felt no great pangs about its continuation,'' Davis told Bruce Berman in *Filmmakers Newsletter*. The partners then decided to document the war's effect on the Vietnamese people in ''an attempt to understand what we have done and what we have become,'' as Davis told Walter Goodman of the *New York Times*. ''[The film] is more psychological than political, and it is not a chronology of the war so much as a study of people's feelings.''

Davis began work on *Hearts and Minds* in 1972, backed by a $950,000 budget from Columbia Pictures. He spent the next year conducting interviews and shooting original footage in Vietnam, the United States, and Paris. Davis recalled to Paul D. Zimmerman in *Newsweek* that he tried unsuccessfully to arrange interviews with such prominent American policymakers as Nixon, Kissinger, and former Secretary of Defense Robert McNamara, but ''none of them believed themselves obliged to account for their actions, not then, not now.'' After adding existing newsreel footage, interviews, and clips from Hollywood fiction films to his new material, the director edited 250 hours of footage into a 115-minute final product.

Hearts and Minds, which *New York Times* reviewer Stephanie Harrington described as ''a montage of the mistakes, foolishness, tragedy and sheer horror in Vietnam contrasted with the self-absorbed complacency of many Americans at home,'' consists of an often chaotic series of images that illuminate the Vietnamese perspective on the war. Rather than following any sort of chronology, Davis instead juxtaposes various images to support his contentions about the immorality of American involvement. The film opens with an idyllic scene in a traditional, rural Vietnamese village, as a horse-drawn cart meanders down a dirt track. Eventually a few American soldiers pass by, but none of the villagers appears to take notice. ''The idea of the opening of the film is to bring you into a different world . . . to suspend the world you are normally familiar with and learn about something else . . . to initiate audiences into the reality of Vietnam,'' Davis explained to Berman.

In one of the most controversial sequences in the film, Davis juxtaposes scenes of a Vietnamese family grieving at a funeral—during which a young boy clutches a framed photograph of the deceased, and the despondent widow must be restrained from climbing into the grave—with an interview with General William Westmoreland, commander of the U.S. troops in Vietnam. Wearing civilian attire and standing in a garden, Westmoreland opines that ''the Oriental does not put the same high value on human life as does the Westerner.'' The film then cuts immediately to the famous footage of a young Vietnamese girl, her body seriously burned, running naked from her napalmed village. By using scenes that directly contradict Westmoreland's statement, several reviewers noted, Davis intentionally undermines his credibility and suggests that it is actually the Americans who are complacent about death.

Another well-known sequence in *Hearts and Minds* involves a festive White House banquet honoring returned American POWs, at which Nixon calls for a round of applause for the pilots who conducted the Christmas bombing of Hanoi. Davis follows this scene with several depicting the consequences of the bombing, such as a hospital reduced to rubble and a father mourning the loss of his two young children. In other sequences, Harrington wrote, Davis ''searches our national myths for the sources of our brutality in Vietnam.'' For example, he juxtaposes violent scenes from American culture—including World War II movies and a high school football game—with scenes showing the brutality and racism of some American soldiers toward the Vietnamese. The film's final scene depicts a Fourth of July parade in Middle America. When a small group of people begin demonstrating on the sideline, the crowd and parade participants jeer and make obscene gestures toward them. After the credits roll, the demonstrators are revealed to be Vietnam veterans protesting their inability to obtain jobs.

Hearts and Minds premiered at the 1974 Cannes Film Festival and received laudatory reviews. ''When I made the movie,'' Davis admitted to Zimmerman, ''I thought people would pay handsomely *not* to be reminded of the war. Cannes was the first indication that I might be wrong.'' Despite the film's success at Cannes, however, Columbia delayed its American release out of concern that it would provoke lawsuits by some of the individuals who appeared onscreen. Indeed, Walt Rostow—a former advisor to Presidents Kennedy and Johnson who is shown arguing with an interviewer who questions his support for American involvement in Vietnam—obtained a temporary restraining order to prevent the film's release but ultimately lost his case. Eventually Warner Bros. purchased the rights to *Hearts and Minds* and made it the first Vietnam documentary to be released by a major distributor.

In its initial, limited release, the film did not attract much attention. But this situation changed dramatically after *Hearts and Minds* received a 1975 Academy

Award as best documentary. In his nationally televised acceptance speech, producer Schneider outraged many Americans by reading "greetings of friendship" from a Vietcong official and referring to the impending "liberation" of South Vietnam by the Communists. NBC affiliates were swamped with calls of protest, and ceremony hosts Bob Hope and Frank Sinatra presented a hasty disclaimer stating that the Academy was not responsible for the political opinions expressed by winners during the show. The disclaimer, in turn, outraged several liberal, antiwar members of the Academy, who took advantage of opportunities later in the broadcast to express their views.

Schneider told Stephen Farber of the *New York Times* that his acceptance speech "wasn't done to create controversy. I simply wanted to take the opportunity to transmit a message to 65 million Americans. The American government's propaganda machinery is very powerful, and the message of the Vietnamese people is usually buried." Nonetheless, Schneider was pleased by all the attention the resulting uproar brought to his message. "Sinatra and Hope are like Walt Rostow in terms of heightening consciousness. Rostow helped the movie and helped the peace movement by trying to censor our film; he made sure that more people knew about it. And Sinatra and Hope are wonderful for the same reason. They call attention to the issues. The more air time that I can take advantage of, the better, because it all helps our cause," he noted to Farber. In fact, the box office receipts for *Hearts and Minds* tripled in Los Angeles and doubled in New York in the weeks following the Academy Awards broadcast.

Both Schneider and Davis were pleased by the reception the film received from audiences. "I have met hundreds of people from the peace movement who said, 'I never thought I could see anything about Vietnam at this stage that could have an effect on me. But the movie really rekindled my concern, and it shed new light,' " Schneider related to Farber. "The film has also had a very direct political effect. We opened the film in Washington, and at that time the debate was on over additional aid to the Thieu government. I know that *Hearts and Minds* had an influence on the consciousness of those Congressmen and Senators who saw it." Davis was particularly gratified by the film's effect on average Americans who did not hold strong opinions for or against the Vietnam War. "They come away with serious questions and they do more thinking as a result of seeing the film," he explained to Zimmerman. "It's this audience that gives me both pleasure as a filmmaker and hope as an American. These are the people I want the film to reach: those who may not have thought very much about the war but who have that peculiarly healthy American trait of doubt."

CRITICAL RECEPTION

True to the controversy that had surrounded it, *Hearts and Minds* received both glowing and scathing reviews upon its release. Zimmerman called it "a thoroughly committed, brilliantly executed and profoundly moving document," and noted that "unlike our leaders who encourage us to put Vietnam behind us,

Davis wants us to confront our feelings about it first and to understand the experience before we bury it. We turn away from this portrait of ourselves at our peril." Similarly, Pulitzer Prize-winning Vietnam correspondent Frances FitzGerald told Harrington that *Hearts and Minds* "is the most moving film I've ever seen on Vietnam, because, for the first time, the camera lingers on the faces of Vietnamese and one hears their voices."

Some reviewers praised the filmmakers' implication that American culture—and therefore average Americans, rather than just government policymakers—was partly to blame for the tragedy in Vietnam. According to *Film Quarterly* writer Bernard Weiner, the film provides "a stunning, searing indictment not only of the American policy makers who enmeshed the U.S. in the Vietnam quagmire, but of America itself and the racist militarist-macho mentality that led and/or permitted those leaders to execute such policy—and, unless changed, will lead inevitably to more such imperialist incursions." In his *Cineaste* review, Biskind added that "*Hearts and Minds* truly brings the war home. In the process, it reveals the furnishings of this home to be shabby and mean, for its target is not only American policy in Vietnam, but the American experience itself. It looks for the sources of the war in the arrogant, violent, hypocritical side of American culture. . . . American rulers, monstrous as they appear in the film, become less authors of a genocidal culture than its agent, no better nor worse than the people they rule."

Other reviewers condemned this aspect of the film and claimed that Davis presented a one-sided picture of the war. "The camera's harrowing examination of soldiers and beggars, or coffinmakers and grieving fathers, displays an abiding sense of pity and outrage. But when the camera swings to the Anglo-Saxon side of the Pacific, compassion is jettisoned," Stefan Kanfer wrote in *Time*. "Nations and wars are too complex for such simplism. . . . And the righteous indignation may tend to blind the documentary filmmaker to his prime task: the representation of life in all its fullness, not only those incidents that conform to his thesis." A reviewer for the *Nation* agreed, noting that *Hearts and Minds* "makes no pretense of being an even-handed report. . . . It operates to arouse hatred against hatred, to induce a gut reaction against gut reactions, and by so doing serves to sustain a morbid emotionalism of the very sort it claims to abominate. . . . We need to armor ourselves with understanding, and to that end the film contributes nothing. Worse, it encourages the luxury of blinding hatred, which becomes a substitute for understanding."

Other criticisms of the film centered around Davis's intentional juxtaposition of certain images in order to make a political point. Some reviewers claimed that this technique manipulated viewers and turned the film into a propaganda piece rather than a documentary. "*Hearts and Minds* is the product of talented filmmakers caught between clashing impulses—to produce a work of art or to advance a political argument," Goodman commented. "When these filmmakers focus on human beings, they give us moments of depth and beauty; when they force a tendentious thesis upon us, they diminish their film. Even if they had resisted the temptation to score elementary points, *Hearts and Minds* would still have been propaganda—but it would have been something much more as well. Peter Davis and his colleagues may have had their hearts in the right place, but they did not trust the minds of their audience.''

M. J. Sobran, Jr., writing in the *National Review*, claimed that the filmmakers conveniently omitted information that would contradict their view of the war. ''There is of course no depiction of Communist savagery, nor any hint that there is such a thing. . . . The filmmakers would acknowledge no suffering, no death, on which they couldn't grind their axe,'' he stated. ''It is this pro-Communist blindness, this refusal to try to see the war whole, that makes this film . . . a cinematic lie.'' Responding to critics who dismissed *Hearts and Minds* as one-sided Communist propaganda, Schneider told Farber, ''I don't understand what that means. Is Picasso's 'Guernica' Communist propaganda? If I say the sun comes up in the east and sets in the west, and we discover that Karl Marx also said that, am I a tool of the Communists? I used to see that kind of thing when the McCarthy investigations were taking place—guilt by association.''

FURTHER READING

Barnouw, Erik. *Documentary: A History of Nonfiction Film*. New York: Oxford University Press, 1993.

Berman, Bruce. ''The Making of *Hearts and Minds*.'' *Filmmakers Newsletter* (April 1975).

Biskind, Peter. Review of *Hearts and Minds*. In *Cineaste* (Fall 1975).

Emerson, Gloria. *Winners and Losers*. New York: Random House, 1976.

Farber, Stephen. ''The Man Who Brought Us Greetings from the Vietcong.'' *New York Times* (May 4, 1975).

Goodman, Walter. ''The False Art of the Propaganda Film.'' *New York Times* (March 23, 1975).

Grosser, David. '' 'We Aren't on the Wrong Side, We Are the Wrong Side': Peter Davis Targets (American) Hearts and Minds.'' In *From Hanoi to Hollywood: The Vietnam War in American Film*, Linda Dittmar and Gene Michaud, eds. New Brunswick, N.J.: Rutgers University Press, 1990.

Hallin, Daniel. *The Uncensored War*. New York: Oxford University Press, 1986.

Harrington, Stephanie. ''First an Undeclared War, Now an Unseen Film.'' *New York Times* (November 17, 1974).

Kanfer, Stefan. ''War-Torn.'' *Time* (March 17, 1975).

Kauffmann, Stanley. Review of *Hearts and Minds*. In *New Republic* (March 15, 1975).

Lipsman, Samuel, and Stephen Weiss. *The False Peace, 1972–1974*. Boston: Boston Publishing Company, 1985.

Osnos, Peter. ''The War and Riverdale.'' In *The Vietnam Legacy*, Anthony Lake, ed. New York: New York University Press, 1976.

Review of *Hearts and Minds*. In *Nation* (April 12, 1975).

Shils, Edward. ''American Society and the War in Indochina.'' In *The Vietnam Legacy*, Anthony Lake, ed. New York: New York University Press, 1976.

Sobran, M. J., Jr., ''Heartless and Mindless.'' *National Review* (June 6, 1975).

Wall, James M. "American Hearts and Minds Deceived." Editorial in *Christian Century* (April 16, 1975).

Weiner, Bernard. Review of *Hearts and Minds*. In *Film Quarterly* (Winter 1974–75).

Zimmerman, Paul D. "Faces of War." *Newsweek* (March 3, 1975).

Home before Morning

Nonfiction

Author: Lynda Van Devanter, with Christopher Morgan

Facts of Publication: New York: Beaufort Books, 1983

The body of literature detailing the experiences of American combat soldiers in the Vietnam War is an extensive one, and these works—whether memoirs, novels, poems, or plays—are widely credited with helping Americans come to a better understanding of the tumultuous experiences of Vietnam veterans. The experiences of the American women who served in Vietnam, however, went largely undocumented until the 1983 publication of Lynda Van Devanter's *Home before Morning: The Story of an Army Nurse in Vietnam*. In subsequent years—aided in part by Van Devanter's activism on behalf of women veterans— the often harrowing experiences of the nurses and other female personnel who endured Vietnam (including civilians with such organizations as the Red Cross and the Agency for International Development) have been studied more closely. This examination has spurred a greater appreciation of the sacrifices they made on behalf of their country.

HISTORICAL BACKGROUND

Government statistics are decidedly lacking in documenting the number of American nurses who served in Vietnam. Some sources have estimated that as many as fifty thousand nurses tended to wounded and dying soldiers in Vietnam, but others contend that only a fraction of that number served there during the war. American women also served in nonmedical capacities, working as secretaries, clerks, air traffic controllers, cartographers, decoders, and photographers. But the most-visible occupations—and the most emotionally draining—were in nursing and other medical fields.

The nurses who cared for the wounded in Vietnam worked under circumstances that were in many respects quite different from those of previous American wars. Advances in medical technology, coupled with the evacuation capacities of helicopters and the proximity of battlefield to hospital, often saved soldiers who would have expired in previous wars. But while the percentage of wounded soldiers who survived in Vietnam was greater than that in conflicts such as the Korean War or World War II, their bodies were far more likely to be fundamentally scarred by the war. "In Vietnam," wrote Laura Palmer in *New York Times Magazine*, "a gunshot wound to the chest was a routine wound. Land mines, grenades, rockets and mortars mauled, maimed and mutilated the youngest soldiers America ever sent into combat." Indeed, the average U.S. soldier in Vietnam was nineteen, about seven years younger than his World War II counterpart.

The thousands of young women who were sent to Vietnam to care for such men "were as prepared for the war as the geese that fly into the engines of a 747," wrote Palmer. "The war the women fought was different [than the war seen on the evening news]. It imploded. There was no film footage of the relentless horror that was hidden in the hospitals." Even nurses with experience in trauma units back in the United States were shocked by the wounds they regularly confronted in Indochina. "[The injuries were] more like a grotesque form of 'can you top this,' because each time you thought you'd seen the ultimate, something else would come along," said Ruth Sidisin in Kathryn Marshall's *In the Combat Zone*. "I remember one young man with beautiful blonde hair who came in blinded and missing one of his arms and both of his legs. He also had a belly wound. Well, thank God he couldn't see my face when he said, 'Nurse, today's my twenty-first birthday.' Because that was one of those times when you just couldn't have let them see it. When you smiled and smiled while you were there taking care of them so that afterward you could go home to your hootch and cry."

Confronted with such wide-scale misery, many nurses struggled with depression and other maladies. "Unlike the soldiers the women nurses had no release from the fear and anger," noted Shelley Saywell in *Women in War*. "The sexual double standard followed them to Vietnam. Women, especially nurses, were expected not only to deal with their own emotion but also to nurture and comfort and understand the emotions of the men they treated and served with. There was little or no psychiatric help for them in Vietnam. Indulging in normal releases, like sex, merely slandered the reputation of women in the army." This latter aspect of the American servicewoman's experience in Vietnam would prove to be a source of lingering pain for many nurses years after their return to America.

The nurses did experience moments of exultation, moments in which their talents and dedication made the difference between life and death for a soldier. But the nightmarish aspects of their experiences in Vietnam often overshadowed such instances, and many women veterans—like their male counterparts—found it difficult to reintegrate themselves into the ''World'' back in America when their tours were up. This difficulty stemmed in large measure from the belief that they had to sublimate their anger and sorrow, just as they had done during their tours. ''The need to talk was perhaps the single most overwhelming need of the men and women who had gone to the Vietnam War,'' wrote Marshall. ''But if talking was hard for the men, it was harder for the women.'' Isolated by their smaller numbers and the inattention of veterans' organizations, women veterans often coped with post-traumatic stress disorder (PTSD) and other fallout from their wartime experiences alone. ''The mind-set from Vietnam is that the grunts were the ones paying the price,'' former Army nurse Joan Furey told Palmer. ''And I don't dismiss that. What I had to learn, and what we have to teach the women we treat now, is that acknowledging the stress of your own experiences does not diminish anyone else's.''

VAN DEVANTER AND VIETNAM

Lynda Van Devanter recalled that she volunteered to go to Vietnam out of a mixture of patriotism and the conviction that her talents could make a difference. After completing the six-week basic training course that was required of all Vietnam nurses, she flew to Saigon in June 1969, the year in which American troop strength in the country was at its peak. She was assigned to the 71st Evacuation Hospital in Pleiku Province, a region close to the Cambodian border that was, she later wrote in her memoir, known as ''an area of heavy combat [in which] the casualties were supposedly unending.''

During the first weeks of her year-long tour, Van Devanter maintained her long-held belief in the legitimacy of America's intervention in Vietnam, but the steady influx of brutally mutilated young soldiers eroded her faith. ''I started listening to the local discontents who railed against Nixon, Congress, the joint chiefs of staff, and the whole U.S. government. Every time another person died on my table, I came one step closer to agreeing with them,'' she wrote in *Home before Morning*. ''I still tried to remind myself that we were in Vietnam to save people who were threatened by tyranny, but that became more and more difficult to believe as I heard stories of corrupt South Vietnamese officials, U.S. Army atrocities, and a population who wanted nothing more than to be left alone so they could return to farming their land.''

The daily grind at the 71st Evacuation Hospital gradually took a toll on Van Devanter. ''As the casualties kept coming in a seemingly endless torrent of human flesh, I began feeling as if I were turning into an old woman. We were living by a different clock in Pleiku, and learning that chronological age has little correlation with how old some people feel. Holding the hand of one dying boy could age a person ten years. Holding dozens of hands could thrust a person past senility in a matter of weeks.'' The war impacted her in other ways as well. She found that a dark hatred for the Vietnamese had blossomed in her heart, and that the vicious nature of the conflict sparked a thirst for companionship that often ended in further heartache.

Upon returning home to the United States at the conclusion of her tour, Van Devanter was rocked by the domestic atmosphere and her inability to put the haunting memories of the war behind her. She felt the same sting of indifference and outright hostility from her countrymen that male Vietnam veterans endured during that period, and she indicated that the passage of years did nothing to ease the pain that had accumulated during her stay at Pleiku. ''For years I tried to talk about it,'' she wrote. ''Nobody listened. Who would have wanted to listen? Mine were not nice, neat stories. . . . The stories, even the funny ones, were all dirty. They were rotten and they stank. The moments, good and bad, were permeated with the stench of death and napalm.''

CREATION OF *HOME BEFORE MORNING*

Van Devanter began work on *Home before Morning* in 1979 as a therapeutic exercise. ''I was hoping somehow to exorcize the Vietnam war from my mind and heart,'' she wrote. But as the work progressed, she found that although the project did not excise the wounds of that conflict, it did help her to gain a greater acceptance of her experiences there. ''My story is only my own, but many other women and men shared similar experiences both during and after the war. I hope to let them know that they are not alone, and that they, too, can find the way back home.''

In the 1980s Van Devanter also emerged as an early and highly visible advocate on behalf of the nurses and other female personnel who served in Vietnam. In November 1980 she assumed leadership of the Vietnam Veterans of America Women's Project, which sought to give both help and recognition to female veterans. Over the next few years a number of other veterans' organizations (such as Disabled American Veterans and the Veterans' Administration-sponsored Vietnam Veterans' Outreach Program) followed suit, increasing their efforts to reach nurses and other women who had been in the war. By the middle of the decade, support groups for women veterans—though scattered—were thriving. In 1993 the Vietnam War service of American women was officially recognized with the dedication of the Vietnam Women's Memorial in Washington, D.C.

CRITICAL REACTION

Home before Morning garnered generally positive reviews from literary critics, though it did not receive nearly the same level of attention as did *Fields of Fire, A Rumor of War*, and other Vietnam combat memoirs. *Atlantic* reviewer Phoebe-Lou Adams, who noted that Van Devanter's book marked one of the first instances in which the experiences of Vietnam nurses had been documented, suggested that the memoir filled that void in powerful fashion: ''Three days after [Van Devanter] arrived in Vietnam, she was at work in an evacuation hospital where enemy sniping and shelling were commonplace, frightening but less distressing than the streams of mangled casualties over whom the staff toiled for twenty-four hours at a stretch, falling asleep in blood-stiffened uniforms only to scramble up and start again. . . . Not much has been reported about the women veterans of Vietnam. Much of this book is sickening, but it should be read.'' Critic Helen Rogan agreed, writing in *Harper's* that ''this book reads like a diary: unguarded, heartfelt. The style can be clichéd or ungainly, and some of the gruesome parts are quite horrible to read. But finally the book is both moving and valuable, for reminding us so vividly that war is indeed hell.''

The publication of *Home before Morning* also marked a turning point for some Vietnam nurses who had returned home and stayed silent about their service, isolated by their outsider status among veterans groups and their conviction that any attempts to broach the subject would be rebuffed. One nurse who had served in Vietnam in the early 1970s recalled in an interview for Marshall's *In the Combat Zone* that the discovery of Van Devanter's memoir had a tremendous impact on her. ''[A Vietnam veteran friend] went home and got this book,'' she said. ''It's *Home before Morning*, which I had never heard of. I took it home and started to read it. Only I couldn't read it. Because every time I read a page I'd start to see things and start to cry. I kept saying to myself, 'I can't believe this. I can't believe someone else is feeling the same things I am.' Because, all those years, I'd thought I was the only one.''

The book did have its detractors, however. Although many Vietnam nurses embraced the book, some nurses argued that Van Devanter exaggerated her experiences. Myra MacPherson noted in *Long Time Passing* that some other nurses—and especially those who maintained their belief in the legitimacy of the war—suggested that Van Devanter distorted her story in order to further her antiwar agenda. Van Devanter flatly rejected such charges. ''These people would obviously prefer that I had written a book that said we were saints and angels and everything was wonderful,'' she told MacPherson. ''They're trying to write revisionist history.''

FURTHER READING

Adams, Phoebe-Lou. Review of *Home before Morning*. In *Atlantic* (May 1983).

MacPherson, Myra. *Long Time Passing: Vietnam and the Haunted Generation*. New York: Doubleday, 1984.

Marshall, Kathryn. *In the Combat Zone: An Oral History of American Women in Vietnam*. Boston: Little, Brown, 1987.

Norman, Elizabeth M. *Women at War: The Story of Fifty Military Nurses Who Served in Vietnam*. Philadelphia: University of Pennsylvania Press, 1990.

Palmer, Laura. ''The Nurses of Vietnam, Still Wounded: Only Now Are They Healing Themselves.'' *New York Times Magazine* (November 7, 1993).

Rogan, Helen. Review of *Home before Morning*. In *Harper's* (May 1983).

Saywell, Shelley. *Women in War*. New York: Viking, 1985.
Van Devanter, Lynda, with Christopher Morgan. *Home before Morning: The Story of an Army Nurse in Vietnam*. New York: Beaufort Books, 1983.
Walker, Keith. *A Piece of My Heart: The Stories of Twenty-Six American Women Who Served in Vietnam*. Novato, Calif.: Presidio, 1985.

In Country

Novel

Author: Bobbie Ann Mason

Facts of Publication: New York: Harper & Row, 1985

In November 1982 the Vietnam Veterans Memorial was dedicated in Washington, D.C. The design of the "Wall," as it was commonly known, had been the subject of intense debate over the previous eighteen months. But the controversy faded with the passing of the years, and the Memorial now stands as one of the country's most revered places, treasured by both comrades and relatives of those who are memorialized there. Three years after the dedication of the Wall, writer Bobbie Ann Mason used the Memorial as the setting for the climactic scene in *In Country*, her novel about the war's impact on one Kentucky family.

HISTORICAL BACKGROUND

In 1979 Jan Scruggs, a Vietnam veteran who still carried shrapnel in his leg from a 1969 rocket-propelled grenade attack, saw the film *The Deer Hunter*. Shaken by the work's story and imagery, he told his wife a day later that he wanted to build a memorial to the American men and women who had died in Vietnam. He envisioned the memorial as one that would make no political statements about the legitimacy of American involvement in the conflict; it would simply pay tribute to the men and women who had perished there. He subsequently established the Vietnam Veterans Memorial Fund in hopes of building the memorial with private donations rather than government funding.

"There was a great deal of difficulty in getting this project off the ground,"

Scruggs recalled in *Writings on the Wall*. "Most Vietnam veterans were primarily concerned with jobs, Agent Orange and other issues relating to themselves. I argued that the recognition a memorial would bring about would help the veterans on other issues. Everyone was skeptical, but I was totally obsessed with the idea of placing the names of all 58,000 Vietnam War deaths on the Memorial."

After a slow start, the fund surged toward its $1 million goal (nearly $10 million was eventually raised). Scruggs and a number of volunteers dedicated many hours to the project, and the U.S. Senate passed a bill that set aside two acres on the Mall in Constitution Gardens—between the Washington and Lincoln memorials—for the proposed memorial. In the summer of 1980 President Jimmy Carter signed the bill into law. In August 1980 it was announced that a nationwide competition would be held to determine the design of the memorial. A jury of eight judges with impressive credentials in the realms of architecture and sculpture was assembled. None of the judges had served in Vietnam, however, a fact that would later be discussed at great length.

On May 1, 1981, nearly one year after the competition had commenced, the jury announced the winner from the more than 1,400 entries that had been submitted. The winning design was created by Maya Lin, a young, Chinese-American art student at Yale University. Lin's design called for a black V-shaped wall of polished granite, on which the names of all dead or missing-in-action Americans from Vietnam would be engraved. The design was a decided departure from the traditional memorial designs with which Americans were familiar, and a firestorm of controversy immediately erupted over its selection. Some people were puzzled by the choice; others were furious about it. A number of national publications denounced the design as a nihilistic affront to those who had fought in the war, and many Vietnam vets spoke up against it as a final slap in the face (opponents of the design described it at various times as a "black gash of shame," "black hole for the dead," and "black flagless pit"). Other veterans defended the design with equal vigor. "The battle had been joined, though the lines were blurred," wrote Vietnam veteran Robert Timberg in *The Nightingale's Song*. "The American Legion endorsed the design; the Marine Corps League withdrew its support, calling the design 'an insult to the memory of those it is intended to memorialize.' . . . Veteran was pitted against veteran."

In an interview with filmmaker Freida Lee Mock for her Oscar-winning documentary, *Maya Lin: A Strong Clear Vision*, Scruggs recalled the controversy and its impact on Lin with sadness. "She won this competition very, very fairly, and very honestly," he said. "She was treated very poorly, some of the opponents made some innuendos about her nationality, about being Asian, that was a very ugly thing. I'm very sorry she had to put up with that." Lin admitted that the turmoil shook her, but she told Jim Sexton in *USA Weekend* that she never lost faith in her vision. "I designed it so that a child a hundred years from now will still be able to go to that piece and have a sober understanding about a high price of the war.''

As the dedication date for the Wall drew near (Veterans Day weekend, 1982), the two sides finally agreed on a compromise in which a statue of three young soldiers representing a cross-section of American ethnicity would be added to the two-acre plot (an American flag was also added to the area). Perhaps inevitably, the statue, which was designed by Frederick Hart, triggered controversy as well. Lin argued that the statue's fundamental stylistic differences with her own work detracted from both pieces, and there was a period when it was uncertain whether the Fund would pay for Hart's statue. Finally, though, the Memorial was dedicated as scheduled, in November 1982. (A statue by sculptor Glenna Goodacre commemorating the service of Vietnam War nurses was added to the grounds in 1993.)

Within months of the dedication of the Wall, a fundamental reappraisal of its merits seemed to take place, as thousands of Americans who had lost family members and friends in the war made their own judgment. ''No one involved with the creation of the Vietnam Veterans Memorial had any idea of how significant it would become,'' wrote Laura Palmer in *Shrapnel in the Heart*. ''Jan Scruggs thought it would initially attract thousands of visitors but then would turn into just another pretty place to play frisbee on the Mall. No one anticipated that nearly twenty million Americans would visit it during its first five years.'' As Palmer and many others have noted, instead of fading anonymously into the capital's forest of statuary, the Vietnam Veterans Memorial became the place where America began to come to terms with the war and its devastating toll.

The Wall, wrote Sexton, ''evokes silence, contemplation, regret and, say those who visit, a kind of healing.'' Indeed, visitors to the Wall have remarked that its interactive elements are a vital component of the overall design. They observe that the Memorial's mirror-like surface, which reflects the faces of its visitors, and the engraved names, which can be touched or traced on paper, provide a sense of intimacy with their lost sons or brothers or buddies that more traditional memorials could never provide. The design also made it possible for visitors to leave offerings—whether flowers, photographs, letters, or other mementos—and such gifts quickly became a part of the memorial as well.

Now, more than twenty years after the fall of Saigon, the Vietnam Veterans Memorial continues to stand as the most heavily visited Park Service site in Washington, D.C. ''How could this memorial have once been the focal point of such controversy?'' wrote Congressman David Bonier in *Writings on the Wall*. ''It is now the most revered monument in Washington. . . . My hope is that as the years move along, this monument will continue to play its healing role and will continue to be the place, above all others, where America remembers the sacrifice of those who served their country with such courage.''

CREATION OF *IN COUNTRY*

Bobbie Ann Mason was already an established short story writer when she began work on *In Country*. Her tale of Samantha—a seventeen-year-old girl from Kentucky—and her uncle Emmett—an emotionally and physically scarred veteran of Vietnam—was originally envisioned as a short story as well, with Emmett serving as a peripheral character. But after she decided to make Samantha's dead father a casualty of Vietnam, the focus of the story—which was shaping up as a novel at this point—turned to the war.

Still, Mason had difficulty confronting the issues surrounding that troubled period. "What did I know?" she told interviewer Eric James Schroeder. "I was a girl, I had never been to Vietnam. I felt intimidated writing about the subject. And questioning a little bit whether I had the right to get into that."

In 1983, though, Mason visited the Vietnam Veterans Memorial. The experience helped her come to terms with the ambivalence she felt about tackling Vietnam as a topic. "I guess this event was a turning point for me because then I felt it was something that touched every American, and I was an American, and I had the right to tell our story," she recalled to Schroeder. "I was able to have [Vietnam] surface in my consciousness at the same time it was starting to come out in everyone else's. The finishing of the wall was a sign of this, and everywhere you started to see people getting concerned. The book became a mirror."

In Country tells the story of Sam, a teenage girl on the cusp of adulthood who lost her father years ago in Vietnam. She lives with her uncle Emmett, an emotionally haunted veteran who also suffers from symptoms associated with exposure to Agent Orange. Sam's interest in the war that killed her father is triggered by the commencement speech at her high school graduation. The speech's message of self-sacrifice and American preeminence echoes themes that were frequently employed during the war, and in the months following graduation Sam's interest in learning about Vietnam becomes obsessive. Her inquiries about Vietnam are rebuffed by Emmett and others in the small town in which she lives, but she perseveres, eventually striking up a relationship with another veteran.

At times Sam's pursuit of an understanding of Vietnam leads her to draw simplistic conclusions about the war and its participants (at one point she erroneously decides that her uncle's current difficulties stem from a war-bred appetite for killing). But as she continues with her struggles to understand the war, she comes to realize that America's experiences in Vietnam had many layers, some of them dark and unsightly, but others based on honorable ideals and human frailties. One night she camps out deep in the woods in an attempt to gain a sense of "grunt" existence. Her experiment is an utter failure, but it does provide her with greater insight into the ghosts that torment her uncle. After finding her, he recounts a harrowing experience from the war in which he was forced to hide underneath the bodies of his comrades to survive. Haunted by his survival, he admits to Sam that "I'm damaged. It's like something in the center of my heart is gone and I can't get it back."

The novel culminates with Sam's visit to the Vietnam Veterans Memorial with her uncle and her paternal grandmother. The dark, sleek wall has a dramatic impact on both Sam and Emmett, still chained to the wounds that the war visited upon him years before. After finding her father's name on the wall, Sam sees her own name—SAM A. HUGHES—embedded in the dark stone. She touches the name tentatively, reflecting on "how odd it feels, as though all the names in America have been used to decorate this wall."

Sam's uncle, meanwhile, "undergoes a more profound, almost phoenix-like rebirth," wrote Robert H. Brinkmeyer, Jr. in *The Southern Literary Journal*. "As he sits cross-legged before the wall, searching out the names of those with whom he fought, 'his face bursts into a smile like flames.' In finally confronting the terrors of his past, Emmett is ready to forge a new life, something he has been resisting since his return from Vietnam."

CRITICAL RECEPTION

In Country received generally favorable reviews, as critics applauded Mason's careful characterizations and her exploration of the still-felt repercussions of the war on America. Patrick Parrinder, writing in the *London Review of Books*, remarked that "*In Country* will doubtless be seen by some readers as uncomfortably moralistic. . . . But this is a courageous and poignant first novel, a moral fable by a writer unafraid of sentiment—the climax comes with the characters' visit to the Vietnam Memorial—and capable also of expressing a precise and disciplined anger." Brinkmeyer concurred, calling the novel a "profound probing of the darker sides of our national experience." He was particularly struck by the struggles of Mason's primary characters—Sam and Emmett—to understand and emerge from their personal and family histories. "For both characters," he wrote, "vision can come not by simply mouthing platitudes of allegiance or praise for heroism, but by grappling with the complexities and dilemmas of their inheritance."

Other reviewers, however, contended that Mason was not wholly successful in her examination of Vietnam's continued impact on American society and its families. Thomas de Pietro, writing in *Commonweal*, noted that "though Mason begins with an admirable goal—to understand the aftershock of that horrible war abroad and those parlous times at home—she ends up trivializing both past and present." He goes on to charge that Mason too often substitutes pop culture references for genuine exposition of her characters' emotions, employing a sort of "emotional shorthand. . . . Next to a pop masterpiece like 'Born in the U.S.A.' or even *M*A*S*H*, *In Country* seems bloated, condescending to its characters, pretentious in its feigned naïveté."

In 1989, four years after the publication of Mason's novel, a film adaptation of *In Country* was released. The film—also called *In Country*—received mixed reviews, but the performances of Bruce Willis (as Emmett) and especially Emily Lloyd (as Sam) were widely praised.

FURTHER READING

Brinkmeyer, Robert H., Jr. "Finding One's History: Bobbie Ann Mason and Contemporary Southern Literature." *The Southern Literary Journal* (Spring 1987).

de Pietro, Thomas. "In Quest of the Bloody Truth." *Commonweal* (November 1, 1985).

Lin, Maya. "America Remembers." *National Geographic* (May 1985).

Mason, Bobbie Ann. *In Country.* New York: Harper, 1985.

Palmer, Laura. *Shrapnel in the Heart: Letters and Remembrances from the Vietnam Veterans Memorial.* New York: Random House, 1987.

Parrinder, Patrick. "Lost in the Funhouse." *London Review of Books* (April 17, 1986).

Schroeder, Eric James. *Vietnam, We've All Been There: Interviews with American Writers.* Westport, Conn.: Praeger, 1992.

Scruggs, Jan. *To Heal a Nation: The Vietnam Veterans Memorial.* New York: Harper & Row, 1985.

———. *Writings on the Wall.* Vietnam Veterans Memorial Fund, 1994.

Sexton, Jim. "Maya Lin: Making Art That Heals." *USA Weekend* (November 1–3, 1996).

Sterba, James P. "Stop That Monument." *National Review* (September 18, 1981).

Timberg, Robert. *The Nightingale's Song.* New York: Simon & Schuster, 1995.

Wolfe, Tom. "Art Disputes War: The Battle of the Vietnam Memorial." *Washington Post* (October 13, 1982).

In Pharaoh's Army

Nonfiction

Author: Tobias Wolff

Facts of Publication: New York: Alfred A. Knopf, 1994

In 1994 acclaimed short-story writer and memoirist Tobias Wolff released *In Pharaoh's Army*, an account of his military service as an advisor to a South Vietnamese army unit during parts of 1967 and 1968. In contrast to many other books and films about the war, in which carnage and death shadow every moment of the narrative, Wolff's memoir included few violent scenes. But the book nonetheless pondered several significant aspects of the war, from the shortcomings of South Vietnamese military officers to the psychological significance of the Tet Offensive to the feelings of guilt and loss that veterans experience when thinking of those comrades who did not survive.

HISTORICAL BACKGROUND

During the latter part of the 1960s, as strategies for prosecuting the war became more ruthless and death tolls—both civilian and military—mounted, grief for lost comrades became an increasingly prevalent aspect of the American soldier's Vietnam experience. Coping with the loss of friendships forged in the heat of boot camp or combat, which was difficult under any circumstances, was made even harder by the suspicion that the sacrifice might be for naught. As Jonathan Shay wrote in *Achilles in Vietnam*, "In victory, the meaning of the dead has rarely been a problem to the living—soldiers have died 'for' victory. Ancient and modern war are alike in defining the relationship between victory and the army's dead, *after the fact*. At the time of the deaths, victory has not yet been achieved, so the corpses' meaning hovers in the void until the lethal contest has been decided.'' Thus, as increasing numbers of people both within and without the American military concluded that the war was going awry, it became difficult for survivors to attach meaning to their comrades' sacrifice.

In some instances, the grieving of soldiers manifested itself in feelings of unfocused rage, emotional withdrawal, or "survivor's guilt" (in which the grieving soldier feels that he should have been the one to die). For other soldiers, the deaths of friends led to troubled meditations on the random way in which the Vietnam War claimed its victims. In one chapter of *In Pharaoh's Army*, for instance, Tobias Wolff recounted three different episodes in which he nearly lost his life, only to be spared by chance. In the last of these episodes, the mere arrangement of soldiers around a table leads the commander of his advisory team to choose another lieutenant rather than himself to enter a firefight as an advisor to reinforcements. The lieutenant is killed a few hours later, an event that leads Wolff to muse that "there were times, not immediately afterward but in the months and years to come, that I myself had the suspicion it should have been me—that Keith [the lieutenant], and Hugh [Wolff's best friend, killed a few months earlier], and other men had somehow picked up my cards and stood in the place where I was meant to stand. . . . All around you people are killed: soldiers on both sides, farmers, teachers, mothers, fathers, schoolgirls, nurses, your friends—but not you. They have been killed instead of you. This observation is unavoidable. So, in time, is the corollary, implicit in the word *instead*: in place of. . . . You don't think it out, not at the time, not in those terms, but you can't help but feel it, and go on feeling it. It's the close call you have to keep escaping from, the unending doubt that you have a right to your own life. It's the corruption suffered by everyone who lives on, that henceforth they must wonder at the reason, and probe its justice.''

WOLFF AND VIETNAM

Wolff joined the U.S. Army in 1964, convinced that military experience was essential if he were to follow in the footsteps of his literary idols. "The men I'd respected when I was growing up had all served, and most of the writers I looked up to—Norman Mailer, Irwin Shaw, James Jones, Erich Maria Remarque, and of course Hemingway," recalled Wolff in *In Pharaoh's Army*. "Military service was not an incidental part of their histories; they were unimaginable apart from it. . . . Experience was the clapper in the bell [for writers], the money in the bank, and of all experiences the most bankable was military service."

This thirst for writing fodder, combined with a desire to achieve a level of respectability in American society that had proven elusive during his troubled childhood, made Wolff a willing addition to the military ranks. He joined the army's Special Forces (Green Berets) but found his confidence draining away as his friends "disappeared into the war." His self-confidence was further shaken during a stint at Officer Candidate School (OCS), where he finished last in his graduating class. "In the end I finished OCS only because . . . I had written a number of satirical songs and sketches for our battery to perform on graduation night," he wrote in *In Pharaoh's Army*. These revues, he suggested, had become a tradition: "There'd be hell to pay if the show was a flop. When the time came for the final cuts to be made in our class it was discovered that I was the only one who could put the whole thing together. They kept me on to produce a farce. That was how I became an officer in the United States Army."

Wolff's tour in Vietnam was delayed further when, in 1966, he was given orders to attend Washington, D.C.'s Defense Language Institute and study the Vietnamese language. A year later—after learning to speak the language "like a seven-year-old child with a freakish military vocabulary"—he went to Vietnam, where he served as a military advisor to an ARVN artillery battalion in the village of My Tho, in the Mekong Delta. He regarded this assignment as a stroke of good fortune, because as he himself admitted in *In Pharaoh's Army*, "I was completely incompetent to lead a Special Forces team. This was adamant fact, not failure of nerve."

Wolff became disillusioned with America's prosecution of the war during his tour, and after his 1968 discharge (with the rank of first lieutenant) he found it immensely difficult to reintegrate into American society. "A sense of deficiency, even blight, had taken hold of me," he recalled in his memoir. "In Vietnam I'd barely noticed it, but here, among people who did not take corruption and brutality for granted, I came to understand that I did, and that this set me apart."

"We didn't spend much time making distinctions between enemies and friends [in Vietnam]," commented Wolff in "After the Crusade," a 1995 *Time* essay. "Entire towns were destroyed, others devastated by our jets and artillery. Most of the dead were civilians. In this way we taught the people—and taught ourselves, once and for all—that we didn't love them and wouldn't protect them, and that we were prepared to kill them all to save ourselves." But Wolff contended that the enemy was also culpable for the carnage visited upon Vietnam's civilian population. "How about the VC?" he wrote in *In Pharaoh's Army*. "I used to wonder. Were they sorry? Did they love their perfect future so much that they could without shame feed children to it, children and families and towns—their own towns? They must have, because they kept doing it."

CREATION OF *IN PHARAOH'S ARMY*

During the late 1970s and early 1980s, Wolff established himself as one of America's most promising writers of short fiction. In 1984 his novella *The Barracks Thief*, which concerned three soldiers stationed stateside during the Vietnam War, was awarded the PEN/Faulkner Award for fiction. Five years later his childhood memoir *This Boy's Life* was published to great acclaim.

Wolff picked up the narrative of his life where *This Boy's Life* left off with *In Pharaoh's Army* (1994), an account of his Vietnam experiences that also includes chapters on his pre- and post-Vietnam life. Arranged in thirteen chapters—each of them largely self-contained sketches of specific experiences and emotions—*In Pharaoh's Army* includes memorable portraits of several men that the author encountered during the Vietnam era. These include Sergeant Benet, the savvy soldier who looked after Wolff upon his arrival in My Tho; the cynical Doc Macleod; the compassionate Sergeant Fisher, whose sense of "duty had swallowed him whole, loneliness, fear, and all"; and Pete Landon, a seemingly perfect Foreign Service officer possessed of a core of moral corruption.

But the primary character remains Wolff himself. A callow officer when he first arrives in Vietnam, he comes to recognize that the war has transformed Vietnam into a place where inhumanity is commonplace and death often strikes in capricious fashion. "Why one man died and another lived was, in the end, a mystery, and we who lived paid court to that mystery in every way we could think of," recalled Wolff. He came to view a gold watch bestowed upon him by his fiancée as a potent totem of good fortune: "It went with me everywhere, rain or shine. That it continued to tick I regarded as an affirmation somehow linked to my own continuance, and when it got stolen toward the end of my tour I suffered through several days of stupefying fatalism."

CRITICAL RECEPTION

Most critics were favorably disposed toward *In Pharaoh's Army*, though a number of otherwise laudatory reviews indicated their authors' belief that its predecessor, *This Boy's Life*, remained the superior of Wolff's two memoirs.

"Wolff's memoir is the most balanced, unapologetic account of the war we are likely to see," wrote Pat C. Hoy II in the *Sewanee Review*. "We hear his reasons for going, see him through his preparation, and experience the beauty of his stories of friendship, as well as his stories of corruption." James Hannah offered similar compliments in the *Nation*, calling the book an "unflinchingly honest and humane . . . chronicle of a particular boy's life and its universal appeal in times of peace and war." *Commonweal*'s Michael O. Garvey was moved to call Wolff "a far better writer than anyone else who has yet tried to describe what happened in Vietnam."

Indeed, nearly all reviewers of *In Pharaoh's Army* praised Wolff for his perceptive character studies, his honest examination of his hopes and fears, and his unsparing assessment of his qualities as an officer. But some critics contended that the book's thirteen self-contained chapters—though possessed of many appealing qualities—did not add up to a completely satisfying whole. "To his credit," wrote Jeff Giles in *Newsweek*, "Wolff doesn't turn the war into a morality play about the loss of innocence, the slaughter of innocents, the horror, the horror and so on. He doesn't do Vietnam in Sensurround. But, while it's plain Wolff doesn't want to push the usual buttons, it's not always clear what buttons he *does* want to push. In its more listless moments, [*In*] *Pharaoh's Army* seems a ramshackle collection of memories not overly concerned with telling a larger story.'' *New York Times Book Review* critic Bruce Bawer, meanwhile, wrote that ''there is a great deal of precise, evocative writing here. Yet on the whole, Mr. Wolff's characteristic literary manner seems rather more suited to a book like *This Boy's Life* than to a war memoir.''

FURTHER READING

Baritz, Loren. *Backfire*. New York: William Morrow, 1985.

Bawer, Bruce. ''A Vietnam Sketchbook.'' *New York Times Book Review* (November 27, 1994).

Garvey, Michael O. ''A Predator of Experience.'' *Commonweal* (May 19, 1995).

Giles, Jeff. ''He's in the Army Now.'' *Newsweek* (October 24, 1994).

Gray, Paul. ''Judging the Man He Was.'' *Time* (October 31, 1994).

Hannah, James. Review of *In Pharaoh's Army*. In *Nation* (November 21, 1994).

Hoy, Pat C., II. ''They Died for Nothing, Did They Not?'' *Sewanee Review* (Summer 1995).

Shay, Jonathan. *Achilles in Vietnam: Combat Trauma and the Undoing of Character*. New York: Touchstone, 1994.

Wolff, Tobias. ''After the Crusade.'' *Time* (April 24, 1995).

———. *In Pharaoh's Army: Memories of the Lost War*. New York: Alfred A. Knopf, 1994.

In Retrospect: The Tragedy and Lessons of Vietnam

Nonfiction

Author: Robert S. McNamara, with Brian VanDeMark

Facts of Publication: New York: Times Books, 1995

In 1968 Secretary of Defense Robert S. McNamara left his position at the Pentagon after seven stormy, controversial years. As the man who had overseen the American military buildup in Vietnam in the 1960s, he had come to be viewed by many in the antiwar movement as a personification of the cold, bureaucratic machine that was feeding America's youth to the war. Indeed, the conflict in Vietnam was sometimes referred to as ''McNamara's War,'' a sobriquet that the secretary once publicly embraced. But by 1967 he was widely regarded as a troubled figure, and his departure from President Lyndon Johnson's cabinet was not a surprise.

Nearly three decades after his departure from the Pentagon, during which time the former defense secretary remained largely silent on the subject of the Vietnam War, McNamara wrote a memoir about those years. The book, called *In Retrospect: The Tragedy and Lessons of Vietnam*, immediately triggered a renewed firestorm of debate over the war and the author's role in it. Some reviewers and readers called McNamara's memoir a courageous one, full of regret and sadness about the way events had unfolded under his direction. The prevailing reaction, however, was far more negative. As Carl Mollins wrote in *Maclean's*, ''seldom has a book provoked the scale of unbridled rage that Robert McNamara unleashed with the publication . . . of a confessional memoir on the U.S. war in Vietnam. Initial reactions exposed a furious sense of betrayal. Anger focused on the fact that McNamara, who played a central role in the war as

U.S. defense secretary from 1961 to 1968, waited three decades to declare publicly what he said presciently but privately at the time: the purposeless war would poison American society and the U.S. image for a long time.''

HISTORICAL BACKGROUND

Robert Strange McNamara came to the Kennedy Administration in 1961 from the Ford Motor Company, where he had been named president only a month earlier (he was the first executive not of the Ford family to ever be named to the position). McNamara and a small group of fellow ''Whiz Kids''—talented military officers who had presided over various statistical operations during World War II—had revived the previously ailing auto giant by initiating a dramatic reorganization and modernization of the company. Kennedy, impressed by McNamara's work at Ford and eager to secure a Republican for his cabinet, offered him the position of secretary of defense. ''Of all the figures that John F. Kennedy chose for his Cabinet, McNamara was the most original and the one with the greatest mystique, being regarded universally with deference and awe,'' wrote Sidney Blumenthal in *New Yorker*. ''He was the new man. He had subdued the world of the modern corporation, and he would now conquer government.'' Deborah Shapley, author of the McNamara biography *Promise and Power*, concurred: ''When John Kennedy had raised hopes for a rational world, the spectacled, soberly dressed McNamara, widely credited with shaping the success of Ford, presented himself as the embodiment of rational policy-making. McNamara's rule would be based on analysis and logic, not politics or emotion, he said. Nobody else used numbers the way McNamara did. They symbolized his supposedly detached, objective approach to policy. [McNamara] stood for quantification and technology when the American romance with both was at its height.''

McNamara quickly made his mark in the Pentagon, instituting major changes in the budgeting, administration, and management of America's military (his strong opposition to nuclear-based military strategies impacted the Pentagon's guiding philosophy as well). Former Undersecretary of State George Ball, who would emerge as one of the Administration's most dedicated ''doves'' during the war, recalled in his book *The Past Has Another Pattern* that ''in any group where Robert McNamara was present, he soon emerged as the dominant voice. I was impressed by his extraordinary self-confidence. . . . Once he had made up his mind to go forward, he would push aside the most formidable impediment that might threaten to slow down or deflect him from his determined course.'' But while a number of the changes initiated by McNamara came to be regarded in many quarters as positive moves, they sometimes triggered conflict with America's military leadership, some of whom came to see him as an autocratic civilian with insufficient regard for their knowledge and experience. In any case, controversy over McNamara's initiatives paled next to growing concern about the widening Vietnam War.

McNamara was confident of victory in Vietnam throughout the early 1960s. In May 1962 he visited Vietnam and, after forty-eight hours, pronounced that "every quantitative measurement . . . shows that we are winning the war." Indeed, George C. Herring, author of *LBJ and Vietnam*, contended that "from McNamara's perspective, Vietnam was to be a test case for the new style of crisis management and the new command system." McNamara reasoned that victory would be easily obtained if the United States and South Vietnam armed themselves with the necessary statistical data about the conflict and acted accordingly. Military and civilian surveys and studies on all aspects of the war— from defoliation to pacification to enemy movements—subsequently proliferated, but many participants in the war would later comment that such statistical analyses were wholly inadequate in measuring qualitative aspects of the war, such as the determination of guerrillas, the despair of civilians, and the frustrations and fears felt by Americans. Some measurements of the war's progress— most notably the "body count" of enemy dead—became controversial in and of themselves. Critics contended that McNamara's reliance on the body count to gauge the war's progress encouraged American and South Vietnamese troops to overstate enemy dead. Others said that reliance on the body count, coupled with U.S. and ARVN uncertainty about the often hazy allegiances of Vietnamese peasants, spurred troops to adopt a more callous—and sometimes brutal—attitude toward the Vietnamese. Peasant women and children who were killed during the war thus were sometimes included in official body count figures, giving rise to the commonplace saying that "if it's dead, it's VC."

Looking back on the war's early years, many observers have concluded that America's civilian and military leadership misread several important aspects of the crisis in Vietnam, especially the conflict's nationalist underpinnings, the Saigon government's fundamental weakness, and the region's strategic importance in the Cold War. McNamara himself concurred with this assessment in his memoirs. He admitted that he did not "understand or appreciate [Vietnam's] history, language, culture, or values" and acknowledged that other administration and military figures shared his ignorance: "When it came to Vietnam, we found ourselves setting policy for a region that was terra incognita. . . . The foundations of our decision making were gravely flawed."

But it was not until late 1965 or 1966 that McNamara experienced his first major doubts about America's ability to win the war. During the first six months of 1965, President Johnson had initiated bombing of North Vietnam and committed U.S. ground forces in South Vietnam. Herring contended that these decisions "marked a major turning point in [Johnson's] war policies and in the civil-military balance. After this point the military became more aggressive, bombarding the civilians with requests for additional troops and an expanded mission." The struggles over military strategy grew increasingly heated, as the Joint Chiefs of Staff (JCS) lobbied for increased troop deployments and more vigorous military action and some Johnson Administration officials commenced their struggle to escape from the current that was pulling the nation into full-fledged war. McNamara and other civilian officials opted instead for a strategy of gradual escalation. "They persisted in believing that slow and carefully measured increases in military pressure would locate that point where the North Vietnamese were convinced that the cost of war would be greater than the potential gain," wrote Herring. "Once the North Vietnamese had been persuaded to stop infiltration of men and supplies, the southern insurgency could be contained."

Antiwar protests against the defense secretary intensified at this time as well. McNamara himself wrote that protests aimed at him had been "sporadic and limited through the fall of 1965 and had not compelled attention." On November 2, 1965, though, a Quaker activist named Norman R. Morrison immolated himself in front of McNamara's Pentagon office window, leaving behind a widow and three young children. This horrific incident marked the beginning of an intensification of protest against McNamara that sometimes left him deeply shaken. Later that November, McNamara made a visit to Vietnam that had a major impact on him. Prior to that visit, wrote Stanley Karnow, author of *Vietnam: A History*, "McNamara had believed firmly in the American crusade in Vietnam. But his attitude altered perceptibly during his quick trip to Saigon. . . . The U.S. combat performance impressed him, yet he was shaken by the evidence that North Vietnamese infiltration into the south had risen so dramatically—and would surely continue. Discarding his customary display of public optimism, he candidly told correspondents in Saigon that 'it will be a long war.' "

Upon his return to the United States, McNamara began to push for negotiations with Hanoi. In December 1965, the Johnson Administration called a temporary cessation in their bombing of North Vietnam, despite the objections of the JCS, in hopes of spurring negotiations with the Communists. The bombing halt failed to produce the desired result, however, and some observers traced McNamara's fall from official grace to this moment. "McNamara's influence began to wane after the December 1965 bombing pause," wrote Herring. "The secretary of defense had pushed the pause and accompanying peace initiative and LBJ, grudgingly and against his better judgment, had endorsed it. When it failed, as Johnson predicted it would, McNamara's infallibility was challenged and the president held him responsible for a major policy failure. After December 1965, moreover, the once indomitable secretary of defense was increasingly skeptical that the war could be won militarily, and as his skepticism grew and more and more manifested itself in his policy recommendations, his influence declined still further." As McNamara's power waned, American military leaders assumed greater control of the war effort.

Though McNamara has elsewhere stated that he did not lose faith in America's ability to win the war until 1966 or 1967, it was clear that his confidence was ebbing, and by the spring of 1966 he was privately pushing for diplomatic rather than military solutions. "As one diplomatic initiative after another fizzled, my frustration, disenchantment, and anguish deepened. I could see no good way to win—or end—an increasingly costly and destructive war," he wrote in *In*

Retrospect. "Looking back, I deeply regret that I did not force a probing debate about whether it would ever be possible to forge a winning military effort on a foundation of political quicksand. It became clear then, and I believe it is clear today, that military force—especially when wielded by an outside power—just cannot bring order in a country that cannot govern itself."

Still, McNamara kept his doubt hidden from the public, even as the military and civilian factions of the Johnson White House deadlocked over alternative military strategies and options to extricate the nation from the war. Paul Hendrickson, author of *The Living and the Dead: Robert McNamara and Five Lives of a Lost War*, wrote that "only astute McNamara-watchers on the inside could begin to detect a different man, who, for swirls of complicated reasons, was going to continue managing the doomed war for the next two years, a war he believed could not be won on the battlefield, while the casualty rates of the dead, dying, wounded, and missing spiked past the 100,000 mark and the country tore apart and his own deep slow incineration went on."

McNamara later attributed his decision to stay with the Administration to his loyalty to Johnson and his hopes that he might be able to influence the course of American involvement in Vietnam. But a public break with U.S. military leaders over bombing strategy accelerated his departure from the Administration. In mid-1967 the hawkish Senate Armed Services Committee's Preparedness Investigating Subcommittee, chaired by Senator John Stennis, called public hearings to consider testimony on the administration's decision to keep the bombing of North Vietnam limited. "The hearings," wrote McNamara, "were intended to pressure the White House to lift the bombing restrictions." Most of those called to testify were top military officers who supported expansion of bombing campaigns in North Vietnam. During the course of his testimony, however, McNamara contradicted the generals who had preceded him, arguing instead that, short of embarking on a course of total annihilation, no amount of bombing would break North Vietnam's will to continue the conflict. "I stressed that the air war in the North was no substitute for the ground war in the South, that bombing would not allow us to win on the cheap," he wrote.

This public split with the Joint Chiefs only added to McNamara's difficulties with the military. It also helped convince Johnson that his defense secretary needed to be replaced. By the fall of 1967 McNamara's increasingly antiwar views had led the president to conclude that, as diplomat (and McNamara successor) Clark Clifford had said, he would either have to change his Vietnam policy or change his secretary of defense. On February 29, 1968—only a few months after the antiwar March on the Pentagon had brought thousands of protestors to the steps of the nation's military headquarters—McNamara left the Administration for a position as head of the World Bank. "I do not know to this day whether I quit or was fired. Maybe it was both," he wrote in *In Retrospect*. "It has since become a common assumption that I was near emotional and physical collapse. I was not."

CREATION OF *IN RETROSPECT*

After his resignation from the Johnson Administration, McNamara refused to discuss Vietnam. When asked why he maintained this silence, given his growing opposition to the war, McNamara told *Newsweek*'s Jonathan Alter that he "wasn't capable" of lending his voice to those trying to stop the war. He elaborated further in his memoirs: "I hesitated for fear that I might appear self-serving, defensive, or vindictive, which I wished to avoid at all costs. Perhaps I hesitated also because it is hard to face one's mistakes."

McNamara's silence on the subject ended in 1984, when, while testifying in General William Westmoreland's libel trial against CBS, he admitted that he had concluded that the war in Vietnam was "unwinnable" as early as 1966 (and possibly even earlier). But he did not publicly speak of the war again until 1995, when *In Retrospect* was published. McNamara cited his growing alarm with "the cynicism and even contempt with which so many people view our political institutions and leaders" as the impetus for writing his memoirs. "We of the Kennedy and Johnson administrations who participated in the decisions on Vietnam acted according to what we thought were the principles and traditions of this nation. We made our decisions in light of those values. Yet we were wrong, terribly wrong."

The book (which was excerpted in *Newsweek*) and McNamara's publicity tour in support of it sparked an explosion of controversy and a revisiting of the war in many of America's media outlets. As Paul Hendrickson observed, "If anything, what *In Retrospect* proved, probably beyond any publisher's cash-register dreams, was that Vietnam hadn't gone away, it was only hiding, seething under the surface. As someone said, the Vietnam War was like malaria—awaiting a new moment. *In Retrospect* was the pin on the new grenade."

CRITICAL RECEPTION

Critical and popular reaction to *In Retrospect* was largely negative. As Sidney Blumenthal wrote in *New Yorker*, "All sides accuse him of betrayal, differing only on when the deed was done. To the antiwar left, the perfidy was in the past: McNamara knew the war was wrong in 1967 but didn't say so when it would have counted." Those who thought the war could have been won were angry as well: "He has blown the whistle on their cherished doctrine that the war was winnable if only the civilians had been steadfast," wrote Blumenthal. "To some veterans, it's in both past and present: then he sent their comrades to die; now he tells them their sacrifice was for naught."

Some people did defend McNamara, contending that expressions of regret—however tardy—should not be dismissed. An editorial in *Commonweal* contended that within the pages of McNamara's memoir one can find "an epic struggle of a bright and focused intelligence at war not only with the limits of knowledge but with the intricacies of the heart and the demands of the moral world. . . . McNamara's memoir is flawed. . . . Nevertheless, he has managed to raise again, almost single-handedly, the questions that still haunt us. . . . Robert S. McNamara has finally spoken the unuttered words of his heart. His book may not be a perfect act of contrition, but it is a courageous act. It is a gift to his country: A nation still at war with itself, still in need of clarifying its vision, promise, and role."

Anne Morrison Welsh, widow of Norman R. Morrison (the Quaker who immolated himself outside McNamara's window three decades earlier), released a statement of support as well: "I am grateful to Robert McNamara for his courageous and honest reappraisal of the Vietnam War and his involvement in it. I hope his book will contribute to the healing process." And William Styron and William Manchester argued in a letter published in the *New York Times* on April 26, 1995, that "No mea culpa deserves such contempt. It is true that his comes late—very late—but it should be saluted, not scorned. . . . America can never be damaged by an act of contrition."

But most commentary on the book and its author was of a far more critical quality. *Atlantic Monthly* editor James Fallows denounced McNamara's book on National Public Radio, saying that "It would have been better to go out silently if you could not find the courage to speak when it would have done your country any good." David Halberstam, author of *The Best and the Brightest* and a longtime McNamara critic, was outraged by the memoir as well. In a long, critical review of *In Retrospect* for the *Los Angeles Times*, Halberstam dismissed the former defense secretary as "a man so contorted and so deep in his own unique self-delusion and self-division that he still doesn't know who he is and what he did at that time." Other critics echoed Halberstam's comments, calling the memoir evasive and devoid of honest introspection.

The *New York Times* offered a particularly harsh analysis of the memoir and its author. The paper's editors devoted a lead editorial to McNamara's book shortly after its publication, excoriating him for his wartime actions and the lateness of his apology: "Mr. McNamara must not escape the lasting moral condemnation of his countrymen. . . . His regret cannot be huge enough to balance the books for our dead soldiers. The ghosts of those unlived circle close around Mr. McNamara. Surely he must in every quiet and prosperous moment hear the ceaseless whispers of those poor boys in the infantry, dying in the tall grass, platoon by platoon, for no purpose. What he took from them cannot be repaid by prime-time apology and stale tears, three decades late."

Finally, Paul Hendrickson summarized the feelings of many of those who read the book when he wrote that, as one read McNamara's memoir, it "began to seem sort of faux—an apology for the wrong things, geopolitical things, strategic things. It was as if a man had said to himself back there in his writing room, okay, I'll apologize to you on the first page—then spend the rest of the book refuting it. While I'm at it I'll yoke everybody else in for the blame. The closer you looked at the book, the more it seemed he was telling you all he did right."

FURTHER READING

Alter, Jonathan. "Confessing the Sins of Vietnam." *Newsweek* (April 17, 1995).

Ball, George. *The Past Has Another Pattern*. New York: W. W. Norton, 1982.

Berman, Larry. *Lyndon Johnson's War*. New York: W. W. Norton, 1989.

Blumenthal, Sidney. "McNamara's Peace." *New Yorker* (May 8, 1995).

Halberstam, David. *The Best and the Brightest*. New York: Random House, 1972.

Hendrickson, Paul. *The Living and the Dead: Robert McNamara and Five Lives of a Lost War*. New York: Alfred A. Knopf, 1996.

Herring, George C. *LBJ and Vietnam: A Different Kind of War*. Austin: University of Texas Press, 1994.

Johnson, Lyndon Baines. *The Vantage Point: Perspectives on the Presidency, 1963–1969*. New York: Holt, Rinehart and Winston, 1971.

Karnow, Stanley. *Vietnam: A History*. New York: Viking Press, 1983.

McNamara, Robert S., and Brian VanDeMark. *In Retrospect: The Tragedy and Lessons of Vietnam*. New York: Times Books, 1995.

"McNamara's Book." Editorial in *Commonweal* (May 5, 1995).

"Mr. McNamara's War." Editorial in the *New York Times* (April 12, 1995).

Mollins, Carl. "Hard Lessons: McNamara Apologized for the Vietnam War." *Maclean's* (April 24, 1995).

Neu, Charles E. Review of *In Retrospect*. In *America* (May 20, 1995).

Shapley, Deborah. *Promise and Power: The Life and Times of Robert McNamara*. Boston: Little, Brown, 1993.

VanDeMark, Brian. *Into the Quagmire: Lyndon Johnson and the Escalation of the Vietnam War*. New York: Oxford University Press, 1991.

The Killing Fields

Film

Director: Roland Joffe

Screenplay: Bruce Robinson; based on the 1980 *New York Times Magazine* article "The Death and Life of Dith Pran," by Sydney Schanberg

Principal Cast: Sam Waterston, Haing S. Ngor, John Malkovich, Julian Sands, Craig T. Nelson

Year of Release: 1984 (Warner Brothers)

On April 17, 1975, the capital of Cambodia, Phnom Penh, fell to the Khmer Rouge. This group of radical Communist insurgents, led by the mysterious Pol Pot, immediately undertook a brutal transformation of Cambodian society. During the next four years, as many as two million of the country's seven million residents were executed by the Khmer Rouge or died of starvation or disease in forced labor camps. Some historians have compared the genocidal rampage perpetrated by the Khmer Rouge to the Nazi holocaust of World War II.

Perhaps the best-known depiction of the horrors that descended upon Cambodia under the Pol Pot regime is the 1984 film *The Killing Fields*. Based on a 1980 *New York Times Magazine* article by correspondent Sydney Schanberg, the film traces the relationship between Schanberg and his Cambodian interpreter and guide, Dith Pran, against the backdrop of war-torn Cambodia between 1972 and 1979. *The Killing Fields*, directed by Englishman Roland Joffe, was popular at the box office and well-received by critics, eventually winning three American and eight British Academy Awards. One of the most notable aspects of the film was the performance of newcomer Haing S. Ngor, a Cambodian physician who drew upon his own harrowing experiences during the war in his Oscar-winning portrayal of Dith Pran.

HISTORICAL BACKGROUND

The people of Cambodia are descended from the ancient Khmer empire that once occupied much of Indochina. The Khmers were pushed from their traditional territory by the expansion of their neighbors, Vietnam and Thailand, until they faced extinction in the early nineteenth century. This threat was averted in 1863, when Cambodia became a French protectorate, though the Khmers retained a basic distrust of their neighbors. After gaining its independence in 1954, Cambodia—which had become known as a peaceful nation, proud of its cultural heritage and agricultural productivity—struggled to steer clear of the Cold War conflicts that enveloped much of the rest of the region. By the early 1960s, however, the Vietnam War increasingly encroached upon Cambodia's borders and drew the reluctant country into the fray. "The ultimate horrors of the Second Indochina War took place not in Vietnam but in Cambodia, a nation that had tried desperately for much of that conflict to maintain its neutrality," Harry G. Summers, Jr. wrote in his *Historical Atlas of the Vietnam War*.

Although Cambodia nominally remained neutral during the Vietnam War, its leader, Prince Norodom Sihanouk, displayed a willingness to shift his allegiance in whatever direction seemed politically expedient. In 1962, the Cambodian ruler allowed North Vietnamese Army (NVA) and Vietcong (VC) forces to set up base camps along his country's eastern border, and in 1965 he severed diplomatic relations with the United States. But by 1969, concerned about the growing Communist presence in Cambodia, Sihanouk appealed to Western powers for help in removing the NVA/VC forces. American President Richard Nixon viewed offensive strikes in Cambodia as a means to disrupt major NVA supply routes, put the allies in a more favorable position during peace talks, and prevent the enemy from taking advantage of the withdrawal of American troops under his Vietnamization program, which was scheduled to begin that June. As a result, Nixon authorized a secret strategic bombing campaign against the enemy border positions, called Operation Menu, on March 18, 1969. Because Nixon had promised a swift end to the conflict during his election campaign, he chose to conceal the mission from many officials in his Administration, as well as the U.S. Congress and the American public. Sihanouk approved the plan on the condition that no Cambodian civilians would be hurt, and a month later he officially reestablished diplomatic relations with the United States.

Sihanouk's change of heart did not go unnoticed by the North Vietnamese or by Communist rebels within his own country. The NVA and VC began training and arming a secretive group of Cambodian Communists, known as the Khmer Rouge, around this time, and later managed to infiltrate about twelve thousand rebels into Phnom Penh to put pressure on Sihanouk. When the prince left the country in March 1970, his prime minister, Lon Nol, took advantage of the ruler's fading popularity to take control of the government. Lon Nol immediately began to crack down on the Khmer Rouge and to lend intelligence support to the American bombing efforts. Sihanouk, angry at Lon Nol for his betrayal, declared his support for the rebels and asked the Chinese government to help restore him to power.

After fourteen months, it became clear that Operation Menu had only encouraged the enemy forces to move westward toward the Cambodian capital of Phnom Penh, and Nixon began to fear that the Communists would gain control of the country. In response, he authorized an incursion of U.S. troops into Cambodia on April 30, 1970. Though the operation was a success from a strictly military perspective—taking eleven thousand enemy lives at a cost of one thousand allied lives, relieving the pressure on the pro-Western Lon Nol government, and pushing back the NVA offensive by two years—it proved disastrous to Nixon's popularity back home in the United States. "Nixon had promised only a couple of weeks earlier that 'the just peace we are seeking' was in sight, yet he had expanded the war," Stanley Karnow wrote in his book *Vietnam: A History.* "The antiwar movement at home, which he had skillfully subdued, suddenly erupted again in the biggest protests to date." One of the most shocking events to occur in the aftermath of the invasion of Cambodia was the killing of four student protesters by National Guard troops on the Ohio campus of Kent State University in May 1970. Congressional opposition to Nixon's war policies also increased at this time. On June 24, 1970, the U.S. Senate repealed the Gulf of Tonkin Resolution, which had served as the original basis for American intervention in the Vietnam War, and forced Nixon to invoke his constitutional powers as commander-in-chief to justify continued U.S. involvement.

Following the withdrawal of American forces in June 1970, Cambodia became embroiled in a bitter, three-year civil war that pitted its military against the Khmer Rouge. During this time, the weak and corrupt Lon Nol government began to totter precariously as the prime minister suffered a series of strokes. The government generally retained the support of the Cambodian peasantry, which tended to be deferential toward authority, but many middle-class citizens—tired of the war and its effect on the nation's economy—began to turn their support toward the Khmer Rouge.

Though the organization and its goals were enshrouded in secrecy, some known Khmer Rouge leaders were intellectuals who had gained the respect of middle-class Cambodians by resisting government corruption in the past. By early 1975, the Khmer Rouge had forced the Cambodian military into a defensive circle around Phnom Penh. After the rebels managed to cut off supply lines to the city in March, Western powers withdrew their diplomats in anticipation of the inevitable. The capital fell to the Khmer Rouge on April 17, 1975.

It quickly became clear that the Khmer Rouge government would be far from the peaceful and benevolent force that many Cambodians had hoped for. The leader of the Khmer Rouge, Saloth Sar (who adopted the *nom de guerre* Pol Pot), had come to embrace a radical Chinese Communist philosophy. His regime immediately set about transforming Cambodia into Democratic Kampuchea by tearing down all remnants of Western influence and mobilizing the peasantry to create an agrarian utopia. "The prairie fire of revolution that swept through Cambodia between 1975 and the beginning of 1979 was one of the fiercest and most consuming in this century of revolutions," David P. Chandler wrote in *The Tragedy of Cambodian History.* "The [Pol Pot] regime abolished money, evacuated cities and towns, prohibited religious practices, suspended formal education, newspapers, and postal services, collectivized eating after 1977, and made everyone wear peasant costumes. Its economic plan called for average national yields of rice that were more than twice as high as those in the most productive areas of Cambodia. The regime proposed to wage a class war and to turn the economy around by abolishing class distinctions, destroying prerevolutionary institutions, and transforming the population into unpaid agricultural workers."

The most insidious part of the "transformation" of Cambodian society that took place under the Khmer Rouge was the murder of untold numbers of Cambodian citizens. During Pol Pot's rule, the formerly placid rice fields that dotted the country's landscape became "killing fields," or mass graves. "The Communists were engaged in exterminating as many as two million Cambodians— a quarter of the population. Most, herded into forced marches or forced labor projects, perished from famine, disease, mistreatment, or exhaustion, and the atrocities included instances of cannibalism. Thousands of middle-class citizens, branded as parasite intellectuals merely because they wore spectacles or spoke a foreign language, were systematically liquidated," Karnow explained. "The Communists proclaimed the advent of their administration Year Zero, the start of a 'new community' that would be cleansed of 'all sorts of depraved cultures and social blemishes.' "

The brutal Pol Pot regime was removed from power in January 1979, when Vietnam mounted a successful invasion of Cambodia. Though the Vietnamese government was aware of many of the atrocities that took place in Cambodia under the Khmer Rouge, they did not invade their neighbor for humanitarian reasons. Instead, Vietnam's actions grew out of their concern that the Khmer Rouge, backed by China, would try to annex parts of Vietnam west of the Mekong River—territory that had once belonged to Cambodia. The Vietnamese did stop the slaughter of Cambodian citizens, however, and established a pro-Soviet government.

Despite the brutality of the Pol Pot regime, the U.S. government—partly in an effort to placate China and partly to punish Vietnam for its pro-Soviet leanings—decried the invasion. Though many members of the American media supported the government's stance, it drew outraged criticism from some quarters. "When the Vietnamese invaded Cambodia and restored some semblance of civilized order to the country early in 1979, the American press, led by the *[New York] Times*, followed the State Department's description of events as an example of Vietnamese expansionism, which posed a threat to Thailand and who

knows what other Southeast Asian refuges of American power,'' Andrew Kopkind wrote in *The Nation*. ''Before long, Pol Pot was an ally and an agent of
the United States, and the horrible history of a decade had been sanitized.''
Vietnamese occupying forces periodically clashed with three different Cambodian factions over the next decade, until the Vietnamese finally withdrew in
September 1989. A formal peace treaty was signed in October 1991, and the
United Nations sponsored elections in Cambodia in May 1993. Sihanouk was
reinstalled as head of a coalition government in September of that year. Even
so, a lasting peace for the battered country was not assured. As of early 1997,
Pol Pot and an estimated ten thousand members of the Khmer Rouge were
reported to be in hiding near the Thai border in western Cambodia.

NGOR AND CAMBODIA

Haing S. Ngor, a Cambodian physician who won an Academy Award as best
supporting actor for his portrayal of Dith Pran in *The Killing Fields*, had personally experienced the horrors of Cambodia under the Khmer Rouge. Ngor's
first encounter with the Khmer Rouge came shortly after the fall of Phnom Penh,
when rebel soldiers burst into the hospital room where he was operating on a
wounded man and asked whether he was a doctor. Realizing that the Khmer
Rouge would kill him if he revealed the truth, Ngor claimed that the doctor had
just stepped out. After the soldiers left, Ngor was forced to abandon his patient
in order to save himself.

Before long, Ngor was herded out of the capital along with its other residents
and forced to become a slave laborer in the Cambodian countryside. He worked
twelve-hour days smashing stones or pulling a plow as armed Khmer Rouge
guards stood by, ready to whip him if he disobeyed their orders. In order to
avoid the certain death that would result if he revealed that he was a learned
professional, Ngor steadfastly maintained that he was an illiterate taxi driver.
''If you know only ABC, Khmer Rouge say, 'You CIA!' They want to wash
your brain,'' he explained to Deirdre Donahue in an interview for *People*. Still,
Ngor endured numerous forms of torture at the hands of the Khmer Rouge. In
one instance, rebel soldiers cut off part of his finger after accusing him of
stealing vegetables from a garden. Another time, after a former colleague identified him as a doctor, Ngor was tied to a post with a plastic bag placed over
his head. Though several others nearby died of suffocation, Ngor's bag was
removed just before he passed out. On another occasion, Ngor was herded into
a small, filthy hut along with 180 other people. The Khmer Rouge then set the
hut on fire and gunned down anyone who ran out. Ngor was one of only 30
people who survived the ordeal by huddling on the floor of the hut.

In 1979, Ngor escaped from the labor camp. He trekked through the mountains of western Cambodia, which were laced with land mines, for four days
without food in order to reach safety at the Thai border. Though he had survived,
his fiancée, father, mother, two brothers, and two sisters had all been killed by

the Khmer Rouge. Ngor spent the next eighteen months in Thailand working as a medic to help Cambodian refugees, then immigrated to the United States in 1980. He became involved with *The Killing Fields* when the movie's casting director, Pat Golden, met him at a Cambodian wedding near Los Angeles and asked him to audition for a part. Director Roland Joffe recalled Ngor's audition to Donahue: "I obtrusively placed a camera about a foot away from his face. Then I asked him to pretend to persuade Pat Golden, reading for Pran's wife, to leave the country. He cried, and he made Pat cry. He did it five times, and he cried five times. At that point, I knew this was an actor, not a gifted amateur."

Ngor drew upon his own harrowing experiences with the Khmer Rouge in playing the role of Dith Pran in *The Killing Fields*. At one point, the filming of a particularly intense scene became so real for Ngor that he ran off the set screaming. International film critics were surprised by the profound depth of his performance, especially since he had never acted before, but Ngor claimed that he had had plenty of practice. "After all, I spent four years in the Khmer Rouge school of acting," he remarked to Donahue. Ngor was pleased with the completed film, which he felt was important in bringing the tragic history of Cambodia to the attention of the world. "I wanted to show the world how deep starvation is in Cambodia, how many people die under Communist regime," he told Donahue. "My heart is satisfied, I have done something perfect." Although Ngor found watching the film so painful that he only managed to sit through it once, he still told Donahue that, compared to his own experience, *The Killing Fields* was "not strong enough, not bad enough, not cruel enough, not violent enough."

Following his success as an actor, Ngor became a vocal opponent of the Khmer Rouge and a prominent figure in efforts to provide humanitarian aid to his homeland. Tragically, he was murdered in 1996 outside his home in Los Angeles, and there are some indications that his death may have come at the hands of Khmer Rouge operatives. "It is a matter of great irony that one who had survived the violence of his homeland Cambodia and who expressed so eloquently and passionately a commitment to peace would die so violently," stated Richard Parkins, director of Episcopal Migration Ministries, a refugee relief organization. "The life of Haing Ngor speaks to survival, courage, and compassion. . . . He was a caring human being who overcame tragedy and committed himself to diminishing the tragedy which had befallen others. It is this legacy that continues to inspire and give this gifted human being immortality."

CREATION OF *THE KILLING FIELDS*

In addition to Ngor's acting debut, *The Killing Fields* provided the feature-film debut of director Roland Joffe, who was trained in British theater and television. Joffe became involved with the film when producer David Puttnam asked his opinion about a script based on Schanberg's article. Impressed by Joffe's enthusiasm for the project, Puttnam soon hired him to direct it.

The film is divided into three parts: The first begins with journalist Schanberg's arrival in Cambodia in 1972 and traces the development of his relationship with his Cambodian guide, Dith Pran, up until the fall of Phnom Penh to the Khmer Rouge; in the second part, Schanberg returns to the United States but is unable to help his friend escape the country, and the action follows Dith Pran's struggles to survive in Cambodia between 1976 and 1978; the third part chronicles Dith Pran's escape to Thailand and his reunion with Schanberg at a refugee camp. Throughout *The Killing Fields*, the camera juxtaposes scenes of the tranquil beauty of the Cambodian countryside with disturbing images of the war.

When Schanberg (played by Sam Waterston) first arrives in Cambodia, he is rather overbearing and dismissive of Dith Pran's talents, even though it is immediately clear to the viewer how much the American reporter must depend upon his guide to do his job effectively. Dith Pran soon helps Schanberg uncover a major story in the heavily populated town of Neak Luong on the Mekong River, where an American B-52 mistakenly dropped twenty tons of bombs, killing 150 civilians and wounding 250 more. The American government at first tries to downplay the event, then attempts to prevent reporters from getting to the scene. But Schanberg is able to break the story about the tragic results of the bombing after Dith Pran manages to sneak him aboard a Cambodian patrol boat.

The film then jumps to March 1975, as Khmer Rouge forces are closing in on Phnom Penh and officials at the American embassy are making plans to leave the country. Schanberg wants to remain in the country to cover the fall of Phnom Penh, and he needs Dith Pran to stay and help. In a pivotal scene, Schanberg—busy at his typewriter—refuses to discuss the matter at length with his friend. Dith Pran yields to Schanberg's subtle pressure, and his family leaves for the United States without him. Shortly after the fall of Phnom Penh, it becomes clear that Cambodia is no longer safe for either foreigners or educated Cambodian natives. When Schanberg and several other Western journalists are captured by a group of young Khmer Rouge guerillas, Dith Pran convinces the soldiers to let them go, thus saving their lives. Schanberg and the others, realizing their immediate need to leave the country, retreat to the French embassy, but they are unable to forge a passport in time to help Dith Pran escape.

The film then follows Dith Pran's struggles to survive in a forced labor camp, where, like Ngor, he survives by pretending to be a peasant taxi driver. In one haunting scene, he tries to escape and must hide in a paddy filled with the decomposing corpses of his countrymen—a literal killing field. During this section, the film occasionally cuts to New York, where Schanberg wins a Pulitzer Prize for his coverage of the Khmer Rouge takeover of Phnom Penh. Though he is pleased about the award, Schanberg is consumed with guilt because he put his career ahead of the safety of his friend. He spends a great deal of time writing letters and contacting relief agencies in a frantic effort to locate Dith Pran and raise public awareness of the situation in Cambodia. Meanwhile, Dith

Pran is recaptured, but he manages to befriend a Khmer Rouge soldier and agrees to carry the soldier's child to safety in Thailand. During their harrowing journey through jungles and over mountains, the child and two traveling companions are killed by a land mine. But Dith Pran finally makes it to a Red Cross outpost on the Thai border, where he is reunited with a joyful Schanberg.

CRITICAL RECEPTION

The Killing Fields was a major success at the box office, both in the United States and overseas. In fact, it remained among the top ten grossing films in the United States for over six months. The film was equally well-received by critics, who bestowed three American Academy Awards (for best supporting actor, best cinematography, and best film editing) and eight British Academy Awards (including best picture and best actor) upon it. Writing in the *National Review*, John Simon called *The Killing Fields* "an important, indeed necessary, film," though he wrote that—particularly in the first half—"it tries to do too much, which leads to oversimplification and superficiality in some areas." Simon had high praise for the second half of the film, however, noting that "*The Killing Fields* rises to those heights where our tears flow even as our blood is chilled. Seldom has man's inhumanity to man been shown with such scrupulously understated harrowingness."

Nation reviewer Andrew Kopkind, who claimed that the film's rendering of events from Schanberg's Western perspective at times tended to distance the viewer from the plight of the Cambodians, nevertheless concluded that "The hideous consequences of Nixon's secret war, the holocaust that followed, and the struggle of an enslaved and decimated people for survival are movingly, and often masterfully, projected on an epic screen." In a review for *Newsweek*, David Ansen commented on how the importance of the film's message overrode the minor flaws in its execution. "The narrative thread often gets lost," he wrote. "This would have been a crippling flaw in most movies, but not here. For the tragedy of the Cambodian civil war is greater than the individual story in the foreground. *The Killing Fields* paints a canvas of ravaged Cambodia so compelling and convincing you can't tear your eyes from the screen."

FURTHER READING

Ansen, David. "A Beautiful Vision of Hell." *Newsweek* (November 5, 1984).
Becker, Elizabeth. *When the War Was Over: The Voices of Cambodia's Revolution and Its People*. New York: Simon and Schuster, 1986.
Chandler, David P. *The Tragedy of Cambodian History: Politics, War, and Revolution since 1945*. New Haven, Conn.: Yale University Press, 1991.
Dith Pran. "Return to the Killing Fields." *New York Times Magazine* (September 24, 1989).
Donahue, Deirdre. "Cambodian Doctor Haing Ngor Turns Actor in *The Killing Fields*, and Relives His Grisly Past." *People Weekly* (February 4, 1985).

Karnow, Stanley. *Vietnam: A History*. New York: Viking, 1983.

Kopkind, Andrew. Review of *The Killing Fields*. In *The Nation* (December 1, 1984).

Manso, Peter, and Ellen Hawkes. "Who Killed Haing Ngor?" *Los Angeles Magazine* (June 1996).

Ponchaud, François. *Cambodia: Year Zero*. New York: Holt, Rinehart, and Winston, 1977.

Schanberg, Sydney H. *The Death and Life of Dith Pran*. New York: Viking Penguin, 1980.

———. "My Life Becomes Reel Life." *Vogue* (December 1984).

Schickel, Richard. "Ordeal of a Heroic Survivor." *Time* (November 5, 1984).

Simon, John. Review of *The Killing Fields*. In *National Review* (December 28, 1984).

Summers, Harry G., Jr. *Historical Atlas of the Vietnam War*. Boston: Houghton Mifflin, 1995.

"Masters of War"

Song

Artist: Bob Dylan

Written by: Bob Dylan

Recorded: April 24, 1963 (Columbia Studios, New York)

Release: May 27, 1963 (on *The Freewheelin' Bob Dylan*, Columbia)

On January 17, 1961—with President-elect John F. Kennedy waiting in the wings—outgoing President Dwight Eisenhower gave a farewell address to the nation that became best remembered for its warning tone. He cautioned the American people to keep an eye on the "military-industrial complex" that had sprung up in the shadow of Cold War fears and warned that its appetite for money and influence presented a potential threat to the country's future.

As the decade unfolded, and the Vietnam War spread across America's newspapers and televisions, Eisenhower's cautionary words came to be remembered more vividly than any of his other utterances. But his words were not the only ones that antiwar protestors took to heart; when songwriter Bob Dylan offered his own apocalyptic musings on the "military-industrial complex" in "Masters of War," the song was seized upon by those who were convinced that America's corporate and military institutions had formed a most unsavory partnership.

HISTORICAL BACKGROUND

The U.S. Economy

John F. Kennedy was elected president in 1960 on a platform that promised, among other things, better U.S. economic performance and increased military spending to close an alleged "missile gap" between America and its Cold War foe, the Soviet Union. After taking office, Kennedy quickly began "one of the most rapid military buildups in peacetime and planned increased spending on the Polaris and Minuteman missiles to reduce the alleged missile gap," wrote Anthony Campagna in *The Economic Consequences of the Vietnam War*. Although this defense buildup—which was supported by the American public— was primarily designed to ensure that the United States maintained a strong position in the Cold War, it also seemed to benefit America's anemic economy (although myriad other factors also played a role in the subsequent economic upturn). As defense spending rose, manufacturers' use of their capacity rose as well. Manufacturers went from an 81 percent rate of utilization in 1962 to a 90 percent rate in 1965. In 1966 the rate climbed even higher, to over 91 percent. Unemployment also dropped as companies sought workers to meet increased demand for product, and a 1964 tax cut provided further fuel for the economy.

By 1966, however, a downturn loomed once again. Expenditures on defense contracts for the Vietnam War dramatically surpassed original estimates in some cases, while the fiscal demands of the Johnson Administration's social program agenda were increasingly felt. The federal government was spending more money than it had, and inflation became a problem. As Gabriel Kolko observed in *Anatomy of a War*, rather than create prosperity, the nation's military budget began to jeopardize American economic expansion: "Internationally, the United States was highly vulnerable. It attempted to play the role of stabilizer of the world economic structure, which was geared to the strength of the dollar, while it simultaneously exported investment funds and goods on the one hand and made costly political and military commitments which undermined its economic role in the world on the other."

Back in December 1965 the Council of Economic Advisors had warned Johnson that "he could not have the Great Society, the war, and price stability unless there was a tax increase," observed Campagna. Johnson resisted, for he remained determined to keep his "Guns and Butter" pledge. But Johnson felt that his position was a difficult one, as he himself acknowledged to Doris Kearns, author of *Lyndon Johnson and the American Dream*: "I knew from the start that I was bound to be crucified either way I moved. If I left the woman I really loved—the Great Society—to get involved with that bitch of a war on the other side of the world, then I would lose everything at home. . . . But if I left that war and let the Communists take over South Vietnam, then I would be seen as a coward and my nation would be seen as an appeaser." Stanley Karnow later commented in *Vietnam: A History* that the president "feared that even the slightest accommodation to the war would compel him to sacrifice some of his domestic programs—and more critically, awaken the public to the costs of the commitment. He wanted to wage the war without paying for it—just as he repeatedly refused to admit that he was escalating the conflict whenever he raised the troop level or stepped up the bombing.'' Tax increase proposals did not get off the ground in Congress, either; tax increases are never politically popular, and some representatives worried that any such increase would be interpreted as a ''war tax'' intended to finance an increasingly controversial war.

But international economic considerations changed matters dramatically in 1968. The growing imbalance in the federal budget, coupled with international concerns about the American prosecution of the war—and the possibility that the war might continue to have a corrosive effect on the U.S. deficit—triggered a drop in the dollar's value in world markets. This drop spurred a corresponding run on purchases of gold, and the situation became so serious that the U.S. Treasury closed the gold market on March 14, 1968. A day later Johnson wrote a letter to European leaders in which he warned that ''these financial disorders— if not promptly and firmly overcome—can profoundly damage the political relations between Europe and America and set in motion forces like those which disintegrated the Western world between 1929 and 1933.'' European bankers held fast, however, and insisted that the United States increase its efforts to nourish the dollar. This international uneasiness was undoubtedly a major factor in the Johnson Administration's decision to reject General Westmoreland's post-Tet troop increase proposal. As Kolko wrote, ''the gold and dollar crisis colored all of Washington's thoughts on responses to the precarious military situation in South Vietnam.'' The United States could no longer afford to run up a deficit; increased military expenditures would have to be offset by cuts elsewhere. Robert Warren Stevens, writing in *Vain Hopes, Grim Realities*, charged that the 10 percent tax surcharge that Congress subsequently passed in 1968 at the urging of the Johnson Administration ''revealed its preference for guns over butter by adding a requirement—unprecedented in U.S. history—that the administration must reduce spending by $6 billion on government programs other than the Vietnam war.''

Defense Contractors and Their Allies

During his farewell address to the nation in early 1961, President Dwight Eisenhower warned the American public about the power of the nation's ''military-industrial complex.'' Eisenhower suggested that this alliance, between the defense department and the U.S. defense industry, increased the stature and health of both groups to the potential detriment of democracy. ''The total influence—economic, political, even spiritual—is felt in every city, every statehouse, every office of the federal government. . . . In the councils of government we must guard against the acquisition of unwarranted influence, whether sought or unsought, by the military-industrial complex. The potential for the disastrous rise exists and will persist," he said. Unruffled by his predecessor's admonition, Kennedy followed through on his promises of increased military expenditures.

Cold War concerns with keeping up with the Soviets accounted for much of America's defense spending in the early 1960s, but as American involvement in Vietnam deepened during the course of the decade, so too did the price tag, and by the late 1960s much of the continually expanding defense department budget was devoted to Vietnam-related expenses. "The official direct cost of the war according to the Office of Budget and Management (OMB) was $140 billion," noted Campagna. "In 1968, the expenditures on the Vietnam War represented approximately 34 percent of all defense spending and in 1969 the proportion rose to 37 percent."

The income of major American military manufacturers naturally rose considerably as U.S. military involvement in Vietnam expanded. Critics of this trend found many targets at which to aim their ire. They pointed out that cost overruns on major weapons systems were epidemic, and charged that defense contractors too often benefited from excessive Pentagon generosity in the form of use of government-owned resources (such as land, machinery, and materials) and patent policy. Regarding the latter issue, critics often pointed to findings of the 1968 congressional Subcommittee on Economy in Government, chaired by Wisconsin Senator William Proxmire. The subcommittee had reported that while the federal government pays for defense-related research and development, it "permits contractors to obtain exclusive patent rights, free of charge, on inventions produced in the performance of government contracts."

"It is likely that the military industrial complex benefited from the war," said Campagna. But, he added, "the military industrial complex should be understood to include organized labor and major universities in the United States." Indeed, critics of the war decried the involvement of a number of leading American universities in military research and development programs, and opponents such as former University of California president Clark Kerr charged that "intellect has . . . become an instrument of national purpose, a component part of the 'military-industrial complex.' " Several universities, however, reacted angrily to accusations that their actions were dishonorable. In 1967, for instance, a Princeton faculty committee contended that the school's involvement in defense-related research "symbolizes a choice by the university to integrate itself into the life of the nation, to relate itself to the pressing problems of contemporary society, and to acknowledge its obligations to the defense of the society of which it is a part."

Organized labor's support for the war, meanwhile, became increasingly fitful as the war dragged on. David Levy remarked in *The Debate over Vietnam* that, "for many Americans of the 1960s, labor's attitude toward the war could be neatly summed up in the person of George Meany, the president of the AFL-CIO and, by virtue of his office, labor's preeminent spokesman." Meany was deeply and outspokenly anti-Communist, and his support for the war was unwavering during both the Johnson and Nixon Administrations. "Under his dominating influence," wrote Levy, "the AFL-CIO issued nine statements endorsing American policy between the Gulf of Tonkin Resolution and February 1968."

But even though many labor leaders and members of the rank-and-file were staunchly prowar in their stances, Campagna pointed out that "individual unions, and other union leaders, such as Walter Reuther, did object to the war and voiced concerns over the morality of war-induced prosperity, even if more employment was created as a consequence." Discontent within union ranks grew as the war continued, and by 1970 a number of union leaders of significance had registered their opposition to the war, including the presidents of the United Auto Workers (UAW) and the Amalgamated Clothing Workers (ACW). Levy noted that the official journal of the Amalgamated Meat Cutters and Butchers even went so far as to publicly question Meany's stance in 1970: "We do not believe that the leader of our great American trade union family speaks for that family in supporting the President in the present war dilemma of our nation."

"There were many reasons for the labor revolt against the war," said Levy. These ranged from an awareness of the growing chasm between labor and their traditional political allies to a belief that "the war was diverting attention and resources from the much-needed social and urban programs that would benefit workers directly. A few suspected that the war was merely a way to enrich big business, the corporate moguls, and, drawing on a venerable antibusiness rhetoric, opposed the war on that ground. For a number of reasons, therefore, American workers also experienced a little civil war in their ranks; within this subcommunity, as within so many others, a deep division had opened."

CREATION OF "MASTERS OF WAR"

Dylan's Rise to Stardom

Bob Dylan (born Robert Zimmerman on May 24, 1941) first arrived in New York in December 1960 with little more than a guitar and a deep interest in American folk music, which had been enjoying a renaissance of sorts over the previous few years. He soon gravitated to Greenwich Village, a bohemian community that served as the epicenter of the folk music world. "Dylan was already up to his earlobes in folk music," wrote Robert Shelton in *No Direction Home*, "and soon his boots were deep into beat poetry."

Over the next several months Dylan became a regular performer on the Village coffeehouse circuit. His performances were heavily peppered with covers of old folk standards—indeed, the folk community frowned on those who did not pay frequent homage to Woody Guthrie and other forebearers—but he also displayed a talent for songwriting that transcended his merely adequate technical abilities. As fellow folksinger Bob Gibson once remarked, "He couldn't play real good. He couldn't sing real good. . . . But you were drawn back." Paul Friedlander noted in *Rock and Roll: A Social History* that Dylan's personality drew mixed reviews as well. "He arrived in the Village unkempt, a folk urchin.

. . . The folk community put him up, fed him, and took care of him. Some would later feel discarded, no longer needed, no longer cultivated as friends. As Dylan became more popular, he became more aloof and sometimes cruel. During legendary drinking sessions, Dylan would unleash brutal sarcastic attacks, putting down friends and other performers. Some left; others returned for more.''

In March 1962, Columbia released Dylan's first album. *Bob Dylan*, a collection of traditional folk songs (and one Dylan original), promptly sank without a trace despite positive newspaper coverage of the spindly singer. A year later Dylan's second album, *The Freewheelin' Bob Dylan*, was released. This album, wrote Friedlander, "unveiled Bob Dylan, poet-prophet, to the world." The album, comprised almost entirely of original compositions, immediately established the artist as a major new force in folk music. The best known of the works on the album was "Blowin' in the Wind," a song that was already fairly well known in folk circles since its lyrics had been published in *Broadside* several months earlier. "Blowin' in the Wind" eventually became one of pop music's biggest songs ever. A few weeks after the release of *Freewheelin'*, Peter, Paul and Mary's version of "Blowin' in the Wind" was released as a single. Within eight business days, the song had sold more than three hundred thousand copies. The civil rights movement seized on the song as an anthem, and the appellation "spokesman of his generation" began to be applied to Dylan for the first time.

No other song on *Freewheelin'* could approach "Blowin' in the Wind" in terms of popular appeal, but reviewers and fans pointed out that other songs on the album staked out similar topical territory. One of these songs was "Masters of War," a Dylan composition that, along with "Blowin' in the Wind" and "A Hard Rain's A-Gonna Fall," heralded a new era in socially relevant popular music.

CRITICAL RECEPTION

"Masters of War" was a startlingly blunt attack on America's military-industrial complex. Written at a time when Cold War tensions were high and the United States' slow slide into Vietnam had already begun, the song accused munitions makers and their political allies of engaging in an unholy swap of innocent blood for money ("You hide in your mansion / As young people's blood / Flows out of their bodies / And is buried in the mud"). Set to an eerie, guitar-driven melody, "Masters" painted a damning portrait of the munitions makers—"You that build the death planes / You that build the big bombs"— and concluded with a final stanza of black triumph in which Dylan envisioned himself watching the funerals of "the masters of war" themselves.

High Fidelity columnist Gene Lees called "Masters of War" a "pessimistic and brutal work." Jon Landau, writing in *Crawdaddy*, called it "a song of deep hatred [in which] neither [Dylan's] own righteousness . . . nor their wickedness is ever questioned." Certainly, the controversial song proved difficult to ignore.

Some listeners slammed "Masters of War" on stylistic grounds, calling its lyrics simplistic, and others found its very sentiments to be deeply offensive. Many left-leaning listeners, by contrast, found the lyrics to be all too sadly accurate. Shelton called the song "a blistering indictment of war profiteers [that] points fingers, in the vein of 1930s plays like *Idiot's Delight* or *Bury the Dead.*"

In the months after the release of *Freewheelin'* and his third album, *The Times They Are A'Changin'* (February 1964), Dylan chafed (and occasionally wilted) under the sometimes suffocating adulation of his rapidly growing legion of fans. As Shelton observed, "Dylan felt he was being pushed, as Guthrie had been, into being a troubadour of the Old Left, a puppet laureate who would respond on call with a song for each cause." Uncomfortable with the expectations of domestic social movements hungry for inspiration, Dylan was also determined to explore non-folk musical avenues. He subsequently added a strong "electric" component to his songs, and by the mid-1960s he had become notorious for his self-conscious efforts to weave a veil of hip mystery around himself via false, evasive, or impenetrable comments about his past, Vietnam, American society, and just about everything else. In typically perverse fashion, Dylan also disowned much of his earlier "protest" material, indicating that the songs had simply been a good way for him to launch his musical career; "Messages are a drag," he told *Playboy* in 1966. By the late 1960s, though, Dylan seemed to concede that his early material had meant a great deal to many people. Dylan remarked in an interview with John Cohen and Happy Traum for *Sing Out!* that writing "Masters of War" was "an easy thing to do. There were thousands and thousands of people just wanting that song, so I wrote it up."

FURTHER READING

Campagna, Anthony S. *The Economic Consequences of the Vietnam War*. New York: Praeger, 1991.

Cohen, John, and Happy Traum. "Conversations with Bob Dylan." *Sing Out!* (October/November, 1968).

Denisoff, R. Serge, and David Fandray. " 'Hey, Hey Woody Guthrie I Wrote You a Song': The Political Side of Bob Dylan." *Popular Music and Society* 5 (1977): 31–42.

Friedlander, Paul. *Rock and Roll: A Social History*. Boulder, Colo.: Westview Press, 1996.

Karnow, Stanley. *Vietnam: A History*. New York: Viking, 1983.

Kearns, Doris. *Lyndon Johnson and the American Dream*. New York: Harper and Row, 1976.

Kerr, Clark. *The Uses of the University*, 4th ed. Cambridge: Harvard University Press, 1995.

Kolko, Gabriel. *Anatomy of a War: Vietnam, the United States, and the Modern Historical Experience*. New York: Pantheon Books, 1985.

Landau, Jon. "John Wesley Harding." *Crawdaddy* (1968).

Lees, Gene. "From *Over There* to *Kill for Peace*." *High Fidelity* (November 1968): 56–60.

Lens, Sidney. *The Military-Industrial Complex*. Philadelphia: Pilgrim Press, 1970.

Levy, David W. *The Debate over Vietnam*, 2d ed. Baltimore: Johns Hopkins University Press, 1995.

McGregor, Craig. *Bob Dylan: A Retrospective*. New York: William Morrow, 1972.

Melman, Seymour. *The Permanent War Economy: American Capitalism in Decline*. New York: Simon & Schuster, 1985.

Shelton, Robert. *No Direction Home: The Life and Music of Bob Dylan*. New York: Beech Tree Books, 1986.

Stevens, Robert Warren. *Vain Hopes, Grim Realities: The Economic Consequences of the Vietnam War*. New York: New Viewpoints, 1976.

Wright, James D. "The Working Class, Authoritarianism, and the War in Vietnam." *Social Problems* 20 (1972).

Meditations in Green

Novel

Author: Stephen Wright

Facts of Publication: New York: Charles Scribner's Sons, 1983

The terrible trauma of the Vietnam War challenged many American soldiers' abilities to cope, both during their tours and afterward, when they faced a difficult readjustment to civilian life. Some instead chose to escape from their problems by using drugs and alcohol, which were available and to a large extent accepted in Vietnam. *Meditations in Green*, the first novel by former military intelligence officer Stephen Wright, details the struggles of one Vietnam veteran to come to terms with his wartime experiences. Drug addiction is a constant theme in the novel, as Wright's protagonist resorts to heroin, both in Vietnam and back home in the United States, to help ease the pain he feels about the war.

HISTORICAL BACKGROUND

Extremely potent varieties of many illicit drugs—including marijuana, LSD, opium, and heroin—were readily available to the American troops in Vietnam. Many soldiers who would not have considered using drugs at home did so during their tours, either as a means of escape from the reality of the war or as a form of resistance against military authority. Though drug use was less common out in the field—where a failure to remain alert could cost lives—it was a popular form of recreation in many rear-echelon support areas, especially during the latter part of the war.

Most studies indicate that drug use among American troops expanded most dramatically in 1968 and 1969, as responsibility for fighting the war shifted from U.S. to ARVN forces in accordance with President Nixon's "Vietnamization" strategy. American troops thus moved to more-secure areas, but this proved a mixed blessing. With many U.S. soldiers confined to heavily fortified garrisons, combat fatalities dropped. But boredom and disillusionment took a heavy toll in some units; marijuana use shot up, and when the Pentagon took steps to curb marijuana use, many troops turned to heroin, which was plentiful. "In the spring of 1970, 96 percent pure white heroin appeared in Saigon; by the end of the year it was everywhere, sold in drugstores and by Vietnamese children on street corners. This junk was so pure and cheap that the troops smoked or sniffed, with only a minority reduced to injection. Its use was not remarkable in Vietnam because smoking was usually a group activity, accepted by almost everyone," Loren Baritz explained in his book *Backfire*. "Nothing in all of military history even nearly resembled this plague. About 28 percent of the troops used hard drugs, with more than half a million becoming addicted. This was approximately the same percentage of high school students in the States who were using drugs, but they were using softer stuff. In Vietnam, grass was smoked so much it is a wonder that a southerly wind did not levitate Hanoi's politburo."

Some sources placed the percentage of American servicemen who used drugs in Vietnam as high as 40 percent and claimed that the U.S. government directly contributed to the problem. These critics argued that the government failed to address the issue out of a sense that the drug trade was necessary to the support of their allies. "In not rooting out the sources of heroin in Laos and Thailand, the government had simply made a calculation that the continued political and military support of those groups profiting from the drug traffic was worth the risk of hooking U.S. soldiers," Paul Starr commented in *The Discarded Army*. The U.S. government naturally disputed these charges.

Still other observers claimed that the media blew the drug issue out of proportion. For example, Wendell S. Merick said in *U.S. News and World Report* that drugs were "less of a problem than statistics show," and that "the vast majority of men smoke only once in a while for kicks" or to relieve tension and boredom.

Nevertheless, some veterans claimed that drug use among American troops contributed to a number of other problems in Vietnam, including fragging (the murder of officers by enlisted men) and racial tension. They claimed that drug use was not only symptomatic of the overall demoralization of the American forces but also provided an excuse for some soldiers to act on their frustrations. "For many GIs fighting a war in Vietnam is so confusing and unassimilable that when they are there they feel as though they are in a dream, that they are not really themselves," Eugene Linden wrote in *Saturday Review*. "Because life there is not real, it becomes acceptable to snort scag and to frag the sarge. That's what your buddies are doing. When the dream stops and you return safely to the States, you will stop—or so goes the dream." One officer admitted to Merick that "Given beer, whisky, or drugs, mixed in with a crowd of blacks and whites, you can have trouble. But you never know which came first—the booze, the drugs, or racial disagreements."

Sadly, some of the soldiers who were introduced to drugs in Vietnam returned home to the United States as addicts. Drug addiction vastly compounded the already difficult reintegration process that Vietnam veterans faced. "The legacy of our demoralized Army in Vietnam is beginning to filter back to the United States with our returning troops," Linden wrote in 1972. "The names of vets are beginning to show up on police blotters in towns around points of disembarkation as soldier/addicts resort to crime to obtain the vastly more expensive American heroin." As a result of such reports, some sectors of the American public came to associate drug addiction with Vietnam veterans, thus creating a harmful stereotype. For as Baritz noted, "Most of the veterans returned home reasonably whole, as whole as returning veterans from earlier wars. The majority were not dopers, did not beat their wives or children, did not commit suicide, did not haunt the unemployment offices, and did not boozily sink into despair and futility."

CREATION OF *MEDITATIONS IN GREEN*

Like the protagonist in *Meditations in Green*, author Stephen Wright served as a military intelligence officer in Vietnam from December 1969 to November 1970. After returning to the United States, Wright earned a bachelor's degree in English from Ohio State University in 1973 and a master's degree from the University of Iowa Writers Workshop in 1975. *Meditations in Green*, his first novel, was published in 1983. Though fictional, the book draws extensively upon Wright's experiences in Vietnam. "Most of the time, people in the novel are pretending to do something, which was the sense we had over there," the author explained to John A. Glusman in the *Christian Science Monitor*. "We thought no matter what you did or had accomplished, what did it matter in the end?"

Meditations in Green tells the story of James Griffin, a disabled Vietnam veteran struggling to readjust to civilian life in a decaying American city. Many aspects of his daily existence—from a cereal called "Crispy Critters" (the slang term for a body charred by napalm) to a perfume called "Charlie" (the slang term for the enemy)—remind him of the horrors he experienced during the war. Throughout the novel, Griffin revisits Vietnam in flashbacks and, at the recommendation of his therapist, attempts to come to terms with his experiences through meditation and gardening. Wright presents his protagonist's memories of the war in the third person and describes his traumatic reintegration into American society in the first person. In addition, the author intersperses fifteen meditations on plants, which provide a "high-relief map of Griffin's internalized postwar battlefield," according to Thomas Myers in *Walking Point*. Both during and after the war, Griffin turns to drugs to help him escape his problems. Though

Wright describes his character's drug addiction in graphic terms, he neither defends nor condemns it.

Spec. Four Griffin begins his tour in Vietnam as a naive, patriotic young man who is less than enthusiastic about serving but willing to do his part to defend democracy. Initially, his job is to interpret aerial photographs, locate enemy strongholds, and evaluate the effectiveness of allied air strikes against them. Later he identifies expanses of thick jungle and orders their destruction with chemical defoliants. The tenor of his existence in a rear-echelon military intelligence unit is described as "incredible boredom punctuated by exclamation marks of orgiastic horror." Griffin increasingly turns to drugs to escape from the tedium: "Marijuana, happily, elevated tolerance levels and seemed to produce a beneficial air-conditioning effect on the body," he explains in the novel.

Over time, Griffin's distance from the combat he charts and interprets begins to gnaw at him, and he volunteers for a dangerous jungle search-and-rescue mission in order to "experience some portion of the madness as his own." The horrors he observes—which include finding the mutilated bodies of the men for whom he is searching dangling from the rotors of their downed helicopter—vividly demonstrate the inaccuracy of his former, removed view of the war. Griffin reacts to the chilling contrast by using more and harder drugs until he becomes addicted to heroin. By this time he has been transformed from a "stupid sweet kid" into a withdrawn and shattered man whose only interest is obtaining a fix. Ironically, it is at this point that his commanding officer praises him as a "model soldier."

After completing a painful withdrawal process, Griffin finds himself returning to drugs shortly after his arrival stateside. He is haunted by his wartime experiences, which seem to permeate every aspect of his daily existence, and he comes to view urban America as another type of war zone. According to Myers, Griffin struggles to be "a survivor who, surrounded by urban decay and trapped within disordered, ghastly memory, can claim some variety of healthy organic life. The threats to this project are not only the residue of what he became in Vietnam, a heroin-addicted, fragmented sensibility, but also the present influences in his unnamed American city that encourage continued dissolution, paranoia, and alienation."

Griffin is assisted in his difficult recovery by Dr. Arden, a combination botanist and pop psychologist known as "the messiah of the advent of vegetable consciousness," who encourages him to visualize himself as a healthy flower. Griffin mediates on the life cycle of plants and takes up gardening, which he sees as the opposite of the defoliation he presided over in Vietnam. He eventually covers the floor of his apartment with humus and grows a flower garden there. Toward the end of the book, one of Griffin's army buddies, Trips, involves him in a convoluted plot to murder a former sergeant who had killed Trips's dog in Vietnam. When Griffin stabs Trips to prevent him from killing the wrong man, then applies medical techniques he learned during the war to save his friend's life, he becomes an unlikely hero.

CRITICAL RECEPTION

Meditations in Green was generally well-received by critics. A reviewer for *Publishers Weekly* described the book as "a savagely clear-eyed study of soldiers escaping from horror into cynicism, hysteria, or madness" and called it "possibly the best story yet to come out of the Vietnam War, the most imaginatively conceived and executed, the most painful and hard-hitting."

Reviewers tended to disagree about the effectiveness of the novel's structure. Some argued that the frequent shifts in time and location, combined with the drug-induced confusion of the narrator, detracted from Wright's message. Tom Graves, writing in the *New Leader*, claimed that the novel wavered "between a gripping, no-nonsense, eye-level look at the war and a William Burroughs-like mush of verbiage that serves the reader little." Though admitting that Wright "forcefully recalls the psychological ravages Vietnam wrought on so many Americans—the debilitating stretches of boredom combined with anxiety that led to heroin addiction, for example, among other acts of self-destruction," Graves charged that "he sabotages even the heart of his story with disorienting shifts in the narrative voice." Glusman, on the other hand, thought the novel's structure added to the reader's sense of "the breakdown of order, the loss of control, the deterioration of character. Its multiple perspectives convey the fragmentation of experience, the shattering effects of war. . . . The structure of *Meditations in Green* may at times be disconcerting, and Wright, like many first novelists, can be seen straining after effect. But it is this consciousness of Vietnam as an abstraction, the recognition of U.S. policy there as stagecraft, that makes his work such an important—and disturbing—contribution to the literature of the war."

Some reviewers felt that Wright's emphasis on drug use was exaggerated in the novel. For example, William Boyd of the *Washington Post Book World* stated that "drug trips, hallucinogenic dreams, zonked-out introspections take the biscuit when it comes to boring reading" and claimed that the detailed passages about drug use in *Meditations in Green* "mar, though not critically, what is otherwise an uneven but on the whole impressive debut and addition to the canon of Vietnam War novels." Other reviewers felt that the novel's portrayal of drug use was realistic and added to the reader's understanding of the war. "Wright's treatment of drug abuse . . . deserves high commendation," Graves commented. "The smell of the dope pipes and the late-night acid trails are reported in ferociously vivid prose that avoids stooping to sensationalism. The author makes it easy for us to understand how so many veterans came home addicts, and easy to give them our sympathy."

Summing up the critical reaction to *Meditations in Green* for the *New York Times Book Review*, Walter Kendrick wrote: "The novel is lurid, extravagant, rhapsodic and horrific by turns—sometimes all at once. Its structure is needlessly complicated, and its superheated prose often gets wearisome. Yet for all its self-conscious excesses, it has overwhelming impact—the impact of an experience so devastating that words can hardly contain it.''

FURTHER READING

Baritz, Loren. *Backfire: A History of How American Culture Led Us into Vietnam and Made Us Fight the Way We Did.* New York: Morrow, 1985.

Boyd, William. "The War That Won't Go Away." *Washington Post Book World* (October 30, 1983).

Figley, Charles R., and Seymour Leventman, eds. *Strangers at Home: Vietnam Veterans since the War.* New York: Praeger, 1980.

Glusman, John A. "Bringing the Field to Us: Superb Novel about Vietnam." *Christian Science Monitor* (November 4, 1983).

Graves, Tom. "A Checkered Novel of Vietnam." *New Leader* (November 28, 1983).

Kendrick, Walter. "Drugged in Vietnam." *New York Times Book Review* (November 6, 1983).

Linden, Eugene. "The Demoralization of an Army: Fragging and Other Withdrawal Symptoms." *Saturday Review* (January 8, 1972).

Merick, Wendell S. "Sagging Morale in Vietnam: Eyewitness Report on Drugs, Race Problems, and Boredom." *U.S. News and World Report* (January 25, 1971).

Myers, Thomas. *Walking Point: American Narratives of Vietnam.* New York: Oxford University Press, 1988.

Review of *Meditations in Green.* In *Publishers Weekly* (August 12, 1983).

Searle, William J., edr. *Search and Clear: Critical Responses to Selected Literature and Films of the Vietnam War.* Bowling Green, Ohio: Popular Press, 1988.

Wright, Stephen. *Meditations in Green.* New York: Scribner's, 1983.

"Ohio"

Song

Artist: Crosby, Stills, Nash & Young

Written by: Neil Young

Recorded: May 21, 1970, at Record Plant Studio 3, Los Angeles

Original Release: June 4, 1970 (as single)

Album Release: August 19, 1974 (on *So Far*, Atlantic)

The song "Ohio" was written and performed only a few short weeks after a deadly confrontation between student protestors and National Guardsmen on the Kent State University campus in Kent, Ohio. The May 1970 clash left four students dead and another nine wounded. It also deepened the already substantial chasm between supporters and critics of America's military presence in Southeast Asia. Many Americans expressed their support of the National Guard's actions at Kent State, but the deaths galvanized protestors. Universities across the land were rocked by new demonstrations against President Nixon's war policies.

Neil Young, a member of the popular musical group Crosby, Stills, Nash & Young (CSNY), wrote the song "Ohio" in one day after seeing photographs in *Life* magazine of the Kent State incident. The song was an outraged condemnation of the shootings. In the liner notes for his album *Decades* Young commented that "it's still hard to believe I had to write this song. . . . Probably the biggest lesson ever learned at an American place of learning." He went on to add that "Ohio" was "recorded totally live in Los Angeles. David Crosby cried after this take."

HISTORICAL BACKGROUND

Nixon Invades Cambodia

Richard Nixon had been elected president of the United States in 1968. His ascension to the presidency had been due in no small measure to his campaign promise to "end the war [in Vietnam] and win the peace." Support for America's involvement in Vietnam had begun to erode by the late 1960s, and antiwar factions in the country grew in popularity and organization during this time.

Stanley Karnow noted in *Vietnam: A History* that "opinion surveys conducted in the spring of 1969 showed that most Americans were willing to give Nixon a chance to cope with Vietnam. But Nixon realized that his approval ratings would slip fast unless he made progress in bringing the boys home. Signs of impatience were already visible in Congress, which the Democrats dominated." On May 14, 1969, Nixon delivered a speech in which he rejected a military solution to the war. At the same time, however, he rejected any compromise that "would amount to a disguised American defeat."

In recognition of public opinion, Nixon did order the withdrawal of some American troops. The Nixon Administration hoped to gradually pull out of Southeast Asia, replacing their presence with South Vietnamese troops as they departed. This effort to gradually turn the prosecution of the war over to the South Vietnamese came to be known as "Vietnamization." Throughout 1969, however, some members of the Nixon Administration—notably Henry Kissinger—argued for increased air strikes against North Vietnam. Nixon resisted such plans, however, on the advice of other administration officials, who feared that such actions would galvanize domestic opposition to the war.

In the fall of 1969 Nixon announced a second troop withdrawal, then followed up with a November speech in which he informed the American people of his plan to end U.S. involvement in Asia via the "Vietnamization" approach. The core of his address, though, was a call for public support: "To you, the great silent majority of my fellow Americans—I ask for your support. Let us be united for peace. Let us be united against defeat. Because let us understand: North Vietnam cannot defeat or humiliate the United States. Only Americans can do that."

The response to the speech was gratifyingly positive for Nixon, who had grown increasingly fed up with the "liberals" who were criticizing the war. A relative lull in the war at the end of 1969 and early 1970 furthered Nixon's position. "The Communists had lost much of their steam, the South Vietnamese were showing signs of assuming responsibility for themselves, and [Nixon] had repatriated more than a hundred thousand young Americans and promised to bring home another hundred and fifty thousand over the next year," reported Karnow. "But in the spring of 1970, determined to demonstrate his power, he plunged into a crazy sequence of events in Cambodia."

In mid-March 1970, Norodom Sihanouk, the ruler of Cambodia, a country on the western border of South Vietnam, was overthrown. By the end of the month the country was a chaotic, deadly mess, and many observers wondered whether Communist forces would eventually gain the upper hand. Nixon was warned that "another large troop withdrawal, imperative for domestic political reasons, would jeopardize the American forces remaining in South Vietnam unless the enemy sanctuaries in Cambodia could be eliminated," wrote Karnow. Moreover, Nixon hoped that an impressive display of American military power would drive the North Vietnamese to accept a compromise and end the conflict.

By late April Nixon gave his approval for a plan to invade Cambodia. On April 30, 1970, Nixon gave a televised address in which he defiantly insisted that "if, when the chips are down, the world's most powerful nation, the United States of America, acts like a pitiful helpless giant, the forces of totalitarianism and anarchy will threaten free nations and free institutions throughout the world." The reality for many critics of the war, however, was that Nixon had broadened the war only weeks after promising that "the just peace we are seeking" was in sight.

College Campuses Erupt in Protest

At Kent State University and other campuses across America, the news of military operations in Cambodia provoked renewed outrage. The *New York Times* reported that "the national antiwar movement, drained of vigor in recent months, seemed . . . to have found a new rallying point and an impetus to renewed protest in President Nixon's announcement. . . . College campuses, the focus of earlier mass demonstrations and protests, were once again the scene of student activities ranging from strikes to window-smashing melees." President Nixon was less than conciliatory toward the protestors, referring to them as "bums" who were "the luckiest people in the world, going to the greatest universities, and here they are burning up the books, storming around about this issue."

Kent, Ohio, was not immune to the repercussions of the move into Cambodia. Indeed, the atmosphere at Kent State University had become quite tense over the previous few years, and Nixon's announcement had a combustible effect on the campus. "Although initially a small movement . . . antiwar protest had not been unknown at the university," wrote Kenneth J. Heineman in *Give Peace a Chance*. Spurred by the student leadership of the Kent Committee to End the War in Vietnam and other groups (Students for a Democratic Society, Young Socialist Alliance), a core of determined antiwar students initiated or took part in many demonstrations on the campus and elsewhere in the mid-1960s, despite fierce opposition from the university administration and the larger community (this opposition sometimes took the form of physical assaults, especially when hawkish Kent State students were involved). "By 1968 the Kent antiwar movement had gained a significant presence on the campus," said Heineman. Moreover, he claimed, "through its hostility to peace activists and unwillingness to prosecute hawkish student vigilantes, the university administration had created an environment conducive to the escalation of violence." Certainly, the atmosphere on the Kent State campus became a polarized one, and tensions were hardly eased in the late 1960s, when the moderate antiwar faction on the campus saw their influence within the movement threatened by more radical elements of the SDS (some of whom became involved with the notorious Weathermen). "With the beginning of the 1969 fall session, [President Robert] White discovered that his efforts to crush student activism had backfired," wrote Heineman. "The cumulative impact of four years of escalating war, as well as university and community hostility towards even the most politically moderate activists, had outraged and mobilized a hitherto unthinkable number of students."

The night after Nixon's address, the Kent community's downtown area was subjected to a large wave of young people who wreaked heavy property damage in the form of smashed windows and small fires. Reports varied concerning the identities and motives of those involved in the destruction. Some blamed "radicals" angry with government policy; others attributed the damage to students or motorcycle gangs. In any event, the events of May 1 convinced Ohio Governor James A. Rhodes to send in the Ohio National Guard to secure the Kent State campus.

On Saturday, May 2, demonstrators on the Kent State campus set fire to the university's ROTC (Reserve Officers Training Corps) building despite the presence of the National Guard. Demonstrators clashed with fellow students and guardsmen until after midnight, when the situation finally calmed down. When the sun rose on May 3, tired National Guardsmen were stationed around many buildings on campus and in town.

Sunday afternoon unfolded quietly on the Kent State campus. One student recalled in James Michener's *Kent State: What Happened and Why* that a guardsman explained that they had been ordered to fraternize with the students to relieve the tension. "They turned the whole campus into one friendly circus. People wandered aimlessly about as if they were in an art gallery."

As dusk fell, however, the atmosphere changed. Guardsmen who had been warned all weekend about possible snipers associated with radical groups grew increasingly tense. Meanwhile, a group of demonstrators gathered to protest a curfew that had been imposed. Aggressive attempts by the National Guard to disperse the crowd—whose leaders at one point unsuccessfully sought to negotiate a meeting with authorities to discuss concerns—soon deteriorated into confusion and fear. Tear gas was utilized, and a number of students were bayoneted. Demonstrators fled back to the dormitories, where many taunted the guardsmen. By this time, campus radicals found their ranks swelled by large numbers of previously uninvolved students who were angered by the events of the evening.

On Monday, May 4, a student rally was scheduled for noon in the campus commons area. President White later stated that "it was hammered at me from all sides that the Guard was in complete command. They told me the noon rally was illegal and they'd break it up." This account differs somewhat from National Guard reports, which contended that it was White who felt that the rally was dangerous, and who insisted that it not be permitted.

At 11:15 A.M., an announcement was made indicating that all outdoor demonstrations had been banned by order of Governor Rhodes. According to Michener, however, the announcement "reached only a small proportion of the students, because the intercom system operated in only certain classrooms and none of the dormitories. But the rally had been forbidden; everyone knew it except the students." Additional efforts to break up the fast-assembling students were made during the next forty-five minutes, but the warnings were either unheard or greeted with catcalls.

By noon, the time when the National Guard force of 113 soldiers moved forward to disperse the crowd, they faced well over a thousand demonstrators (some observers placed the number considerably higher). Efforts to clear the area through the use of tear gas proved ineffective because of the direction of the wind; indeed, a number of demonstrators hurled canisters back at the guardsmen. The soldiers were pelted with rocks and bricks as well, although many of these missiles fell short of their intended targets. The Guard marched on, splintering off to deal with various groups of demonstrators.

One contingent of the Guard eventually decided to return to the burned-out ROTC building to regroup. Angry and frustrated with the demonstrators, many of whom vented an unrelieved stream of verbal abuse at the soldiers, the guardsmen began to trudge up a big hill to return to the ROTC building. At 12:24 P.M., though, guardsmen on the trailing right flank suddenly stopped and wheeled around to the right to face a contingent of students, most of whom were about seventy yards away. They dropped their rifles to the ready position. A single shot rang out, followed closely by a loud, crackling volley that echoed across the campus. Though many of the twenty-eight guardsmen who fired shot their weapons into the air, some guardsmen—either out of anger or fear—fired directly into the crowd. By the time the gunfire ceased, thirteen bodies were scattered over the grass and the distant parking area. Four students were dead and nine others were wounded.

At the sound of the gunfire, "some of the students dived to the ground, crawling on the grass in terror," reported the *New York Times*. "Others stood shocked or half crouched, apparently believing the troops were firing into the air. . . . The youths stood stunned, many of them clustered in small groups staring at the bodies."

A tense stand-off followed. Many students demanded immediate retribution, but they were finally convinced to disburse by several faculty members and student leaders who feared further violence. "But a bizarre atmosphere hung over the campus," reported the *New York Times*. "A Guard helicopter hovered overhead, grim-faced officers maneuvered their men to safeguard the normally pastoral campus, and students, dazed, fearful and angry, struggled to comprehend what had happened and to find something to do about it.''

By early in the evening the entire campus had been sealed off, and roadblocks had been erected around the town to prevent anyone from entering. A court injunction was issued that ordered all students to leave the campus. Many left via thirty-six university buses that took them to airports in Cleveland or Columbus. ''And so the huge blue and gray buses pulled up to arbitrary loading points while weeping girls and young men, paralyzed with rage at what they had seen, piled in for one of the most mournful caravans ever to start from a university town,'' wrote Michener.

Predictably, news of the deaths of the four Kent State students—Jeffrey Miller, Allison B. Krause, William Schroeder, and Sandra Lee Scheuer—shocked college campuses across the country. ''In thirteen seconds of gunfire, Kent State became an international symbol of antiwar protest and government repression,'' remarked Heineman. ''As the wounded and dead lay upon the ground, the strike movement initiated to protest the American military invasion of Cambodia immediately increased: 4,350,000 students at 1,350 universities and colleges participated in demonstrations against the shootings and the escalation.'' A number of the demonstrations turned violent, and many universities subsequently closed for the year (an estimated 536 campuses were shut down completely, 51 for the remainder of the academic year).

Elsewhere, however, large numbers of people angry with the widespread unrest were unmoved by the deaths of the students. In Kent the local newspaper ''had to reserve a full page, day after day for several weeks [for] one of the most virulent outpourings of community hatred in recent decades. It seemed as if everybody in the Kent area suddenly wanted to unburden himself of resentments against young people, colleges and education which had been festering for years,'' wrote Michener. Not even the four dead students—none of whom had been known as radicals—were spared. Indeed, vicious and baseless rumors about the students proliferated and were passed on with gusto. For his part, President Nixon deplored the deaths within hours of the shootings, though he suggested that the student protestors should shoulder some of the blame. A White House statement remarked that the incident ''should remind us all once again that when dissent turns to violence, it invites tragedy.'' Later in the evening, Vice President Spiro Agnew characterized the shootings as ''predictable'' in public comments largely devoted to criticizing activist leaders. These leaders, he insinuated, had introduced ''traitors and thieves and perverts and irrational and illogical people [into] our midst.''

Investigations into the shootings were launched by several state and federal law enforcement agencies. National Guard spokesmen initially claimed that the shootings had taken place in reaction to a sniper attack, but no evidence of this claim was ever found, and this possibility was soon dismissed. Investigators then tried to determine if anyone had given the order to fire, but no definitive conclusion was drawn.

No guardsmen were punished for the shootings at Kent State, noted Joseph Kelner and James Munves in *The Kent State Coverup*, despite the fact that the attack had taken place ''before hundreds of witnesses, the events documented by photographs; despite the fact that President Nixon's Scranton Commission had termed the shootings 'unnecessary, unwarranted and inexcusable'; and despite the fact that every other impartial group that had looked into the incident . . . had declared the shootings unjustifiable.'' In 1979 the parents of each of the four dead students received $15,000 and an apology from Ohio's governor and the state National Guard in an out-of-court settlement of a civil suit.

CREATION OF ''OHIO''

Crosby, Stills & Nash was an enormously popular rock group in the late 1960s and early 1970s. Comprised of David Crosby, Steven Stills, and Graham Nash, the group sometimes also included the Canadian-born Neil Young. This incarnation of the group—known as Crosby, Stills, Nash & Young (CSNY)—produced the band's second album, which was released on March 11, 1970.

The band went out to tour in support of the album, but tentatively broke up in Chicago as a result of bitter backstage disagreements. David Crosby and Neil Young retreated to a friend's house. Once there, Young read a magazine account of the recent Kent State shootings. After reading the article, he was silent for a long time. Crosby recalled in his autobiography *Long Time Gone* that ''I watched Neil Young see, really *see* that famous picture of the girl kneeling over the dead kid, looking up as if to say, 'Why?' I handed him the guitar and watched him write the song. I got on the phone and called the guys in L.A. and said, 'Book the studio, man. This is it. Get the studio time tonight. I don't care where. This is important.' I got Neil to the airport and we got on a plane and we flew down.'' According to Graham Nash, the recording was done within fifteen minutes. ''Ohio'' was released as a single about two weeks later.

Crosby later commented that, ''for me 'Ohio' was a high point of the band, a major point of validity. There we were, reacting to reality, dealing with it on the highest level we could—relevant, immediate. It named names and pointed the finger. It said 'Nixon.' I was so moved by it that I completely lost it at the end of the song.''

''Ohio'' was the first song of a political nature that Young had ever written, a fact that Crosby attributed to the songwriter's fundamental approach to music: ''Neil had the stance I have now,'' Crosby observed in Johnny Rogan's biography *Neil Young*. ''I don't think musicians should go and seek stands out. . . . I think that music is for fun. But when something slaps you in the face personally, you have to respond to it. And Kent State was too damn much. They'd gone too far. Even Neil couldn't stand it. He had to respond to it. It was a genuine and honest a thing as you could ask for. It wasn't us going out and seeking stands to take that made us look good. He was just honestly reacting to what hit him in the face. It blew his mind. He couldn't believe they'd shot those kids. It was too much.''

CRITICAL RECEPTION

"Ohio" was released as a single on June 4, 1970. Another CSNY song called "Find the Cost of Freedom" was selected as the B-side. The band knew that "Ohio" would arouse controversy upon its release. "I don't think they'll touch it," Crosby said in *Rolling Stone*, referring to the nation's radio stations. "This one names names."

"Did 'Ohio' have any lasting impact?" wrote David Downing, author of *Neil Young: The Man and His Music*. "Many radio stations did refuse to play it, and Vice-President Agnew was moved by it to denounce rock music as anti-American, but you could still buy the record at the local store." For his part, Downing called the song an eloquent testimonial to the anger that so many people felt at the time, not just about "the events at Kent State or of the wider Indo-Chinese situation, but of politics in the Western world in general."

"The music and the performance more than matched the lyric," wrote Downing. "The bass rumbled with anger, the vocals and guitars cried with passion. . . . It was CSN & Y's best record. It said everything there was to say, said it powerfully, beautifully."

Others saw "Ohio" as a warning. *Christian Century* contributor Charles E. Fager wrote, "anyone who wants to understand what it was that sent one-third of the nation's colleges into an unprecedented paroxysm of protest in the spring should listen to 'Ohio.' " Though critical of the musical arrangement, Fager insisted that "in only two-and-a-half minutes the song captures and reinforces the chilling outrage that has recently swept across U.S. campuses. It has the same powerful effect as some posters I saw in Harvard Square the morning following the disaster at Kent State—posters depicting four black coffins resting above the word INCREDIBLE, with the IN crossed out in red. That art was also untidy and hastily produced—and thereby somehow more powerful."

FURTHER READING

Crosby, David, with Carl Gottlieb. *Long Time Gone: The Autobiography of David Crosby*. New York: Doubleday, 1988.

Downing, David. *Neil Young: The Man and His Music*. New York: De Capo Press, 1995.

Fager, Charles E. "Chilling Outrage." *Christian Century* (August 19, 1970).

Heineman, Kenneth J. " 'Look Out Kid, You're Gonna Get Hit!': Kent State and the Vietnam Antiwar Movement." In *Give Peace a Chance: Exploring the Vietnam Antiwar Movement*, Melvin Small and William D. Hoover, eds. Syracuse: Syracuse University Press, 1992.

Karnow, Stanley. *Vietnam: A History*. New York: Viking Press, 1983.

Kelner, Joseph, and James Munves. *The Kent State Coverup*. New York: Harper & Row, 1980.

Kifner, John. "4 Kent State Students Killed by Troops." *New York Times* (May 5, 1970).

Michener, James A. *Kent State: What Happened and Why*. New York: Random House,
    1971.
Onis, Juan de. "Nixon Puts 'Bums' Label on Some College Radicals." *New York Times*
    (May 2, 1970).
Rogan, Johnny. *Neil Young: The Definitive Story of His Musical Career*. New York:
    Proteus Books, 1982.
Semple, Robert B., Jr. "Nixon Says Violence Invites Tragedy." *New York Times* (May
    5, 1970).
"Tin Soldiers & Nixon's Coming." *Rolling Stone* (June 25, 1970).
Wells, Tom. *The War Within: America's Battle over Vietnam*. Berkeley: University of
    California Press, 1994.

"Okie from Muskogee"

Song

Artist: Merle Haggard

Written by: Merle Haggard

Recorded: 1969

Album Release: December 1969 (on *Okie from Muskogee,* Capitol)

In the months prior to the release of "Okie from Muskogee," the country music world had been largely silent on the topic of the Vietnam War. A few years earlier, in the mid-1960s, a number of prowar songs had been recorded by country artists. The lyrics of these songs typically embraced two major themes: the bravery of American soldiers and the moral bankruptcy of antiwar protestors and draft dodgers. Several of these songs were warmly received in the South (as well as other areas of the country) because numerous Southern communities were staunch supporters of the Vietnam War and adhered to its anti-Communist underpinnings. Moreover, some white Southerners equated antiwar activists with the leaders of the civil rights movement, whom they blamed for the social upheavals that convulsed much of the South in the 1950s and 1960s. As a result, country and folk/rock acts—which were more likely to express liberal views— exchanged fire over Vietnam and other social issues confronting the nation. The clash between the two camps provided observers with yet another gauge to study the growing cultural polarization taking place across America.

In 1967 and 1968, however, as American military involvement in Vietnam intensified and domestic clashes over Vietnam policy escalated, Nashville was quiet. Finally, in December 1969, Capitol Records released Merle Haggard's

"Okie from Muskogee." Earlier country songs had commented on the nation's antiwar community in much harsher terms, but "Okie" tapped into a reservoir of pent-up demand. It was embraced by proponents of the war and quickly assumed anthemic status among America's "Silent Majority."

HISTORICAL BACKGROUND

Partisan pro-Vietnam songs first appeared on country music labels in mid-1965. Often touted as a response to the protest songs that were growing in popularity at the same time, these songs equated patriotism with support for America's involvement in Vietnam. As Jens Lund noted in "Country Music Goes to War," the liner notes for one 1965 anthology of country war songs proudly proclaimed that "it is significant that Country Music artists have never been identified with the so-called 'protest' songs or 'Peace Marches' . . . right or wrong, Country music stands with our Country."

By early 1966, the *Billboard* country music chart included five songs that addressed the Vietnam conflict, including "Hello Viet Nam" and "Keep the Flag Flying," by Johnny Wright; "What We're Fighting For," by Dave Dudley; and Ernest Tubbs's "It's for God and Country and You, Mom." These were quickly followed by such songs as "Wish You Were Here, Buddy," a Pat Boone song that mirrored the pro-Vietnam crowd's growing hostility toward dissenters. Lund observed that "Wish You Were Here, Buddy," also reflected the growing conservative stereotype of "the dissenter as an unwashed, immoral bum." Other artists offered rhetoric that was even more explosive. For example, Marty Robbins, who campaigned for George Wallace in 1968, recorded a song called "Ain't I Right" under the name Johnny Freedom. The song, said R. Serge Denisoff in *Sing a Song of Social Significance*, argued "that the fight against Communism would be best carried out by attacking civil rights marchers, college students, and liberal United States senators." Most country musicians were not so extreme in their support for the war, but there was no mistaking the prowar leanings of the industry and its Southern fan base. Indeed, the sentiments expressed in country music lyrics merely expressed the prevailing (though by no means) universal attitudes of most Southern communities. As Myra MacPherson remarked in *Long Time Passing: Vietnam and the Haunted Generation*, "decade after decade, the South had given up its young to war. For the poor, military life was a way up and out; for the middle class and the elite, military academies were citadels of respect and honor. Even when Vietnam tarnished the military in many eyes, to die for God and Country was a Southern, flag-waving, honorable sentiment. They were often called 'rebels' in Vietnam and some flew their Confederate flags on their tanks. Some were bigoted and dumb and mean. Some were gentle and bright and brave. And they were all over Vietnam."

By early 1966, when Barry Sadler's hugely successful "The Ballad of the Green Berets" appeared, Vietnam songs were comfortably ensconced on the country music charts. Many leading artists also made public appearances at gatherings designed to galvanize public support for the war effort. The country music industry thus presented a largely unified front in support of involvement in Vietnam, and it tolerated little dissent within its ranks. Lund noted that after country artist Glen Campbell recorded ''Universal Soldier''—a pacifist song—in the summer of 1965, he was strongly rebuked by the country music community. Campbell subsequently did his best to get back in the industry's good graces, proclaiming that draft-card burners should be executed and promising to record only ''red-blooded American'' songs from that point on.

CREATION OF "OKIE FROM MUSKOGEE"

Merle Haggard was born on April 6, 1937, in Bakersfield, California. Buffeted by poverty—the family lived in a converted boxcar when Haggard was an infant—and the death of his father when he was nine years old, Haggard turned to a life of train hopping and petty crime as a teenager. Brushes with the law became progressively more serious until he was thrown into San Quentin Prison in 1957. Nearly three years later he was released, determined to make it as a musical performer. Over the next several years he rode a couple of songs to the top of the country charts, aided by both his talent and the aura of his hard-scrabble personal history. By the late 1960s, Haggard's blue-collar tales of hard-luck poverty, lonesome prison cells, rambling drifters, and traditional values had made him a cross-over artist with significant appeal in both country and folk music camps.

''Okie from Muskogee'' was originally intended ''as a lighthearted commentary on the generation gap,'' said James Cobb in the *Journal of Popular Culture*. Inspired by a Muskogee road sign and subsequent musings about the inhabitants' preferred smoking materials, Haggard later said that the song only took him about twenty minutes to write. The song's political flavor was unmistakable, however. The lyrics combined down-home homages to patriotism with blunt rebukes of the protest movement and its excesses.

POPULAR RECEPTION

After its release in December 1969, ''Okie from Muskogee'' was immediately appropriated by conservatives and Southern whites eager for a song that encapsulated many of their feelings of pride, anger, and bewilderment. The song, said Cobb, ''paid tribute to militant 'hippie-haters' and generally reconfirmed the traditionalism and authoritarianism long associated with the South and country music.'' One of Haggard's first public performances of the song was at a concert at Fort Bragg, North Carolina. He was initially stunned by the audience's roaring approval of the song, but he quickly found that the reception was the same wherever he went. In the wake of ''Okie,'' wrote Denisoff, ''Haggard's songs [were] requested by the President, highlighted the July 4th pro-Vietnam Honor America Day rally in Washington, and evoked near hysteria at many concerts both North and South of the Mason-Dixon line.'' Indeed, President Nixon even wrote Haggard a letter congratulating him on the song.

The wild popularity of ''Okie'' naturally spawned a flood of country songs expressing similar patriotic, antihippie sentiments, including Ernest Tubbs's ''It's America (Love It or Leave It)'' and Haggard's own ''The Fightin' Side of Me.'' None, however, could match the overwhelming popularity of ''Okie from Muskogee.'' The Country Music Association eventually bestowed best song, album, and single awards on ''Okie'' for 1969.

For his part, Haggard expressed some ambivalence about the song's status as a rallying cry for conservatives and war supporters. The song was immensely profitable for the singer, but critics noted that Haggard's philosophy had always appeared to be grounded more in traditionalism than in hard-core conservatism. In any case, he fended off overtures from Wallace supporters and other right-wing groups who sought him out after the release of ''Okie,'' and in subsequent recordings he returned to the gambling, rambling tales of the working class that had first vaulted him to stardom.

FURTHER READING

''Artists Support U.S. Servicemen in Viet Nam.'' *Billboard* (January 8, 1966).

Cobb, James M. ''From Muskogee to Luckenbach: Country Music and the Southernization of America.'' *Journal of Popular Culture* (Winter 1982).

DeBenedetti, Charles. *An American Ordeal: The Antiwar Movement of the Vietnam Era.* Syracuse: Syracuse University Press, 1990.

Denisoff, R. Serge. *Sing a Song of Social Significance.* Bowling Green, Ohio: Bowling Green University Popular Press, 1972.

Denisoff, R. Serge, and Richard A. Peterson, eds. *The Sounds of Social Change: Studies in Popular Culture.* Chicago: Rand McNally, 1972.

Gottschalk, Earl, Jr. ''Love It or Leave It: New Patriotic Music Wins Fans, Enemies.'' *Wall Street Journal* (August 16, 1970).

Haggard, Merle, with Peggy Russell. *Sing Me Back Home: My Life.* New York: Times Books, 1981.

Kendrick, Alexander. *The Wound Within: America in the Vietnam Years, 1945–74.* Boston: Little, Brown, 1974.

King, Florence. ''Red Necks, White Socks and Blue Ribbon Fear.'' *Harper's* (July 1974).

Lund, Jens. ''Country Music Goes to War: Songs for the Red-Blooded American.'' *Popular Music and Society* (Summer 1972).

MacPherson, Myra. *Long Time Passing: Vietnam and the Haunted Generation.* New York: Doubleday, 1984.

Wells, Tom. *The War Within: America's Battle over Vietnam.* Berkeley, Calif.: University of California Press, 1994.

Paco's Story

Novel

Author: Larry Heinemann

Facts of Publication: New York: Farrar Straus Giroux, 1986

In the years following the Vietnam War, it became clear that thousands of American veterans had not been wholly able to leave the war behind. Often operating in an environment of social isolation, they struggled to accept what they had seen and done in the war. Some were unsuccessful in those efforts, succumbing to debilitating feelings of depression and anger and resorting to self-destructive actions ranging from substance abuse to suicide. The difficulties experienced by these veterans initially contributed to a negative stereotype of the Vietnam veteran that was particularly prevalent in the 1970s and early 1980s. But as time passed and the body of research on veterans grew, Americans became aware that the problems of many of these men and women could be traced back to an acknowledged psychological malady: post-traumatic stress disorder (PTSD), also known as post-traumatic stress syndrome (PTSS).

One of the best-known examinations of PTSD and its sometimes-crippling impact on the American Vietnam veteran was undertaken by author and Vietnam vet Larry Heinemann, who became an outspoken critic of the war—and of America's indifference to returning veterans—in the years following America's final withdrawal. His book *Paco's Story*, which won a National Book Award, concerns a PTSD-afflicted veteran and his experiences in a small Midwestern town.

HISTORICAL BACKGROUND

Although many Vietnam veterans successfully readjusted to life back in the United States after concluding their tours, others found it difficult to come to terms with their wartime experiences. Successful readjustment was predicated on many factors, including level of exposure to combat, military preparedness, age, attitude toward the war, circumstances of involvement (volunteer versus draftee), family support, personality characteristics, and the period in which one served (studies indicate that veterans who served in the late 1960s and early 1970s—a period often characterized as one of particular demoralization in the armed forces—had greater difficulty adjusting to postwar life than did those who served earlier in the conflict).

Unfortunately, for many veterans struggling with their Vietnam experiences, the environment back in the United States did little to alleviate matters. In fact, the domestic environment often exacerbated the situation. As Myra MacPherson noted in *Long Time Passing: Vietnam and the Haunted Generation*, the Vietnam War was a "particularly dehumanizing" war for its participants. Some were dogged with doubts about the morality of American actions there, and others were shaken by methods that were employed in its prosecution. Those who survived returned home only to find a country indifferent to them. "They were immigrants from something so repugnant to their own people that it had to remain locked in their own hearts and minds," said MacPherson. Critics charge that this apathy far too often extended into the medical community. Indeed, the Veterans Administration—and America's larger medical community—has been roundly criticized for its inattention to those veterans who struggled with the psychological repercussions of their service upon returning to their native country.

The passage of years, though, spurred a growing recognition of the difficulties that some veterans were having in coming to terms with and making sense of their Vietnam experiences. In 1980, the American Psychiatric Association officially acknowledged that many troubled veterans were suffering from a legitimate psychological malady: post-traumatic stress disorder (PTSD). Since that time, estimates of the number of veterans afflicted with PTSD have ranged from half a million to more than eight hundred thousand, with cases ranging from those completely debilitated by their experiences to those whose seemingly healthy integration back into American society had been disrupted by a sudden traumatic episode. As Senator Alan Cranston noted in his foreword to *Trauma and the Vietnam War Generation*, "PTSD is known among clinicians as a spectrum disorder, and the effect on a person's life can vary greatly—from dampening an individual's ability to participate in life to the fullest degree to total incapacitation when suicide appears to be the only hope of escape."

Authorities point out that post-traumatic stress is a result not of the stressful events themselves but of the inability to satisfactorily come to terms with those events. Characteristic behavioral symptoms of PTSD "may be understood as the persistence of past traumatic experience in the present physiology, psychology, and social relatedness of the survivor,'' wrote PTSD specialist Jonathan Shay in *Achilles in Vietnam*. These include intrusive reexperiences of the traumatic event(s), whether through conscious recollection or dreams; alcohol and drug abuse; unfocused rage; despair and depression; social isolation from family, friends, and country, often because of what Shay termed a ''persistent expectation of betrayal and exploitation''; and inability to put wartime survival instincts to rest.

HEINEMANN AND VIETNAM

Heinemann recalled in his essay ''What Shall We Tell Our Children about Vietnam?'' that he went to Vietnam in March 1967, ten months after submitting to the draft, with what he termed ''soul-deadening dread.'' Stationed first in Cu Chi, and then at Dau Tieng, he endured more than a dozen firefights during his first nine months there. *Chicago Tribune Magazine* writer Jeff Lyon noted that the last three months of Heinemann's tour were even worse, because he saw combat every day: ''Month by month he turned from a nice, unmotivated suburban kid into a self-preservation machine.'' Heinemann later told Lyon that ''combat does that to you. You have to take what's good about yourself and put it away. I became a hard son of a bitch; we all did. I mean, you get an interesting fix on how mean you can be over there. I wanted to kill. I wanted to keep everyone away from me. I just wanted to get home from that g——— place at any price.''

Heinemann participated in several well-known military operations during his tour, most notably Operation Junction City, a search-and-destroy operation that was among the largest and most-ambitious efforts carried out by the U.S. military during the war. The 1967 operation, which took place near the Cambodian border in a region of southwestern South Vietnam known as War Zone C, resulted in some of the fiercest clashes of the entire war. He also took part in a huge battle around the time of the Tet Offensive that he was later stunned to see depicted in Oliver Stone's film *Platoon* (he eventually learned that Stone's battalion had also taken part in the battle upon which the scene was based).

Heinemann completed his tour and returned home to the United States in March 1968, but even though he was relieved to have survived the ordeal in Vietnam, he found it difficult to reintegrate himself into American society. He later explained in a 1991 letter to Ronald Baughman for *American Writers of the Vietnam War* that ''throughout that spring and summer, and fall, I had the distinct feeling that I had come back to a place that was not mine, anymore, that this was not my time; that I was so changed, transformed, that I would never be able to rediscover whatever was left of my humanity.'' At one point he turned to a local Veterans Administration hospital for help in dealing with his feelings of delayed stress and nervousness, but he later characterized the treatment there as wholly inadequate.

Heinemann subsequently turned to writing and literature, and by the early 1970s he had established himself as an English professor. He had also begun work on a story about Vietnam that would become his first novel, the critically acclaimed *Close Quarters*. "I think that my original impulse and ambition to write came from my undeniable urge to tell the story of the war, with no tasteful dashes, no polite euphemisms, no ellipses," he told Baughman. "It sounds impossibly corny now, but 23 years ago good friends of mine were dead for a lie, and I thought I owed them that much."

Indeed, over the years Heinemann's feelings of bitterness and betrayal led him to become one of the most outspoken of the Vietnam veterans who would write about their wartime experiences. "They told us this was a good war, a righteous war, and it wasn't," he told Lyon. "It was one of the most evil things I've ever been a party to. . . . What could possibly have been redeeming about corrupting an entire culture from the ground up? The worst thing was we really corrupted ourselves. We threw away something that was good in us. As a people, we squandered something very important in Vietnam, and it has to do with our own good opinion of ourselves and our generosity of heart."

CREATION OF *PACO'S STORY*

Armed with a publisher's advance of $10,000—thanks largely to the positive response to *Close Quarters*—Heinemann began work on *Paco's Story* in 1979. He worked slowly, though, until he left his teaching position at Columbia in a dispute with the department head. Suddenly armed with much more free time— and looming bills—Heinemann completed the book quickly, and it was published in 1986.

Paco's Story concerns the experiences of Paco Sullivan, a Vietnam veteran who is the only member of his company to survive a horrific barrage of artillery fire during a firefight. The novel's narrative voice is provided by a ghost or ghosts from that fallen company, a device that most critics would later cite as pivotal in establishing and maintaining the novel's distinctive, disturbing tone.

Paco, who lies sprawled among the dead for two days until found by a medic (who is himself profoundly changed by his discovery), returns to the United States with both physical and emotional scars. Paco's shattered body has been cobbled back together with pins, screws, and stitches, but his mind is haunted by the nightmarish memories of the war. He attempts to cauterize his psychic wounds through alcohol and painkillers, but memories of the war continually intrude. After leaving a veterans' hospital, Paco jumps on an interstate bus and instructs the driver to take him as far as the last of his meager savings will allow. He is subsequently deposited in a small town called Boone, where he manages to secure a dishwashing job at a local diner called the Texas Lunch. The veteran is isolated from the town's self-absorbed populace by his past— and the scars that serve as grim emblems of that time. A few of the towns-people—Ernest, the owner of the diner, and Cathy, his neighbor—are attracted to the haunted Paco, but for the most part his stay only increases his sense of alienation. Paco spends his evenings alone, struggling with his tortured memories of the war.

CRITICAL REACTION

When it first appeared, Heinemann's book garnered gratifying reaction from most reviewers. "*Paco's Story*, brief and with a remarkable intensity, presses the social claims of those who died literally, and those who survived but whose history, for all the place it has today, might as well be dead," wrote *Los Angeles Times Book Review* critic Richard Eder. "Heinemann writes of the two universes that coexist in our country: the large one that can't remember, the small one that can't forget." *Washington Post Book World* reviewer Duncan Spencer was similarly impressed: "Heinemann's story is to tell us how one gets PTSD (Post Traumatic Stress Disorder), and the answer is by being systematically brutalized by terror, disorganization, pain, lack of leadership—in short the conditions prevalent for much of the time in the field in Vietnam. . . . In the jungle recollections which drift through the book like evil-smelling smoke, Heinemann's experience of Vietnam as a grunt pours out onto the page like wasted agony, pitiful and resonant."

But despite the positive reviews, *Paco's Story* "was hardly on the tip of everybody's tongue," in the words of Lyon. Thus, when Heinemann's book was announced as the surprise winner of the 1987 National Book Award, it triggered a furor among some members of the literary community. Notable among those that expressed their displeasure with the choice was the *New York Times*, which had not even published a review of Heinemann's novel in its *Book Review* until the day before the ceremony. A week after the award was presented, Michiko Kakutani wrote a critical *New York Times* piece titled "Did *Paco's Story* Deserve Its Award?" in which she commented that "Mr. Heinemann's writing is insufficiently powerful, his vision too myopic, to effectively turn [Paco Sullivan] into the sort of mythic Lazarus-like figure that might otherwise engage our passions." *New York Review of Books* contributor Robert Tower was dismissive as well, remarking that "in that [the book] tries, in somewhat blatant fashion, to exploit the reader's most accessible and predictable responses of revulsion, pity, and guilt, *Paco's Story* is, I think, essentially a sentimental novel." Other critics came to Heinemann's defense, however, dismissing the negative comments as the grousing of an overly self-important literary establishment. *TriQuarterly* editor Reginald Gibbons, for instance, wrote that "*Paco's Story* is a wonderful piece of work, even if it did win the National Book Award. . . . The novel has the feeling of having been written small piece by piece; it is filled with grief, fierceness and a dignity wrestled continuously out of the grip of the despair and hopelessness that won't ever let go entirely, after those days of violent death, but which books like this oppose and transform into life again."

FURTHER READING

Baughman, Ronald. "Larry Heinemann." *American Writers of the Vietnam War*, Volume 9 of *Dictionary of Literary Biography Documentary Series*. Detroit: Gale Research, 1991.

Eder, Richard. Review of *Paco's Story*. In *Los Angeles Times Book Review* (December 7, 1986).

Gibbons, Reginald. Review of *Paco's Story*. In *TriQuarterly* (Winter 1988).

Heinemann, Larry. *Close Quarters*. New York: Farrar Straus Giroux, 1977.

———. *Paco's Story*. New York: Farrar Straus Giroux, 1986.

———. "Syndromes: Making One's Way, Again, through Vietnam." *Harper's* (July 1991).

———. "What Shall We Tell Our Children about Vietnam?" In *What Shall We Tell Our Children about Vietnam?*, William McCloud, ed. Norman: University of Oklahoma Press, 1989.

Kakutani, Michiko. "Did *Paco's Story* Deserve Its Award?" *New York Times* (November 16, 1987).

Kulka, Richard A. et al. *Trauma and the Vietnam War Generation*. New York: Brunner/Mazel, 1990.

Legacies of Vietnam: Comparative Adjustment of Veterans and Their Peers, 5 vols. New York: Center for Policy Research, 1981.

Lifton, Robert J. *Home from the War*. New York: Simon and Schuster, 1973.

Lyon, Jeff. "Author 1st Class." *Chicago Tribune Magazine* (February 7, 1988).

MacPherson, Myra. *Long Time Passing: Vietnam and the Haunted Generation*. Garden City, N.Y.: Doubleday, 1984.

Shay, Jonathan. *Achilles in Vietnam: Combat Trauma and the Undoing of Character*. New York: Touchstone, 1994.

Spencer, Duncan. "When the War Was Over." *Washington Post Book World* (January 18, 1987).

Towers, Robert. "All-American Novels." *New York Review of Books* (January 21, 1988).

Platoon

Film

Director: Oliver Stone

Screenplay: Oliver Stone

Principal Cast: Charlie Sheen, Willem Dafoe, Tom Berenger, Keith David, John C. McGinley, Forest Whitaker, Kevin Dillon

Year of Release: 1986 (Orion)

As American involvement in Vietnam dragged on through the late 1960s and the body count spiraled upward, morale sagged in many sectors of the U.S. military. Factors commonly cited for this decline included the frustrating nature of the conflict, America's flawed attrition-driven prosecution of the war, tour rotation logistics (many critics felt that the one-year tour in Vietnam had a negative impact on unit cohesion and individual willingness to engage the enemy), the conflict's "working class war" trappings, military corruption and profiteering, and the chaotic environment back home in the United States. These factors led many soldiers to conclude that they were locked in a bloody stalemate, and some GIs became convinced that the sacrifices made by U.S. soldiers would ultimately be for naught.

Oliver Stone's film *Platoon* provided a powerful depiction of the deteriorating environment in some American fighting units. Stone, who served in Vietnam from the fall of 1967 to the end of 1968, documented many aspects of this decline: strained race relations, drug use, "fragging" (the intentional killing of American personnel—usually officers—by other U.S. soldiers), resentments between career soldiers—"lifers"—and draftees, and brutality. But the film, which was nominated for eight Academy Awards (it won four, including Best Picture and Best Director), is perhaps best known for its depiction of the struggle that U.S. soldiers waged to adhere to a moral code of conduct in a frighteningly corrosive environment.

HISTORICAL BACKGROUND

The downturn in the performance of the U.S. military in Vietnam in the late 1960s and early 1970s was evident throughout much of the country. Some soldiers continued to perform at a high level, despite the terrifying environment in which they found themselves, but other platoons were crippled by drug use, internal tensions, and the growing suspicion that they were putting their lives on the line for nothing. By early 1971, said journalist Leon Daniel in *The Bad War*, "it seemed to me that morale had deteriorated significantly. You had senior NCOs (non-commissioned officers) evacuating themselves for alcoholism—lifers, not just grunts. There was large-scale dope use. The talk of fragging was rampant. I never could pin down any fragging incident hard enough to write about it, but it was going on. And there were cases of mutiny, units that refused to go forward. In the end I came to believe that the war was destroying the U.S. Army." Colonel Robert Heinl offered a similar assessment in a 1971 issue of *Armed Forces Magazine*: "The morale, discipline and battleworthiness of the U.S. Armed Forces are, with a few salient exceptions, lower and worse than at any time in this century and possibly in the history of the United States," he charged.

Military leaders and conservative supporters of American involvement in Vietnam often cited factors beyond the military's control for this collapse in performance. It was commonly charged, for instance, that restraints imposed by indecisive politicians and the American antiwar movement prevented them from securing victory, a state of affairs that ultimately had a terribly dispiriting impact on soldiers. Another reason cited by the army for the breakdown in discipline was that its difficulties simply reflected the turbulent environment back in the United States. Drug abuse, racial tensions, and confrontations with authority were on the upswing in the streets of America; because the army replenished itself with infusions of men taken from such an environment, it was inevitable that these blemishes would eventually manifest themselves in the U.S. military.

Others, however, argued that many of the U.S. military's internal difficulties were due to failures of American military leadership. "Because the U.S. Army saw fit to remain ignorant of the theory and oblivious to the practice of guerrilla warfare, its reward was an internal chaos of AWOLs, fraggings, drug problems, combat refusals, and resignation of its best and brightest," claimed Cecil B. Curry (writing as Cincinnatus) in his *Self-Destruction: The Disintegration and Decay of the United States Army during the Vietnam Era*. "Morale and dedication and ethical behavior disintegrated within the officer corps of the army and deteriorated throughout the structure. Disillusionment became epidemic. Its ultimate reward was discord of unparalleled ferocity and defeat 'with honor.' ''

Critics of U.S. military leadership frequently cited the tour rotation set up in Vietnam as a particularly destructive factor. Many veterans and other observers, such as Richard A. Gabriel and Paul L. Savage, authors of *Crisis in Command*, contended that ''the rotation policies operative in Vietnam virtually foreclosed the possibility of establishing fighting units with a sense of identity, morale and strong cohesiveness. The assignment of individual, as opposed to *unit*, DEROS (Date Estimated Return Overseas Service) dates, plus the frequent rotation of officers, made it clear that the policy was virtually every man for himself.'' Critics also contended that the one-year tour of duty pushed American casualties upward because competent, experienced troops were always being replaced with raw troops. Finally, critics of the U.S. military performance in Vietnam charged that these troops often reported to officers who were more concerned with advancing their career than with winning the war. As Lieutenant Colonel William L. Hauser wrote in his book *America's Army in Crisis*, ''widespread allegations of manipulation of statistical indicators, unseemly pursuit of rank and decorations, and 'ticket-punching' careerism—even if some of the critics appear to have come into court with unclean hands—are too damning to be ignored.''

The breakdown in discipline and performance in some army units made it that much more difficult for individual soldiers to maintain their ethical and moral bearings. Many did so despite the disintegrating environment in which they found themselves, but others compromised—or discarded—their ideals during their tours of Vietnam's war-blasted countryside. ''A lot of men found their compassion in the war,'' wrote Michael Herr in *Dispatches*, ''some found it and couldn't live with it, war-washed shutdown of feeling, like who gives a fuck. People retreated into positions of hard irony, cynicism, despair, some saw the action and declared for it, only heavy killing could make them feel so alive. And some just went insane, followed the black-light arrow around the bend and took possession of the madness that had been waiting there in trust for them for eighteen or twenty-five or fifty years.''

Fragging

Perhaps the single most chilling manifestation of demoralization among U.S. troops was the practice of fragging. Debate about the seriousness and frequency of these incidents continues to rage, but there is no question that it became a concern in the latter years of American involvement in Vietnam. Reports of bounties on officers circulated with increasing frequency in 1967 and 1968 (primarily in the Mekong Delta region), and by 1969 the U.S. Army had admitted knowledge of at least two hundred fragging incidents. Eugene Linden, writing in the *Saturday Review* in January 1972, said that ''fragging has ballooned into intra-Army guerrilla warfare, and in parts of Vietnam it stirs more fear among officers and NCOs than does the war with 'Charlie.' '' Linden noted that in

1970 and 1971, another 363 fragging cases had been documented, yet "officers in the Judge Advocate General Corps have estimated that only about 10 percent of fraggings end up in court." James William Gibson contended in *The Perfect War* that "commanders had nothing to gain by reporting attacks against either themselves or other officers and noncommissioned officers in their units, since fraggings indicated failures in leadership." Gibson speculated that they thus filed misleading cause-of-death reports, and "the Pentagon in turn tried to minimize those few reports they did receive by counting only grenade-caused casualties, literal 'fraggings,' rather than including attacks on superiors by all means, including the use of rifles and machine guns, and the sabotage of helicopters." Postwar surveys indicated that fragging incidents were underreported as well. Sociologist John Helmer, for instance, reported in his book *Bringing the War Home* that 58 percent of Vietnam veterans that he interviewed indicated that they personally knew of a fragging incident in their unit directed against NCOs or officers.

The vast majority of those targeted by their fellow soldiers for execution were officers. As one Vietnam veteran told Curry, "too often [officers] made decisions when simply not aware of what was involved—they hadn't been there long enough or were too stupid to know better—yet they had the power to enforce their decisions no matter what it cost those who had to carry them out." Thus, as self-preservation became the guiding factor in some soldiers' tours, it too often combined with the general breakdown in discipline to create a deadly willingness to remove perceived threats to that survival.

But Vietnam also saw a disturbing number of fragging incidents in rear-echelon areas where dangers were minimal. On a number of occasions, the lives of officers or NCOs in rear areas were taken or endangered with little or no provocation. As one JAG (Judge Advocate General) lawyer told Linden, "Rear-echelon fraggings are a complete mystery to me. All it takes is a 'How are you, Joe?' and bang, somebody will shoot you."

By the early 1970s, the specter of fragging had cast a chilling shadow over the U.S. Army's control of its troops in Vietnam. Some observers claimed that the issue even influenced the military's prosecution of the war by the early 1970s. "Through intimidation by threats—verbal and written—and scare stories, fragging is influential to the point that virtually all officers and NCOs have to take into account the possibility of fragging before giving an order to the men under them," charged Linden. David Cortright, author of *Soldiers in Revolt*, agreed, contending that "the unexpected appearance of a grenade pin or the detonation of a harmless smoke grenade frequently convinced commanders to abandon expected military standards. Once a commander was threatened by or became the actual target of a fragging, his effectiveness and that of the unit involved were severely hampered."

STONE AND VIETNAM

Stone's first experiences in Indonesia took place in 1965, when, at the age of eighteen, he fled Yale University for a teaching position at a Catholic school for Chinese students in a Saigon suburb. Upon arrival in Saigon, he became intoxicated with the city's exotic atmosphere, which was heightened further by the influx of American soldiers onto its streets. The setting provided ample fodder for Stone's interest in writing, and before long he was working furiously on a novel. He eventually returned to Yale, but after Simon and Schuster rejected his massive novel, "I gave up," Stone told *Time*'s Richard Corliss. Wracked with self-doubt and a feeling that he was not meeting his father's expectations, "I joined the Army. They'd cut my hair, and I'd be a number. To me the American involvement was correct. My dad was a cold warrior, and I was a cold-war baby. I knew that Viet Nam was going to be *the* war of my generation, and I didn't want to miss it."

Pushing for infantry duty in Vietnam, Stone was assigned to the 2nd Platoon of B Company, 3rd Battalion, 25th Infantry Division. In September 1967 he joined his platoon out by the Cambodian border. "My first day in Viet Nam," Stone recalled to Corliss, "I realized, like Chris in *Platoon*, that I'd made a terrible mistake. It was on-the-job training: Here's your machete, kid; you cut point. You learn if you can, and if not you're dead. Nobody was motivated, except to get out. Survival was the key. It wasn't very romantic."

Stone quickly learned that platoons were often plagued by factionalism and disunity. "On one side were the lifers, the juicers [heavy drinkers], and the moron white element," he told Corliss. "On the other side was a progressive, hippie, dope-smoking group: some blacks, some urban whites, Indians, random characters from odd places. . . . They were out to survive this bummer with some integrity and a sense of humor. I fell in with the progressives—a Yale boy who heard soul music and smoked dope for the first time in his life."

Stone spent the next fifteen months in Vietnam before returning to the United States. A significant amount of this time was spent "in country" with the 25th infantry; he also spent some of his tour in Saigon and with a Long Range Reconnaissance Platoon (LRRP) of the 1st Cavalry. His time with the 25th infantry ended in January 1968, when he was wounded for a second time, but by then he had a wealth of sobering battlefield experiences under his belt. Stone later noted that many of the major events that take place in *Platoon*, from an ugly atrocity sequence in a Vietnamese village to the climactic battle scene, were based on his own experiences with the 25th. He also claimed that "fragging" incidents such as the one included in the film were far more commonplace than the military would admit. "[Fragging] happened a lot," he told *Playboy*'s Marc Cooper. "We knew that there was no moral objective from day to day—that there was no victory in sight. And you're out on the front lines. What are you going to do? Risk your life and get killed for this? So that was the source of the tension leading to the murders and the fraggings. The officer corps—not just the officers but especially the top sergeants—were pretty much hated, most of them.''

Upon being transferred to the 1st Cavalry in April 1968, Stone met the two men who would serve as the models for Elias and Barnes, the two archetypal sergeants who would struggle for the heart and mind of Chris Taylor in *Platoon*. Barnes, he later mused in *Platoon: Screenplay*, was ''the best soldier I ever saw, except possibly for Elias.'' But whereas Elias was able to keep his moral bearings in the war, ''there was a sickness in [Barnes], he wanted to kill too much.''

Finally, around Thanksgiving 1968, Stone returned to the United States, where he had difficulty reconciling his wartime experiences with his perception that most of his countrymen were indifferent to the whole Vietnam issue. ''Nobody was fighting the war,'' he told Riordan. ''The problem wasn't the hippies or the protestors. They were a very small group. It was the mass indifference. Nobody cared. That was what hurt. People were going about the business of making money. The whole problem with Vietnam was that Johnson never made it a war. Either you go to war or you don't go to war. You just don't send poor kids and draftees and let the college kids stay in college. That divides the country.''

CREATION OF *PLATOON*

Upon returning to America, Stone secured a degree in film from New York University and launched his career in movies as a scriptwriter. In the mid-1970s he began work on the script that would become *Platoon*. ''Essentially what I wanted to say was, Remember. Just remember what that war was,'' he remarked to Corliss. ''I wanted to make a document of this forgotten pocket of time. I felt Viet Nam was omitted from history books.'' The finished product, however, was shunned by the studios, who felt that Stone's grim Vietnam vision would be box office poison.

As time passed, however, circumstances changed. Other films dealing with Vietnam proved successful, and Stone's work on *Salvador*, a critically acclaimed film about a journalist's experiences in war-torn El Salvador, gave him added legitimacy. By October 1985 the filmmaker had secured financing for *Platoon*; the film would finally be made.

Stone went to extraordinary lengths to make the film as realistic as possible. He shot the movie in the Philippines, and prior to production he made all the actors go through an arduous two-week training session at the hands of a decorated Vietnam veteran, Marine Dale Dye (who also served as the film's technical advisor). ''The idea was to fuck with their heads so we could get that dog-tired attitude, the anger, the irritation, the casual way of brutality, the casual approach to death. What I remember most about Vietnam and what a lot of guys remember is the tiredness,'' he said in Riordan's biography. ''We wanted to immerse the cast in the Vietnam infantryman's life, his way of thinking, talking, and moving." Actor Charlie Sheen, who played Stone's alter-ego, Chris Taylor, in the film, later told Riordan that "my respect for the guys who served in Vietnam escalated seven hundred percent [after the training]," and Tom Berenger, who played Sergeant Barnes, told Riordan that "the training gave me a sense of how awful the war must have been. The jungle is an ass-kicker. . . . After this, one guy said, it would be hard to go back to making Twinkies commercials. It was kind of like playing 'Army,' but when it was over we were all cranky, blistered, hollow-eyed—and ready to start filming."

The film opens in September 1967, as soldier Chris Taylor (Sheen) arrives in Vietnam. He joins his infantry unit, which is soon snaking through the mysterious jungles of Vietnam. Taylor quickly sees that the platoon, nominally headed by a lieutenant, is actually dominated by two sergeants: Elias (played by Willem Dafoe), a compassionate but skilled soldier, and Barnes (Berenger), an intimidating, heavily scarred man who eventually emerges as a figure of amorality and implacable violence. Taylor is quickly wounded in a frightening clash with the enemy, and during his convalescence he sees evidence of a chasm that exists in the platoon between the followers of Elias and Barnes.

Taylor rejoins the platoon, and in a subsequent foray, the death of two platoon members triggers a bloody assault on a nearby village. Taylor is momentarily drawn into the ugliness, but he snaps out of it, only to watch in horror as a fellow soldier bashes in an old villager's head. Taylor subsequently stops several other soldiers from raping a young Vietnamese woman, but the village is destroyed by Barnes and his followers. Elias is horrified by the violence, and upon returning to their base, he makes it clear that he intends to press charges against Barnes. As the individual platoon members choose whether to side with Barnes or Elias, Taylor remains undecided; he admires Elias's moral convictions, but is attracted too to the aura of ruthless invulnerability that hangs over Barnes.

A short time later the platoon is ambushed, but they fight their way out of it. Elias dispatches several enemy soldiers, but his pursuit of the VC soon takes him away from the rest of the platoon. Taylor's efforts to find Elias are cut short by Barnes, who orders him to return to the evacuation area. Barnes subsequently tracks Elias down and shoots him three times. Afterward Barnes returns to the platoon, telling Taylor that he found Elias's body. The platoon then jumps on the evacuation helicopters, but as they swing up into the sky, Taylor sees Elias stumble out of the jungle, pursued by Vietcong soldiers. Elias is shot down by the VC, his arms raised to the heavens.

Taylor subsequently attempts to convince others that Barnes was responsible for Elias's death, only to have the sergeant berate him. The two men clash, and Barnes appears to be on the verge of killing the young soldier until he is reminded of the consequences of such an action. A short time later, the platoon's position is overrun by enemy soldiers, and the captain calls in air strikes on his own position. Barnes, who used the confusion of battle to hunt down Taylor, is hit by an incoming strike just before he can kill the enlisted man.

Taylor wakes the next morning, hurt but alive. Wandering around the now quiet battlefield, he comes upon a seriously wounded Barnes. Ignoring Barnes's instructions to go find a medic, Taylor points his rifle at the sergeant. Barnes abruptly barks out an order—"Do it!"—and Taylor kills him. The film ends with a tearful Taylor looking over the battlefield from his seat in another helicopter, as a voice-over muses on the struggle that the two sergeants waged for his soul.

CRITICAL REACTION

The critical response to *Platoon* was overwhelmingly positive. "Oliver Stone's impassioned, mournful *Platoon* is the kind of Vietnam picture that many of us have longed for and also, in secret, dreaded," wrote David Denby in *New York*. "Stone has told the familiar young soldier's story without copping out on the ineradicable bitterness and confusion of the Vietnam War." *New York Times* critic Vincent Canby called the film "possibly the best work of any kind about the Vietnam War since Michael Herr's vigorous and hallucinatory book *Dispatches*." *Time*'s Richard Corliss wrote that Stone "has created a time-capsule movie that explodes like a frag bomb in the consciousness of America, showing how it was back then, over there. . . . Stone has proved that a film can still roil the blood of the American body politic." Many reviewers were particularly struck by *Platoon*'s stark depictions of some of the most controversial and intensely debated aspects of the American soldiers' performance in Vietnam. Internal dissension, drug use, fragging, brutality, climate, and the enemy's elusive and deadly qualities all had a corrosive effect on American military performance, and all are given attention in the film. And Stone's ability to re-create the unique nature of that war—in which weeks of numbing boredom give way to sudden conflagrations of dizzying violence—was praised in many quarters. Terrence Rafferty wrote in *The Nation* that the film's "straightforward genre-picture intensity makes all the other film treatments of the subject look evasive and superficial." Corliss claimed that "more than any other film, *Platoon* gives the sense—all five senses—of fighting in Viet Nam. . . . The film does not glamourize or trivialize death with grotesque special effects. But it jolts the viewer alive to the sensuousness of danger, fear and war lust."

A minority of reviewers offered harsher assessments of the film. John Podhoretz, writing in the conservative *Washington Times' Insight*, called the film a "repellent" work that defamed American soldiers, and *New Yorker* critic Pauline Kael wrote that "[Stone] lacks judgment. Just about everything in *Platoon* is too explicit, and is so heightened that it can numb you and make you feel jaded." A number of critics took issue with the symbolism in Stone's depictions of the saintlike Elias and the nihilistic Barnes as well. But most agreed that whatever its faults, *Platoon* painted a powerful, convincing portrait of the physical and moral challenges that confronted American soldiers in Vietnam.

Opinion of the film was also generally positive among those who experienced Vietnam firsthand. Many veterans agreed that Stone did a remarkable job of re-creating the atmosphere out in Vietnam's "Indian country," and some people who were there, such as journalist David Halberstam, were unstinting in their praise for the picture. "*Platoon* is the first real Viet Nam film," he wrote in the *New York Times*. "*Platoon* is historically and politically accurate. . . . I think the film will become an American classic. Thirty years from now, people will think of the Viet Nam War as *Platoon*."

Such a possibility disturbed some veterans, though, who contended that Stone painted an excessively grim picture of American behavior in the war. Citing the village atrocity sequence in the film in particular, they voiced concerns that viewers would regard *Platoon* as the story of *every* infantryman who served in Vietnam. "Most of [the veterans] agreed that *Platoon* looked and felt so much like the war that it brought back the sensory experience of it in an almost overpowering way, yet they resented the way it portrayed how soldiers handled the horrors they encountered," wrote James Riordan. "The simple truth is that each veteran has his own view of the war." For his part, Stone took pains to make it clear that the film was based on his experiences, not those of anyone else. "I'm not going to be so pretentious as to say this is *the* Vietnam War movie. I think there are many more that can be done. There are a thousand stories. A million stories."

FURTHER READING

Bennett, Leslie. "Oliver Stone—Easing out of Violence." *New York Times* (April 13, 1987).

Canby, Vincent. "Film: The Vietnam War in Stone's 'Platoon.' " *New York Times* (December 19, 1986).

Cooper, Marc. "*Wall Street*: An Interview on Jungle Warfare with Oliver Stone." *Playboy* (February 1988).

Corliss, Richard. "*Platoon*: Viet Nam, the Way It Really Was, on Film." *Time* (January 26, 1987).

Cortright, David. *Soldiers in Revolt: The American Military Today*. Garden City, N.Y.: Anchor Press/Doubleday, 1975.

Curry, Cecil B. (as Cincinnatus). *Self-Destruction: The Disintegration and Decay of the U.S. Army in Vietnam*. New York: W. W. Norton, 1981.

Denby, David. "Bringing the War Back Home." *New York* (December 15, 1986).

Gabriel, Richard A., and Paul L. Savage. *Crisis in Command: Mismanagement in the Army*. New York: Hill and Wang, 1978.

Gibson, James William. *The Perfect War: The War We Couldn't Lose and How We Did*. Boston: Atlantic Monthly Press, 1986.

Halberstam, David, and Bernard E. Trainor. "Two Who Were There View 'Platoon.' " *New York Times* (March 8, 1987).

Hauser, William L. *America's Army in Crisis: A Study in Civil-Military Relations*. Baltimore: Johns Hopkins University Press, 1973.

Heinl, Robert. "The Collapse of the Armed Forces." *Armed Forces Magazine* (June 1971).

Helmer, John. *Bringing the War Home: The American Soldier in Vietnam and After*. New York: Free Press, 1974.

Herr, Michael. *Dispatches*. New York: Alfred A. Knopf, 1977.

Kael, Pauline. "Platoon." *New Yorker* (January 12, 1987).

Kagan, Norman. *The Cinema of Oliver Stone*. New York: Continuum, 1995.

Linden, Eugene. "The Demoralization of an Army: Fragging and Other Withdrawal Symptoms." *Saturday Review* (January 8, 1972).

Riordan, James. *Stone: The Controversies, Excesses, and Exploits of a Radical Filmmaker*. New York: Hyperion, 1995.

Stone, Oliver. "One from the Heart." *American Film* (January/February 1987).

———. *Platoon: Screenplay*. New York: Vintage Books, 1986.

Willenson, Kim. *The Bad War: An Oral History of the Vietnam War*. New York: New American Library, 1987.

The Quiet American

Novel

Author: Graham Greene

Facts of Publication: London: Heinemann, 1955; New York: Viking, 1956

Although British author Graham Greene's 1955 novel *The Quiet American* pre-dated direct American military involvement in Vietnam by several years, it eventually earned wide acclaim for its accurate prediction of the tragic results of that involvement. The book aroused a great deal of controversy upon its initial publication, however: Condemned by many American reviewers for its perceived anti-American bias, it was embraced by officials of the Soviet Union for the same reason. The novel is set during the First Indochina War, when the Communist-led Vietminh forces sought to liberate Vietnam from French colonial rule. Greene, who made several trips to Vietnam as a journalist between 1951 and 1954, created this story of personal rivalry, political intrigue, and moral ambiguity based on his own experiences during this period.

HISTORICAL BACKGROUND

Vietnam has a long history of struggle against repressive rule by other nations. The region that eventually became known as Vietnam was first conquered by China in 111 B.C., which marked the beginning of one thousand years of Chinese rule. During this time, the Vietnamese people gradually took on distinctive cultural characteristics and developed a separate identity from the Chinese. After gaining their independence in A.D. 939, the Vietnamese faced persistent incursions by China and various other neighbors through the mid-1400s. Over the next 250 years, the Vietnamese people expanded their territory to the south until it approximated the boundaries of modern Vietnam. The nation was unified politically for the first time under the Nguyen dynasty in 1802. According to Gary R. Hess in his book *Vietnam and the United States*, this event helped give the Vietnamese "a sense of patriotism unique among the peoples of Southeast Asia."

Around this time, Indochina increasingly became the target of European expansionism. French missionaries and traders had worked in Vietnam for several decades by 1858, when France undertook an invasion that required nearly forty years to complete. In 1897 Vietnam became part of French Indochina, a colony that also included Laos and Cambodia. The colonial rulers divided Vietnam into three political units, instituted repressive laws, changed many aspects of its culture, and exploited its natural resources. "Civil liberties were not recognized, and political parties were virtually prohibited," Hess explained. "When combined with the economic policies that prevented the rise of a substantial Vietnamese middle class, the effect of French policy was to preclude the development of a liberal, Western-oriented political movement."

Rise of the Vietminh

The Communist Party began to exert some influence in Vietnam during the 1930s, when Ho Chi Minh organized peasants in protests against their treatment by the French. After these protests were violently suppressed by the colonial powers at a cost of ten thousand Vietnamese lives, the Communist Party seemed to disappear, but in fact its leaders remained active and created a broadly based nationalist movement. When France was overrun by Germany during World War II, Vietnamese nationalists saw it as an opportunity to seek independence and established an organization, the Vietminh, for that purpose. But shortly after the attack on Pearl Harbor in 1941, Japan assumed control over much of Southeast Asia, including Vietnam. The Vietminh led the Vietnamese resistance against Japan and were instrumental in providing the Allies with intelligence reports about Japanese activities in Indochina. Immediately following Japan's surrender in 1945, the Vietminh-led independence movement, known as the August Revolution, swept quickly across Vietnam from north to south. On August 30 Emperor Bao Dai—the last member of the Nguyen dynasty, who had collaborated with both the French and the Japanese—abdicated in favor of Ho Chi Minh, thus granting the Vietminh government legitimacy in the eyes of the Vietnamese people. On September 2 Ho formally declared his nation's independence in a statement that included many passages from the American Declaration of Independence.

In this and many other ways, Ho downplayed his Communist philosophy and cultivated the favor of the United States. Knowing that President Franklin Roosevelt was an avowed anticolonialist, he counted on American support for the independence movements in Southeast Asia. In fact, Roosevelt made several statements early in the postwar period indicating that he wanted to end Western colonialism around the world. Over time, however, the politics of the peace process and the beginning of the Cold War diminished the American commitment to this cause. "Ironically, the foundation of the First Indochina War had been laid in part by the United States, whose inflated anti-colonialist rhetoric . . . had raised false expectations throughout Asia," Harry G. Summers, Jr. wrote in his *Historical Atlas of the Vietnam War.* "When these expectations were not realized, there was a rejection of . . . the American model . . . and a move toward the model provided by Vladimir Lenin."

The British were given control over the postwar status of Indochina in 1945, and they did not object when France sought to reclaim its former colonies. The United States, not wishing to alienate its allies and concerned about the Communist leanings of the Vietminh, went along with the plan. "Within the context of the period, the United States was disinclined to underwrite Ho, a veteran Communist opposed to France," Stanley Karnow explained in *Vietnam: A History.* "Thus it was that two decades before its commitment of combat troops there, the United States began to sink into the Vietnam quagmire." Fearing that a Communist takeover of Vietnam would lead to the spread of Communist influence throughout Indochina, the United States grew resigned to supporting French policy. "To U.S. policymakers Vietnam stood as the key to the entire region, for if the Viet Minh . . . succeeded, that would enhance the prospects for Communist success in Thailand and the newly independent Philippines, Indonesia, and Burma. Economic problems and political insecurity in these countries seemingly facilitated the appeal of communism and weakened resistance to external pressures," Hess noted.

The First Indochina War

The Vietminh, lacking international recognition and support, soon signed a compromise agreement in Paris that made Vietnam a "free state" within the French Union. But the two sides inevitably disagreed about the particulars of the arrangement. In 1946, the French began military actions to retake control of Vietnam. During the early years of this conflict, which became known as the First Indochina War, French troops generally defeated Vietminh forces in open battles and gained control of most major cities, but the Vietminh prevailed in guerilla warfare and controlled a great deal of the countryside.

Seeking to draw the nationalist sentiments of the Vietnamese people away from the Vietminh, the French reinstalled Bao Dai as emperor and created a puppet government around him in 1949. The U.S. government viewed this development as a positive step toward self-rule for the Vietnamese. In fact, some American advisors had been working covertly to develop a "third force" in the country that would provide Vietnamese nationalists with an alternative to the French colonialists and the Communist Vietminh. The implementation of the "Bao Dai solution" prompted the United States to begin giving direct assistance to France in 1950. Though this aid had totaled $775 million by the end of 1952, the French continued to suffer embarrassing defeats at the hands of the Vietminh. In addition, China was able to lend its support to the Vietminh after the end of the Korean War in 1953. At this time, the French decided to negotiate an end to the unpopular conflict—which had caused 150,000 French casualties, cost half of the nation's annual defense budget, and weakened its position in Europe.

Dien Bien Phu

As the time to negotiate a settlement drew near, both sides tried to bolster their positions through military actions. General Vo Nguyen Giap, the commander of the Vietminh forces, showed his power by launching an attack on Laos from the remote northwestern village of Dien Bien Phu. Though the Vietminh quickly retreated, the move alarmed the French. The French thus settled on Dien Bien Phu as the center of their last-ditch effort to improve their negotiating position. Hoping to draw the Vietminh into a set-piece battle and destroy a large part of their forces as quickly and decisively as possible, the French dropped paratroopers into the valley surrounding the village in the fall of 1953. "It was an incredible gamble," Bernard B. Fall wrote in *Hell in a Very Small Place: The Siege of Dien Bien Phu*, "for upon its success hinged not only the fate of the French forces in Indochina and France's political role in Southeast Asia, but the survival of Vietnam as a non-Communist state."

The French forces soon took over the village and established a central garrison and several supporting artillery bases, but the Vietminh maintained control over the surrounding mountains and were able to prevent supplies from reaching the valley. Giap took the French by surprise in March 1954 by attacking and gaining control of the artillery bases, then laying siege to the garrison. The desperate French government appealed to the United States for help in the form of bombing runs over Vietminh positions, but President Dwight Eisenhower ultimately decided not to intervene. The siege ended with a Vietminh victory on May 7, 1954, the same day that peace talks were to begin in Geneva, Switzerland. Fall called Dien Bien Phu "one of the truly decisive battles of the twentieth century. . . . The whole 'tone' of the conflict, as it were, had changed. One of the sides in the conflict had lost its chance of attaining whatever it had sought to gain in fighting the war. This was true of the French after they had lost the Battle of Dien Bien Phu." The outcome of the battle also had significant effect on the tone of the later conflict with the United States, as Fall explained: "Twelve years later, the North Vietnamese were still unafraid to take on the best forces the United States [could] muster."

Although the U.S. government viewed the French defeat in the First Indochina War as a major setback in preventing the spread of Communism, most Vietnamese saw it instead as a nationalist victory over the forces of Colonialism. As Greene noted in his *New Republic* piece "Last Act in Indo-china," "The war in Vietnam did not begin as a Communist war, and the victory of Dien Bien Phu was welcomed at heart by every Vietnamian, in the South as well as the North." Nevertheless, the Geneva agreements that ended the First Indochina War "temporarily" divided Vietnam at the seventeenth parallel. The division was originally intended to allow the various forces involved in the conflict to regroup, and the country was to have been reunified through national elections in 1956. The Vietminh consented to the arrangement in hopes of avoiding U.S. intervention.

Thus the Communist Vietminh controlled North Vietnam, and the United States and its allies sought to establish a strong, non-Communist government in South Vietnam. Concerned that nationwide elections would result in the installation of a Communist government, they also scuttled the scheduled elections. As a result, the boundary line dividing the nation remained in place. Ngo Dinh Diem, who was anti-French and anti-Communist, was named premier of South Vietnam and bolstered with $1.2 billion in U.S. aid over the next five years. But Diem alienated many of his people by establishing a dictatorship rather than enacting real reforms. North Vietnamese leaders, with significant support from nationalists in the South, reacted by making plans to reunify Vietnam. "Their struggle was seen as a continuation of the struggle against the French and their puppet Bao Dai. The French and Bao Dai were gone, but in their place were the Americans and Diem," Hess explained. The Americans, determined to hold the line against Communism, soon found themselves supporting the Diem government in a war against the North Vietnamese Army and the Vietminh nationalists, whom the Americans referred to as the Vietcong. Within a few years, the American involvement escalated from providing monetary aid to the Diem government, to providing military advisors to South Vietnam, to the full-scale commitment of U.S. troops during the Second Indochina War.

GREENE AND VIETNAM

Though Graham Greene eventually gained renown as one of the most widely read English novelists of the twentieth century—as well as a prominent literary critic, screenwriter, and journalist—his career began slowly. His first two novels went unpublished, and he had to work feverishly throughout the 1930s in order to pay off debts to his publishers. His earliest literary success came in 1932 with the thriller *Stamboul Train* (later published as *The Orient Express*). During World War II, Greene served with the counterintelligence arm of the British Secret Service. Afterward, still doubting his talents as a novelist, he accepted a contract with MGM as a screenwriter. During the 1950s, Greene traveled to war-torn areas of Malaya, Kenya, and Vietnam as a journalist. He explained in *Ways of Escape* that he wanted "to visit troubled places, not to seek material for novels but to regain the sense of insecurity which I had enjoyed in three blitzes on London."

Greene first went to Vietnam in 1951—during the midst of the war between the French and the Vietminh—to visit his old friend Trevor Wilson, who was then the British Consul in Hanoi. He immediately fell in love with the region. "In Indochina I drained a magic potion, a loving-cup," he recalled in his introduction to *The Quiet American*. "The spell was first cast, I think, by the tall elegant girls in white silk trousers, by the pewter evening light on flat paddy fields, where the water-buffaloes trudged fetlock-deep with a slow primeval gait, the French perfumeries in the rue Catina, the Chinese gambling houses in Cholon, above all by that feeling of exhilaration which a measure of danger brings to the visitor with a return ticket." Greene returned to Vietnam that fall and made three more trips in subsequent years, each time producing journal and magazine articles about the First Indochina War. "I suspect my ambivalent attitude to the war was already perceptible [in these articles]—my admiration for the French Army, my admiration for their enemies, and my doubt of any final value in the war," he admitted in the novel's introduction.

During one visit to Vietnam, Greene met and developed a deep respect for the Communist leader of the Vietminh. "Ho Chi Minh gave an impression of simplicity and candor, but overwhelmingly of leadership. There was nothing evasive about him: this was a man who gave orders and expected obedience and also love. The kind remorseless face had no fanaticism about it," Greene wrote in "Last Act in Indochina." "I am on my guard against hero worship, but he appealed directly to that buried relic of the schoolboy. . . . I regretted I was too old to accept the rules or believe what the school taught."

CREATION OF *THE QUIET AMERICAN*

Greene did not initially intend to turn his experiences in Vietnam into a novel. However, he changed his mind after attending a party thrown by a French colonel. "I shared a room that night with an American attached to an economic aid mission—the members were assumed by the French, probably correctly, to belong to the CIA. My companion bore no resemblance at all to Pyle [the title character of *The Quiet American*]—he was a man of greater intelligence and of less innocence, but he lectured me all the long drive back to Saigon on the necessity of finding a 'third force in Vietnam.' I had never before come so close to the great American dream which was to bedevil affairs in the East," he explained in the introduction. "So the subject of *The Quiet American* came to me, during that talk of a 'third force' on the road through the delta, and my characters quickly followed." The book includes a great deal of direct reportage based upon Greene's own experiences. For example, the author actually attended the press conferences in Hanoi that are described in the novel, and he also went on a "vertical" bombing mission against the Vietminh and saw a canal full of bodies at Phat Diem.

The action in the novel takes place between late 1951 and early 1952, just as it begins to appear that the French colonial powers might ultimately be defeated by the Vietminh. It anticipates not only the French defeat at Dien Bien Phu but also the tragic results of the American military intervention nearly a decade later. In his book *Understanding Graham Greene*, R. H. Miller described *The Quiet American* as a drama about a "lovely, highly civilized country as it moved rapidly toward the overthrow of its French colonial lords and the resultant dangers such a political change presented to the United States, who chose as a matter of policy to regard Vietnam as the key to a free Southeast Asia." The American government reacts to the possibility that the Communists will gain control of Vietnam by cultivating a third political force in the country—largely through the work of CIA operatives—as a pro-American alternative to the French and the Vietminh.

Greene's multilayered story traces the personal rivalry that develops between two very different men against this historical backdrop. *The Quiet American* begins when the title character, a 32-year-old, Harvard-educated idealist named Alden Pyle, is found murdered under a bridge in Saigon. The mystery surrounding his death is gradually unraveled by the narrator, a cynical, middle-aged British reporter named Thomas Fowler, as he thinks back upon the course of his relationship with the young American. Pyle had ostensibly come to Vietnam as part of the American Economic Aid Mission. As Fowler describes him upon his arrival, "He was determined . . . to do good, not to any individual person, but to a country, a continent, a world. Well, he was in his element now, with the whole universe to improve." Pyle bases his political philosophy, which involves introducing a third force into the French-Vietminh conflict, on the writings of the fictional theorist York Harding, author of such tomes as *The Role of the West* and *The Challenge to Democracy*. In contrast, Fowler resolves to remain objective and detached from the events he witnesses. "The human condition being what it was, let them fight, let them love, let them murder, I would not be involved," he states in the novel. "I took no action—even an opinion is a kind of action."

The two main characters become rivals for the affection of a Vietnamese woman, Phuong. At the beginning of the novel Phuong is Fowler's mistress, but Pyle falls in love with her soon after his arrival. When Fowler is unable to obtain a divorce from his estranged wife, Phuong leaves him and goes to live with Pyle, who offers to marry her and take her to the United States. The tension between the two men reaches a peak when they are stranded in the countryside together one night and take refuge in a sentry tower. When the tower comes under attack by the Vietminh, Fowler's leg is broken and Pyle saves his life.

Over time, Fowler becomes increasingly aware of Pyle's true mission in Vietnam. As a covert CIA operative, the young American provides plastic explosives to a terrorist group led by General The. The and his followers set bombs in populous areas of Saigon—causing the deaths of numerous civilians—and blame the destruction on the Vietminh. These acts are meant to erode the Communists' base of support and promote The as a viable third force in the conflict. Pyle is able to dismiss the suffering the bombings cause because he believes that his actions will help gain a victory for democracy. Fowler eventually recognizes that, in his political innocence, the young American is even more dangerous than the terrorists he supports. "Innocence always calls mutely for protection when we would be so much wiser to guard ourselves against it: innocence is like a dumb leper who has lost his bell, wandering the world, meaning no harm," the narrator relates. When Fowler witnesses the aftermath of one of the terrorist bombings, he finds himself unable to adhere to his policy of noninvolvement. Believing that Pyle must be stopped, he agrees to set up the young American for a Communist assassination plot. Though Phuong returns to Fowler after Pyle's death, the reporter remains unhappy, haunted by feelings of guilt about his role in the murder.

As *Literature/Film Quarterly* editor James M. Welsh indicated in *Masterplots*, "*The Quiet American* can be read as a political and moral meditation on the beginning stages of the United States' involvement in Southeast Asia. . . . The large-scale political thesis [is that] American interference in the internal affairs of another country can only result in suffering, death, and defeat, and is not morally justifiable because of abstract idealism." Discussing the message contained in the novel in his book *Graham Greene*, John Atkins noted that the author himself "did not make the mistake of political innocents in believing that guns can defeat Communism, especially foreign guns. The people must be allowed to take up a position from which Communism will not appear enticing."

CRITICAL RECEPTION

Greene's decidedly unflattering portrayal of Americans and negative commentary on the U.S. government's political aims ensured that *The Quiet American* would not be popular with American critics upon its release in 1955. John Lehmann of the *New Republic* called it "one of the most icily anti-American books I have ever read," adding that "the world today is full of desperate idealists who take manslaughter in their stride, and by no means all of them carry American passports." Some reviewers interpreted Greene's stance as pro-Communist and pointed out that the author had joined the Communist Party as a student at Oxford University thirty years earlier (though Greene dismissed this incident as a "prank," it had nevertheless resulted in his being denied a visa to enter the United States in 1952). Particularly controversial was Greene's implicit blaming of the American government for an actual terrorist bombing that took place in Saigon. Adding fuel to the fire, *The Quiet American* received high praise within the Soviet Union and was excerpted in the newspaper *Pravda*. Given all the controversy and suspicion that surrounded the novel, "It is no wonder, then, that Greene's warning about Vietnam was not taken seriously in the United States, even though later events tended to substantiate the wisdom of his political analysis," Welsh commented.

Greene responded to the criticism by reminding readers of Fowler's biases and warning them not to equate him with his unreliable narrator. "Those who have read my war articles on Indochina will know that I am myself by no means a neutralist,'' he remarked to Robert Clurman in the *New York Times Book Review*. ''I share certain of Fowler's views, but obviously not all of them—for instance, I don't happen to be an atheist. But even those views I share with Fowler I don't hold with Fowler's passion because I don't happen to have lost a girl to an American!'' In a 1959 reassessment of the novel published in *Renascence*, R. E. Hughes stated that ''once the reader recognizes that Fowler is not Greene's *alter ego*, but a character being observed and criticized by both reader and author, then the novel as chauvinism disappears, and the novel as art emerges.''

In fact, many later analyses of Greene's work praised various aspects of *The Quiet American*, from the elaborately constructed mystery of its plot to the unforgettable detail of its descriptions of war. But the main aspect of the work that attracted attention was the accuracy of Greene's predictions about the nature and consequences of American involvement in Vietnam. Calling *The Quiet American* ''an astonishing novel of political prophecy,'' Welsh noted that in it ''Greene summarizes the lesson of Vietnam fully ten years before the American government expanded its military commitment to fill the vacuum left by the defeated French.'' Other reviewers noted that the book heavily influenced later literary interpretations of the war. ''The shadow cast over the entire American corpus of Vietnam works by Greene's 1955 work . . . is indeed a large one, for the mixtures of fact and imagination, minute observation and historical connection, reportage and prophecy set an early standard for fiction of that war and placed before American writers a workable model of the contemporary historical novel of extraordinarily high levels of vision and control,'' Thomas Myers wrote in *Walking Point*. ''In *The Quiet American*, he succeeded in offering a symbolic prophecy of the next eighteen years of American commitment in Indochina, a cultural adventure whose hubris concerning political and social engineering principles could be read finally as the most tragic but preventable discrepancy between means and ends.''

FURTHER READING

Atkins, John. *Graham Greene*. London: Calder and Boyars, 1957.

Boardman, Gwenn R. *Graham Greene: The Aesthetics of Exploration*. Gainesville: University of Florida Press, 1971.

Clurman, Robert. ''In and Out of Books.'' *New York Times Book Review* (August 26, 1956).

Dunn, Peter M. *The First Vietnam War*. New York: St. Martin's Press, 1985.

Fall, Bernard B. *Hell in a Very Small Place: The Siege of Dien Bien Phu*. Philadelphia: Lippincott, 1967.

Greene, Graham. ''Last Act in Indochina.'' *New Republic* (May 9, 1955 [part 1], May 15, 1955 [part 2]).

———. *The Quiet American*. London: Heinemann, 1955.

———. *A Sort of Life*. New York: Simon and Schuster, 1971.

———. *Ways of Escape*. London: Bodley Head, 1980.

Hess, Gary R. *Vietnam and the United States: Origins and Legacy of War*. Boston: Twayne, 1990.

Hughes, R. E. "*The Quiet American*: The Case Reopened." *Renascence* (Autumn 1959).

Karnow, Stanley. *Vietnam: A History*. New York: Viking, 1983.

Lehmann, John. "The Blundering, Ineffectual American." *New Republic* (March 12, 1956).

Miller, R. H. *Understanding Graham Greene*. Columbia: University of South Carolina Press, 1990.

Myers, Thomas. *Walking Point: American Narratives of Vietnam*. New York: Oxford University Press, 1988.

O'Prey, Paul. *A Reader's Guide to Graham Greene*. New York: Thames and Hudson, 1988.

Sherry, Norman. *The Life of Graham Greene*. New York: Viking, 1989.

Summers, Harry G., Jr. *Historical Atlas of the Vietnam War*. Boston: Houghton Mifflin, 1995.

Rambo: First Blood, Part II

Film

Director: George Pan Cosmatos

Screenplay: Sylvester Stallone, James Cameron

Principal Cast: Sylvester Stallone, Richard Crenna, Charles Napier, Julia Nickson

Year of Release: 1985 (Tri-Star)

The mid-1980s are commonly viewed as a time when the American public, long haunted by Vietnam and other national disappointments, experienced a rejuvenation of national pride and self-confidence. Debates about the health and character of this reinvigoration, however, were ubiquitous, and they intensified with the 1985 release of Sylvester Stallone's *Rambo: First Blood, Part II*, a film that tells the tale of an embittered Vietnam veteran who slaughters dozens of Communist foes while on a POW rescue mission.

HISTORICAL BACKGROUND

The decade of the 1970s has been characterized as a period of retrenchment and disillusionment in America. Historians and social critics contend that such factors as the Vietnam War, the Watergate scandal, the Middle East oil crisis, the ever-present threat of Communism, and the demoralizing Iranian hostage affair all combined to erode American confidence in itself and its status as the world's preeminent nation.

Ronald Reagan, who defeated incumbent Jimmy Carter in the 1980 election for the presidency of the United States, was troubled by this deterioration in the nation's self-image. ''The previous administration for some reason had accepted the notion that America was no longer the world power it had once been, that it had become powerless to shape world events,'' he wrote in his autobiography, *An American Life*. ''Consciously or unconsciously, we had sent out a message to the world that Washington was no longer sure of itself, its ideals, or its commitments to our allies, and that it seemed to accept as inevitable the advance of Soviet expansionism, especially in the poor and underdeveloped countries of the world.''

Reagan signaled his determination to reverse this apparent slide in national self-perception in his 1981 inaugural address, when he remarked that the nation's ''era of self-doubt was over.'' Many historians have since observed that the timing of Reagan's pronouncement could not have been better. As journalist Haynes Johnson wrote in *Sleepwalking through History: America in the Reagan Years*, ''Ronald Reagan's inauguration brought together two contradictory but complementary strains of pessimism and optimism present in the United States in 1981: a deep sense of frustration, compounded by a series of political, economic, and military failures at home and abroad that struck at the nation's self-confidence and self-esteem, and a corresponding yearning to believe that a more successful period of national strength was dawning.'' Over the course of the next several years, Reagan's unfaltering expression of faith in the merits of conservative patriotism proved to be a soothing balm for America's wounds, at least among a significant percentage of the electorate. Even his detractors admitted that he was adept at rekindling the nation's self-confidence, though they also contended that this revitalization too often strayed into the realm of excessive nationalism.

Reagan—Vietnam Hawk

During the 1980s the Reagan Administration became well known for its adherence to antitax and antiregulatory philosophies, but it became equally recognized for its fiercely anti-Communist foreign policy philosophy. This was particularly evident in its active opposition to Communist groups in Third World nations (especially El Salvador and Nicaragua). Reagan's conservative views on Communism had been formed decades before. He had been an unapologetic hawk during the Vietnam War, when he had served as governor of California. During that conflict he had characterized student protestors at Berkeley and elsewhere as immoral and ignorant. He also favored lifting restrictions on bombing targets in North Vietnam, and once suggested that the best way to prosecute the war was to reduce Vietnam to a ''parking lot.'' Years later, as president, he intimated on several occasions that the American soldiers who had served in Vietnam had lost because of a failure of will back home. Indeed, this interpretation of the war came to be voiced with increased frequency and conviction by right-wing politicians and opinion-makers during the Reagan era.

Reagan supporters maintained that his unwavering championing of traditional

American values and his efforts to instill national pride were significant factors in the reevaluation of Vietnam veterans that took place during the 1980s. But despite Reagan's often kind words for Vietnam veterans—and his heavy spending on military programs—the Reagan Administration was heavily criticized in some quarters for the impact that its domestic budget cuts had on Vietnam veterans.

STALLONE AND VIETNAM

After Sylvester Stallone's Rambo character appeared on movie screens, speculation mounted about the reasons why the actor, who came of draft age during the war, had not served in the armed forces. A column by nationally syndicated newspaper columnist Mike Royko, in which he charged that Stallone had actually worked to avoid the draft, added to the controversy. Stallone, though, insisted that the accounts were false. "I'm sure [Royko] is a good writer, but he got his facts wrong on this one," Stallone said in a *Rolling Stone* interview with Nancy Collins. "I was here in '67, at the height of the war. I went to Dade College and then the University of Miami. I went for my draft twice, and they wouldn't let me in—once for hearing and once for feet. I have flat feet, fallen arches, superbly fallen, like Rome. And they said no. I went there ready and willing to go. I was very opposed to draft dodging."

Stallone, who characterized himself as patriotic but apolitical in mid-1980s interviews, expressed pride in the Rambo films and in the widespread perception that the character had come to symbolize newly rejuvenated American pride, at the same time dismissing critics who complained that this patriotism was in reality a virulent strain of jingoism. "You say am I the Jane Fonda of the right?" he said in an interview with Richard Grenier for the *New York Times*. "Listen. I'm not right wing. I'm not left wing. I love my country. I stand for ordinary Americans, losers a lot of them. They don't understand big, international politics. Their country tells them to fight in Vietnam? They fight."

Stallone acknowledged that Rambo was a character likely to draw controversy, remarking to Grenier that when the early footage of the first Rambo film, *First Blood*, came in, "we were scared to death. This Rambo character looked nihilistic, almost psychopathic." But he claimed that over the course of the two pictures, he and the other creative people associated with the film managed to imbue the character with a human element. "Nobody could do all the things he does. He's far bigger than life. But he's a megaphone. He's telling you that men who fought for their country, and a lot of them lost their lives, deserve to be honored."

Asked to account for Rambo's tremendous popularity, Stallone told Collins that "we just happened to come along at the right time. . . . This country has really needed to flex its muscles. This country is like a child that developed too quickly and became self-conscious of its power. The other little nations were pulling at us, saying, 'You're bullying. Don't tread on us.' So we pulled back.

. . . And what happened, as usual, is people took kindness for weakness, and America lost its esteem. Right now, it's just flexing. You might say America has gone back to the gym.''

CREATION OF *RAMBO: FIRST BLOOD, PART II*

The character of Vietnam veteran John Rambo was created by writer David Morrell, who published the first book of his exploits, *First Blood*, in 1972. The novel, which featured a body count that the author later characterized as "virtually uncountable," garnered some interest from Hollywood, but the proposed film languished until 1981, when Sylvester Stallone of *Rocky* fame agreed to take the lead role.

The film opened in the fall of 1982 to large, enthusiastic audiences who ignored the many reviewers who found the film to be emotionally manipulative and ultimately insulting to veterans. *First Blood* concerns John Rambo, a hollow-eyed drifter and Vietnam vet who, after learning that his last friend from the war has died of cancer (from exposure to Agent Orange), is hassled by the red-necked sheriff (played by Brian Dennehy) of a small town in the Pacific Northwest. The sheriff, who sees the stranger as an unsightly vagrant, attempts to remove him from the town, but these efforts prove disastrous. The harsh treatment visited upon Rambo by the sheriff's men triggers a flashback to his torture-filled days as a POW, and he subsequently escapes, leaving battered deputies in his wake. The violent clash soon triggers a war between Rambo—who turns out to be a veteran of a Special Forces unit—and various law enforcement agencies, including the National Guard. The battle ends only after Rambo's old commander, Colonel Trautman (Richard Crenna), is brought in to defuse the situation. Rambo finally surrenders, crying out that "you just don't turn it off," a reference to his terrible experiences in Vietnam.

The sequel, *Rambo: First Blood, Part II* (commonly known as *Rambo II*), continued with the first film's basic setup—lone warrior battles against incredible odds—but transposed the action to Vietnam. The film opens with Colonel Trautman (Crenna again) arranging Rambo's release from prison, where he has presumably been ensconced since the conclusion of *First Blood*. The colonel informs Rambo that he can gain his freedom if he consents to go on a secret reconnaissance mission in Vietnam to search for possible American POWs. Rambo agrees to the deal, though he bitterly adds, "Do we get to win this time?"

Rambo is subsequently flown to Thailand, where he is briefed by the mission's leader, Murdock (Charles Napier), and sent on his way. Rambo soon learns, however, that the mission is a fake one. The government task force wants the search to be unsuccessful, thus putting the aggravating POW issue to rest with the American people once and for all. Instead, Rambo actually finds a group of POWs. Murdock quickly abandons him, and he is subsequently captured by the Communists. His Vietnamese and Soviet captors subject him to a gauntlet of horrible torture, but he escapes with the help of a young Vietnamese woman named Co (Julia Nickson). Her murder at the hands of a Vietnamese officer, however, sends Rambo on a vengeful killing spree. After decimating large numbers of Vietnamese and Soviet troops, Rambo successfully delivers the POWs from imprisonment in a commandeered Soviet helicopter. He subsequently slays his chief Communist enemies, including the officer who killed Co, and then confronts the cowardly Murdock. But though he thoroughly humiliates Murdock, he lets him live in order to relay ominous warnings to his superiors.

CRITICAL RECEPTION

Rambo: First Blood, Part II was an enormous box office hit. During its first three weeks alone it grossed about $70 million (the film, which cost $27 million to make, would eventually gross an estimated $275 million worldwide). Studio executives quickly seized on the film's popularity, launching a wide array of "Rambo-gear" merchandise that proved quite popular. "Rambomania is spreading faster than the fire storms set by the hero's explosive warheads," wrote *Time*'s Richard Zoglin in 1985. "Hollywood megahits of summers past have flooded the market with such whimsical souvenirs as furry Gremlins and cuddly E.T.s. This year stores are stocking up with war paraphernalia: a $150 replica of Rambo's high-tech bow and arrow, Rambo knives and an assortment of toy guns." The name Rambo became a ubiquitous presence in editorial cartoons and late night monologues as well.

Many critics granted that the film delivered the action-packed goods that its audience expected, albeit in simplistic, cartoonish fashion. But discussion of the film tended to center far more often on the perceived significance of the film's popularity—and the merits of the ideology it championed—than on Stallone's acting ability or George Pan Cosmatos's direction. The prevailing critical and scholarly response to the film in these areas was negative.

Some commentators contended that *Rambo II* was popular not only because it offered a perversely comforting explanation for the American defeat in Vietnam (America lost because of a cowardly and duplicitous government and a paralyzed public rather than because of troop shortcomings) but also because it provided an alternative ending to that conflict, with America emerging triumphant. Martha Bayles wrote in the *New Republic* that "Stallone taps popular patriotism, but he also taps darker emotions, such as the resentment many veterans feel toward their government for not waging war against North Vietnam to the hilt, and toward their countrymen for ridiculing or ignoring their sacrifices." Film scholar Kevin Bowen offered a similar assessment in *From Hanoi to Hollywood*, contending that films like *Rambo II* "make a direct association between the marginalized status of veterans and a war lost due to a failure of will in America brought about by liberals, radicals, and self-serving government officials." Critics like Bowen also argued that *Rambo II* and its cinematic cousins were exploitive in nature. "These films exploit the marginal positioning of veterans and the anger it causes to serve a particularly conservative political view," Bowen remarked. "They represent no serious attempts to come to terms with the complex experience of the war and the postwar period, their goal being a simple-minded, income-producing revisionism that feeds on the pain of veterans and makes dangerous overtures to a new heroic image."

Others, however, speculated that the United States' embrace of Stallone's heroic icon had some therapeutic dimensions. As historian Stanley Karnow told Zoglin, "in general, the public feels that Vietnam was a tragedy, an experience they don't want to repeat. But at the same time, there's an attempt to find some redeeming aspects in it. Movies can turn a defeat into victory; you can achieve in fantasy what you didn't achieve in reality." Budra added that even though the film utilizes a "convenient myth" (failure of domestic will) to explain the American defeat in the war, it nonetheless had some cathartic qualities: "Rambo, in liberating himself, his countrymen and his friends, is liberating the American conscience, held captive, emasculated, since the Vietnam war." *Newsweek*'s appraisal of Rambo's impact was even more succinct; the magazine remarked that Stallone had "brought the hero back to the forefront of American mythology."

Some academics contended that *Rambo: First Blood, Part II*, though highly critical of America's *prosecution* of the war, also legitimized American *involvement* in the conflict. As Gaylyn Studlar and David Desser wrote in *Film Quarterly*, "The need to believe in the MIAs [depicted in *Rambo II*] gives credence to the view that the Vietnamese are now and *therefore have always been* an inhuman and cruel enemy. Vietnam's alleged actions in *presently* holding American prisoners serves as an index of our essential rightness in fighting such an enemy *in the past*. Moreover, our alleged unwillingness to confront Vietnam on the MIAs issue is taken to be an index of the government's cowardice in its Vietnam policy. . . . Within its formula of militaristic zeal, *Rambo* sustains an atmosphere of post-Watergate distrust of government."

Finally, a number of critics argued that the film's anti-Communist tone, coupled with its repudiation of weak-willed Americans, served to support the Reagan administration's foreign policy stances in Nicaragua, El Salvador, and elsewhere during the 1980s. Critic Gregory A. Waller observed in *From Hanoi to Hollywood* that "*Rambo*'s representation of the Third World works ideologically by positing a thoroughly entrenched Soviet presence and by denying the existence of politicized 'native' masses. . . . In this way the film corroborates aspects of the Reagan administration's public posture, while still remaining 'critical' of America's treatment of Vietnam vets." Journalist David Ignatius expressed similar sentiments in an essay in *The Reagan Legacy*: "The Rambo movies of the mid-1980s provided an easy caricature for Ronald Reagan's foreign policy. Here was the raw imagery of American power, a nation seemingly free at last from the pain and self-doubt of Vietnam, personified by a muscular hero with an oversize machine gun. The 'America Is Back' theme of the Rambo movies was pure Reagan.'' Some observers even speculated that the film's anti-government rhetoric reflected the administration's disenchantment with ''big government'' and its proclaimed intentions to lessen the role of government in American life. But supporters of the administration's foreign policy initiatives and governing philosophy rejected such comparisons, dismissing them as superficial and inaccurate.

FURTHER READING

Bayles, Martha. ''The Road to Rambo III: Hollywood's Visions of Vietnam.'' *New Republic* (July 18, 1988).

Blumenthal, Sidney, and Thomas Byrne Edsall, eds. *The Reagan Legacy*. New York: Pantheon, 1988.

Bruning, Fred. ''A Nation Succumbs to Rambomania.'' *Maclean's* (July 29, 1985).

Budra, Paul. ''*Rambo* in the Garden: The POW Film as Pastoral.'' *Literature/Film Quarterly* 18, no. 3 (1990).

Collins, Nancy. ''The *Rolling Stone* Interview: Sylvester Stallone.'' *Rolling Stone* (December 19, 1985).

Dittmar, Linda, and Gene Michaud, eds. *From Hanoi to Hollywood: The Vietnam War in American Film*. New Brunswick, N.J.: Rutgers University Press, 1990.

Grenier, Richard. ''Stallone on Patriotism and *Rambo*.'' *New York Times* (June 6, 1985).

Hoberman, J. ''The Fascist Guns in the West.'' *American Film* (March 1986).

Johnson, Haynes. *Sleepwalking through History: America in the Reagan Years*. New York: Norton, 1991.

Kopkind, Andrew. Review of *Rambo: First Blood, Part II*. In *Nation* (June 22, 1985).

Morrell, David. *First Blood*. New York: Ballantine, 1982.

Reagan, Ronald. *An American Life*. New York: Simon and Schuster, 1990.

Studlar, Gaylyn, and David Desser. ''Never Having to Say You're Sorry: *Rambo*'s Rewriting of the Vietnam War.'' *Film Quarterly* (Fall 1988).

Zoglin, Richard. ''An Outbreak of Rambomania.'' *Time* (June 24, 1985).

The Real War

Nonfiction

Author: Jonathan Schell

Facts of Publication: New York: Pantheon Books, 1987

During the latter part of the 1960s, voices from across America's political spectrum expressed growing concerns that the U.S. military's counterinsurgency strategies in South Vietnam were fundamentally flawed. Critics contended that these programs, designed to reverse patterns of Communist infiltration in villages and the larger countryside, were instead wreaking far heavier damage on the country's civilian population. Their contentions were supported by field reports such as the ones filed by Jonathan Schell, who published several articles on the prosecution of the war in *New Yorker* in 1966 and 1967. His detailed reports, which covered a number of American military operations in the South Vietnamese countryside, sparked a great deal of controversy when they appeared, because they cast those operations in a decidedly unfavorable light. Soon after their original publication, Schell's *New Yorker* pieces were put together in two critically acclaimed books, *The Village of Ben Suc* (1967) and *The Military Half: An Account of Destruction in Quang Ngai and Quang Tin* (1968). Nearly twenty years later, those two books were combined with another Schell essay in a collection titled *The Real War: The Classic Reporting on the Vietnam War.*

HISTORICAL BACKGROUND

"The United States in Vietnam unleashed the greatest flood of firepower against a nation known to history," wrote historian Gabriel Kolko in *Anatomy of a War*. "The human suffering was monumental. The figures on all aspects of this enormous trauma are inadequate, and between 1968 and 1970 the refugee reporting system alone underwent three major revisions. The Pentagon's final estimate of killed and wounded civilians in South Vietnam between 1965 and 1972 ran from 700,000 to 1,225,000, while Senate numbers for the same period were 1,350,000."

American firepower also took a tremendous toll on the land itself. "In the seven-year period from 1965 to 1971 the area of Indochina, a region slightly larger than Texas, was bombarded by a tonnage of munitions amounting to approximately twice the total used by the U.S. in all the theaters of World War II," reported Arthur H. Westing and E. W. Pfeiffer in *Scientific American* (other estimates put the tonnage of bombs even higher; *Time*, for instance, contended in 1995 that U.S. fliers dropped seven million tons of bombs, nearly three times the total tonnage dropped in World War II and Korea combined). "From the air some areas in Vietnam looked like photographs of the moon." Indeed, "by the end of the war there were an estimated 21 million bomb craters in South Vietnam," wrote James William Gibson in *The Perfect War: The War We Could Not Lose and How We Did*. "Air force planes sprayed 18 million gallons of herbicide containing dioxins on some six million acres—around one-seventh of South Vietnam's total land area, and a much higher proportion of its most fertile cropland and richest forests. An additional 1,200 square miles of territory were bulldozed flat, stripped of all life."

Thousands of Vietnam's rural villages—which Frances FitzGerald characterized as "the essential community of Vietnam" in her book *Fire in the Lake*—were washed away by this onslaught. In many regions of South Vietnam, the village way of life, already weakened by French colonialism, proved unable to withstand the impact of the various pacification and counterinsurgency programs that were instituted by the ARVN (Army of the Republic of Vietnam) and the United States military during the war. Indeed, by 1972 perhaps half of the nation's rural population had been relegated to refugee status.

The forerunner of these pacification/counterinsurgency initiatives, the Strategic Hamlet Program, was launched in 1962 by South Vietnam President Ngo Dinh Diem. The program involved removing villagers from their ancestral lands and placing them in fortified hamlets especially built to house the communities. The strategy reflected a recognition that some rural villages served not only as bases of operations for the Vietcong but also as a major source of troop replenishment (though the VC sometimes resorted to coercion or outright terrorism to gain these new recruits). The program was designed to free the peasant population from Vietcong intimidation, but security measures proved inadequate, and the VC continued to hold sway in many of the hamlets. The U.S. military endeavored to make improvements to the program in the mid-1960s, but by 1966 the program was regarded as a failure and allowed to die.

The Strategic Hamlet Program was an unpopular one among the Vietnamese peasant population, but other pacification and counterinsurgency measures undertaken by the American and South Vietnamese militaries proved even more disruptive. In fact, said Kolko, "counterinsurgency and pacification efforts became interchangeable conceptions, centering on the military and technical means for physically controlling the population." And after a time, as frustration over the enemy's effective use of guerrilla tactics mounted, the Americans and South Vietnamese resorted to increasingly ruthless tactics to eliminate the villages from the enemy's arsenal. Their concern about the villages was well-founded. As FitzGerald noted, "in many regions—and those where the greatest U.S. military effort was made—the unarmed peasants actively and voluntarily cooperated with the [National Liberation] Front troops, giving information, carrying supplies, laying booby traps. Where, then, was the distinction between 'soldiers' and 'civilians'? In many regions 'the Viet Cong' were simply the villagers themselves; to 'eliminate the Viet Cong' meant to eliminate the villages, if not the villagers themselves, an entire social structure and a way of life."

As the lines between the enemy and the peasant population blurred, the villagers were increasingly regarded as foes rather than apolitical bystanders, and a new philosophy emerged that reflected that reappraisal. FitzGerald wrote that "with the arrival of the American troops [in Vietnam] the U.S. command had largely given up hope for the conventional pacification schemes, the aim of which was to drive the NLF out of the villages and to secure the villagers' loyalty to the government. The new attempt would be to destroy the villages and, as it were, dry up the 'water' where the 'fish' of the Liberation forces swam in their element." Increasingly ruthless and violent methodologies aimed at neutralizing the rural population as a factor in the war soon emerged. The effectiveness of some programs—such as the controversial Phoenix Program, which sought to "neutralize" Vietcong operatives in the villages—is still a subject of considerable debate, but others were unequivocal failures.

American search-and-destroy operations (later euphemized to search-and-clear) left dozens of burning villages in their wake, and encounters with villagers with murky allegiances sometimes resulted in death at the hands of U.S. troops who knew from bitter experience that the enemy in Vietnam sometimes took the form of children or elderly people. Civilian deaths subsequently increased, fueled by uncertainty in the field and the Pentagon's increased willingness to bring military might to bear. Military critics contended that these efforts to neutralize the villages actually served to drive the Vietnamese toward the Vietcong. One U.S. soldier echoed these sentiments in Mark Lane's *Conversations with Americans*: "A friend of mine in A company, which was our sister company, said one time that when A company goes into a friendly village, if it's not VC when they go into it, it's VC when they leave."

But air operations took an even greater toll on South Vietnam's rural population. Defoliation programs and bombing campaigns obliterated large stretches of the countryside, including valuable croplands and forests. These threats, coupled with the forcible evacuation of villagers from targeted areas by U.S. ground troops, produced a refugee population of immense size and a dramatic downturn in the percentage of South Vietnamese living in rural areas (some studies estimate that the percentage of South Vietnam's population living in urban centers swelled from 20 to 40 percent during the 1960s). Many were relegated to refugee camps that often assumed prisonlike characteristics. Indeed, stories of hunger, poverty, and generally miserable conditions in the camps were ubiquitous.

The various pacification programs undertaken by U.S. and South Vietnamese officials were too often ineffectual in addressing the physical, emotional, and economic wounds suffered by the villagers. The impact of these endeavors, which ranged from food distribution to propaganda dissemination, paled next to that of the "Zippo raids," napalm strikes, and other counterinsurgency measures that they had experienced out in the countryside. As Jonathan Schell wrote in *The Military Half*, "many optimistic Americans, including reporters as well as military men and civilian officials, tended to set off the destruction caused by the military effort against the construction resulting from civil-affairs effort, seeing the two results as *separate but balanced* 'sides' of the war." But Schell pointed out that the people who received food allotments and the people who saw their villages go up in flames were one and the same. "The Vietnamese civilians felt the effects of the two programs not as two abstract 'sides' of the war but as a *continuing experience in the single reality of their daily lives*," he wrote. "From their point of view, the aid given them by the Americans and the South Vietnamese government amounted to only a tiny measure of compensation . . . for enormous losses and suffering."

Critics of U.S. policymakers thus charged that in their zeal to neutralize rural communities as VC centers and recruiting bases, American officials pursued policies that in effect pushed a significant percentage of South Vietnam's peasant class into the arms of the Communists. These critics contended that the strategies America employed to prosecute the war convinced many villagers that the Communists were the side most likely to restore a measure of stability and security to their lives. As Vietnam veteran and author Tobias Wolff wrote in his essay "After the Crusade," the real battle for control of South Vietnam "was for the trust and loyalty of the common man. We knew this, but our anger and fear kept getting the best of us. Why didn't they get behind us? Why didn't they care that we were dying for them? Yet every time we slapped someone around, or trashed a village, or shouted curses from a jeep, we defined ourselves as the enemy and thereby handed more power and legitimacy to the people we had to beat."

SCHELL AND VIETNAM

Jonathan Schell was a twenty-four-year-old postgraduate student in January 1967, when he accompanied American military forces in their advance on Ben Suc, a farming village of four thousand to six thousand Vietnamese located about thirty miles from Saigon. Ben Suc was reputed to be a headquarters for Vietcong troops of the "Iron Triangle," a region northwest of Saigon that boasted a large VC presence. The move on Ben Suc—which was part of Operation Cedar Falls, a much larger operation designed to clear the Iron Triangle of VC—began on January 8. The American forces encountered no major resistance in Ben Suc, and they quickly took control of the hamlet. After forcibly evacuating the villagers to refugee camps, the Americans destroyed the village. Reports submitted by Schell and other reporters on the razing of Ben Suc sparked a roar of protest from the U.S. antiwar movement, which called the incident emblematic of the United States military's disregard for the Vietnamese population. The U.S. military defended the operation, noting that the VC had lost over one thousand men to death or capture and that the Communists had been forced to flee the Iron Triangle. Ultimately, however, the success of Operation Cedar Falls proved fleeting, because the Vietcong resumed activity in the area soon thereafter.

Several months later, Schell began investigating the effectiveness of Task Force Oregon, a search-and-destroy military operation that included American, ARVN, and Korean forces. The task force's targets were VC or North Vietnamese Army (NVA) personnel located in Quang Ngai Province (and to a lesser extent the provinces of Quang Tin and Binh Dinh), but as Schell and many other observers would later suggest, the operation may have been most devastating to the civilian population in those provinces. Schell traveled throughout large areas of Quang Ngai and Quang Tin during the summer of 1967, and he also flew on several occasions in the forward air-control planes that guided American bombing runs in those provinces. Schell concluded that operations such as Task Force Oregon, which reduced much of the terrain to a wasteland and turned many Vietnamese civilians into refugees, had virtually destroyed the two provinces.

CREATION OF *THE REAL WAR*

Schell's accounts of Operation Cedar Falls and Task Force Oregon first appeared in several issues of *New Yorker*, but they were quickly collected in book form. *The Village of Ben Suc*, which collected his *New Yorker* articles on the attack on Ben Suc and its aftermath, was published in late 1967. Schell's articles on the provinces of Quang Ngai and Quang Tin were published in book form a year later as *The Military Half: An Account of Destruction in Quang Ngai and Quang Tin*. The two books, both of which were published by Knopf, subsequently came to be regarded as important documentation of the war's toll on Vietnam's civilian population. Nearly twenty years later, the two works were combined in a book entitled *The Real War: The Classic Reporting of the Vietnam War*. The volume included a new essay written by Schell called ''The Real War,'' in which the author offered his interpretation of the war and its central characteristics.

Writing in ''The Real War,'' Schell contended that America's efforts to win the Vietnam War were doomed by certain fundamental contradictions between its ultimate goals and the methodologies it chose—or was forced to use—to reach those goals. He claimed that as the war broadened, and efforts to create a self-sustaining government in Saigon faltered, "the temptation for the Americans to take things into their own hands was overwhelming. Yet if they did the South Vietnamese, shunted aside, would grow even weaker, for the more the Americans did things for the South Vietnamese the more dependent they became—a self-defeating result, since the point of the exercise was to strengthen them." He suggested that as time passed, South Vietnam's reliance on the United States assumed abjectly dependent dimensions. "If the Americans didn't step in and hold the government together, it would collapse. But if they did step in, whatever independent strength it had was still further weakened and the regime's chances of ever standing on its own were further reduced. It's not an exaggeration to say that the whole American effort in Vietnam foundered on this contradiction."

Schell wrote that the war also reflected a profound divergence between America's ultimate vision for the country and the practical effects of the military operations that were unleashed to realize that vision. "In South Vietnam, [American] victories were won at the expense of pulverizing the country physically, providing a poor foundation for the creation of the strong, independent regime in the South that American policy required. The moral absurdity of 'destroying' the society we were trying to 'save' was often pointed out; the strategic absurdity of the same policy was less often noted." But although Schell was in many respects critical of the American military, which he claimed had no strategy "other than to punish the enemy so severely that it would simply give up," he also argued that South Vietnam's weak government was an albatross that no army could overcome. "In politics, as in nature, there are forces that clear the scene of organisms whose strength has declined to a certain point," he wrote in "The Real War." "Again and again, the Saigon regime declined to that point and beyond. Again and again, it came to the end of its natural life. . . . But again and again the United States hoisted the cadaver to its feet and tried to breathe artificial life into it. Like a ghost that is denied a grave to rest in, this regime stalked the earth posthumously." Finally, Schell asserted that time was a critical factor in the war's outcome. All the principals involved, from Hanoi to Saigon to Washington, D.C., knew that a day would come when the United States would depart from Vietnam. Whereas the U.S. military needed to *win*—and quickly, given the toll that the war was taking on American society—the Communists only had to *endure*, secure in the knowledge that the Americans would one day return home.

CRITICAL RECEPTION

Both *The Village of Ben Suc* and *The Military Half* were cited as further evidence that the U.S. effort in Vietnam had gone seriously awry. Several reviewers contended that the incidents described in the works had a devastating cumulative effect, in part because Schell took pains to the report the incidents without offering his own commentary or criticism. Others, however, argued that Schell chose to write about events that were not representative of the war effort in Vietnam. These critics, many of them hailing from the Administration or the military, contended that incidents such as the one at Ben Suc were aberrations; defenders of Schell's work, however, have pointed out that similar accounts of wholesale and arbitrary destruction proliferated as the war dragged on.

Perhaps inevitably, debate over the legitimacy and prosecution of the war itself flavored some of the reaction to Schell's work within the literary community. For instance, *Saturday Review* contributor Charles A. Hogan wrote that Schell's book on the assault on Ben Suc "is guaranteed to turn hawks into doves." *New York Times Book Review* critic John Mecklin offered a largely laudatory review as well, though he charged that the reporter sometimes shaded events in a "reprehensible" manner in order to support his picture of the war. Despite such reservations, however, Mecklin concluded that "Schell . . . has produced one of the most disturbing books yet published on American errors and stupidities in dealing with the Vietnamese people. . . . His account of what happened is written with a skill that many a veteran war reporter will envy, eloquently sensitive, subtly clothed in an aura of detachment, understated, extraordinarily persuasive. . . . It should be read with the caveat that it tells only a small part of the story, but it nevertheless performs a public service in suggesting how poorly American military commanders—even today, thirteen years after Dienbienphu—understand the nature of Asian guerrilla warfare."

The Military Half was warmly received as well, though defenders of U.S. military policy once again suggested that Schell gave too much weight to isolated incidents. *National Review* writer Steven C. Schueller was among those who suggested that *The Military Half* provided an inaccurate portrait of the larger war. He acknowledged Schell's writing and reporting skills, but maintained that the reporter had only "witnessed action in a limited area," thus echoing the complaints of those who had criticized *The Village of Ben Suc*. Many others defended Schell's work, however, insisting that his books provided an all-too-accurate glimpse into the situation across all of Vietnam. "His report of what he saw and experienced confirms that in certain parts of South Vietnam we have, by the indiscriminate use of our enormous fire-power, virtually destroyed entire regions that were once inhabited by large peasant populations," wrote Hal Dareff in *Saturday Review*. "I know no book which has made me angrier and more ashamed," Jonathan Mirsky noted in *The Nation*. "When Jonathan Schell published *The Village of Ben Suc* some reviewers twisted madly, attempting to explain away the destruction of a village of 3,800 as an unfortunate but probably *isolated* incident. . . . At the end of *The Military Half* Schell describes the elimination of the coastal village of Tuyet Diem, and the transportation of its 1,600 inhabitants. By this time our outrage has been overstrained by the endless killing and burning."

FURTHER READING

Andradé, Dale. *Ashes to Ashes: The Phoenix Program and the Vietnam War*. Lexington, Mass.: Lexington Books, 1990.

Buckingham, William A., Jr. *Operation Ranch Hand: The Air Force and Herbicides in Southeast Asia, 1961–1971*. Washington, D.C.: Office of Air Force History, 1982.

Dareff, Hal. "Uphill Fight for the 'Other War.' " *Saturday Review* (July 13, 1968).

Dillin, John. "The War in One Small Village." *Christian Science Monitor* (December 2, 1967).

FitzGerald, Frances. *Fire in the Lake: The Vietnamese and the Americans in Vietnam*. Boston: Atlantic-Little, Brown, 1972.

Gibson, James William. *The Perfect War: The War We Couldn't Lose and How We Did*. Boston: Atlantic Monthly Press, 1986.

Grinter, Lawrence E. "South Vietnam: Pacification Denied." *Southeast Asia Spectrum* (July 1975).

Herrington, Stuart A. *Silence Was a Weapon: The Vietnam War in the Villages*. Novato, Calif.: Presidio Press, 1982.

Hogan, Charles A. "Another Lidice." *Saturday Review* (November 4, 1967).

Kolko, Gabriel. *Anatomy of a War: Vietnam, the United States, and the Modern Historical Experience*. New York: Pantheon, 1985.

Lane, Mark. *Conversations with Americans*. New York: Simon and Schuster, 1970.

Littauer, Ralph, and Norman Uphoff, eds. *The Air War in Indochina*. Boston: Beacon Press, 1972.

Mecklin, John. "Moving Day in Vietnam." *New York Times Book Review* (October 29, 1967).

Mirsky, Jonathan. "The Root of Resistance." *Nation* (August 5, 1968).

Schell, Jonathan. *The Real War: The Classic Reporting on the Vietnam War*. New York: Pantheon, 1987.

Westing, Arthur H., and E. W. Pfeiffer. "The Cratering of Indochina." *Scientific American* (May 1972).

Westmoreland, William. *A Soldier Reports*. Garden City, N.J.: Doubleday, 1976.

Wolff, Tobias. "After the Crusade." *Time* (April 24, 1995).

A Rumor of War

Nonfiction

Author: Philip Caputo

Facts of Publication: New York: Henry Holt, 1977

In March 1965 the United States dramatically escalated its stake in Vietnam as it launched the Operation Rolling Thunder bombing campaign and introduced U.S. ground troops into the conflict. Marine Lieutenant Philip Caputo was a part of this first deployment, a period that proved pivotal in the "Americanization" of the war. Caputo later wrote about his experiences in *A Rumor of War*, one of the most celebrated of the memoirs to come out of the Vietnam War.

HISTORICAL BACKGROUND

The Tonkin Gulf Incident and "Americanization" of the War

By the spring of 1964, Johnson Administration concerns about the shaky South Vietnamese government—and a corresponding increase in Communist control of the nation's countryside—led the United States to increase the size of its financial and military aid to South Vietnam. Direct U.S. involvement began in the summer of 1964, after a mysterious clash at sea that remains a subject of controversy to this day. On August 2 the Navy destroyer USS *Maddox*, stationed in the Gulf of Tonkin, was attacked by three North Vietnamese patrol torpedo (PT) boats. The *Maddox* fended off the assault with the help of the USS *Ticon-*

deroga, an aircraft carrier, scoring several hits on the PT boats. This episode marked the first direct confrontation between U.S. and North Vietnamese forces. A day later a second destroyer, the USS *Turner Joy*, joined the *Maddox* in the gulf.

On the evening of August 4 the *Maddox*, citing intercepted radio messages and ominous radar sightings, alerted the *Ticonderoga* to an impending North Vietnamese attack. The Americans subsequently launched an assault in the direction of the radar contacts, notifying Washington of the clash. But within a short period of time it became clear that there was significant doubt about whether the Communists had ever truly attacked. Pilots from the *Ticonderoga* admitted that they had seen no signs of the alleged vessels, and inexperienced sonar operators and stormy weather were mentioned as possible factors for the supposed PT boat sightings. A revised report acknowledging the Americans' uncertainty about the evening's events—though still insisting that "the [North Vietnamese] ambush was bona fide"—was subsequently cabled to Washington.

Many people, such as Admiral James B. Stockdale, who provided air cover for the destroyers from the *Ticonderoga* that evening, would later insist that subsequent military and political decisions made by the United States were made in response to a nonexistent attack. "In Washington what comes in over the teletype is that there are North Vietnamese PT boats in such and such an area of the ocean," he recalled in *The Bad War: An Oral History of the Vietnam War.* "But it's one thing to accept that as a fact and another to be on the scene listening to hesitant, heavily qualified, stammering people on radios trying to disabuse themselves of a hell of a lot of doubt about the reality of the situation. That was Tonkin Gulf."

President Lyndon B. Johnson, who had been criticized in some quarters for a perceived weak response to the first North Vietnamese attack, seized on the August 4 cables. He ordered a retaliatory strike against the Communists. This assault, against four North Vietnamese PT boat bases and an oil storage depot, destroyed nearly half of the nation's PT boat fleet. On August 5 Johnson sent the so-called "Tonkin Gulf Resolution" to Congress for approval. The bill was designed to give the president authority to "take all necessary measures to repel any armed attack against the forces of the United States and to prevent further aggression." The bill was passed in the Senate by an 88 to 2 vote; it breezed through the House of Representatives by a unanimous 416 to 0 vote. The bill marked the dawning of a new level of American entanglement in Vietnam.

Over the next several months, the Johnson Administration cited the Tonkin Gulf Resolution as authorization for a number of controversial steps that accelerated U.S. involvement in Vietnam, including the Rolling Thunder aerial bombing campaign against North Vietnam. (Operation Rolling Thunder, which was launched in March 1965 after a VC attack on a U.S. air base at Pleiku, would continue, with occasional stops, for the next eight years.) Johnson Administration officials also used the resolution to commit U.S. ground forces to Vietnam.

The Introduction of U.S. Troops into Vietnam

The first U.S. combat troops were stationed in Vietnam in March 1965. By the end of the year, U.S. troop strength stood at 184,000, an increase of approximately 800 percent from the beginning of the year, when approximately 23,000 U.S. military personnel had been stationed there.

By 1965 some U.S. policymakers were reassessing their initial impressions that the Communist enemy in Vietnam could be easily dealt with. These observers were sobered both by the seemingly never-ending instability in Saigon as well as the surprisingly effective guerrilla tactics of the resilient VC. But many policymakers—and the soldiers themselves—felt that with the introduction of U.S. ground troops, the war would finally begin to unfold as ultimately expected; namely, with an American victory.

General William C. Westmoreland, commander of the American troops in Vietnam, initially used the infusion of U.S. soldiers to secure strategically important areas around Saigon and along the coastline. He also launched a series of "search-and-destroy" operations into South Vietnam's Central Highlands. These were designed to hound the VC down and head off any attempts by the enemy to cut South Vietnam in half. All too often, however, these expeditions took a far greater toll on the U.S. soldiers than on their VC foes. These early patrols—long, uncomfortable slogs through unforgiving terrain in search of an elusive, deadly enemy—would prove to be a sort of harbinger of the experiences of thousands of American soldiers in the years that followed.

CAPUTO AND VIETNAM

Philip Caputo arrived in Vietnam on March 8, 1965, as part of the 9th Marine Expeditionary Brigade, the first U.S. combat unit that was sent into the country. Over the ensuing sixteen months Caputo's perspective on the war changed dramatically. Like his compatriots, Caputo arrived in Vietnam armed with great confidence that, now that the U.S. military had decided to step in, the war would be won quickly and decisively. "I guess we believed in our own publicity—Asian guerrillas did not stand a chance against U.S. Marines—as we believed in all the myths created by that most articulate and elegant mythmaker, John Kennedy," Caputo wrote in *A Rumor of War*. "If he was the King of Camelot, then we were his knights and Vietnam our crusade. There was nothing we could not do because we were Americans, and for the same reason, whatever we did was right."

As the months went by, however, the nature of the conflict—what Caputo termed "the formless war against a formless enemy"—began to gnaw at the psyches of the soldiers stationed in Vietnam, and Caputo was no exception. The young officer's doubts about the prosecution of the war intensified in June 1965, after he was reassigned—over his objections—from his infantry officer position to a posting at regimental headquarters. He spent the next several months engaged in administrative work; his stay included a stint as regimental casualty reporting officer that was by turns surrealistic and demoralizing.

In November 1965 Caputo was finally transferred back to an infantry company. "My convictions about the war had eroded almost to nothing," he wrote. "I had no illusions, but I had volunteered for a line company anyway." Citing boredom and his disgust with his casualty-tracking assignment, Caputo welcomed his return to the front, where "the rights or wrongs of the war aside, there was a magnetism about combat. You seemed to live more intensely under fire. Every sense was sharper, the mind worked clear and faster. Perhaps it was the tension of opposites that made it so, an attraction balanced by revulsion, hope that warred with dread."

But the growing deadliness of the war, coupled with the frustrations of pursuing an enemy who regularly faded into the jungles and hamlets of the region, hardened Caputo as it did so many other U.S. soldiers. Caputo's tour in Vietnam culminated with an ugly incident wherein Caputo sent a team of his best men into a Vietnamese village to kidnap (and, it was understood, kill) two VC, only to learn that one of the slain was actually the informer who first alerted the platoon to the VC presence in the village. A military investigation into the actions of Caputo and his men ensued, but the only punishment meted out to any of them was a letter of reprimand that was put in Caputo's file.

After being discharged from the Marines, Caputo joined the antiwar movement back in the United States, but he admitted that his confused feelings about the conflict rendered him a fairly passive member of the movement. He became a journalist, and in 1975 he returned to Vietnam to cover the fall of Saigon as a reporter for the *Chicago Tribune*.

CREATION OF *A RUMOR OF WAR*

Caputo began *A Rumor of War* in 1967, but he did not complete the work until the fall of 1976. Discussing the length of time it took him to complete the memoir, Caputo remarked in a postscript to the 1996 edition of the book that "my thoughts and emotions were too fractured by the war to set them down on paper coherently. I had a story to tell and a profound need to tell it, but I wasn't ready to write it. I needed the distance only time could give." Still, although he often worked on the book in fits and starts, he never let the work die. Spurred in part by his anger at the penchant that both right- and left-leaning observers had for reducing veterans and their Vietnam experiences to stereotypes, he refused to allow his busy journalistic schedule to wholly bury the project. As Caputo wrote in his postscript, "as the citizens of a democracy, the noisy patriots and protestors had a right to their opinions about Vietnam but not, it seemed to me, to the smug righteousness with which they voiced them, because they hadn't been there. . . . I wanted *A Rumor of War* to make people uncomfortable—in effect, to blow them out of their snug polemical bunkers into the confusing, disturbing emotional and moral no-man's-land where we warriors dwelled. . . . Above all, I wanted to communicate the moral ambiguities of a conflict in which demons and angels traded places too often to tell one from the other.''

After suffering gunshot and shrapnel wounds during a reporting assignment in Lebanon in October 1975, Caputo was forced into a period of convalescence that enabled him to complete much of the work on the book. In May 1977 *A Rumor of War* was published. Though he was proud of the book, Caputo was convinced that it would cause nary a ripple in the book world. Instead, it proved stunningly popular with both critics and the public.

CRITICAL RECEPTION

A Rumor of War quickly came to be regarded as a classic memoir of Vietnam. Critical reaction to Caputo's book was almost entirely positive, and many reviewers offered effusive praise. William Styron wrote in the *New York Review of Books* that ''some of Caputo's troubled, searching meditations on the love and hate of war, on fear, and the ambivalent discord that warfare can create in the hearts of decent men, are among the most eloquent I have read in modern literature. . . . His is the chronicle of men fighting with great bravery but forever losing ground in a kind of perplexed, insidious lassitude—learning too late that they were suffocating in a moral swamp.'' *New York Times Book Review* critic Theodore Solotaroff was similarly impressed. Solotaroff remarked that ''the ultimate effect of this book is to make the personal and the public responsibility merge into a nightmare of horror and waste experienced humanly by the Caputos and inhumanly by the politicians and generals. Out of the force of his obsession with the war and his role in it, Caputo has revealed the broken idealism and suppressed agony of America's involvement. *A Rumor of War* is the troubled conscience of America speaking passionately, truthfully, finally.''

The swirl of publicity that surrounded Caputo in the wake of the release of *A Rumor of War*, however, ultimately had a debilitating impact on the writer. Besieged by the American media, veterans' organizations, and hundreds of others whose lives had been changed by Vietnam in one respect or another, Caputo found it immensely difficult to ''cope with the transformation of what had been an intensely personal and private experience . . . into public property.'' A nationwide book tour in support of his memoir quickly degenerated into a nightmarish experience, as the author turned to alcohol to fend off growing exhaustion and anxiety attacks, some of which he later attributed to a nagging sense of guilt that he was profiting from the misery that the war had engendered in thousands of Americans and Vietnamese. He finally suffered a self-described nervous collapse and was admitted to the psychiatric ward of a hospital, where he found himself relieved to be out of the public's field of vision. He was released after several days and quickly resumed his journalistic career.

FURTHER READING

Berman, Larry. *Planning a Tragedy: The Americanization of the War in Vietnam*. New York: W. W. Norton, 1982.

Caputo, Philip. *Indian Country*. New York: Bantam, 1987.

————. *A Rumor of War*. New York: Henry Holt, 1977; Owl Books, 1996.

Goulden, Joseph C. *Truth Is the First Casualty: The Gulf of Tonkin Affair—Illusion and Reality*. Chicago: Rand-McNally, 1969.

Johnson, Lyndon B. *The Vantage Point: Perspectives of the Presidency, 1963–1969*. New York: Holt, Rinehart & Winston, 1971.

Kahin, George McT. *Intervention: How America Became Involved in Vietnam*. New York: Knopf, 1986.

Karnow, Stanley. *Vietnam: A History*. New York: Viking, 1983.

Lewy, Guenter. *America in Vietnam*. New York: Oxford University Press, 1978.

Myers, Thomas. *Walking Point: American Narratives of Vietnam*. New York: Oxford University Press, 1988.

Solotaroff, Theodore. "Memoirs for Memorial Day." *New York Times Book Review* (May 29, 1977).

Styron, William. "A Farewell to Arms." *New York Review of Books* (June 23, 1977).

Willenson, Kim. *The Bad War: An Oral History of the Vietnam War*. New York: New American Library, 1987.

Windchy, Eugene G. *Tonkin Gulf*. Garden City. N.Y.: Doubleday, 1971.

Song of Napalm

Poetry Collection

Author: Bruce Weigl

Facts of Publication: New York: Atlantic Monthly Press, 1988

During the 1970s American literature received an infusion of new poetry from Vietnam War veterans still grappling with their memories of that conflict. Though many of the early poems that spoke to these experiences were flawed, characterized by technical mediocrity and overreliance on raw emotion, several collections—either anthologies or collected works of one poet—unveiled poems of uncommon perception and power. As critic Philip Beidler remarked in his *Re-writing America*, "the experience of Vietnam brought forth the work of combat poets speaking the nightmare of war with a new wisdom of horror and abandonment." During the 1970s and 1980s, Vietnam veteran Bruce Weigl emerged as one of the most accomplished of these poets, and his 1988 collection *Song of Napalm* further burnished his reputation as one of America's foremost chroniclers of the war. "Vietnam was Bruce Weigl's war, and it was ours," observed Dave Smith on the book's jacket. "But we have not had it so well seen, so grittily felt, so permanently expressed until Weigl's *Song of Napalm*."

HISTORICAL BACKGROUND

The first enduring collections of poetry by Vietnam War veterans were published in 1972. Prior to that time, the American public's exposure to poems about the conflict had been largely limited to the antiwar verse of such stateside poets as Allen Ginsberg, Denise Levertov, Robert Bly, Galway Kinnell, and

Robert Duncan. But 1972 saw the publication of the first major anthology of veterans' poetry—*Winning Hearts and Minds*—as well as two other significant collections of poems, Michael Casey's *Obscenities* and D. C. Berry's *saigon cemetery*. Subsequent collections of note published during the 1970s included MacAvoy Layne's *How Audie Murphy Died in Vietnam* (1973), Bryan Alec Floyd's *The Long War Dead* (1976), and Walter McDonald's *Caliban in Blue* (1976). These collections, coupled with the works of Bruce Weigl, John Balaban (1974's *After Our War*), Yusef Komunyakaa (1986's *Dien Cai Dau*), and W. D. Ehrhart (1975's *A Generation of Peace* and 1984's *To Those Who Have Gone Home Tired*), further enriched the canon of Vietnam War poetry.

Of these latter writers, Ehrhart made particularly varied contributions to Vietnam War literature. In addition to penning some of the finest poetry to emerge from the Vietnam War, he compiled and edited several highly regarded anthologies of veteran poetry; written a trilogy of critically acclaimed, highly polemical memoirs (1983's *Vietnam-Perkasie*, 1986's *Marking Time*—published in 1989 as *Passing Time*—and 1995's *Busted*); and contributed important critical essays on Vietnam War poetry. Ehrhart's many contributions led Beidler to remark that ''Ehrhart's career as a Vietnam author in his generation will always be of singular significance . . . in ways for which conventional criticism will never provide an adequate account.''

Many critics have commented on the unique qualities of much of the poetry penned by Vietnam veterans—qualities unique even when compared to the verse of poets of earlier wars. These characteristics are frequently attributed to the grim nature of the conflict itself and the often-demoralizing environment to which soldiers returned after completing their tours. ''The veteran's recourse [when discussing the war] is an anti-poetry stripped of transfiguring metaphor but enriched by the accuracy of a witnessing moral vision,'' wrote Lorrie Smith in *American Poetry Review*. ''Its content is empirical rather than idealistic, its epiphanies sardonic rather than transcendant. Indeed, most Vietnam veteran poets shun the traditional affirmations and consolations of lyricism. Their motives are decidedly to instruct rather than to delight—a stance entirely appropriate for a subject which is, after all, political.'' But Beidler, Smith, and other critics have observed that, over time, the finest of these poets have published work that moved far beyond reporting to more complex and lyrically accomplished examinations of the war's moral and political underpinnings.

But though the works of poets such as Balaban, Ehrhart, McDonald, Komunyakaa, and Weigl outshine those of most other Vietnam veterans, Ehrhart commented that the cathartic qualities of writing poetry make the process worthwhile for all of its practitioners. ''One might venture to say that the act of writing these poems—even the worst of them—is an act of cleansing,'' he wrote in his essay ''Soldier-Poets of the Vietnam War.'' ''One would like to think that the soul of the nation might somehow be cleansed thereby, but that is hardly likely. More realistically, one hopes that in writing these poems, the poets might at least have begun to cleanse their own souls of the torment that was and is

Vietnam. Surely, in the process of trying, the best of them have added immeasurably to the body and soul of American poetry.''

WEIGL AND VIETNAM

Bruce Weigl served in the U.S. Army in Vietnam from 1967 to 1970. He returned home to America with a Bronze Star and many haunting memories of the conflict. By the mid-1970s he had become an English professor and a published poet (his first two chapbooks of poetry—*A Sack Full of Old Quarrels* and *Executioner*—were both published in 1976) and in 1979 he published *A Romance*, his first book-length collection. Although some of Weigl's poetry of the 1970s and early 1980s reflected his experiences in the war, he turned to his working-class upbringing in the industrial Midwest for much of his inspiration. Taking note of this, Ehrhart suggested in ''Soldier-Poets of the Vietnam War'' that Weigl's early collections showed a reluctance ''to confront the war directly, relying time and again on dreams, illusions and surreality . . . almost as if, even after 11 years, the war is still too painful to grasp head-on. Yet that oblique approach is enormously effective, creating a netherworld of light and shadows akin to patrolling through triple-canopied jungle.''

The publication of 1985's *The Monkey Wars* established Weigl as one of the nation's most eloquent chroniclers of Vietnam. As with his previous collections, many of the poet's works in *The Monkey Wars* did not explicitly deal with the war. ''And yet, there is an overwhelming impression in these four collections that the Vietnam War is *the* central event that governs a life, albeit a subterranean or, more precisely, subliminal influence,'' said Vince Gotera in *Radical Visions: Poetry by Vietnam Veterans*. ''As Weigl writes about Toledo, Ohio, or his grandparents, or the ancestral fields of Eastern Europe, or his marriage to a Japanese American, the ubiquitous ghost of the Vietnam War implies an urgent need for catharsis, purgation, or 'cleansing.' '' Reviewers contended that, with *The Monkey Wars*, this need to address the ''ghost'' of Vietnam took on new urgency and depth. ''Weigl images the war as a monkey on his back—a tenacious memory, potent and insidious as a drug; a carnivalesque *Doppelgänger*, both intimate and repugnant,'' wrote Smith. Ehrhart, meanwhile, remarked in ''Soldier-Poets'' that the war poems included in the collection tackled the subject with a new level of directness. Weigl's ''poetic vision,'' Ehrhart concluded, is both ''compelling and vibrant.''

CREATION OF *SONG OF NAPALM*

Weigl finally made Vietnam the explicit fulcrum for his next poetry collection, 1988's *Song of Napalm*. Melding the Vietnam poems of *A Romance* and *The Monkey Wars* with new poems about the war and its impact on its participants, he created a thematically unified document of that conflict's toll on himself, his fellow veterans, and his country. ''Divided into three sections entitled 'Sailing to Bien Hoa,' 'Song of Napalm,' and 'The Kiss,' the overall movement of the book is roughly equivalent to the emotional development of a soldier in Vietnam,'' wrote Gotera. ''The loss of innocence and romanticism (the surreal hopefulness of the poem 'Sailing to Bien Hoa') in the cauldron of the 'Nam'; the ambiguities and ironies inherent in the return to the World (imaged through the cynicism and despair voiced by the poem 'Song of Napalm'); and the synthesis and possibility of hope implied in 'The Kiss.' ''

CRITICAL RECEPTION

Song of Napalm was widely regarded as an outstanding addition to the canon of Vietnam War literature upon its publication, and as further proof of Weigl's prowess as a poet. Readers praised the poems in the volume as hauntingly evocative, honest meditations on Vietnam and its lingering presence in his life. Author Larry Heinemann remarked on the book's jacket that, while reading *Song of Napalm*, he became ''struck with something close to awe for the resilience of the human body and the human heart.'' Robert Schultz wrote in the *Hudson Review* that ''Weigl renders the terrible beauty of a sensibility which denies nothing, forgets nothing, and refuses to cease being human.'' Vince Gotera, meanwhile, contended in *Radical Visions* that *Song of Napalm* was a rarity in that it portrayed ''the absurdity and horror of Vietnam without sacrificing lyrical aesthetics.''

Novelist Robert Stone offered a particularly passionate commentary in praise of Weigl's Vietnam poetry in his introduction to the book. ''*Song of Napalm* is poetry performed in defiance of physical and moral death,'' he asserted. Lauding the poems of *Song of Napalm* as replete with vitality and ''incantatory power,'' Stone wrote that ''Bruce Weigl's poetry is a refusal to forget. It is an angry assertion of the youth and life that was spent in Vietnam with such vast prodigality, as though youth and life were infinite. Through his honesty and toughmindedness, he undertakes the traditional duty of the poet: in the face of randomness and terror to subject things themselves to the power of art and thus bring them within the compass of moral comprehension.''

FURTHER READING

Barry, Jan, and W. D. Ehrhart, eds. *Demilitarized Zones: Veterans after Vietnam.* Perkasie, Penn.: East River Anthology, 1976.

Beidler, Philip. *Re-Writing America: Vietnam Authors in Their Generation.* Athens, Ga: University of Georgia Press, 1991.

Ehrhart, W. D. ''Soldier-Poets of the Vietnam War.'' In *America Rediscovered: Critical Essays on Literature and Film of the Vietnam War*, Owen W. Gilman and Lorrie Smith, eds. New York: Garland, 1990.

————, ed. *Unaccustomed Mercy: Soldier-Poets of the Vietnam War.* Lubbock: Texas Tech University Press, 1989.

Felstiner, John. ''American Poetry and the War in Vietnam.'' *Stand* 19, no. 2 (1978).

Gotera, Vince. *Radical Visions: Poetry by Vietnam Veterans*. Athens: University of Georgia Press, 1994.

Jones, Roger D. "Bruce Weigl." In *American Poets since World War II, Third Series*, Vol. 120 of *Dictionary of Literary Biography*. Detroit: Gale Research, 1992.

Schultz, Robert. Review of *Song of Napalm*. In *Hudson Review* (Spring 1989).

Smith, Lorrie. "A Sense-Making Perspective in Recent Poetry by Vietnam Veterans." *American Poetry Review* (November/December 1986).

Weigl, Bruce. *The Monkey Wars*. Athens: University of Georgia Press, 1985.

———. *Song of Napalm*. New York: Atlantic Monthly Press, 1988.

———. "Welcome Home." *Nation* (November 27, 1982).

Sticks and Bones

Play

Author: David Rabe

First Production: February 10, 1969, at Varsey Theatre, Villanova University, Villanova, Pennsylvania

When playwright David Rabe returned to the United States from Vietnam in 1967, he was rocked by the surrealistic quality of his rapid reimmersion into American society. He was not alone in his disorientation; soldiers such as Rabe often went from the jungles of Vietnam to their family living rooms in as little as forty-eight hours; deprived of time to adjust psychologically to their change in circumstances, some vets struggled mightily to return to the rhythms of daily existence in America. "Strange things began to happen to me," Rabe recalled. "Everybody seemed totally removed from the war." Drawing on the sense of dislocation and isolation he felt upon his return, Rabe subsequently penned one of America's most controversial works about the Vietnam War, *Sticks and Bones*.

HISTORICAL BACKGROUND

Nearly 520,000 Americans who served in the Vietnam War were officially classified as disabled for either psychological or physical reasons. Diagnosis of physical wounds was easy, but diagnosis of psychological damage visited upon veterans was sometimes a more difficult undertaking. Consequently, observers note that the actual number of vets who were psychologically damaged in fundamental ways by the war may be even higher.

One of America's first researchers into what would become known as "post-traumatic stress syndrome," a malady closely associated with Vietnam, was Robert J. Lifton, professor of psychiatry at Yale and author of *Home from the War*. "What distinguishes Vietnam veterans from the rest of their countrymen is their awesome experience and knowledge of what others merely sense and resist knowing, their suffering on the basis of that knowledge and experience, and, in the case of anti-war veterans, their commitment to telling the tale," he said.

Christian Appy, author of *Working-Class War*, remarked that much of the anguish experienced by some who took part in the war "had its most wrenching impact . . . after their return to the United States. Away from the war, veterans found it difficult to numb themselves to the suffering they endured, witnessed, and inflicted. The radical contrast between the misery left in Vietnam and the comfortable abundance of most Americans often triggered such anguish."

Reentry into American society and into family networks was traumatic for veterans for other reasons as well, such as the disorienting rapidity with which such reentry was accomplished and the sense of "otherness" that reintegration often engendered. Some families, of course, found such homecomings to be disconcerting as well, their minds troubled by the flickering images of the war that flashed across their television screens. Most veterans and their families found that the war—even if not discussed—was a constant presence in the household.

Recalling discussions with veterans, Lifton remarked that "above all, the men had the impression that their parents did not want to hear or know about the extent of horror, absurdity, and corruption they had experienced in Vietnam. Many felt that their parents had been much more comfortable with them when they put on the uniform than when they threw it off. . . . Not that parents necessarily favored the war—a large number had apparently soured on it—but rather, as one of the men put it, 'They just didn't want me to do anything to rock the boat.' The 'boat' they didn't want rocked was the whole set of institutional arrangements and conventional cultural images and forms, within which one is expected to sit quietly over the course of a life's voyage."

RABE AND VIETNAM

In his afterword to 1993's *The Vietnam Plays*, a two-volume collection of his Vietnam works, David Rabe contended that the war marked a "turning point" in American society. "Since the end of the war the level of violence accepted as routine in this society has risen steadily, and there are times when I think that the war was . . . the launch pad that fired us into this lethal drift. At other times I see Vietnam less as a cause and more as a symptom of a comprehensive tradition of slaughter that must be understood as a constant in all history, ours included." He confessed, however, that he had profound doubts about whether America's potentially instructive experiences in Vietnam were taken to heart.

"We saw graphic depictions of the massive reach of war's destructive powers—body bags, burning villages, and ditches full of corpses. The poison was not so much that we did what we did as the way we denied that we were doing what we could see ourselves doing on television," he wrote. "The Vietnam War, in its conduct and in the obfuscation proclaimed as its recognition and exegesis, was a seedbed, I think. A watershed. It was the swamp where history paused and could have shown us who we were and who we were becoming. In its flash and violence it was a probe into the depths, an X ray knifing open the darkness with an obscene illumination against whose eloquence we closed our eyes."

Drafted into the U.S. Army, Rabe served from January 1965 to January 1967 as a specialist fourth class. He spent the last eleven months of his service in Vietnam, where he was assigned to a support group for hospitals. Rabe's time in Vietnam had a tremendous impact, because even though he never personally experienced combat, the war's violence was all about him. Many of his observations concerned the chilling nature of the war and its dehumanizing effect on participants. As James Patterson noted in a short biography of the playwright, Rabe once commented that "you don't realize how young most of our army is over there until you see them, troops fresh off the line, standing around some bar like teenagers at a soda fountain, talking coolly about how many of their guys got killed in the last battle." He admitted, however, that Vietnam's more-surreal aspects also had a darkly fascinating quality. "I'll tell you what it was like," he once said. "It was a carnival—exciting, vulgar, obscene."

After returning to the United States in January 1967, Rabe received his M.A. degree in theater from Villanova University. His first major production was *The Basic Training of Pavlo Hummel*, a well-received play about a disturbed American soldier's experiences during his military training and in Vietnam. In preparing his follow-up play, *Sticks and Bones*, Rabe tapped into the disconcerting sense of disorientation that he had felt when he first returned to the United States after completing his tour. An early version of the play was produced at Villanova in 1969, but the final version of *Sticks and Bones* was unveiled at Joseph Papp's Public Theatre. Then, in September 1971, the drama moved on to Broadway.

CREATION OF *STICKS AND BONES*

During the late 1960s and early 1970s, the American theatrical community—both its artists and its audiences—appeared to be more receptive to commentaries on the Vietnam War than was the American public at large. Citing plays such as Megan Terry's *Viet Rock*, Barbara Garson's *MacBird*, Ron Cowen's *Summertree*, and the controversial musical *Hair*, N. Bradley Christie remarked in *Search and Clear* that theatrical audiences were for the most part receptive to such works. "This trend," he wrote, "embodied the theater community's opposition to the war, or perhaps the theater merely viewed 'the hot war' as a vehicle for rejuvenating a business in decline. Who was producing and patronizing these plays, anyway? Certainly they attracted numbers of people whose affluence and/or ingenuity had spared them a tour in Vietnam. Whatever the reasons, the theater and its patrons seemed ready, or at least willing, to confront the volatile issues raised by America's involvement in Indochina a full decade before works in more popular media became best sellers or box-office hits.''

Homecoming plays—works dealing with the efforts of war veterans to reintegrate themselves into the lives of their families and the larger American society—proved a popular subset of this larger group of Vietnam-related plays. Examples of such works include *Bringing It All Back Home* (by Terrence McNally), *An Evening with Dead Essex* (Adrienne Kennedy), *The Burial of Esposito* (Ronald Ribman), and *Medal of Honor Rag* (Tom Cole). "The plays, to a greater or lesser degree, all deal with problems of reintegration and acceptance,'' said J. W. Fenn, author of *Levitating the Pentagon*. "Yet, of all the homecoming works, David Rabe's *Sticks and Bones* . . . is the most critical to an appreciation of the problems of cultural alienation and the difficulties faced by the American veteran in the process of reassimilation.''

Sticks and Bones tells the tale of a blinded Vietnam veteran named David who is deposited back at his home in the United States by a surly sergeant. There he is reunited with his father, Ozzie, his mother, Harriet, and his brother, Ricky, caricatures of the prototypical "All-American'' family of *Ozzie and Harriet*, a popular television series in the 1950s and 1960s. David's return proves to be an unsettling event for all involved; he remains haunted by the war and by the Vietnamese girlfriend—Zung—whom he left behind, whereas his parents and brother view his return as a threat to the cultural myopia and smug assumptions upon which they have constructed their identity as a family.

As the play progresses, and the family proves unwilling or unable to address the unseen baggage that David has brought home with him, tensions between him and his family deepen. David attacks the reputation of Hank Grenweller, a family friend of mythic qualities whose efforts on behalf of Ozzie and Harriet have made him a beloved figure in their home. "Grenweller has both a specific and an abstract role in the life of the family: his physical presence and influence in the affairs of the family is acknowledged by all its members, yet he is also a paradigm for American culture, its essence and its potential,'' wrote Fenn. The family, meanwhile, rebukes David for his miscegenation with Zung, whose silent, ghostly presence floats in and out of the play.

By the latter stages of the drama, the entire family's faith in the trappings of its materialistic existence has been shaken to its core by David and his memories of the war. Ozzie, in particular, is struggling to maintain his patriarchal authority and his belief in the convictions that have guided his life. Snared in a mood of dark euphoria, Ozzie finally perceives the ghost of Zung in the room. Infuriated by her presence, he strangles her, setting the stage for the drama's climactic scene. The family, galvanized by its instinct for self-preservation, gathers around David and persuades him to kill himself for the good of their little community. They provide him with a razor to slit his wrists and a bowl and towels to ensure that the suicide will not be a messy one. As the family members look on expectantly, David bleeds to death on stage. With the threat to the family removed, Ozzie, Harriet, and Ricky turn to one another with assurances: "He's happier"; "We're all happier."

CRITICAL RECEPTION

Sticks and Bones was a controversial play that garnered significant adverse commentary. Judgments were often predicated on the reviewer's interpretation of Rabe's message. Many critics who perceived it as antiwar and/or anti-American slammed it for those reasons. Others, though, criticized if for perceived flaws in execution. *New York Times* critic Walter Kerr, for instance, commented that "the play stands still. David comes home unapproachable, remains unapproachable. We don't know whether his hatred is for the war they've permitted, for the racist attitudes that have kept him from bringing the girl home, or simply for their ordinariness. . . . Lacking movement, the play simply repeats the things it does well until it tires us with them." James Patterson also found fault with the play on stylistic grounds: "The contrasting bursts of poetry, parody, and pathos do not cohere; the writing is compelling but the mixture of the obvious and the obscure is, finally, unsatisfying."

Others, though, were more impressed. *Saturday Review* contributor Henry Hewes wrote that "occasionally in the theater one finds a play that drives deeper into the despair of existence than can be stated in clichés. David Rabe's *Sticks and Bones* is one such, and although I cannot fully comprehend its meaning, I am aware that it is invading with freshness and honesty some of the most painful ambiguities that afflict contemporary America." Clive Barnes of the *New York Times* concurred, calling the play "a poet's vision of the disaster of moral bankruptcy."

For his part, Rabe commented in the 1973 introduction to a book containing *Sticks and Bones* and *Pavlo Hummel* that "an 'anti-war' play is one that expects, by the very fabric of its executed conception, to have political effect. I anticipated no such consequences from my plays, nor did I conceive them in the hope that they would have such consequences. I have written them to diagnose, as best I can, certain phenomena that went on in and around me. It seems presumptuous and pointless to call them 'anti-war' plays."

In 1973 *Sticks and Bones*, which won a Tony Award for best play, became the subject of controversy once again. The CBS television network had made plans to televise a production of the play on March 9, only to indefinitely postpone the showing in the face of objections from U.S. officials and dozens of CBS affiliate stations who announced that they would not broadcast the play. After several months of delay, however, CBS showed the play on August 17, albeit in a poor time slot. Nearly 70 CBS stations refused to air the play, and Rabe recalled that the lack of sponsors forced the network to broadcast a blank screen in place of commercials.

FURTHER READING

Alter, Nora M. *Vietnam Protest Theatre: The Television War on Stage*. Bloomington, Ind.: Indiana University Press, 1996.

Appy, Christian G. *Working-Class War: American Combat Soldiers and Vietnam*. Chapel Hill, N.C.: University of North Carolina Press, 1993.

Barnes, Clive. "David Rabe Presents 'Sticks and Bones.' " *New York Times* (November 8, 1971).

Beidler, Philip D. *American Literature and the Experience of Vietnam*. Athens: University of Georgia Press, 1982.

Christie, N. Bradley. "David Rabe's Theater of War and Remembering." In *Search and Clear: Critical Responses to Selected Literature and Films of the Vietnam War*, William J. Searle, ed. Bowling Green: Bowling Green University Popular Press, 1988.

Fenn, J. W. *Levitating the Pentagon: Evolutions in the American Theatre of the Vietnam War Era*. Newark: University of Delaware Press, 1992.

Kerr, Walter. "Unmistakably a Writer—Why, Then, Does His Play Stand Still?" *New York Times* (November 14, 1971).

Figley, Charles R., and Seymour Leventman, eds. *Strangers at Home: Vietnam Veterans since the War*. New York: Praeger, 1980.

Hewes, Henry. "Only Winter Is White." *Saturday Review* (November 27, 1971).

Lifton, Robert Jay. *Home from the War: Vietnam Veterans, Neither Victims nor Executioners*. New York: Simon and Schuster, 1973.

MacPherson, Myra. *Long Time Passing: Vietnam and the Haunted Generation*. Garden City, N.Y.: Doubleday, 1984.

Marin, Peter. "Coming to Terms with Vietnam." *Harper's* (December 1980).

Patterson, James A. "David Rabe." In *Dictionary of Literary Biography, Volume 7: Twentieth-Century American Dramatists*. Detroit: Gale Research, 1981.

Rabe, David. *The Vietnam Plays*, 2 vols. New York: Grove, 1993.

Schroeder, Eric James. *Vietnam, We've All Been There: Interviews with American Writers*. Westport, Conn.: Praeger, 1992.

The Things They Carried

Short story collection

Author: Tim O'Brien

Facts of Publication: Boston: Seymour Lawrence/Houghton Mifflin Co., 1990

The Things They Carried is a collection of interrelated stories set in Vietnam that examine the nature of war and the struggle of its participants to maintain their humanity in the face of atrocities and tragedies. Classification of Tim O'Brien's book—a hybrid of fact and fiction that has novel elements—is difficult. The author himself simply refers to *The Things They Carried* as a "work of fiction," although it features characters that are based on people who actually served with him in Vietnam. In addition, most of the stories are set in Quang Ngai Province, the area of Vietnam in which the author served his tour of duty. Critics have, for the most part, put aside the question of labeling the work, devoting their time instead to an examination of the book's contents. In that regard, *Minneapolis Star and Tribune* critic Dan Carpenter echoed the thoughts of many when he called *The Things They Carried* "an epic prose poem of our time, deromanticizing and demystifying and yet singing the beauty and mystery of human life over its screams and explosions, curses and lies."

HISTORICAL BACKGROUND

The province of Quang Ngai was a deadly region through much of the Vietnam War. Located in central Vietnam on the South China Sea, it was often the site of VC activity and a target of American firepower. The notorious My

Lai Massacre, in which hundreds of Vietnamese villagers were executed by American soldiers, took place in the region.

"Quang Ngai Province was home to one of Vietnam's fiercest, most recalcitrant, most zealous revolutionary movements," O'Brien commented in *New York Times Magazine*. "Independent by tradition, hardened by poverty and rural isolation, the people of Quang Ngai were openly resistant to French colonialism as far back as the nineteenth century and were among the first to rebel against France in the 1930s. The province remained wholly under Vietminh control throughout the war against France; it remained under Vietcong control, at least by night, throughout the years of war against America."

As a stronghold of Vietcong support (in 1965 the South Vietnamese government considered abandoning the provincial capital), the Quang Ngai area of Vietnam suffered enormous punishment throughout the duration of the conflict. By 1965 entire villages in the area were destroyed, "reduced to rubble or grotesque skeletons by two months of bombardment from aircraft and point-blank shelling by the five-inch guns of Seventh Fleet destroyers," according to Neil Sheehan, author of *A Bright Shining Lie*. Often the villages were designated as enemy areas solely on the basis of their geographic location in Vietcong-controlled areas.

The next year brought no relief for the region. Instead, a number of deadly clashes erupted between Marine forces and Vietcong guerrillas, who were supported by the local peasants as well as North Vietnamese troops who streamed down from the Annamite Mountains of western Quang Ngai Province. In the spring of 1967, the American presence increased with the introduction of Task Force Oregon, an army division sent into the area to replace the Marines.

By 1967 large areas of the province had been decimated. Jonathan Schell, a young reporter with *New Yorker*, provided details on the activities in the province in the fall of 1967. After consulting military maps, pilots, officers, and Saigon officials, he reported that 70 percent of the estimated 450 hamlets in Quang Ngai Province had been obliterated. The human toll was significant as well. Schell reported that a volunteer British doctor who had endured three years in Quang Ngai estimated that the total civilian casualty rate for the province, including the dead and the lightly wounded, was about fifty thousand annually.

The high casualty rate in the region was due in part to the reluctance of the peasantry to travel to refugee camps, where conditions were often wretched. Instead, many returned to their firebombed communities and took up residence in underground bomb shelters. These peasants, along with the villagers who resided in relatively unscathed communities along Route 1, a major road that ran along the coast of the South China Sea, maintained their presence in the province throughout the conflict.

O'BRIEN AND VIETNAM

In February 1969 pfc (private first class) Tim O'Brien arrived in Quang Ngai Province. A radio-telephone operator for the 198th Infantry Brigade, O'Brien spent three or four days a month at a base called LZ Gator, which included a mess hall, medical facilities, machine shops, supply depots, barracks, and entertainment clubs. LZ Gator "was our castle," O'Brien recalled in *New York Times Magazine*. "Not safe, exactly, but far preferable to the bush. . . . There were hot showers and hot meals, ice chests packed with beer, glossy pinup girls, big, black Sony tape decks booming 'We gotta get out of this place' at decibels for the deaf." O'Brien and the rest of his Alpha Company unit spent most of their time out in the countryside on patrol, however. As the hours and days accumulated, "Alpha Company began to regard Quang Ngai itself as the true enemy—the physical place, the soil and paddies. What had started for us as a weird, vicious little war soon evolved into something far beyond vicious, a hopped-up killer strain of nihilism, waste without want, aimlessness of deed mixed with aimlessness of spirit."

As the soldiers of Alpha Company engaged in their mostly fruitless search for the enemy, they grew accustomed to the devastated terrain of Quang Ngai Province. "The wreckage was all around us, so common it seemed part of the geography, as natural as any mountain or river," O'Brien remarked. "Wreckage was the rule. Brutality was S.O.P. [standard operating procedure]. Scalded children, pistol-whipped women, burning hooches, free-fire zones, body counts, indiscriminate bombing and harassment fire, villages in ash, M-60 machine guns hosing down dark green tree lines and any human life behind them."

The constant peril of active duty in Vietnam, though, also increased O'Brien's appreciation of life. "Vietnam was more than terror. For me, at least, Vietnam was partly love. With each step, each light-year of a second, a foot soldier is always almost dead, or so it feels, and in such circumstances you can't *help* but love. You love your mom and dad, the Vikings, hamburgers on the grill, your pulse, your future—everything that might be lost or never come to be. Intimacy with death carries with it a corresponding new intimacy with life," O'Brien said in *New York Times Magazine*. He went on to describe a friend from his platoon, a young black man named Chip who wrote letters to O'Brien's sister while O'Brien reciprocated with correspondence to Chip's sister. "In the bush . . . nothing kept us apart. 'Black and White,' we were called. In May of 1969, Chip was blown high into a hedge of bamboo. Many pieces. I loved the guy, he loved me. I'm alive. He's dead. An old story, I guess."

CREATION OF *THE THINGS THEY CARRIED*

In 1968 Minnesota native O'Brien graduated from Macalester College with a full academic scholarship to Harvard, only to be drafted. After completing his tour of duty—in which he received the Purple Heart and was promoted to the rank of sergeant—he returned to the United States to resume his education. "They process you out of the army in about two hours," remarked O'Brien in an interview with Michael Coffey for *Publishers Weekly*. "Say the pledge of allegiance, get in a taxicab, get on a plane, take off your uniform in the toilet and fly to Minnesota. It was over, in a day and a half—from Vietnam, to Seattle, to Minnesota. It was fast and effortless, just like gliding out of a nightmare." As he embarked on a career as a novelist, however, he found that "my passion as a human being and as a writer intersect in Vietnam, not in the physical stuff but in the issues of Vietnam—of courage, rectitude, enlightenment, holiness, trying to do the right thing in the world," he told *Publishers Weekly.*

The Things They Carried was O'Brien's fifth book, and though a number of his previous works had garnered favorable reviews—*Going After Cacciato* is widely regarded as a classic—this collection of stories/chapters attracted a new level of critical attention and acclaim. The eighteen tales contained in *The Things They Carried* range from stories of robust size to short anecdotes. All of the stories are narrated by a character named Tim O'Brien, an alter-ego of the author who has been fictionalized to an uncertain degree. The stories are interrelated, for they describe the experiences of the members of a single platoon before, during, and after the war. In several instances the stories, served up without regard to chronology, contradict information provided in other parts of the narrative. "As a reader makes his or her way through the book and gradually finds the same stories being retold with new facts and from a new perspective," wrote Steven Kaplan in *Understanding Tim O'Brien*, "it begins to become apparent that there is no such thing for O'Brien as the full and exact truth." Robert R. Harris commented on this aspect of the collection as well: "Are these [multiple versions of events] simply tricks in the service of making good stories? Hardly. Mr. O'Brien strives to get beyond literal descriptions of what these men went through and what they felt. He makes sense of the unreality of the war—makes sense of why he has distorted the unreality even further in his fiction—by turning back to explore the workings of the imagination, by probing his memory of the terror and fearlessly confronting the way he has dealt with it as both soldier and fiction writer."

CRITICAL RECEPTION

The Things They Carried quickly came to be regarded by many critics as a seminal work about the American experience in Vietnam. *Los Angeles Times* reviewer Richard Eder wrote that "the best of these stories—and none is written with less than the sharp edge of a honed vision—are memory as prophecy." Peter S. Prescott of *Newsweek* concurred, proclaiming that "half a dozen of these stories—the longer ones—are simply marvelous. Wars seldom produce good short stories, but two or three of these seem as good as any short stories written about any war." *New York Times Book Review* contributor Robert R. Harris observed that "by moving beyond the horror of the fighting to examine with sensitivity and insight the nature of courage and fear, by questioning the role that imagination plays in helping to form our memories and our own versions of truth, he places *The Things They Carried* high up on the list of best fiction about *any* war."

Although the collection as a whole was widely hailed, several stories in *The*

Things They Carried garnered particular attention. The title story lists the myriad items that soldiers carry into battle, ranging from the common (cigarettes, machine guns, canned peaches) to the personal (love letters, comic books). The latter items are totems of sorts, keepsakes from their lives back in America. As Harris commented, though, the story is really about the emotions that the soldiers carry with them: grief, terror, love, longing, and regret.

"On the Rainy River" relates the agonized indecision of a young draftee who spends a week weighing his options from the shores of a northern Minnesota lake, as Canada beckons on the other side. Another story, titled "The Man I Killed," combines a "stunned description of a Vietnamese torn apart by O'Brien's grenade with a detailed, imaginary biography of the dead man," wrote Julian Loose in the *Times Literary Supplement*. Another story—"Sweetheart of the Song Tra Bong"—chronicles a seventeen-year-old American girl "who is flown to Vietnam by her boyfriend only to become enraptured with the most horrific rituals of war," said *Publishers Weekly*. "From the innocence of a high school cheerleader she is transformed into a frightening image of war's incalculable madness. When last seen, she is disappearing into the jungle wearing a necklace of human tongues." Whereas *Sewanee Review* contributor Clayton W. Lewis cited "Sweetheart of the Song Tra Bong" as one example of several stories in the collection that "dissolve into clever artifice," other critics counted the story as one of the collection's finest. Other chapters in *The Things They Carried* were touted as well. Lewis called "How to Tell a True War Story" "as intelligent as it is profound and one of the most brilliant war memoirs I have read." Such sentiments were voiced by others as well.

In reviewing the eighteen stories that comprise *The Things They Carried*, Kaplan observed that the book "is O'Brien's expression of his love of story-telling as an act that can wrestle tolerable and meaningful truths from even the most horrible events." *Booklist* critic John Mort called it a "compassionate, complex, magnificent novel of self-acceptance and renewal." Certainly it solidified O'Brien's reputation as one of America's most talented and honest writers on the war in Vietnam. For his part, O'Brien termed *The Things They Carried* an antiwar book. He explained to *Publishers Weekly* that "my hope is that when you finish the last page of this book, or any book, there is a sense of having experienced a whole life or a constellation of lives; that something has been preserved which, if the book hadn't been written, would have been lost, like most lives are."

FURTHER READING

Baughman, Ronald. Interview with Tim O'Brien. In *American Writers of the Vietnam War*, Volume 9 of *Dictionary of Literary Biography Documentary Series*. Detroit: Gale Research, 1991.

Coffey, Michael. "Tim O'Brien." *Publisher's Weekly* (February 16, 1990).

Eder, Richard. Review of *The Things They Carried*. In *Los Angeles Times* (March 11, 1990).

Harris, Robert R. Review of *The Things They Carried*. In *New York Times Book Review* (March 11, 1990).

Kaplan, Steven. *Understanding Tim O'Brien*. Columbia, S.C.: University of South Carolina Press, 1994.

Lewis, Clayton W. "Chronicles of War." *Sewanee Review* (April 1991).

Loose, Julian. Review of *The Things They Carried*. In *Times Literary Supplement* (June 29, 1990).

Mort, John. "The Booklist Interview: Tim O'Brien." *Booklist* (August 1994).

O'Brien, Tim. *If I Die in a Combat Zone, Box Me Up and Ship Me Home*. New York: Delacorte, 1973.

————. *The Things They Carried*. Boston: Seymour Lawrence/Houghton Mifflin, 1990.

————. "The Vietnam in Me." *New York Times Magazine* (October 2, 1994).

Prescott, Peter S. Review of *The Things They Carried*. In *Newsweek* (April 2, 1990).

Schell, Jonathan. *The Real War: The Classic Reporting on the Vietnam War*. New York: Pantheon, 1987.

Sheppard, R. Z. "Need for Faces." *Time* (March 19, 1990).

The 13th Valley

Novel

Author: John M. Del Vecchio

Facts of Publication: New York: Bantam, 1982

Upon arriving in Vietnam, all American soldiers—and especially those assigned to infantry units—struggled to adjust to their new environmental circumstances. This was a formidable task, for as Michael Herr observed in *Dispatches*, it generally entailed "getting used to the jungle or the blow-you-out climate or the saturating strangeness of the place which didn't lessen with exposure so often as it fattened and darkened in accumulating alienation." Indeed, infantry duty in Vietnam involved exposure to a wide variety of physical discomforts, from inhospitable weather to tenacious insects to ambush-friendly terrain that left soldiers physically and emotionally exhausted at the end of each day.

John M. Del Vecchio, who served as a Marine combat correspondent in Vietnam in 1970 and 1971, was determined to capture the grim flavor of the "grunt's" daily existence in that exotic locale when he began work on his critically acclaimed first novel, *The 13th Valley*. "Even the earthworms over there—I remember digging a foxhole and coming across an earthworm that was three feet long and as big around as a garter snake," he told interviewer Ronald Baughman in *American Writers of the Vietnam War*. "Very, very different and hard to imagine. One of the things that I try to do in *The 13th Valley* is to put the reader there."

HISTORICAL BACKGROUND

"The Puritan belief that Satan dwelt in Nature could have been born here [in Vietnam], where even on the coldest, freshest mountaintops you could smell jungle and that tension between rot and genesis that all jungles give off," wrote Michael Herr in *Dispatches*. Such observations reflected the sense, pervasive among many American infantrymen, that the formidable terrain and climate of Vietnam constituted yet another enemy. "Vietnam is a beautiful country," conceded James R. Ebert in his *A Life in a Year: The American Infantryman in Vietnam, 1965–1972*, "but it proved to be almost impervious to American technology and it was particularly adept at sapping the physical endurance of American soldiers. . . . The reality that typified the existence of the field soldier in Vietnam was not so much combat with enemy forces as it was the day-to-day hardships, fatigue, and frustration of living and coping in that harsh and hostile environment."

One of the primary sources of discomfort for the American foot soldier in Vietnam was the insect life that thrived throughout the country, especially during the monsoon season. Fire ants, whose painful bites burnt and stung, were a constant bane. Thick clouds of mosquitoes bedeviled troops as well. One soldier recalled in an interview with Ebert how, while trying to sleep on the edge of a rice paddy, "the mosquitoes got so bad I eventually ended up sleeping with everything but my face under the water. I put the gas mask bag over my face and that is how I spent the night. I just couldn't stand it." Perhaps the most dreaded nonhuman foes, however, were the leeches, which could be found in great numbers in the country's swamps, paddies, and jungles. Horror stories abounded of encounters with the blood-sucking creatures, and the American soldier's revulsion toward them led to frequent stops to check one's legs, chest, armpits, or crotch area for unwelcome passengers.

Infantry duty took a heavy physical toll as well. "Even the hardiest veterans found humping synonymous with agony," wrote Ebert. "The region of the country a soldier operated in—the rugged terrain of the Central Highlands, the swamps of the Delta, the jungle, rice paddies, coastal strip, or near the DMZ—didn't seem to matter. Each possessed some quality that made patrolling there a tedious experience." A soldier's heavy pack load did nothing to relieve the situation, either. Whether a soldier was making his way through dense elephant grass that left his arms criss-crossed with cuts or maneuvering through swamps that left him soaked from head to foot, he had to carry his supplies with him. Necessary weapons, ammunition, C-rations, clothing, canteens, and other gear all had to be carried in the field via rucksacks, and soldiers quickly learned to be ruthless in discarding nonessential items. Good packs were highly valued, and some Marines appropriated NVA packs—which had wider straps and more pockets—when possible.

The appearance of infantry units that returned from the field to their base camp was often a distinctly bedraggled one, and not only because of the conditions that they encountered. Jungle boots and fatigues wore out quickly out in the field, and in some cases replacements were difficult to secure. This inadequate protection from the country's elements inevitably took its toll on the physical condition of soldiers, whether manifested in ''jungle rot'' or other maladies.

The physical exertion associated with infantry duty, coupled with the constant threat of enemy attack, made it difficult for soldiers to keep their spirits up. ''There was a lot of depression going with the constant strain of humping and firefights,'' recalled one soldier in *Brothers: Black Soldiers in the Nam.* ''We were so down half the time we didn't know what we were going to do next, and we didn't care. We lost spirit 'cause we were just out there humping. Our [unit's] motto was 'Drive on.' No matter what happened, no matter what came down, we just drove on.''

DEL VECCHIO AND VIETNAM

Del Vecchio served as a combat correspondent to the 101st Airborne Division near Hue for the Armed Forces newspaper *The Screaming Eagle* from June 1970 to April 1971. He commonly worked out in the field, or ''boonies,'' for three-to five-day periods in that capacity, gathering information on troop activities and reporting on battles. Del Vecchio's excursions, which involved eating, sleeping, and turns at the ''point'' (leading patrols down potentially deadly trails) with his fellow soldiers, gave him ample familiarity with the hazards of jungle combat in Vietnam. He was eventually awarded a Bronze Star for heroism for his service.

Years after America's ill-fated involvement in Vietnam ended, Del Vecchio remained certain of the legitimacy of the United States' efforts in that country, and proud of his military service. ''Our intentions in Vietnam, as far back as the 1950s, were the right ones,'' he told Baughman. ''I believe that at that time the basic character of America was one of integrity and honesty and altruism and a true belief that we could help other people and other nations develop a system of government that truly respected human rights.''

Del Vecchio also contended that the American military has been unjustly criticized for its performance during the Vietnam War. ''The military was much better than the limits set on it,'' he told Baughman. ''I'm not saying that there weren't incidents. The stuff that's been written and that's been said about atrocities and drug use and racial tensions and incompetence, most of that's true—as *incidents*. As *emphasis*, however, most of it becomes false.'' Although Del Vecchio acknowledged that some American soldiers behaved badly—whether out of stupidity or immorality or mental breakdowns—he maintained that the vast majority conducted themselves with distinction. ''The American military in Southeast Asia was basically very honest and competent and hardworking and doing the job that it was asked to do,'' he said.

CREATION OF *THE 13TH VALLEY*

Del Vecchio worked on the massive *The 13th Valley* for much of the 1970s, a decade that saw him wander from coast to coast, taking a variety of jobs. He endured a torrent of rejections from agents and publishers when he first sent the manuscript out, and by December 1980 he had declared that if no one expressed interest in the book by the end of the year, he would stick it in a drawer and forget about it. A few days after Christmas, however, an agent contacted him.

The agent delivered the manuscript to the editor-in-chief of Bantam Books, and within a week the publisher had signed a contract with Del Vecchio. As the publication date for *The 13th Valley* drew near, in-house enthusiasm for the book remained high. Vietnam literature was finally emerging as a legitimate genre in publishing at that time, and Bantam felt that Del Vecchio's epic tale would be a worthy addition to that growing list.

The 13th Valley provides a detailed account of a two-week clash that erupts when a battalion of the 101st Airborne is helicopered into a remote valley near the northern border of South Vietnam to take out a North Vietnamese Army (NVA) headquarters. The novel is set in 1970—a period of the war in which, according to some accounts, some American units became frighteningly dysfunctional—but the soldiers of Del Vecchio's Company A comprise a united group possessed of a strong sense of duty. Racial tensions and debates about the value of their presence are presented (the company's all-purpose credo is the bitter ''It don't mean nothin' ''), but the basic unity of the group is not in doubt, even when they confront the potentially divisive fears and physical discomforts that accumulate with each step taken deeper into the valley.

The novel's primary characters are Sergeant Daniel Egan, First Lieutenant Rufus Brooks, and James ''Cherry'' Chelini, a radio-telephone operator. Egan is in some respects an archetype of the American soldier of cinematic myth: a brave, talented, and cynical warrior possessed of a deep commitment to his fellow ''boonierats'' and the execution of their mission. Brooks, meanwhile, is the company's highly respected African American commander, an intelligent, confident officer thoroughly dedicated to his men. The third principal player in Del Vecchio's drama, however, is less admirable. Cherry, a new arrival to Vietnam, proves unable to handle the ominous jungle environment into which he has been thrust. The war quickly produces a dangerous mental collapse in the young soldier, who comes to embrace the savagery around him. By novel's end, noted John Hellmann, author of *American Myth and the Legacy of Vietnam*, ''Cherry [has entered] fully into Vietnam in a blasphemous, nihilistic love of destruction and death.''

The 13th Valley ends in horrific fashion. The NVA base is destroyed, but the company suffers terrible losses from a new wave of foes. As the survivors are frantically helicoptered out, Egan and Brooks—both of whom were seriously wounded while trying to rescue their fellow soldiers—are left behind on a hillside strewn with dead bodies and the flaming wreckage of downed helicopters.

The novel's final scene is a ceremony in which the survivors of Company A are assured that their comrades' sacrifices were not in vain. Cherry, his mind still blackened by his experiences, attempts to mock the tribute by muttering "It don't mean nothin'," only to be harshly cut off by the new commander: "Don't say it, soldier."

CRITICAL RECEPTION

The 13th Valley was highly praised for its authenticity and sense of place. "There have been a number of excellent books about Vietnam," wrote Joe Klein in the *New York Times Book Review*, "but none has managed to communicate in such detail the day-to-day pain, discomfort, frustration, and exhilaration of the American military experience in Vietnam. . . . [Stylistic] lapses are relatively few, and pale before the wealth and power of the details the author provides— the step-by-step subtlety involved in walking point on a jungle patrol, the constant physical discomfort, claustrophobic heat alternating with freezing rain, running sores, jungle rot, diarrhea, immersion foot, mosquitoes." Poet Bruce Weigl agreed (though he echoed the thoughts of a number of other reviewers with his criticism of the book's "stilted philosophizing"): "Through these men we come to share unimaginable torments as they make their way through a no-man's land infested with banana spiders and huge mosquitoes, where they live with dysentery, brutal heat, heavy packs and the knowledge that each step may be their last. . . . This is such a powerful and remarkable book, that its author's excesses are quickly forgotten. It is with consummate skill that Del Vecchio carefully and slowly draws us into the other-worldliness of jungle warfare."

Reviewers also praised the book's sympathetic characterizations and its portrait of combat brotherhood. *Vietnam War Stories* author Tobey Herzog called *The 13th Valley* "a tribute . . . to the skills and self-sacrifice of the American soldiers fighting in Vietnam." Critic Thomas Myers, writing in *Modern Fiction Studies*, remarked that Del Vecchio's novel provided an antidote to other, more simplistic accounts of the war and its participants. "Del Vecchio argues effectively through Egan, Brooks, and a number of other characters that, despite the high levels of cultural confusion and historical ambiguity that enveloped the war, simplistic portraiture of the American soldier in Vietnam as either a debased purveyor of atrocity or an uncomprehending victim is inaccurate, ineffective fictional strategy," wrote Myers. "Del Vecchio offers both a comprehensive corrective to reductive recreations of the war and an admission that no single appraisal can be complete."

FURTHER READING

Baldwin, Neil. "Going After the War." *Publishers Weekly* (February 11, 1983).
Baughman, Ronald. Interview with John M. Del Vecchio (June 19, 1991). In *American Writers of the Vietnam War*, Volume 9 of *Dictionary of Literary Biography Documentary Series*. Detroit: Gale Research, 1991.

Bourne, Peter G. *Men, Stress, and Vietnam*. Boston: Little, Brown, 1970.

Del Vecchio, John M. *The 13th Valley*. New York: Bantam, 1982.

Ebert, James R. *A Life in a Year: The American Infantryman in Vietnam, 1965–1972*, Novato, Calif.: Presidio, 1993.

Hellmann, John. *American Myth and the Legacy of Vietnam*. New York: Columbia University Press, 1986.

Herr, Michael. *Dispatches*. New York: Alfred A. Knopf, 1977.

Herzog, Tobey C. *Vietnam War Stories*. New York: Routledge, 1992.

Klein, Joe. "A Novelist's Vietnam." *New York Times Book Review* (August 15, 1982).

Myers, Thomas. "Diving into the Wreck: Sense Making in *The 13th Valley*." *Modern Fiction Studies* (Spring 1984).

Plummer, William. " 'Moby Dick' in Vietnam." *Newsweek* (July 26, 1982).

Weigl, Bruce. "Reliving the Vietnam Experience." *Virginian-Pilot* (August 29, 1982).

"We Gotta Get Out of This Place"

Song

Artist: The Animals

Written by: Cynthia Weil and Barry Mann

Release: August 1965 (MGM)

During the course of the Vietnam War, many rock and roll songs that were hits back in the United States proved popular among American troops as well, but for dramatically different reasons. Whereas a song's popularity in the States was often based on its melody, the personality of the artist, and other factors that had little to do with lyrical content (although that could be a factor as well), certain songs became popular at American bases in Vietnam precisely because their lyrics seemed to encapsulate certain basic impressions about the nature of the war and the feelings of its participants. One of the most popular of these songs was undoubtedly The Animals' "We Gotta Get Out of This Place," a work that became an anthem of sorts among American troops. But other songs became immensely popular as well, as American soldiers appropriated various works whose lyrical content, when transposed onto the jungles of Vietnam, reflected their feelings of disillusionment, homesickness, anger, and pain.

HISTORICAL BACKGROUND

Les Cleveland noted in his *Dark Laughter: War in Song and Popular Culture* that during the 1960s, a time in which both Vietnam and civil rights issues emerged as emotionally explosive topics in America, "contemporary popular

music [became] related directly to the passions and anxieties of an entire generation of people to the point where, in the hands of the peace movement, it
became a political weapon." Antiwar songs such as "I Ain't Marchin' Anymore" by folksinger Phil Ochs (who also penned a number of other outspokenly
antiwar songs), "Alice's Restaurant" by Arlo Guthrie, and "Saigon Bride" by
Joan Baez were all embraced by the protest movement. In November 1967 a
new antiwar song by the group Country Joe and the Fish called "The I-Feel-
Like-I'm-Fixin'-To-Die Rag" was released. The antiwar movement welcomed
it enthusiastically, transforming it into what H. Ben Auslander called "an un-
official marching song." (Not all antiwar songs were universally loved by protestors, however; Barry McGuire's "Eve of Destruction," though quite
successful commercially, was a controversial song within the antiwar movement.
"Folk purists universally condemned the song as a transparent attempt to cash
in on both the growing national concern over the Vietnam War and the popularity of protest music at the time," wrote Michael Schumacher in *There But
for Fortune*, a biography of Ochs. "Others argued that, while the song was far
from being an artistic wonder, 'Eve of Destruction' was valid for its ability to
get listeners to focus on a crucial issue.")

The controversy that swirled around these songs—and the songs themselves—
filtered quickly across the sea to Vietnam and the troops stationed there. When
not out in the bush, American soldiers had ready access to radio broadcasts,
tape recorders, and stereos, and armed with these technological advances, camps
pulsed with the music being made back in their native land. Armed Forces radio,
Radio Hanoi, and underground radio stations helmed by disaffected GIs all
flooded the country with the latest in American music. "The proliferation of
electronic media meant that troops were exposed to the popular culture of the
homeland in greater volume, especially its commercial music," wrote Cleveland.
"The military command was unable to control the mass media sufficiently to
screen out the dissident sounds of protest." But veteran Lee Ballinger remarked
in Dave Marsh's *Rock & Roll Confidential* that "despite what some may choose
to think, rock and roll was never fundamentally *anti*war; it was a soundtrack
for the entire process, of which opposition was only a part."

Indeed, many of the most popular songs among American troops were nominally apolitical, though they touched on subjects of great importance to soldiers.
Songs of homecoming (Peter, Paul and Mary's "Leaving on a Jet Plane," Simon
and Garfunkel's "Homeward Bound," Bobby Bare's "Detroit City") or those
that provided idyllic images of America (Otis Redding's "[Sittin' On] the Dock
of the Bay," Glen Campbell's "Galveston") were quite popular. The popularity
of these songs, wrote critic David E. James, stemmed from "the polysemy of
[their] lyrics, their availability for investment with individual or group significance." Troops also embraced a number of songs that trafficked in darker, more
electric material, such as Creedence Clearwater Revival's "Run through the
Jungle" and The Rolling Stones' "Paint It Black." The popularity of such
artists as Jimi Hendrix, The Doors, and The Rolling Stones in Vietnam stemmed

from their ferocious sound as well as the nihilistic and/or anarchic sentiments evident in some of their lyrics; such qualities struck many soldiers as grimly appropriate to the environment in which they found themselves.

Finally, Vietnam triggered an explosion of music composed by the American soldiers themselves. These performers often appropriated the melodies of well-known songs, but their lyrics were strikingly original. These songs, whether performed in Saigon bars or far-off firebases, addressed the Vietnam experience with a directness and authority that could not be duplicated by recording artists back in "the World" (the United States). *New York Times* reporter David Gonzalez noted that, "unlike the electric rock or brassy soul music often associated with the war, this style featured simple voices accompanied by acoustic guitars and harmonics that could change from playful to achingly haunting." The subject matter of this material varied widely, moving from sneering characterizations of rear-echelon personnel ("Saigon Warrior") to evaluations of South Vietnamese political instability ("Let's Do It") to criticisms of America's military leadership ("Our Leaders"). Finally, the war's violence and devastation led to the penning of a number of songs that, in the words of Gonzalez, "probed a psychic territory as dark as the skies the pilots zoomed through, with exaggerated aggression that would make civilians blanch and titles like 'Strafe the Town and Kill Them All' or 'Napalm Sticks to Kids.' "

CREATION OF "WE GOTTA GET OUT OF THIS PLACE"

The British musical group The Animals was formed in 1963 when singer Eric Burdon joined forces with a Newcastle-upon-Tyne area band known as the Alan Price Combo. The first incarnation of The Animals—which consisted of Burdon, pianist Price, guitarist Hilton Valentine, drummer John Steel, and bass player Chas Chandler—quickly caused a stir in rhythm and blues circles for its explosive stage performances, but the band remained relatively unknown in the United States until 1964, when it released a cover version of the classic Josh White song "House of the Rising Sun." The song vaulted the band to the top of the charts around the world, and several more respectable hits quickly followed.

Perhaps the most memorable of these follow-up hits was "We Gotta Get Out of This Place." Originally written as an antipoverty song by Cynthia Weil and Barry Mann, The Animals gave it a raucous, hard-charging flavor that proved popular with the record-buying public. The Animals maintained their immense popularity through the mid-1960s, but by 1967 the band was stumbling, hamstrung by the hedonistic life-style favored by some band members and a corresponding drift away from its musical roots.

The band subsequently broke up, and the musicians went in different directions. Burdon formed a new group called Eric Burdon and the New Animals that dedicated itself to the "West Coast sound" that Jefferson Airplane and

The Grateful Dead had popularized. Chas Chandler moved on to manage the Jimi Hendrix Experience.

POPULAR RECEPTION

At the height of the band's popularity, The Animals were mentioned in the same breath as The Beatles and The Rolling Stones. This was due to both the band's energetic stage act and the anthemic status that a few of their songs—most notably "House of the Rising Sun" and "We Gotta Get Out of This Place"—achieved.

Although the latter song was certainly popular in the United States (it reached number 13 on the *Billboard* singles charts), its impact was far greater in Vietnam. Years after its release, the song remained a staple in Saigon jukeboxes and fire base tape players. Indeed, the lyrics of the song—which spoke longingly of the unnamed narrator's thirst for an alternative to his present situation—neatly and simply encapsulated much of the despair and desperation felt by American servicemen in Vietnam, and its raucous sound lent sing-a-longs a cathartic quality absent from more sedately paced songs.

Both during and after the war some observers from both military and civilian backgrounds have speculated that such songs had a corrosive impact. Les Cleveland, for instance, commented that "as a source of oppositional ideology, songs like the Animals' 'We Gotta Get Out of This Place' may have contributed to the demoralization of some of the troops in Vietnam." Others, though, contended that the disillusionment stemmed from more-tangible aspects of the American soldier's environment, and that the popularity of "We Gotta Get Out of This Place" and other songs of its ilk was simply a reflection of the hopes, fears, and experiences of those soldiers.

FURTHER READING

Auslander, H. Ben. " 'If Ya Wanna End War and Stuff, You Gotta Sing Loud': A Survey of Vietnam-Related Protest Music." *Journal of American Culture* (Summer 1981).

Ballinger, Lee. "Deja Vu." In *Rock & Roll Confidential*, Dave Marsh, ed. New York: Pantheon, 1985.

Cleveland, Les. *Dark Laughter: War in Song and Popular Culture*. Westport, Conn.: Praeger, 1994.

———. "Soldiers' Songs: The Folklore of the Powerless." *New York Folklore*, Vol. 13, 1987.

Fish, Lydia. "General Edward G. Lansdale and the Folksongs of Americans in the Vietnam War." *Journal of American Folklore* (October/December 1989).

Gonzalez, David. "From Smoky Saigon Bars to Stateside Concerts." *New York Times* (November 7, 1993).

James, David E. "The Vietnam War and American Music." In *The Vietnam War and*

American Culture, John Carlos Rowe and Rick Berg, eds. New York: Columbia University Press, 1991.

Schumacher, Michael. *There But for Fortune: The Life of Phil Ochs*. New York: Hyperion, 1996.

"When Rock Went to War." *Veteran* (February 1986).

Winners and Losers

Nonfiction

Author: Gloria Emerson

Facts of Publication: New York: Random House, 1976

In 1970 *New York Times* reporter Gloria Emerson was assigned to cover the Vietnam War. The veteran journalist, who had spent a year in Saigon back in 1956, was stunned by the decimated state of the country and its people. She returned to the United States in 1972, deeply shaken by her Vietnam experiences and convinced that America's political leaders were culpable for much of the misery in Indochina. Emerson found it difficult to put her wartime experiences behind her, so she finally decided to write a book about the war. The result was 1976's *Winners and Losers: Battles, Retreats, Gains, Losses and Ruins from a Long War*, a collection of private musings and detailed interviews with American and Vietnamese men, women, and children whose lives had been irrevocably changed by the war.

HISTORICAL BACKGROUND

The Vietnam War marked the first occasion when large numbers of women journalists provided coverage of a war. Indeed, more than seventy women reported on the Vietnam War at some point in the conflict, observed Virginia Elwood-Akers in *Women War Correspondents in the Vietnam War, 1961–1975*. "Although women made up a small percentage of the hundreds of journalists who were accredited as war correspondents during the long years of the Vietnam War," she wrote, "their role was not unimportant. Women reported for such major news media as the *New York Times*, the National Broadcasting Company, the Associated Press, *The Christian Science Monitor, Newsweek*, and United Press International. They won numerous journalistic awards, including a Pulitzer Prize. They were deeply involved in the controversy which raged—and still rages—over whether coverage of the war was accurate or distorted to favor one point of view or another.'' Elwood-Akers also noted that of the dozens of women correspondents who reported from Vietnam, three were wounded in action, four were taken prisoner, and two were killed in action.

Veteran war correspondent Georgette Meyer ''Dickey'' Chapelle, who arrived in South Vietnam in 1961, was the first American woman to report from South Vietnam, but she was followed quickly by American reporter Beverly Deepe, French journalist Suzanne Labin, and Marguerite Higgins, the famous and controversial American correspondent who had received a Pulitzer Prize for her coverage of the Battle of Inchon during the Korean War. Higgins, like Chapelle, was steadfastly anti-Communist in her outlook, and she quickly ran afoul of David Halberstam, Charles Mohr, and other reporters who had filed stories critical of South Vietnam's government. Their clashes, however, did not arise from philosophical differences about the American presence in Vietnam; at this early juncture of the war, the consensus among the American press corps in Saigon was that the U.S. presence was justified. Rather, disputes among the correspondents centered on their dramatically different impressions of the war. Higgins and other reporters—most notably Joseph Alsop—felt that Halberstam, Neil Sheehan, and others were filing unnecessarily gloomy dispatches, and Higgins and Alsop were not averse to registering objections to their colleagues' coverage in their own stories.

By the mid-1960s, women correspondents—though still in the minority—were not regarded as an oddity, though some U.S. military personnel tried to discourage them from accompanying troops on dangerous operations, out of either a sense of paternalism or a preoccupation with bathroom logistics. Nonetheless, social mores governing women's role in society were changing swiftly, and ambitious and talented reporters—whatever their gender—recognized that Vietnam was becoming the top story in American and around the world. As reporter Elaine Shepard acknowledged in a note to Elwood-Akers, ''I would have gone to Vietnam if I'd had to swim over with my typewriter between my teeth.''

A number of notable women correspondents arrived in Vietnam from 1965 to 1967, a period of steadily increasing troop deployments. These correspondents included Shepard, Helen ''Patches'' Musgrove, Philippa Schuyler, and Frances FitzGerald, who became one of the press corps' most vocal critics of the war. But ''despite the cherished belief . . . that women are inherently anti-war, several female journalists fervently supported American involvement in South Vietnam, and went so far as to advocate escalation of the war and invasion of North Vietnam,'' noted Elwood-Akers. Indeed, ''the subjects of their writing ranged from cool reports of battle to sentimental accounts of civilian tragedy. . . . Their politics covered the spectrum from Philippa Schuyler's fervent anti-Communism to Madeleine Riffaud's equally fervent Marxism. Some were advocates of a style of journalism which allows for no personal opinion; others wrote in a highly emotional and dramatic style which bordered on fiction.''

As the size of the press corps in Vietnam continued to grow in the months leading up to the January 1968 Tet Offensive, the number of women correspondents increased as well. Indeed, a number of notable women reporters— Elizabeth Pond (a reporter with the *Christian Science Monitor* who, along with two colleagues, was held captive in Cambodia for more than five weeks); Georgie Annie Geyer (*Chicago Daily News*); Kate Webb (a UPI reporter who was erroneously reported as dead during a three-week period of captivity); Margaret Kilgore (UPI); Oriana Fallaci, Jurate Kazickas, and Gloria Emerson (*New York Times*)—all arrived in South Vietnam between 1967 and 1970. In addition, the writers Susan Sontag and Mary McCarthy, both of whom were well-known for their antiwar stances, paid well-publicized visits to North Vietnam in the months immediately following Tet. By this time, many women correspondents stationed in Indochina had become convinced that America's intervention in the region was fundamentally flawed, but this growing consensus was not attributable to their gender; indeed, their disillusionment was shared by many of their male counterparts.

EMERSON AND VIETNAM

Gloria Emerson first traveled to Vietnam in 1956. Leaving behind a job as a reporter for the women's section of the *New York Journal American*, she arrived in Saigon with a thirst for adventure and a conviction that America's growing involvement in the country's affairs was legitimate: ''In Vietnam that first year I thought it splendid that the Americans were making a democracy in South Vietnam,'' she recalled in *Winners and Losers*. ''It was part of our national tidying-up of the world. Eight years later I finally knew better. Fifteen years later the real punishment came when I went back to Vietnam and could not believe it was the country where I once had been.''

Emerson returned to the United States in 1957, securing a position as a reporter at the *New York Times*. In 1960 she relocated to Europe with her husband and joined the newspaper's Paris bureau. When she had first arrived at the *Times*, she had been relegated to assignments on ''women's news,'' but by the latter part of the 1960s, she had moved on to higher-profile assignments, including the Nigerian civil war in 1968 and the troubles in Northern Ireland in 1969. In 1970 she returned to Vietnam, where she spent the next two years.

Profoundly disturbed by the decimated state of the country, Emerson devoted much of her time to providing coverage of the war's effect on the Vietnamese people. Traveling throughout the war-torn countryside, she penned numerous articles on their plight, and in 1971 she won the George Polk Memorial Award for her reporting. The often critical tone of her articles, however, soon drew fire back home from conservatives unhappy with the media's coverage of the war. Gerry Kirk, for instance, charged in *National Review* that the *New York Times* reporter was "breaking Tokyo Rose's record for the transmission of unadulterated bad news from a war in which the U.S. was engaged." Her articles on poor Vietnamese refugees and foolish American officers were controversial in some quarters, but Emerson was most severely criticized for an incident in which she accompanied a group of Vietnamese youths on an ultimately unsuccessful firebombing mission against U.S. military personnel.

By the time Emerson departed Vietnam, she was convinced that the war was a horrible mistake. "Nothing is simple here for the Americans or the South Vietnamese," she wrote in *McCalls* in 1971. "The blame and the guilt, the guilt and the blame, and always the surprise that it turned out as miserably as this, covers us all."

CREATION OF *WINNERS AND LOSERS*

Emerson returned to the United States in 1972, but as she indicated in *Winners and Losers*, she remained haunted by experiences in Vietnam. "Turn the corner, people said to me in a kindly fashion. Forget the war. But I could not stop writing about it. Each time one more piece was published, there was always mail from men I did not know at all and did not ever meet." She subsequently decided to exorcise the demons she carried with her from the war by writing a book about the conflict. "I went out on my own to collect evidence of what the war had done, as someone might go for the first time into a huge forest to collect leaves and branches, moss and soil, to take back and study," she wrote in *Winners and Losers*. During her travels, which took her across both the United States and Vietnam, she interviewed all manner of American and Vietnamese people whose lives had been impacted by the war. In some instances, those that she interviewed offered perceptive, thoughtful remarks on the war and its shattering effect on their families and themselves. Other encounters, however, proved less rewarding, and this too became a theme in Emerson's work: "This is how it went so often for me: people could not talk for very long about Vietnam any more than they could talk about the weather and the reasons for it. Asking them how they felt about the war, I have heard stories about termites, the evil of welfare, diets that did not work, poor bus service, abortion, the horrible costs of feeding cattle and teenagers. . . . Sometimes I do not sleep well at all, wondering what it is that I am finding out and why some people insisted that after Vietnam nothing would ever be the same again."

CRITICAL RECEPTION

Winners and Losers, which won a National Book Award, was hailed by many as a powerful document of the war when it was published in 1976. Emerson's book, however, was not universally loved. Some critics took her to task for poor organization or an overzealous tone; others contended that though the author dwelled at some length on American abuses of power in Vietnam, she ignored atrocities and other deplorable actions committed by the enemy.

Most reviewers, however, were impressed with Emerson's passion and sympathetic with her struggle to come to terms with her wartime experiences. "[Emerson's] pictures of a devastated country and its people are vivid, unsentimental, and unsparing," remarked *Atlantic* critic Amanda Heller in a fairly representative review. "Whatever private demons drove Gloria Emerson to assemble this book, her intention is that it serve as a public record of the war in Vietnam. In that purpose it succeeds. It is impossible not to be shocked and moved by the innumerable horrors and personal tragedies recounted herein." Philip Beidler offered a similar assessment in his *American Literature and the Experience of Vietnam*, although he suggested that Emerson's passion for her subject matter too often assumed self-righteous dimensions. "There is plenty in the book, to be sure, that is not mere polemic," wrote Beidler. "In moments, she quite literally captures the whole war, comprehends it all somehow within a single brilliant image. . . . What remains troublesome about *Winners and Losers*, nevertheless, is that so much of the time it will not, as *Dispatches*, for instance, almost always does, allow the truth to tell itself. . . . Nearly everything Emerson sees, everything she senses and says about the experience of Vietnam, we now know to have been essentially correct. She is 'right.' The difficulty of *Winners and Losers* even as exposé or polemic is that this 'right' or 'true' vision of things seems so often to be much more of an imposition than a discovery."

But many reviewers contended that any polemical excesses on Emerson's part were eclipsed by the fundamental power of her message. *Newsweek*'s Walter Clemons, for instance, called *Winners and Losers* a "magnificent book. . . . She believes, quite correctly, that many of us are as lazily willing to forget the Vietnam War as we were slow to wake up to its horror while it was happening." C. D. B. Bryan was similarly impressed. Writing in the *Saturday Review*, he commented that although Emerson "succeeds brilliantly in exposing what the war did" to both Americans and Vietnamese, "what I found most moving was the obvious evidence of what the war had done to Miss Emerson herself. Her book dances with such exquisite agility on a tightrope between abysmal madness and pain that she recreates exactly our nation's schizophrenia throughout those endless, dreadful years."

FURTHER READING

Beidler, Philip D. *American Literature and the Experience of Vietnam*. Athens: University of Georgia Press, 1982.

Braestrup, Peter. *Big Story: How the American Press and Television Reported and Interpreted the Crisis of Tet 1968 in Vietnam and Washington*. Boulder, Colo.: Westview Press, 1977.

Bryan, C. D. B. Review of *Winners and Losers*. In *Saturday Review* (February 5, 1977).

Clemons, Walter. Review of *Winners and Losers*. In *Newsweek* (January 10, 1977).

Edwards, Julia. *Women of the World: The Great Foreign Correspondents*. Boston: Houghton Mifflin, 1988.

Elwood-Akers, Virginia, ed. *Women War Correspondents in the Vietnam War, 1961–1975*, Metuchen, N.J.: Scarecrow Press, 1988.

Emerson, Gloria. "Hey, Lady, What Are You Doing Here?" *McCall's* (August 1971).

———. "Wearied by the War." *Newsweek* (January 3, 1994).

———. *Winners and Losers: Battles, Retreats, Gains, Losses and Ruins from a Long War*. New York: Random House, 1976.

Fenton, James. Review of *Winners and Losers*. In *New York Times Book Review* (January 16, 1977).

FitzGerald, Frances. *A Fire in the Lake: The Vietnamese and the Americans in Vietnam*. Boston: Atlantic-Little, Brown, 1972.

Hallin, Daniel C. *"The Uncensored War": The Media and Vietnam*. New York: Oxford University Press, 1986.

Heller, Amanda. Review of *Winners and Losers*. In *Atlantic* (March 1977).

Higgins, Marguerite. *Our Vietnam Nightmare*. New York: Harper & Row, 1965.

Johnson, DeWayne B. "Vietnam: Report Card on the Press Corps at War." *Journalism Quarterly* (Spring 1969).

Kilgore, Margaret. "The Female War Correspondent in Vietnam." *Quill* (May 1972).

Kirk, Gerry. "As Seen by Gloomy Gloria." *National Review* (April 20, 1971).

Other Notable Works
Concerning the Vietnam War

FILMS

Fictional Films

Air America—directed by Roger Spottiswoode, Guild / Carolco, 1990

Alamo Bay—directed by Louis Malle, Tri-Star, 1985

Ashes and Embers—directed by Haile Gerima, Mypheduh Films, 1982

Bat 21—directed by Peter Markle, Tri-Star, 1988

Big Wednesday—directed by John Milius, Warner Bros., 1978

Billy Jack—directed by T. C. Frank, Warner Bros., 1971

Birdy—directed by Alan Parker, Tri-Star, 1984

The Boys in Company C—directed by Sidney J. Furie, Columbia, 1977

China Gate—directed by Samuel Fuller, 20th Century Fox, 1957

Cutter's Way—directed by Ivan Passer, United Artists, 1981

Distant Thunder—directed by Rick Rosenthal, Paramount, 1988

84 Charlie MoPic—directed by Patrick Duncan, New Century / Vista, 1989

Five Gates to Hell—directed by James Clavell, 20th Century Fox / Globe Enterprises, 1959

Flight of the Intruder—directed by John Milius, Paramount, 1990

Forrest Gump—directed by Robert Zemeckis, Paramount, 1994

Four Friends—directed by Arthur Penn, Filmways, 1981

Friendly Fire—directed by David Greene, ABC-TV, 1979

Gardens of Stone—directed by Francis Ford Coppola, Tri-Star Pictures, 1987

Good Morning, Vietnam—directed by Barry Levinson, Touchstone Pictures, 1987

Gordon's War—directed by Ossie Davis, 20th Century Fox, 1973

Hair—directed by Milos Forman, United Artists, 1979

Hamburger Hill—directed by John Irvin, Paramount, 1987

Heaven and Earth—directed by Oliver Stone, Warner Bros., 1993

Heroes—directed by Jeremy Paul Kagan, Universal, 1977

Jacknife—directed by David Jones, Vestron / King's Road Entertainment, 1989

Jacob's Ladder—directed by Adrian Lyne, Tri-Star, 1990

Missing in Action—directed by Joseph Zito, Cannon Films, 1984

1969—directed by Ernest Thompson, Entertainment / Atlantic, 1988

Off Limits—directed by Christopher Crowe, 20th Century Fox, 1988

Operation C.I.A.—directed by Christian Nyby, Allied Artists, 1965

Purple Hearts—directed by Sidney J. Furie, Ladd Company, 1984

The Quiet American—directed by Joseph L. Mankiewicz, United Artists, 1958

Rolling Thunder—directed by John Flynn, American International Pictures, 1977

Running on Empty—directed by Sidney Lumet, Warner Bros, 1988

Some Kind of Hero—directed by Michael Pressman, Paramount, 1982

The Stone Killer—directed by Michael Winner, Columbia, 1973

The Strawberry Statement—directed by Stuart Hagmann, MGM, 1970

Streamers—directed by Robert Altman, United Artists, 1983

Taxi Driver—directed by Martin Scorsese, Columbia, 1976

Tracks—directed by Henry Jaglom, Rainbow, 1976

Trial of the Catonsville Nine—directed by Gordon Davison, Melville Productions, 1972

Twilight's Last Gleaming—directed by Robert Aldrich, Allied Artists, 1977

The Ugly American—directed by George Englund, Universal-International, 1962

Uncommon Valor—directed by Ted Kotcheff, Paramount, 1983

The Visitors—directed by Elia Kazan, Associated Artists, 1972

Welcome Home—directed by Franklin J. Schaffner, Rank, 1989

Welcome Home, Soldier Boys—directed by Richard Compton, 20th Century Fox, 1972

When You Comin' Back, Red Ryder?—directed by Milton Katsela, Columbia, 1979

Who'll Stop the Rain?—directed by Karel Reisz, United Artists, 1978

Documentaries

ABC Scope: The Vietnam War (68-part series)—ABC News, 1966–1968

The Anderson Platoon—directed by Pierre Schoendoerffer, Films, Inc., 1967

Another Part of the Family—directed by Paul Ronder, Summer Morning Films / Museum of Modern Art, 1971

The Battle of Khe Sanh—U.S. Department of Defense, 1969

The Bloods of Nam—directed by Wallace Terry, PBS Video, 1986

The Boat People—directed by Andrew Lack, CBS News, 1979

Christmas in Vietnam—directed by Joe Gorsuch, CBS News, 1965

The Class That Went to War—directed by Richard Gerdau, ABC News, 1977

The Court-Martial of William Calley—CBS News, 1971

Dear America: Letters Home from Vietnam—directed by Bill Couturie, HBO Films, 1987

Eyewitness: Diem's War—or Ours?—directed by Bob Quinn, CBS News, 1961

A Face of War—directed by Eugene Jones, International Historic Films, 1967

Fulbright: Advice and Dissent—CBS News, 1966

Going Back: A Return to Vietnam—directed by David Munro, Bullfrog Films, 1982

Hearts of Darkness—directed by Fax Bahr w/ George Hickenlooper, ZM Productions / Zoetrope Studios, 1991

How Far Home: Veterans after Vietnam—directed by Bestor Cram, Northern Lights, 1983

In the Year of the Pig—directed by Emile de Antonio, Cinetree / New Yorker Films, 1969

Inside North Vietnam—California Newsreel, 1968

Introduction to the Enemy—directed by Christine Burill, IPC Films, 1974

Letter to Jane (French)—directed by Jean-Luc Godard and Jean-Pierre Gorin, New Yorker Films, 1972

Maya Lin: A Strong Clear Vision—directed by Freida Lee Mock, Sanders & Mock / American Film Foundation, 1995

Morley Safer's Vietnam: A Personal Report—CBS News, 1967

No Vietnamese Ever Called Me Nigger—directed by David Loeb Weiss, Paradigm Films / Cinema Guild, 1968

The People's War—Third World Newsreel, 1969

Sad Song of Yellow Skin—directed by Michael Rubbo, Film Board of Canada / Films Inc., 1970

The Selling of the Pentagon—directed by Peter Davis, CBS News, 1971

Television's Vietnam: The Impact of Media and *The Real Story*—directed by Douglas Pike and W. E. Crane, Accuracy in Media, 1985

The Uncounted Enemy: A Vietnam Deception—directed by George Crile, CBS News, 1982

Vietnam: A Television History (13 hour-long episodes)—Films Inc., 1983

Vietnam: An American Journey—directed by Robert Richter, First Run Films, 1980

Vietnam Requiem: Vets in Prison—directed by Jonas McCord and Bill Couturie, Direct Cinema, 1982

Vietnam: The 10,000 Day War (Canadian series, 26 half-hour episodes)—Nelson Entertainment, 1982

Waiting for Cambodia—PBS Video, 1988

Westmoreland on Vietnam—CBS News, 1966

When Johnny Comes Marching Home—ABC News, 1971

Why Vietnam?—U.S. Directorate for Armed Forces Information and Education/International Historic Films, 1965

Winter Soldier—Third World Newsreel, 1972

SONGS

"The 'A' Team," recorded by Barry Sadler, RCA, 1966

"Alice's Restaurant," recorded by Arlo Guthrie, Reprise, 1967

"Bad Moon Rising," recorded by Creedence Clearwater Revival, Fantasy, 1969

"Ball of Confusion," recorded by The Temptations, Motown, 1970

"Battle Hymn of Lt. Calley," recorded by Terry Nelson and C Company, Plantation, 1971

"Blowin' in the Wind," recorded by Peter, Paul, and Mary, Warner Bros., 1963

"Bring the Boys Home," recorded by Freda Payne, Invictus, 1971

"Broken Barricades," recorded by Procul Harum, A&M, 1971

"Bummer," recorded by Harry Chapin, Elektra, 1975

"Camouflage," recorded by Stan Ridgeway, IRS, 1986

"Chicago," recorded by Graham Nash, Atlantic, 1971

"Coming Home Soldier," recorded by Bobby Vinton, Epic, 1966

"The Cruel War," recorded by Peter, Paul, and Mary, Warner Bros., 1966

"Dawn of Correction," recorded by The Spokesmen, Decca, 1966

"Draft Dodger Rag," recorded by Phil Ochs, Elektra, 1965

"Draft Morning," recorded by The Byrds, Columbia, 1968

"Draft Resister," recorded by Steppenwolf, ABC/Dunhill, 1970

"The End," recorded by The Doors, Elektra, 1967

"Eve of Destruction," recorded by Barry McGuire, Dunhill, 1965

"The Fightin' Side of Me," recorded by Merle Haggard, Capitol, 1970

"Fox Hole," recorded by Television, Elektra, 1978

"Front Line," recorded by Stevie Wonder, Motown, 1982

"Gallant Men," recorded by Everett McKinley Dirksen, Capitol, 1966

"Galveston Bay," recorded by Bruce Springsteen, Columbia, 1996

"Give Peace a Chance," recorded by John Lennon, Apple, 1969

"Goodnight Saigon," recorded by Billy Joel, Columbia, 1983

"A Hard Rain's A-Gonna Fall," recorded by Bob Dylan, Columbia, 1963

"He Wore a Green Beret," recorded by Nancy Ames, Epic, 1966

"I Ain't Marching Anymore," recorded by Phil Ochs, Elektra, 1965

"I Don't Wanna Be a Soldier," recorded by John Lennon, 1971

"The I-Feel-Like-I'm-Fixin'-To-Die Rag," recorded by Country Joe and the Fish, Vanguard, 1967

"Kill for Peace," recorded by The Fugs, ESP, 1966

"Lyndon Johnson Told the Nation," recorded by Tom Paxton, Elektra, 1965

"Machine Gun," recorded by Jimi Hendrix, Capitol/EMI, 1970

"Military Madness," recorded by Graham Nash, Atlantic, 1971

"My Uncle," recorded by The Flying Burrito Brothers, A&M, 1972

"19," recorded by Paul Hardcastle, Chrysalis, 1985

"One Tin Soldier," recorded by Coven, Warner Bros., 1971

"Open Letter to My Teenage Son," recorded by Victor Lundberg, Liberty, 1967

"Paint It Black," recorded by The Rolling Stones, Decca, 1966

"Peace Train," recorded by Cat Stevens, A&M, 1971

"Run through the Jungle," recorded by Creedence Clearwater Revival, Fantasy, 1970

"Saigon Bride," recorded by Joan Baez, Vanguard, 1967

"Sam Stone," recorded by John Prine, Atlantic, 1971

"Scarborough Fair/Canticle," recorded by Simon and Garfunkel, Columbia, 1966

"Shut Out the Light," recorded by Bruce Springsteen, Columbia, 1985

"Singing in Vietnam Talking Blues," recorded by Johnny Cash, Columbia, 1971

"Sky Pilot," recorded by The Animals, MGM, 1968

"Soldier's Last Letter," recorded by Merle Haggard, Capitol, 1971

"Still in Saigon," recorded by The Charlie Daniels Band, Epic, 1982

"Stop the War," recorded by Edwin Starr, Gordy, 1970

"Straight to Hell," recorded by The Clash, Epic, 1982

"Talking Vietnam," recorded by Phil Ochs, Elektra, 1964

"Talking Vietnam Pot Luck Blues," recorded by Tom Paxton, Elektra, 1968

"To Susan on the West Coast Waiting," recorded by Donovan, Epic, 1969

"2 + 2," recorded by Bob Seger, Capitol, 1968

"The Universal Soldier," recorded by Buffy Sainte-Marie, Vanguard, 1965

"The Unknown Soldier," recorded by The Doors, Elektra, 1968

"Vietnam," recorded by Jimmy Cliff, A&M, 1970

"Vietnam Blues," recorded by J. B. Lenoir, L&R, 1966

"Vietnamerica," recorded by The Stranglers, A&M, 1980

"Vietnamese Baby," recorded by The New York Dolls, Mercury, 1973

"Vietnow," recorded by Rage against the Machine, Epic, 1996

"Waist Deep in the Big Muddy," recorded by Pete Seeger, Legacy, 1967

"War," recorded by Edwin Starr, Gordy, 1970

"The War Is Over," recorded by Phil Ochs, A&M, 1968

"War Song," recorded by Neil Young and Graham Nash, Reprise, 1972

"What We're Fighting For," recorded by Dave Dudley, Mercury, 1965

"Where Have All the Flowers Gone," recorded by The Kingston Trio, Capitol, 1962

"White Boots Marching in a Yellow Land," recorded by Phil Ochs, A&M, 1968

"William Butler Yeats Visits Lincoln Park and Escapes Unscathed," recorded by Phil Ochs, A&M, 1968

"The Willing Conscript," recorded by Tom Paxton, Elektra, 1965

"Wish You Were Here, Buddy," recorded by Pat Boone, Dot, 1966

LITERATURE

Fiction

The Alleys of Eden—Robert Olen Butler (New York: Horizon Press, 1981).

The American Blues—Ward Just (New York: Viking Press, 1984).

The Bamboo Bed—William Eastlake (New York: Simon and Schuster, 1969).

The Barracks Thief—Tobias Wolff (Hopewell, N.J.: Ecco Press, 1984).

Better Times Than These—Winston Groom (New York: Summit Books, 1978).

The Big V—William Pelfrey (New York: Liveright, 1972).

Body Count—William Turner Huggett (New York: Putnam, 1973).

Bravo Burning—Donald Tate (New York: Scribner, 1986).

Buffalo Afternoon—Susan Fromberg Schaeffer (New York: Knopf, 1989).

Captain Blackman—John Williams (Garden City, N.Y.: Doubleday, 1972).

Close Quarters—Larry Heinemann (New York: Farrar, Straus, Giroux, 1977).

Democracy—Joan Didion (New York: Simon and Schuster, 1984).

Dog Soldiers—Robert Stone (Boston: Houghton Mifflin, 1974).

A Dream with No Stump Roots in It: Stories—David Huddle (Columbia: University of Missouri Press, 1975).

The Embassy House—Nicholas Proffitt (New York: Bantam, 1986).

Firefight—Joseph Ferrandino (New York: Soho, 1987).

First Blood—David Morrell (New York: Evans, 1972).

For the Sake of All Living Things—John Del Vecchio (New York: Bantam, 1990).

Forrest Gump—Winston Groom (Garden City, N.Y.: Doubleday, 1986).

Fragments—Jack Fuller (New York: Morrow, 1984).

Free Fire Zone—Rob Riggan (New York: Norton, 1984).

Gardens of Stone—Nicholas Proffitt (New York: Carroll & Graf, 1983).

A Good Scent from a Strange Mountain: Stories—Robert Olen Butler (New York, Henry Holt, 1993).

The Green Berets—Robin Moore (New York: Crown, 1965).

Highways To War—Christopher J. Koch (New York: Viking, 1995).

In the Lake of the Woods—Tim O'Brien (Boston: Seymour Lawrence/Houghton Mifflin, 1994).

Incident at Muc Wa—Daniel Ford (Garden City, N.Y.: Doubleday, 1967).

Indian Country—Philip Caputo (New York: Bantam, 1987).

The Land of a Million Elephants—Asa Baber (New York: Morrow, 1970).

The Laotian Fragments—John Clark Pratt (New York: Viking Press, 1974).

The Last Ambassador—Bernard Kalb and Marvin Kalb (Boston: Little, Brown, 1981).

The Lionheads—Josiah Bunting (New York: George Braziller, 1972).

Machine Dreams—Jayne Anne Phillips (New York: Dutton, 1984).

No Bugles, No Drums—Charles Durden (New York: Viking Press, 1976).

On Distant Ground—Robert Olen Butler (New York: Knopf, 1985).

On the Way Home—Robert Bausch (New York: St. Martin's Press, 1982).

One Very Hot Day—David Halberstam (Boston: Houghton Mifflin, 1967).

The Phantom Blooper—Gustav Hasford (New York: Bantam, 1990).

Sand in the Wind—Robert Roth (Boston: Little, Brown, 1973).

Stringer—Ward Just (Boston: Little, Brown, 1974).

Sun Dogs—Robert Olen Butler (New York: Horizon Press, 1982).

The Traitors—John Briley (New York: G. P. Putnam's Sons, 1969).

The Ugly American—William Lederer and Eugene Burdick (New York: Norton, 1958).

War Games—James Park Sloan (Boston: Houghton Mifflin, 1971).

We're Not Here—Tim Mahoney (New York: Delta Books, 1988).

Why Are We in Vietnam?—Norman Mailer (New York: Putnam, 1967).

Nonfiction (Memoirs and Oral Histories)

An American Requiem: God, My Father, and the War that Came Between Us—James Carroll (New York: Houghton Mifflin, 1996).

And A Hard Rain Fell—John Ketwig (New York: Macmillan, 1985).

The Bad War—Kim Willenson (New York: New American Library, 1987).

Born on the Fourth of July—Ron Kovic (New York: McGraw-Hill, 1976).

Brothers in Arms—William Broyles, Jr. (New York: Knopf, 1986).

Chickenhawk—Robert Mason (New York: Viking, 1983).

Everything We Had—Al Santoli (New York: Random House, 1981).

For Self and Country—Rick Eilert (New York: Morrow, 1983).

G.I. Diary—David Parks (New York: Harper & Row, 1968).

Happy Hunting Ground—Martin Russ (New York: Atheneum, 1968).

If I Die in a Combat Zone, Box Me Up and Ship Me Home—Tim O'Brien (New York: Delacorte, 1973).

In Love and War—Jim and Sybil Stockdale (New York: Harper & Row, 1984).

In the Combat Zone: An Oral History of American Women in Vietnam—Kathryn Marshall, ed. (Boston: Little, Brown, 1987).

The Killing Zone—Frederick Downs (New York: Norton, 1978).

Long Time Passing: Vietnam and the Haunted Generation—Myra MacPherson (New York: Doubleday, 1984).

M—John Sack (New York: New American Library, 1966).

Nam—Mark Baker (New York: Morrow, 1981).

Passing Time—W. D. Ehrhart (Jefferson, N.C.: McFarland, 1989).

Payback—Joe Klein (New York: Knopf, 1984).

Remembering Heaven's Face—John Balaban (New York: Poseidon Press, 1991).

Reunion: A Memoir—Tom Hayden (New York: Random House, 1988).

RN: The Memoirs of Richard Nixon—Richard M. Nixon (New York: Warner, 1979).

A Soldier Reports—William Westmoreland (Garden City, N.Y.: Doubleday, 1976).

These Good Men—Michael Norman (New York: Crown, 1990).

365 Days—Ron Glasser (New York: George Braziller, 1971).

To Bear Any Burden—Al Santoli (New York: Dutton, 1968).

Unfriendly Fire—Peg Mullen (Iowa City: University of Iowa, 1995).

The Vantage Point: Perspectives of the Presidency 1963–1969—Lyndon B. Johnson (New York: Holt, Rinehart and Winston, 1971).

Vietnam Diary—Richard Tregaskis (New York: Holt, Rinehart and Winston, 1963).

Vietnam-Perkasie—W. D. Ehrhart (Jefferson, N.C.: McFarland, 1983).

War Year—Joe Haldeman (New York: Holt, Rinehart and Winston, 1972).

When Heaven and Earth Changed Places—Le Ly Hayslip (New York: Doubleday, 1989).

White House Years—Henry Kissinger (Boston: Little, Brown, 1979).

Poetry Collections

After the Noise of Saigon—Walter McDonald (Amherst: University of Massachusetts Press, 1988).

Caliban in Blue—Walter McDonald (Lubbock, Tex.: Texas Tech University Press, 1976).

Carrying the Darkness: American Indochina—The Poetry of the Vietnam War—W. D. Ehrhart, ed. (New York: Avon, 1985).

Copacetic—Yusef Komunyakaa (Middletown, Conn.: Wesleyan University Press, 1984).

Demilitarized Zones—Jan Barry and W. D. Ehrhart, eds. (Montclair, N.J.: East River Anthology, 1976).

Dien Cai Dau—Yusef Komunyakaa (Middletown, Conn.: Wesleyan University Press, 1986).

A Generation of Peace—W. D. Ehrhart (New York: New Voices Publishing, 1975).

Highway Number One—James M. Cantwell (Smithtown, N.Y.: Exposition Press, 1983).

How Audie Murphy Died in Vietnam—McAvoy Layne (Garden City, N.Y.: Anchor Books, 1973).

The Long War Dead: An Epiphany—Bryan Alec Floyd (New York: Avon, 1976).

The Monkey Wars—Bruce Weigl (Athens: University of Georgia Press, 1985).

Obscenities—Michael Casey (New Haven, Conn.: Yale University Press, 1972).

A Poetry Reading against the Vietnam War—Robert Bly and David Ray, eds. (Madison, Min.: The Sixties Press, 1966).

Returning Fire—D. F. Brown (San Francisco: San Francisco State University Press, 1984).

A Romance—Bruce Weigl (Pittsburgh: University of Pittsburgh Press, 1979).

saigon cemetery—D. C. Berry (Athens, Ga: University of Georgia Press, 1972).

Shell Burst Pond—Richard E. Baker (Tacoma, Wash.: Rapier Press, 1972).

To Those Who Have Gone Home Tired—W. D. Ehrhart (New York: Thunder's Mouth Press, 1984).

Unaccustomed Mercy: Soldier-Poets of the Vietnam War—W. D. Ehrhart, ed. (Lubbock, Tex.: Texas Tech University Press, 1989).

Vietnam Poems—John Balaban (Oxford, England: Carcanet Press, 1970).

Vinh Long—Perry Oldham (Meadows of Dan, Va: Northwoods Press, 1976).

War Story—Gerald McCarthy (Trumansburg, N.Y.: The Crossing Press, 1977).

Winning Hearts and Minds—Jan Barry, Basil T. Paquet, and Larry Rottmann, eds. (Brooklyn: 1st Casualty Press, 1972).

Plays

The Basic Training of Pavlo Hummel in *The Basic Training of Pavlo Hummel/Sticks and Bones*—David Rabe (New York: Viking 1973).

Botticelli—Terrence McNally (New York: Dramatists Play Service, 1968).

The Burial of Esposito in *Passing Through from Exotic Places*—Ronald Ribman (New York: Dramatists Play Service, 1970).

The Dramatization of 365 Days—H. Wesley Balk (Minneapolis: University of Minnesota Press, 1972).

5th of July—Lanford Wilson (New York: Dramatists Play Service, 1982).

The Final War of Olly Winter—Ronald Ribman (New York: CBS Television Network, 1967).

G. R. Point—David Berry (New York: Dramatists Play Service, 1980).

Home Front—James Duff (New York: Dramatists Play Service, 1985).

How I Got That Story—Amlin Gray (New York: Dramatists Play Service, 1981).

Indians—Arthur Kopit (New York: Hill and Wang, 1969).

Macbird—Barbara Gorson (New York: Grove Press, 1967).

Medal of Honor Rag—Tom Cole (New York: Samuel French, 1977).

Miss Saigon—Alain Boublil and Claude-Michel Schonberg (Milwaukee: Hal Leonard, 1990).

Moonchildren—Michael Weller (New York: Delacorte Press, 1972).

Still Life—Emily Mann (New York: Dramatists Play Service, 1982).

Strange Snow—Stephen Metcalfe (New York: Samuel French, 1983).

Streamers—David Rabe (New York: Knopf, 1977).

Summertree—Ron Cowan (New York: Random House, 1968).

Tracers—John DiFusco (New York: Hill and Wang, 1986).

Viet Rock in *Viet Rock and Other Plays*—Megan Terry (New York: Simon and Schuster, 1967).

Index

About the Authors

KEVIN HILLSTROM and LAURIE COLLIER HILLSTROM are partners in Northern Lights Writers Group. Their other books include *International Dictionary of Films and Filmmakers: Directors, Biography Today: Environmental Leaders*, and *Small Business Encyclopedia*.

ISBN 0-313-30183-2

90000>

EAN

9 780313 301834

HARDCOVER BAR CODE